Pierson v. Post, The Hunt for the Fox

The 1805 New York foxhunting case *Pierson v. Post* has long been used in American property law classrooms to introduce law students to the concept of first possession by asking how one establishes possession of a wild animal. In this book, Professor Angela Fernandez retells the history of the famous fox case, from its origins as a squabble between two wealthy young men on the South Fork of Long Island through its appeal to the New York Supreme Court and entry into legal treatises, law school casebooks, and law journal articles, where it still occupies a central place. Professor Fernandez argues that the dissent is best understood as an example of legal solemn foolery. Yet it has been treated by legal professionals, the lawyers of its day, and subsequent legal academics in such a serious way, demonstrating how the solemn and the silly can occupy two sides of the same coin in American legal culture and history.

Angela Fernandez is a legal historian at the Faculty of Law, University of Toronto, and a member of that University's Department of History.

Cambridge Historical Studies in American Law and Society

Recognizing legal history's growing importance and influence, the goal of this series is to chart legal history's continuing development by publishing innovative scholarship across the discipline's broadening range of perspectives and subjects. It encourages empirically creative works that take legal history into unexplored subject areas, or that fundamentally revise our thinking about familiar topics; it also encourages methodologically innovative works that bring new disciplinary perspectives and techniques to the historical analysis of legal subjects.

Series Editor

Christopher Tomlins, *University of California, Berkeley*

Previously published in the series:

William Kuby, *Conjugal Misconduct: Defying Marriage Law in the Twentieth-Century United States*

Justin Desautels-Stein, *The Jurisprudence of Style: A Structuralist History of American Pragmatism and Liberal Legal Thought*

Angela Fernandez, *Pierson v. Post, The Hunt for the Fox: Law and Professionalization in American Legal Culture*

Rebecca E. Zietlow, *The Forgotten Emancipator: James Mitchell Ashley and the Ideological Origins of Reconstruction*

Robert Daniel Rubin, *Judicial Review and American Conservatism: Christianity, Public Education, and the Federal Courts in the Reagan Era*

Matthew Crow, *Thomas Jefferson, Legal History, and the Art of Recollection*

Oren Bracha, *Owning Ideas: The Intellectual Origins of American Intellectual Property, 1790–1909*

Anne Twitty, *Before* Dred Scott: *Slavery and Legal Culture in the American Confluence, 1787–1857*

Leia Castañeda Anastacio, *The Foundations of the Modern Philippine State:*
Imperial Rule and the American Constitutional Tradition in the Philippine Islands, 1898–1935

Robert Deal, *The Law of the Whale Hunt: Dispute Resolution, Property Law, and American Whalers, 1780–1880*

Sandra F. Vanburkleo, *Gender Remade: Citizenship, Suffrage, and Public Power in the New Northwest, 1879–1912*

Reuel Schiller, *Forging Rivals: Race, Class, Law, and the Collapse of Postwar Liberalism*

Ely Aaronson, *From Slave Abuse to Hate Crime: The Criminalization of Racial Violence in American History*

Stuart Chinn, *Recalibrating Reform: The Limits of Political Change*

Ajay K. Mehrotra, *Making the Modern American Fiscal State*
Yvonne Pitts, *Family, Law, and Inheritance in America:* A Social *and Legal History of Nineteenth-Century Kentucky*
David M. Rabban, *Law's History*
Kunal M. Parker, *Common Law, History, and Democracy in America, 1790–1900*
Steven Wilf, *Law's Imagined Republic*
James D. Schmidt, *Industrial Violence and the Legal Origins of Child Labor*
Rebecca M. McLennan, *The Crisis of Imprisonment: Protest, Politics, and the Making of the American Penal State, 1776–1941*
Tony A. Freyer, *Antitrust and Global Capitalism, 1930–2004*
Davison Douglas, *Jim Crow Moves North*
Andrew Wender Cohen, *The Racketeer's Progress*
Michael Willrich, City of Courts, *Socializing Justice in Progressive Era Chicago*
Barbara Young Welke, *Recasting American Liberty: Gender, Law and the Railroad Revolution, 1865–1920*
Michael Vorenberg, *Final Freedom: The Civil War, the Abolition of Slavery, and the Thirteenth Amendment*
Robert J. Steinfeld, *Coercion, Contract, and Free Labor in Nineteenth Century America*
David M. Rabban, *Free Speech in Its Forgotten Years*
Jenny Wahl, *The Bondsman's Burden: An Economic Analysis of the Common Law of Southern Slavery*
Michael Grossberg, *A Judgment for Solomon: The d'Hauteville Case and Legal Experience in the Antebellum South*

Pierson v. Post, The Hunt for the Fox

Law and Professionalization in American Legal Culture

ANGELA FERNANDEZ
University of Toronto

CAMBRIDGE
UNIVERSITY PRESS

CAMBRIDGE
UNIVERSITY PRESS

University Printing House, Cambridge CB2 8BS, United Kingdom

One Liberty Plaza, 20th Floor, New York, NY 10006, USA

477 Williamstown Road, Port Melbourne, VIC 3207, Australia

314-321, 3rd Floor, Plot 3, Splendor Forum, Jasola District Centre, New Delhi - 110025, India

79 Anson Road, #06-04/06, Singapore 079906

Cambridge University Press is part of the University of Cambridge.

It furthers the University's mission by disseminating knowledge in the pursuit of education, learning and research at the highest international levels of excellence.

www.cambridge.org
Information on this title: www.cambridge.org/9781107039285
DOI: 10.1017/9781139600163

First published 2018

A catalogue record for this publication is available from the British Library

Library of Congress Cataloging in Publication data
NAMES: Fernandez, Angela, 1973–
TITLE: Pierson v. Post : the hunt for the fox / Angela Fernandez, University of Toronto.
DESCRIPTION: Cambridge, United Kingdom ; New York, NY, USA : Cambridge University Press, 2018. | Series: Cambridge historical studies in american law and society | Includes bibliographical references and index.
IDENTIFIERS: LCCN 2017055391 | ISBN 9781107039285 (hardback)
SUBJECTS: LCSH: Pierson, Jesse, – Trials, litigation, etc. | Post, Lodowick, – Trials, litigation, etc. | Property – New York (State) – History – 19th century – Cases. | Foxes Law and legislation – New York (State) – History – 19th century – Cases. | Property – United States – Philosophy.
CLASSIFICATION: LCC KF228 .P455 F47 2018 | DDC 346.74704–dc23
LC record available at https://lccn.loc.gov/2017055391

ISBN 978-1-107-03928-5 Hardback

To poor Reynard

"The Foxe to the Huntesman"

If dogs had tong at will to talke in their defence,
If brutish beast might be so bold, to plead at barre for pence,
If poore Tom troth might speake, of all that is amysse,
Then might would beare no right a down: then me would pardon this,
Which I must here declare. Then quickly would be known,
That he which deales with strangers faults, should first amend his owne.
Thus much my selfe may say, thus much my selfe can proue,
Yet whiles I preache beware the Geese, for so it shall behoue.
I sigh (yet smyle) to see, that man (yea master man)
Can play his part in pollicie, as well as Raynard can.
And yet forsoth the Foxe is he that beares the blame,
But two leggd Foxes eate the ducks, when foure legs beare the name.
A wonder is to see, how people shoute and crye,
With hallowes, whoupes, and spitefull words, when I poore Fox go by.
Lay on him cryes the wife, downe with him sayes the childe,
Some strike, som chide, some throw a stone, som fal & be defilde [...]
These faults with many moe, can wicked men commit,
And yet they say that Foxes passe, for subtletie and wit.
But shall I say my minde? I neuer yet saw day,
But euery town had two or three, which Rainards parts could play.
So that men vaunt in vaine, which say they hunt the Foxe,
To kepe their neighbors poultry free, & to defende their flockes,
When they them selues can spoyle, more profit in an houre,
Than Raynard rifles in a yere, when he doth most deuoure.
No, no, the minds of men, which still be vainely bent,
Must haue their change of Uenerie, as first the Hare in Lent,
The Hart in Sommers heate, and me poore Foxe in cold:
But wherto serue these sundry sports, these chases manyfold?
Forsoth to feede their thoughts, with drags of vaine delight,
Whereon most men do muse by day, wheron they dream by night.

They must haue costly clothes, they must haue deintie fare,
They must haue couches stuft with doune, they must haue all in square.
They must haue newfound games, to make the laugh their fill,
They must haue foules, they must haue beasts, to bayt, to hunt, to kyll.
And all (when all is done) is nothing else but vayne,
So Salomon the wiseman sayd, and so sayes Raynerd playne.

George Gascoigne, *The Noble Arte of Venerie* (1575)

Contents

Figures

Acknowledgments

I wish to acknowledge and thank local historians and others in Southampton, Bridgehampton, East Hampton, and Riverhead, including Ann Sandford, Mary Cummings, Henry Moëller, Julie Greene, Marci Vail, Rosanne Barons, Ned Smith, Sharon A. Pullen, Zachary N. Studenroth, and Christopher Robinson. Also Libby Fannon, Tammy Sweda, and Laura Rissone.

I also thank librarians and archivists at State and University institutions, especially Helen Weltin, Joseph Van Nostrand, Bruce Abrams, Whitney Bagnell, Gerald W. Cloud, Sharon Pullen, Jeff Sohn, Mary Person, and Lia Apodaca at the Library of Congress.

Librarians at my home institution at the University of Toronto's Bora Laskin Law Library provided tremendous assistance, especially Faculty Services Librarian Sooin Kim and Access Services Coordinator Sufei Xu. Reference and Research Librarian Alexia Loumankis worked closely with me to create a temporary exhibit featuring an electronic copy of the Judgment Roll in *Pierson* (https://www.law.utoronto.ca/news/what-does-fox-say-prof-angela-fernandez-makes-accessible-original-judgment-roll-in-famous) and to make these scanned files permanently available through the University of Toronto (https://dataverse.scholarsportal.info/dataset.xhtml?persistentId=doi:10.5683/SP/3HJKJ7). Digital Services and Reference Librarian Susan Barker provided a great deal of help with the images in the book. I made every effort to contact the holders of copyright of these images where it was necessary to do so.

I owe a special expression of gratitude to Christopher Tomlins, series editor for the Cambridge Historical Studies in American Law and Society, for his substantive input, editorial care and attention, patience, and moral support in bringing the book to press. Thanks also to others who helped in the process at Cambridge University Press, including Senior Commissioning Editor Deborah Gershenowitz and her assistant Kristina Deusch, Content Manager Robert Judkins, copy editor Brian Black, and Project Managers Sri Hari Kumar Sugumaran and Sunantha Ramamoorthy.

Legal history mentors and colleagues have had a lot of input over the years and I thank them heartily, especially Robert W. Gordon. I want also to thank Stephen Waddams, Dirk Hartog, Alfred Brophy, Philip Girard, Jim Phillips, Dan Ernst, Laura Edwards, Susanna Blumenthal, Andrea McDowell, David Tanenhaus, Charles Donahue, Paul Halliday, Jim Oldham, Neil Duxbury, Stuart Banner, Andrew Buck, Christopher Schmidt, Darlene Johnston, G. Blaine Baker, Sung Yup Kim, Chris Beauchamp, and Elizabeth Dale.

Retired New York historian Donald M. Roper, who really knows how to put gold in his footnotes.

Literature colleagues, especially Mary Nyquist, Sharif Youssef, Karen J. Cunningham, Greig Henderson, and Kim Yates at the Jackman Humanities Institute.

On matters as various as Syriac translation, Polish names, handwriting analysis, and Freemasonry, Amir Harrak, Jack B. Tannous, Piotr Wrobel, A. K. Singla, and Thomas M. Savini.

My University of Toronto law school colleagues not already mentioned, especially Mariana Prado (who saved me from relegating the discovered Judgment Roll to a footnote), Lisa Austin (in whose property class I would lecture about *Pierson* and she would introduce me as the person in the world who knows the most about this case, an auspicious honor!), Karen Knop (who introduced me to the viral song and video "What Does the Fox Say?" https://www.youtube.com/watch?v=jofNR_WkoCE), my former Dean Mayo Moran, Denise Reaume, Peggy Radin, Martha Shaffer, Bruce Chapman, Michael Trebilcock, Abraham Drassinower, Simon Stern, Markus Dubber, and my current Dean Edward Iacobucci for his support getting the project finished. My thanks go also to my faculty assistant Nancy Bueler.

Various stages of the work benefited greatly from presentations at the Stanford-Yale Junior Faculty Forum; the Toronto Legal History group; the Tel Aviv University Legal History Workshop; Faculty Workshops at the Faculty of Law, University of Toronto; the American Bar Foundation/ Illinois Legal History Seminar; and the Australia and New Zealand Law and History Society.

Research students, especially Alex Zavaglia, Chris Shorey (for finding the link between *Pierson* and the Supreme Court of Canada's *Frederick Gerring Jr.* v. *R.*, arguably Canada's *Pierson* v. *Post*), and Maya Bielinski (for *Titus Andronicus* research and for assistance with the specialized literary terms in Chapter 2).

Students in "Legal Archaeology: Studies in Cases in Context," especially the group in 2016 for their careful reading of the text and bevy of useful suggestions.

All errors are of course my own.

The picture on the cover is by British animal painter Cecil Aldin, one of the illustrations Aldin did for Neils Heiberg's charming yet alarming *White-Ear and Peter: The Story of a Fox and a Fox-Terrier* (London: Macmillan and Co., 1912, reprinted by London: Forgotten Books, 2015), 149. Aldin gave his dogs so much personality and his foxes so little, as he was a foxhunting enthusiast and Master of the Hounds and had likely habituated himself to seeing the fox as a prize, an object to pursue rather than a proper subject. I chose "Eagle carries Half Dead/ Dying Fox" (forgiving it is British and it is from the twentieth century) more for the eagle than for the fox. You are meant to imagine that the eagle is American.

My process of coming to appreciate the fox as subject rather than hunted object came late. It began to develop in the wonderful company of a Working Group Sarah Amato and I first organized at the Jackman Humanities Institute at the University of Toronto in 2014 we called "Animals in the Law and Humanities." This is where I met Mary Nyquist and she pointed out the *Titus Andronicus* connection to Livingston's use of the phrase "saucy intruder," which made so clear the theme of gendered violence and its connection to hunting. I received excellent feedback on draft chapters from fellow historians in the group, Sarah Amato, Matt Brower, and Sean Hawkins. I learned much from law members Lesli Bisgould, Ziyaad Mia, Kristine Connidis, Jennifer Nedelsky, Man Ha Tse, John Enman-Beech, Nadia Lambek, Camille Labchuk, and Jessica Eisen, who gallantly took over organizing an unfunded version of the group in 2017-2018 while I was on leave. Erika Ritter, Stefan Dolgert, Tracy McDonald, Anne Milne, Lisa Kramer, Amy Ratelle, Nicole D'Aoust, Avra Epstein, Linda Bronfman, Kelly Struthers Montford, and Will Kymlicka have all been excellent conversationalists on animal issues.

My ex-husband Matias Milet provided much support throughout our ten years of marriage, and our dearly loved daughter, Isabel Fernandez-Milet, the little wily precious animal who is in everything I do.

I want to thank also my friend Nick Wright, founder of Animal Justice Canada, who was a tremendous source of love and light through many dark and challenging situations that arose in the last years I was working on the book.

Very sadly both my father and my mother passed away while the book was in its final stages of production. I wish they had been able to see it completed and my father especially could have held it in his hands. My mother would have been equally proud. The book's humanism and eclecticism are very much her influence.

Introduction

Pierson v. Post (1805) is a famous (and some might say infamous) leading American property law case. It had its origins in a dispute over possession of a wild fox that occurred on a beach on early nineteenth-century Long Island between the sons of two wealthy families from the Hamptons. A young man named Nathan Post, who was engaged in hunting a fox "with dogs and hounds," and another young man, Jesse Pierson, who intervened in the hunt and killed that fox.[1] It has been used in law school classrooms for over a hundred years to introduce students to the concept of possession, read by literally tens of thousands of law students each year. As one modern property casebook puts it, "[s]o many students have begun their legal studies with *Pierson v. Post*, it is almost unbelievable that an American-educated lawyer would be unfamiliar with it."[2] And, according to the online database HeinOnline, it has been referenced in nearly eight hundred law journal articles and other secondary legal sources to date.[3]

Pierson poses the following question in stark terms: Who has first possession of a wild animal (a fox) – the person pursuing it (Post) or the person who actually kills and takes it (Pierson)? A majority of the New York Supreme Court in 1805 sided with the interloper, Pierson – referred to memorably by the dissenting judge, Henry Brockholst Livingston, as "a saucy intruder."[4] Despite Livingston's often witty protest, the majority decision in *Pierson* became a serious precedent in

[1] *Pierson v. Post*, 3 Cai. R. 175 (N.Y. Sup. Ct., 1805), 175.

[2] Susan Fletcher French and Gerald Korngold eds., *Cases and Text on Property*, 6th ed. (New York: Aspen, 2015), 71.

[3] The count of citations up to July 21, 2015, was 783.

[4] *Pierson*, 181.

the common law world for what became known as the capture rule: an unowned or so-called fugitive resource such as a wild animal – or air, or oil and gas, or ground water – becomes owned only when it is tamed or controlled or captured and is thereby effectively reduced to possession.[5] In a hunt, even in the case of an imminent taking by one who is publicly or notoriously engaged in the chase (like Post), the animal can and often does escape; so the clearest manifestation of control is to kill it (as Pierson did). Killing the animal constitutes best possession. This is sometimes referred to as a "bright line" rule, said to be clearer and easier to apply than the allegedly "fuzzy" standard of an imminent taking that might still go awry. Yet it is acknowledged even by those who think the capture rule is a good one from the perspective of clarity and the promotion of beneficial competition that it encourages overconsumption and waste in an environmental context, as individuals seek to capture and hold more of an unowned natural resource than they need or can process and use in order to be the effective owner of it and exclude others from it. The capture rule has been called "cataclysmic" for nonhuman animals given the lessons of the North American bison and the American passenger pigeon.[6]

Governments are free to legislate around the capture rule and they have in places like Texas where its use for oil and gas fields would have created waste and a free-for-all of vast proportions.[7] The same is true of groundwater regulation in hot dry states like Texas and California.[8] Wild animals too were placed under state ownership for their protection and management.[9]

[5] William Blackstone wrote of wild animals (animals *ferae naturae*) and "the very elements, of fire or light, of air, and of water" that "they are of a vague and fugitive nature, and therefore can admit only of a precarious and qualified ownership, which lasts so long as they are in actual use and occupation, but no longer." *Blackstone's Commentaries on the Laws of England* (Oxford: Clarendon Press, 1765–69): Book 2 *The Rights of Things* (1766), 395 (emphasis added) (http://avalon.law.yale.edu). Subsequent references to Blackstone's *Commentaries* come from the Avalon edition.

[6] See Rance L. Craft, "Of Reservoir Hogs and Pelt Fiction: Defending the *Ferae Naturae* Analogy Between Petroleum and Wildlife," 44 *Emory Law Journal* (1995): 697–733, 715–18.

[7] See ibid., 712 ("During the 1920s, the Federal Oil Conservation Board estimated that extraction under the rule of capture yielded recovery rates of 20–25% of total petroleum deposits, where 85–90% recovery rates were possible with controlled drilling").

[8] See e.g. Burke W. Griggs, "Does Groundwater Management Work?" 15 *Kansas Journal of Law and Public Policy* (2005–2006): 391–405, 393 (noting that the capture rule from *Pierson v. Post* "itself [...] ran wild" in the Western United States, in Texas forcing regulations on producers in order to save them from themselves, and in the San Joaquin Valley of California, groundwater pumping dropped land surface levels by nearly thirty feet).

[9] See Craft, "Of Reservoir Hogs and Pelt Fiction," 726–27 (explaining that in the 1930s states began to take seriously the conservation required to protect depleted wildlife stocks,

Yet in an unlegislated environment, *Pierson* and the capture rule is often the default or first-stop common law rule – the wasteful rule that values the animal killer/capturer over the mere pursuer.

Of the thirty-three American cases included in Appendix A, "Citation History," that cite to *Pierson*, nineteen relate to wild animals and the rest to a wide array of other topics. This low number of citations and the limited impact of *Pierson* as a working precedent stand in sharp contrast to the fame and notoriety given to *Pierson* by its regular appearance in law school classrooms through prominent inclusion in law school casebooks. Probably for this reason and due to its inherently fertile philosophical nature it has been and remains a touchstone in American law journal articles. Significant numbers of citations appear on articles written about intellectual property, the property status of human body parts, and, perhaps surprisingly, home-run baseballs hit into the stands that become the object of contentious dispute.[10] As the editor of a symposium on the

providing funding for enforcement and establishing licensing requirement and hunting seasons). See also Michael C. Blumm and Lucus Ritchie, "The Pioneer Spirit and the Public Trust: The American Rule of Capture and State Ownership of Wildlife," 35 *Environmental Law* (2005): 673–720 (defending state ownership of wild animals and giving an account of its survival in American constitutional law).

[10] On intellectual property see e.g. Shantanu C. Pathak, "The AIA and the First-to-File Provision: Consequences and Constitutionality," 28 *Temple International and Comparative Law Journal* (2014): 115–46, 126–27 (noting that the 2011 US patent law overhaul takes its cue from *Pierson v. Post* in following a "first in time, first in right" principle, where first in time means the capture of first-to-file, rather than first-to-invent, the older rule that required more investigation to determine which of two rivals invented first, described as too "fuzzy" when compared against "bright-line notice"). Intellectual property use of *Pierson* became common in the 1990s. See e.g. Scott A. Chambers, "Exhaustion Doctrine in Biotechnology," 35 *IDEA: The Journal of Law and Technology* (1994–95): 289–330, 292-93 (wondering if escaped transgenic material such as laboratory mice and wind pollinated genetically modified grain crops would qualify as *ferae naturae* and be subject to the capture rule).

On property in human body parts, see e.g. Radhika Rao, "Property, Privacy, and the Human Body," 80 *Boston University Law Review* (2000): 359–460, 375 (referring to *Pierson* for the idea that may have animated a particular case that "severed body parts – much like oil, water, wild animals, and other migratory resources – become free for 'capture' by the first person who recognizes this commercial potential and puts them to productive use").

On baseballs, see e.g. Paul Finkelman, "Fugitive Baseballs and Abandoned Property: Who Owns the Home Run Ball?" 23 *Cardozo Law Review* (2001-2002): 1609–33, 1629; Patrick Stoklas, "*Popov v. Hayashi*, a Modern Day *Pierson v. Post*: A Comment on What the Court Should Have Done with the Seventy-Third Home Run Baseball Hit by Barry Bonds," 34 *Loyola University Chicago Law Journal* (2002–2003): 901–43, 910–12, 932–40; Jason Cieslik, "There's a Drive ... Way Back ... It Might be ... It Could Be ... Another Lawsuit: *Popov v. Hayashi*," 20 *Thomas M. Cooley Law Review* (2003):

rule of capture in the journal *Environmental Law* in 2005 put it, "the universal implications of capture" as they are traditionally explored by law professors through topics such as oil and gas, wildlife, cattle grazing rights, and public land use will play a role in facing twenty-first century problems of "new capture possibilities – such as new territory on other planets, genome sequencing techniques, or power generated from tidal flows."[11]

How anyone comes to own anything in a world, a state of nature, where no one owns anything, was traditionally explored through the concept of occupation or *occupatio*. Blackstone discussed how thinkers such as Grotius and Pufendorf asserted that a tacit assent gave occupation the ability to turn what would be an illegitimate taking from the common property of mankind into a legitimate personal appropriation, and how those like Barbeyrac and Locke thought "that the very act of occupancy, alone, being a degree of bodily labour, is from a principle of nature justice, without any consent or compact, sufficient of itself to gain a title."[12] Blackstone noted, with some impatience, that this was "[a] dispute that favours too much of nice and scholastic refinement! However, both sides agree in this, that *occupancy* is the thing by which the title was in fact originally gained."[13] Hence, occupation and how one effectively became a "first taker" was an extremely important starting point in an understanding of legal property, and of how anyone comes to be acknowledged as an owner of anything.[14]

TEXT, SOURCES, AND ARGUMENT: A FIRST FORAY

The question of how one owns a piece of property that wanders free – and really is not yet any one's property – was traditionally explored in Ancient Roman law and by later civil and natural law thinkers through the hypothetical of the wild animal, such as a boar or a bear or whatever animal that culture or country had an interest in hunting and was familiar to the educated male readers of the legal or philosophical text. The usual rhythm in these texts was the following: there are two kinds of property, real (or unmovable) property (i.e. land) and personal (or movable)

605–38, 626–27. See also Amy Beckham Osborne, "Baseball and the Law: A Selected Annotated Bibliography, 1990–2004," 97 *Law Library Journal* (2005): 335–70.

11 Frank Lupo, "Introduction Symposium: The Rule of Capture and its Consequences," 35 *Environmental Law* (2005): 647–48, 648.

12 Blackstone, *Commentaries*, 2: 8. 13 Ibid. (emphasis added). 14 Ibid., 9.

property – the latter known as chattels in the common law, but movable property was the civil law term. Of the second kind, namely, property that moves, ownership is either absolute or qualified. Only a qualified property might be had in items that are owned by no one and subject to the use of all (*res communes*) such as light, air, the sea, and running water. Wild animals (or animals *ferae naturae*) are capable of individual appropriation but they too, unlike a domestic animal that would be owned absolutely, are qualified property that must be reduced to a first possession or occupation in order for the ownership right to be absolute and capable of excluding others.[15] And so the question arises: What degree of control is necessary in order for that first possession or occupation to be established? Was wounding required? If so, did it need to be mortal wounding? What if a trap was used? Did it need to be an inescapable trap?

Unlike domesticated animals where loss of possession would not result in loss of ownership, wild animals or animals *ferae naturae* had to remain in the power or control of the first occupant otherwise ownership of them would be lost – hence the qualified nature of the ownership.[16] This explains Pierson's lawyers' reliance on the passage from Justinian's *Institutes* (Book 2, Chapter 12), which stated that:

> Wild beasts, birds, fish, and all the animals which are bred either in the sea, the air or upon the earth, do, as soon as they are taken, become instantly by the law of nations, the property of the captor [. . .] But, tho' wild beasts, or fowl, when taken, are esteemed to be the property of the captor, whilst they continue in his custody, yet, when they have once escaped and recovered their natural liberty, the right of the captor ceases, and they become the property of the first, who seizes them.[17]

[15] "[T]hings *res communes* are available for the use of all [. . .] but cannot, by their nature, become the property of any person or persons. Things *res nullius* can become the property of a person or persons" but had either never been owned or had been abandoned by their previous owner. See Prue Taylor, *An Ecological Approach to International Law: Responding to Challenges of Climate Change* (London; New York: Routledge, 1998), 270.

[16] See Blackstone, *Commentaries*, 2: 389 ("animals, which have in themselves a principal and power of motion, and (unless particularly confined) can convey themselves from one part of the world to the another"), 390 (the tame or domestic animal has an *animus revertendi*, or habit of returning, and so can be owned absolutely, i.e. it remains in continuous occupation or possession so long as it returns; whereas one can only have a qualified property in the wild animal).

[17] I rely here on a translation of the *Institutes* that early Americans would have had access to, namely *D. Justiniani Institutionum Libri Quatuor: The Four Books of Justinian's Institutions, translated into English, with notes, by George Harris LL.D.*, 2nd ed. (London, Printed by J. Purser, 1761), Book Two, Chapter 1, section 12, pp. 4–5. This is the edition listed in Herbert A. Johnson, *Imported Eighteenth-Century Law Treatises in American Libraries, 1700–1799* (Knoxville: University of Tennessee Press, 1978), 18.

Application of this passage to the situation in *Pierson* was ambiguous, as Post (at least according to Livingston) was allegedly about to take the animal and was certainly in continued pursuit of it; the fox had not been caught and escaped from him as the Justinian point hypothesized.[18] Blackstone too seemed to have in mind the situation of capture and escape when he discussed animals *ferae naturae* as a species of qualified property. He wrote that the property in a wild animal "ceases the instant they are out of possession: for, when no man is engaged in their actual occupation, they become again common, and every man has an equal right to appropriate them to his own use."[19]

There were other authors who agreed that the degree of control Livingston at least thought Post had, imminent taking, especially if it included wounding or trapping, was sufficient. The ancient Roman jurist Trebatius was of this view. And, indeed, Justinian did include reference to Trebatius: his views of the effect of wounding were mentioned in Gaius's discussion of the occupation of a wild animal, a passage included in Justinian's longer work, the *Digest*.[20] However, the *Digest* was

It was also included in David Hoffman, *A Course of Legal Study: Respectfully addressed to the students of law in the United States* (Baltimore: Coale and Maxwell, 1817), 269.

[18] The rest of the passage in Chapter 12 reads: "And they are understood to have recovered their natural liberty, if they have run or flown out of sight; and even if they are not out of sight, when it so happens, that they can not without difficulty be pursued and retaken." *Institutes*, 5. Charles Donahue points out that this passage is inconclusive on the *Pierson* facts. See Charles Donahue Jr., "*Animalia Ferae Naturae*: Rome, Bologna, Leyden, Oxford and Queen's County, N.Y." in Roger S. Bagnall and William V. Harris eds., *Studies in Roman Law: In Memory of A. Arthur Schiller* (Leiden: E. J. Brill, 1986), 39–63, 41–42. See also Charles Donahue Jr., "Noodt, Titius, and the Natural Law School: The Occupation of Wild Animals and the Intersection of Property and Tort" in J.A. Ankum, J.E. Spruit and F.B.J. Wubbe eds., *Satura Roberto Feenstra* (Fribourg: Presses Universitaires de Fribourg, 1985) 609–29, 610.

[19] Blackstone, *Commentaries*, 2: 395. Pierson's citation to Blackstone is to a later point in the text in the next chapter, p. 403, to support the point that occupation is indispensable to create title in an animal *ferae naturae*. This is not the best passage to cite from Blackstone on the point, which is made more emphatically and directly in the previous chapter; but there is a passage at p. 403 on wild animals that mentions they are qualified property and the chapter is titled "Of Title to Things Personal by Occupancy." See *Pierson*, 176; Blackstone, *Commentaries*, 2: 403.

[20] F. De Zulueta trans., *Digest 41, 1 & 2* (Oxford: Oxford University Press, 1920), 10 ("It has been asked whether a wild beast, which has been so wounded that it can be captured, at once becomes the property of the wounder. Trebatius held that it becomes his property at once, and is considered his so long as he keeps up its pursuit, but that, if he gives up its pursuit, it ceases to be his, and once more becomes the property of the first taker [. . .] The usual opinion has been that the animal only becomes a man's property if he actually captures it, since many things may occur to prevent his capturing it; and this is the truer view").

a complicated text and much harder to come by in the United States than the *Institutes*. Post's lawyer, Cadwallader David Colden, probably did not have access to it.[21] Section 13 of the *Institutes*, which Pierson's lawyer, Nathan Sanford, cited, simply said that even wounding was insufficient, as "many accidents frequently happen; which prevent the capture."[22] The author of the majority opinion, Justice Daniel Tompkins, did discuss wounding at length.[23] The point is not made explicitly but the line of reasoning seems to be that if wounding, even serious wounding, did not establish possession, then mere pursuit would not.[24] The focus of the majority opinion is that all the authorities agree that mere pursuit was not enough.

So was *Pierson* a case of mere pursuit? The majority decision certainly treated it as if it were. Tompkins wrote in his majority decision: "The case now under consideration is one of mere pursuit."[25] This is noteworthy as Post's lawyer, Colden, conceded in his argument that there would be no occupation in the wild animal if there had only been pursuit. He said

[21] See Alan Watson, "Introduction to Law for Second-Year Students?" 46 *Journal of Legal Education* (1996): 430–44, 440 (discussing *Pierson*'s failure to refer to the *Digest*, noting that *Institutes* was the go-to source for Americans and the "*Digest* was often simply not readily to hand or was thought too difficult"). There is no listing for the *Digest* in Johnson, *Imported Eighteenth-Century Law Treatises in American Libraries*. David Hoffman discusses how much more complex the *Digest* or *Pandects* are than the *Institutes*. See Hoffman, *A Course of Legal Study*, 265. See also 89 ("It seemed wise to the great digester of the Roman law, to arrange and abridge in the Institutes [...] the multifarious learning of the Code and Pandects").

[22] *Pierson*, 176; George Harris (1761) translation of the *Institutes*, 5. Donahue thinks this passage is also inconclusive. See Donahue, *Animalia Ferae Naturae*," 42–43; Donahue, "Noodt, Titius, and the Natural Law School," 610–11.

[23] There was disagreement amongst the authorities as to the effect of wounding, Pufendorf conceding reluctantly that yes it gave the original striker a right while the pursuit continued and Bynkershoek agreed. Tompkins understood Barbeyrac to be in agreement, at least on this point, that "mortal wounding [...] by one not abandoning his pursuit [...] may [...] be deemed possession of him." *Pierson*, 178. Like Justinian, Grotius thought that wounding was not enough but snares, nets or traps might be so long as the instruments themselves are in the person's power and the animal is trapped so that it cannot escape. See *Pierson*, 179. The quotes from Grotius are in Latin. To examine the passages in English in their original context, see Hugo Grotius, *The Law of War and Peace (De Jure Belli ac Pacis)*, Louise R. Loomis trans. (New York: Walter J. Black, 1949), 121–22.

[24] Donahue writes that "[s]urely if a wounded animal does not become 'yours' even if the wounding enables you to capture it, then *ipso fortiori* pursuit alone, even pursuit that would have resulted in capture, is not sufficient, absent capture. This is clearly the line of reasoning that impressed the majority of the *Pierson* court, but even this line, though plausible, is not inevitable." Donahue, *Animalia Ferae Naturae*," 42–43; Donahue, "Noodt, Titius, and the Natural Law School," 610.

[25] *Pierson*, 179.

"I admit [...] that pursuit alone does not give a right of property in animals *ferae naturae*".[26] This point is difficult (if not impossible) to see in many casebook reproductions of *Pierson*, which omit the lawyers' arguments and jump straight to Tompkins's majority opinion.[27] Livingston wrote that property in wild animals could be acquired "without bodily touch or manucaption, provided the pursuer be within reach, or have a *reasonable* prospect (which certainly existed here) of taking."[28] Post's lawyer and Livingston spoke as if this was a situation of some kind of hot pursuit. It was certainly not a situation in which the animal was captured and lost or pursuit was difficult (the points addressed in Chapter 12 of the *Institutes*) or where the claim was based on wounding alone (spoken to in Chapter 13 of the *Institutes*). There is no suggestion that there was any wounding of the fox (minor or mortal) and so much of what Tompkins writes about in the majority decision is not really on point. True, if wounding were not enough, mere pursuit could not be; but the question was whether something more than mere pursuit, i.e. hot pursuit, was sufficient. The majority left that question undecided. Indeed, they outright ignored it, even though that was the case put to them by Post, and to which Livingston took himself to be speaking.

Moreover, although Post's lawyer, Colden, admitted that pursuit alone would be insufficient, he argued that "manucaption," actually taking an animal, was "only one of many means, to declare the intention of exclusively appropriating that, which was before in a state of nature."[29] So long as it continued, this declaring of the intention to take was "equivalent to occupancy."[30] So what was required was pursuit plus continued following. "It is all the possession the nature of the subject admits," Colden argued, "it declares the intention of acquiring dominion, and is as much to be respected as manucaption itself."[31] Colden relied on Barbeyrac, an annotator of Pufendorf, as authority for saying that an actual taking was not required.[32]

In addition to Barbeyrac, Colden might also have invoked the authority of the great late eighteenth-century French treatise writer Robert-Joseph

[26] Ibid., 176.

[27] I provide many examples of casebooks excluding the lawyers' arguments in Chapter 7, including those that do not indicate anything has been removed with ellipses. This matches the current-day practice of not including the arguments of the lawyers in reports of cases but it was controversial to do so at the time. See Chapter 6 on reporters for more discussion of this point.

[28] *Pierson*, 182 (emphasis in the original). [29] Ibid., 176. [30] Ibid.

[31] Ibid., 176–77.

[32] Ibid., 177 ("The contrary idea requiring actual taking, proceeds, as Mr. Barbyrac observes, in Puffendorf, B. 4. C. 6. S. 10., on a 'false notion of possession'").

Pothier. Pothier was a legal scholar of tremendous significance, generally thought to have made the codification of the *droit commun* in the French Code in 1804 possible as a result of the series of legal treatises he wrote starting in the 1760s.[33] He had himself produced an authoritative version of Justinian's *Digest*.[34] On the wild animal point, Pothier agreed with the Roman law as it was explained by Trebatius and the old law of the Salians (old customary German law), which favored hot pursuit, understanding it as more civilized (*plus civil*) and what was followed in practice (*est suivi dans l'usage*).[35] But Pothier's property treatise was not available in an English translation, which would explain Colden's failure to refer to it. Pufendorf's *Law of Nature and Nations* was available in English, and in an edition that included Barbeyrac's notes on the text.

Pufendorf defined "the most early Occupant" as "he who lays hold on such a thing before others, or gets the start of them in putting in his Claim to it."[36] Barbeyrac wrote in his note "that taking Possession actually (*Occupatio*) is not always absolutely necessary to acquire a thing that

[33] See Charles Sumner Lobingier, "Napoleon and his Code," 32 *Harvard Law Review* (1918): 114–34, 119–20, 119 n. 19 (noting the influence of Pothier, especially his book on obligations on the law of contracts and how much the treatises simplified the work of the framers of the Code, creating a kind of advance commentary on the Code). See also Robert Taschereau, "Pothier," 3 *La Revue du Barreau de la province de Québec* (1943): 165–78, 174 (stating that nearly the totality of the Code Napoleon was drawn from Pothier's works, nothing that France might have codified anyway but it would have been a different code without him, and despite the fact that he died thirty years earlier and did not work on the Code directly, Pothier was its veritable creator having provided its paths, material, principles, definitions, and organization).

[34] It was a three-volume work published in Paris in 1748 under the title *Pandectea Justinianae in novum ordinem digestae*. See J.E. de Montmorency, "Robert-Joseph Pothier and French Law," 13 *Journal of the Society of Comparative Legislation* (1913): 265–87, 278–79. The *Pandects* were another name for the *Digest*.

[35] See Robert-Joseph Pothier, *Traités du droit de domaine de propriété, de la possession, de la prescription qui resulte de la possession*, vol. 10, *Oeuvres Complètes de Pothier*, M. Siffrein ed. (Paris: Chez Chanson, Imprimeur-Libraire, 1821), 18. Pothier set Trebatius against Gaius on the wounding point. The property treatise was Pothier's last published treatise, first published in 1771–72. See de Montmorency, "Robert-Joseph Pothier and French Law," 282.

[36] Samuel Pufendorf, *Law of Nature and Nations: Or, a General System of the Most Important Principles of Morality, Jurisprudence, and Politics. In eight books. Written in Latin by the Baron Pufendorf ... Done into English by Basil Kennett, ... To which is prefix'd, M. Barbeyrac's prefactory discourse, ... Done into English by Mr. Carew, ... To which are now added, all the large notes of M. Barbeyrac, translated from his fourth and last edition: together with large tables* (London: Printed for J. and J. Bonwicke, R. Ware, J. and P. Knapton, S. Birt, T. Longman [and others], 1749), 386 (Book 4, Chapter 6 "Of Occupancy," section 2).

belongs to no body."[37] If he "makes known to others his Design to seize upon a thing [. . .] he may then acquire the original Property without any actual Possession" but "he must be within Reach of taking what he declares his Design to feixe on."[38] Now Pierson's lawyer, Sanford, retorted that "[t]he only authority relied on is that of an annotator," as if the opinion of a mere commentator should not be given much weight.[39] However, Barbeyrac's annotations on Pufendorf's text were highly esteemed by early Americans, many of whom, like the mentor of John Adams, thought them superior to the Pufendorf text they annotated.[40] Pothier favored Barbeyrac over Pufendorf on the hot pursuit point.[41] If the text had been in circulation in an English translation in the way many of Pothier's other works were, one would have expected to see Colden cite it and for it to carry serious weight with a court inclined to decide the case on the basis of learned authority, as the *Pierson* court appeared to be.

Tompkins agreed with Barbeyrac "[t]o a certain extent," writing that "as far as Barbeyrac appears to me to go, his objections to Puffendorf's definition of occupancy are reasonable and correct. That is to say, that actual bodily seizure is not indispensable to acquire right to, or possession of wild beasts."[42] Mortal wounding would do, Tompkins seems to suggest, as would a net, trap, or snare that was in the hunter's power and made the animal's escape impossible. Tompkins says this is "the full extent of Barbeyrac's objection to Puffendorf's definition [. . .] as can reasonably be inferred from the words or ideas expressed by Barbeyrac in his notes."[43] Barbeyrac "is far from averring that pursuit alone is sufficient," Tompkins wrote.[44] And "[t]he case now under consideration is one of mere pursuit."[45]

[37] Ibid., n. 2. [38] Ibid. [39] *Pierson*, 177.

[40] See Daniel R. Coquillette, "Justinian in Braintree: John Adams, Civilian Learning, and Legal Elitism, 1758–1775" in Daniel R. Coquillette ed., *Law in Colonial Massachusetts, 1630–1800: A Conference held 6 and 7 November 1981 by the Colonial Society of Massachusetts* (Boston, MA: Colonial Society of Massachusetts, 1984), 359–418, 382 n. 7 (John Adams wrote of his mentor, Jeremiah Gridley: "He was a great Admirer of Barbeyrac: thought him a much more sensible and learned Man than Puffendorf"). See also Christopher P. Rodgers, "Continental Literature and the Development of the Common Law by the King's Bench: c. 1750–1800" in Vito Piergiovanni ed., *The Courts and the Development of Commercial Law* (Berlin: Duncker and Humblot, 1987), 161–94, 169 (noting that '[t]he most frequently used edition of Pufendorf was that by Barbeyrac, whose own commentary on the text was itself cited with approval in a number of cases").

[41] Pothier, *Traités du droit de domaine de propriété* in *Oeuvres Complètes*, 10: 18.

[42] *Pierson*, 178. [43] Ibid., 179. [44] Ibid., 178. [45] Ibid., 179.

In other words, Tompkins simply did not respond to Post's lawyer's point that Barbeyrac was putting forward a hot pursuit rule or at least one based on imminent taking (Barbeyrac's idea that the claimant "must be within Reach of taking what he declares his Design to feixe on") and this was not specific to wounding or nets, traps, and the like, points Tompkins brought in from Grotius that are not present in Barbeyrac.[46] This was clearly a strategy to confine and contain the point from Barbeyrac that Post's lawyer Colden was making, namely, that it was sufficient for the claimant to be within the "Reach of taking" the animal. It left undecided the real point of contention in the case; namely, if it was *not* a case of mere pursuit or pursuit with wounding (minor or mortal), could the first pursuer nonetheless acquire a right when the chase had been knowingly disrupted?

Most scholars have (understandably) inferred that a right could not be acquired by hot pursuit, given that the court accepted Justinian's preference for a rule of absolute taking or capture – the capture rule for which *Pierson* is most often taken to stand. However, this is no more than an inference: strictly speaking, the majority decision actually left the situation of an imminent taking undecided, not something that is generally appreciated when *Pierson* is understood as having rejected the hot pursuit rule in favor of the capture rule.

These conceptual and textual gaps (and leaps) in the majority decision might help to explain why we see a strongly worded dissent in the case. The question asked had not actually been answered: If Post was, using Barbeyrac's words, within "the Reach of taking" the fox, did he have a claim against Pierson, who, knowing he was pursuing it, swooped in and took it? However, rather than seriously taking Tompkins to task for his interpretation of Barbeyrac (as he certainly might have), Livingston made fun of the whole approach the lawyers and Tompkins adopted, their game of he-who-cites-the-best-authority-takes-the-prize. Such deference to authority would have agitated Livingston, who, we will see, was an expert in areas of the law intimately tied to civil law authorities and well appreciated that this was an overly simplistic approach to foreign sources. The sources were difficult. They were often at variance. Livingston would have been of the view that they ought to be adopted on the basis of *what* they said, not *who* said what in a different time and place. However, not troubled enough to write a serious peroration on the topic, or perhaps believing indirect chastisement to be more effective

[46] Ibid.

(and more polite with lawyers who had the sophistication Sanford and Colden possessed) and certainly more entertaining, Livingston cloaked his jabs (at the lawyers and at Tompkins) in wit, creating an unusual dissent that this book takes as its starting point. However, before we turn to that dissent we need a bit more ground clearing.

TEXT, SOURCES, AND ARGUMENT: SOME INITIAL QUESTIONS

Early American conditions required careful thinking of what parts of foreign law, British and continental, were appropriate to adopt in which circumstances. This was a tricky business. It was not simply a question of finding the source from a foreign authority that jurists considered to be the best and adopting it because it was the most authoritative. Received wisdom about hierarchies of sources and writers (Justinian is better than Barbeyrac, or Barbeyrac is better than Pufendorf, or Pothier is better than pretty much anyone) had been established in different times, in places as various as the Roman Empire and late eighteenth-century France. What was important in an early American context was *why*: why this rule over that one, that was the true ground for the most persuasive reasons for going one way rather than another.[47] British common-law rules had always been treated that way by colonists, who adopted the parts of it they liked and left the rest behind.[48] After the Revolution, British influence remained extremely important but, politically at least, the onus had shifted. It was perfectly legitimate (especially politically) to demand an explanation of why this British institution (e.g. a Court of Equity) was still relevant to a newly independent nation, or why a system of estates premised on holding land of the Crown still made sense, or why English cases would be considered controlling on American courts.[49] French

[47] The "why" is a powerful trope in early American legal reasoning. See e.g. Noah Webster on the English rule prohibiting a man from marrying his deceased wife's sister, arguing that this rule should be rejected. "Explanation of the Reasons, why Marriage is Prohibited between Natural Relations" (Hartford, July, 1789) in *A Collection of Essays and Fugitive Writings on Moral, Historical, Political and Literary Subjects by Noah Webster Jun.* (Boston: I. Thomas and E.T. Andrews, 1790), 322–24.

[48] See Angela Fernandez, "Record-Keeping and Other Troublemaking: Thomas Lechford and Law Reform in Colonial Massachusetts," 23 *Law and History Review* (2005): 235–77.

[49] See John M. Murrin, *Anglicizing an American Colony: The Transformation of Provincial Massachusetts* (New Haven, CT: Yale University Press, 1966); *Anglicizing America: Empire, Revolution, Republic*, Ignacio Gallup-Diaz, Andrew Shankman and David J. Silverman eds. (Philadelphia: University of Pennsylvania Press, 2015).

writers and philosophers became more popular given the suspect nature of British sources, although they too attracted some negative reaction.[50] And in this *mélange* or mix, the more plural the sources, the more important it was for jurists to have a clear sense of why one rule was adopted in one time and place, why a different rule in another time and place, and what was, all things considered, the best way to go.[51] When multiple choices were on offer, in the eighteenth-century Enlightenment era mindset inherited by these intellectuals, there had to be a reasoned way to choose between them.

The *Pierson* court seemed to favor best-authority over reason-giving. The lawyers at least were certainly arguing as if this were the case, and Tompkins did not correct them, purporting also to base his decision on Barbeyrac (even though it was not the point from Barbeyrac that Post's lawyer had presented), and on Grotius and Justinian (even though he was misreading them). Livingston's own cavalier turn in *Pierson*, specifically discussing authorities like Justinian and Barbeyrac in a flippant way, might well have been a way of objecting to Tompkins's tactics, effectively throwing up his hands and making fun of the whole approach. For instance, Livingston wrote in the dissent that the dispute ought to "have been submitted to the arbitration of sportsmen, without poring over Justinian, Fleta, Bracton, Puffendorf, Locke, Barbeyrac or Blackstone."[52] He rejected Justinian, as "his code was compiled many hundred years ago, and it would be very hard indeed, at the distance of so many centuries, not to have a right to establish a rule for ourselves."[53] "After mature deliberation," he wrote, "I embrace [the opinion] of Barbeyrac," by which he meant the point about the pursuer being within the reach of taking the animal.[54]

[50] See John H. Langbein, "Chancellor Kent and the History of Legal Literature," 93 *Columbia Law Review* (1993): 547–94, 567–68 (discussing the "strong sentiment of hostility to things English" expressed in statutes in New Jersey and Kentucky prohibiting the citation in court of any post-1776 English decisions); Charles Warren, *History of the Harvard Law School and of Early Legal Conditions in America* (New York: Lewis Publishing, 1908), 250–51 (explaining that in Boston and New York Federalists continued to see all things French as "Jacobin" given the French Revolution and conservative feelings about democracy).

[51] And so, as Lawrence Friedman explains, Americans abandoned English practices such as primogeniture, the seal, and feoffment with livery of seizin ("the turf and twig – clearly had to go"). See Lawrence M. Friedman, *A History of American Law*, 3rd ed. (New York: Simon and Shuster, 2001), 171 (abolishing primogeniture from the South); 205–6 (abolishing the seal in most states); 172 (abolishing turf and twig when delivering seizin).

[52] *Pierson*, 180. [53] Ibid., 181. [54] Ibid.

Blackstone warned of the "innumerable tumults" that would result from a variety of persons striving to get first occupation of the same thing and fighting over who had actually gained it."[55] He wrote specifically of the things that must "unavoidably remain in common" such as light, air, water, and wild animals that "disturbances and quarrels would frequently arise among individuals, contending about the acquisition of this species of property by first occupancy."[56] Although not explicitly referred to in the text, Tompkins appears to have been inspired by a thought similar to Blackstone's when he wrote that he would side with Pierson "for the sake of certainty, and preserving peace and order in society." Otherwise disputes between competing first occupants "would prove a fertile source of quarrels and litigation."[57] Hence, Pierson, the "saucy intruder," triumphed over the first pursuer, Post.[58] To the majority, *Pierson* was a case of mere pursuit, in which the animal might well have gotten away; whereas Livingston saw it, as Colden had framed it, as a case of hot pursuit, continuous with a declared intention and ability to take the animal.

When James Kent came to write his famous *Commentaries on American Law* in the 1820s he would have felt that, like Pothier and other learned legal commentators dating back to Justinian, he needed to discuss the situation of the first taker of qualified property, the paradigm example of which was a wild animal, an animal *ferae naturae*, and how one became an owner of it through occupation. However, like the majority opinion, Kent dodged and weaved around the difficult issue, namely, the *minimum* amount of control needed on the continuum between serious uninterrupted pursuit and various degrees of capture (wounding, trapping, and, finally, death). Like Tompkins, Kent presented *Pierson* as a case of mere pursuit. This was the easy case; mere pursuit was not sufficient. The more difficult case was hot pursuit and whether (and when) that was sufficient. Was Barbeyrac wrong to use the standard of within "the Reach of taking"? Was Justinian right to require an actual taking? Was an actual taking required? Despite Kent, many later influential commentators came to understand *Pierson* as a case that held an actual taking was required. It is important to see that this is not actually what Kent said in the *Commentaries*.

Kent's annotations on the second edition of the *Pierson* report, published in 1814, indicate that he knew there was a contrary view on actual taking in Pothier. Kent's reference to Pothier is written next to the part of

[55] Blackstone, *Commentaries*, 2: 4. [56] Ibid., 2: 14–15. [57] *Pierson*, 179.
[58] Ibid., 181.

Tompkins decision that reads "[i]t therefore only remains to inquire whether there are any contrary principles, or authorities, to be found in other books, which ought to induce a different decision" (see Figure I.1).[59] Kent wrote here that Pothier's view was that "[t]he animal must be brought within the power of the pursuer." He then wrote at the bottom of the page that "[a]lmost all the modern civilians agree that the Beast must have been brought within the reach or power of the pursuer" (see Figure I.1). However, "reach or power" did not mean actual taking. Kent wrote, using the same words he used in the Commentaries: "actual taking may not in cases be requisite, but all agree that mere pursuit without bringing the animal within the power of the party is not sufficient."[60]

We do not know precisely when these annotations were written – certainly sometime after 1814 and probably before 1827, when Kent's discussion of *Pierson* appeared in Volume 2 of the *Commentaries*. What Kent says in the *Commentaries* substantially tracks what he wrote in the annotations with a few key differences.[61] First, he did not discuss or cite to Pothier, signaled by Kent's own annotation to Pothier as an authority to the contrary (see Figure I.1). This was despite the fact that Kent did own a complete set of Pothier's works and used Pothier's property law treatise elsewhere in Volume 2 of the *Commentaries*.[62] This is a noteworthy omission because a citation to Pothier not agreeing with the majority opinion would hardly redound to its glory or benefit. We will see below why Kent would have been keen to augment the majority and avoid undermining it. Kent did,

[59] I have been unable to identify which edition of Pothier's complete works Kent was using. From the annotation, it would appear to be one with the property treatise in volume 17. Kent's library listing above has the set at twenty-six volumes. However, the only twenty-six volume set I have been able to locate is by Saint-Albin Berville, which does not contain property in volume 17. Kent has been known to be a little sloppy in his citations and we may have here an example of that. On this last point, see Alan Watson, "Chancellor Kent's Use of Foreign Law" in Mathias Reimann ed. *The Reception of Continental Ideas in the Common Law World, 1820–1920* (Berlin: Duncker and Humblot, 1993), 45–62. I have relied on the more popular and widely available Siffrein edition of Pothier's complete works, where the property material is in volume 10.

[60] See Figure I.1; James Kent, vol. 2, *Commentaries on American Law* (New York: O. Halsted, 1827), 282.

[61] One minor difference is that Kent changed "Almost all the modern civilians agree" to "Almost all the jurists on general jurisprudence agree." See Figure I.1; Kent, *Commentaries*, 2: 282

[62] See *Kent Family Papers, Diaries, and Notebooks*, 1824–1843, Butler Rare Book Room and Manuscript Library, Columbia University, New York City, New York. "Catalogue of his Library." Vol. 8: 92 ("Works of Pothier 26 vols (French)"); Kent, *Commentaries*, 2: 43 n. b; 2: 273 n. c; 2: 294 n. b. See also *Curtis v. Groat*, 6 Johns. 168 (N.Y. Sup. Ct., 1810), 170 (this case is identified as *per curiam* but it was likely written by Kent).

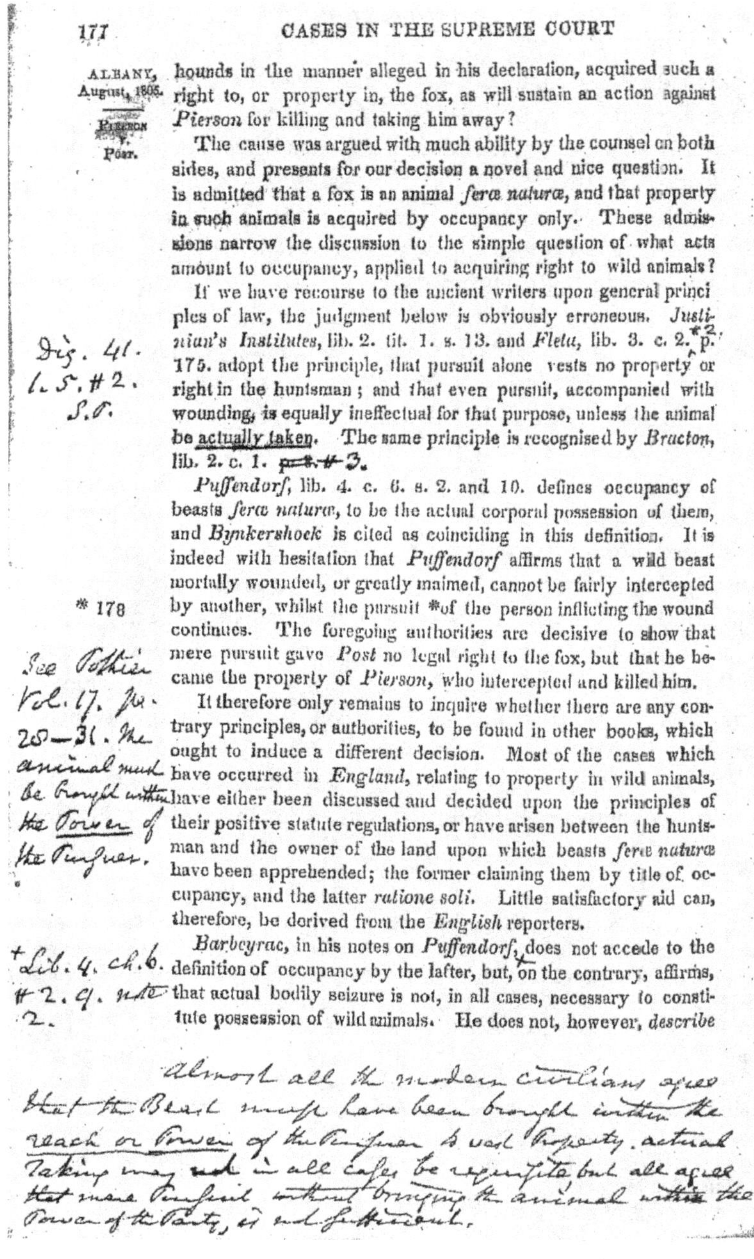

177 CASES IN THE SUPREME COURT

ALBANY, August, 1805. PIERSON v. POST.

hounds in the manner alleged in his declaration, acquired such a right to, or property in, the fox, as will sustain an action against *Pierson* for killing and taking him away?

The cause was argued with much ability by the counsel on both sides, and presents for our decision a novel and nice question. It is admitted that a fox is an animal *feræ naturæ*, and that property in such animals is acquired by occupancy only. These admissions narrow the discussion to the simple question of what acts amount to occupancy, applied to acquiring right to wild animals?

Dig. 41. l. 5. #2. S.P.

If we have recourse to the ancient writers upon general principles of law, the judgment below is obviously erroneous. *Justinian's Institutes*, lib. 2. tit. 1. s. 13. and *Fleta*, lib. 3. c. 2. p. 175. adopt the principle, that pursuit alone vests no property or right in the huntsman; and that even pursuit, accompanied with wounding, is equally ineffectual for that purpose, unless the animal be actually taken. The same principle is recognised by *Bracton*, lib. 2. c. 1. ~~p. 8.~~ #3.

Puffendorf, lib. 4. c. 6. s. 2. and 10. defines occupancy of beasts *feræ naturæ*, to be the actual corporal possession of them, and *Bynkershoek* is cited as coinciding in this definition. It is indeed with hesitation that *Puffendorf* affirms that a wild beast mortally wounded, or greatly maimed, cannot be fairly intercepted by another, whilst the pursuit *of the person inflicting the wound continues. The foregoing authorities are decisive to show that mere pursuit gave *Post* no legal right to the fox, but that he became the property of *Pierson*, who intercepted and killed him.

* 178

See Pothier Vol. 17. pa. 28–31. the animal must be brought within the Power of the Pursuer.

It therefore only remains to inquire whether there are any contrary principles, or authorities, to be found in other books, which ought to induce a different decision. Most of the cases which have occurred in *England*, relating to property in wild animals, have either been discussed and decided upon the principles of their positive statute regulations, or have arisen between the huntsman and the owner of the land upon which beasts *feræ naturæ* have been apprehended; the former claiming them by title of occupancy, and the latter *ratione soli*. Little satisfactory aid can, therefore, be derived from the *English* reporters.

+Lib. 4. ch. 6. #2. 9. note 2.

Barbeyrac, in his notes on *Puffendorf*,+ does not accede to the definition of occupancy by the latter, but, on the contrary, affirms, that actual bodily seizure is not, in all cases, necessary to constitute possession of wild animals. He does not, however, *describe*

Almost all the modern civilians agree that the Beast must have been brought within the reach or Power of the Pursuer to vest Property. actual Taking may not in all cases be requisite but all agree that mere Pursuit without bringing the animal within the Power of the Party, is not sufficient.

FIGURE 1.1 Kent's annotations reproduced from James Kent's copy of George Caines, 2nd ed., vol. 3, *New-York Term Reports of Cases Argued and Determined in the Supreme Court of that State* (New York: Van Winkle & Wiley Printers, 1814), 177. New York State Library, Manuscripts and Special Collections, Albany, NY.

however, bring in the idea of power or *puissance*, which was probably suggested to him by Pothier. Hence, Kent left out Pothier by name (and citation that would support a contrary view) but brought in his concept of power, noting that actual taking was not required but mere pursuit was insufficient.

A second important difference between what Kent wrote in the annotation at the bottom of the page on his copy of *Pierson* and the way these ideas were expressed in the *Commentaries* is that the annotation used the phrase "the reach or power of the pursuer" (see Figure I.1). Kent left "reach" out of the *Commentaries* formulation, where he wrote instead about the "power of the pursuer."[63] Why is that significant? Barbeyrac used the word "reach" in his phrase, "the Reach of taking," the part of Barbeyrac the majority opinion in *Pierson* simply did not address and which Post's lawyer had argued was all that was needed for Post's successful occupation of the fox that Pierson was legally required to respect. Livingston also used the word "reach" when he characterized the case as a situation of hot pursuit (not mere pursuit), i.e. where the fox was *within reach* ("property in animals *ferae naturae*, may be acquired without bodily touch or manucaption, provided the pursuer be *within reach*, or have a reasonable prospect (which certainly existed here) of taking").[64] If Kent was keen to augment rather than undermine the majority opinion, it would make sense for him to leave out the "reach" that animated the opposing view and its supporting authorities and cut against the majority decision.

The majority in *Pierson* and Kent in the *Commentaries* were keen to present *Pierson* as a situation of mere pursuit, something that was both true and, crucially, not true. Post's hunt was *mere* pursuit in the sense that it did not involve wounding or trapping, and so was *only* pursuit; however, it was not *mere* in the sense of being very far away, neither hot nor imminent, at least according to Post's lawyer, Colden. Tompkins's majority opinion traded heavily on the ambiguity surrounding what was meant by *mere*: the pursuit was *mere* in the sense of not involving trapping and wounding. Post's lawyer would certainly have agreed with that, as there was no suggestion wounding or traps played any role on the facts, with the exception of the final (and only) wound Pierson inflicted on the fox when he bludgeoned it to death. The ambiguity has not been appreciated by scholars of *Pierson*. The case is hardly the model of clarity that later twentieth- and twenty-first century legal scholars have tried to turn it into.

[63] Kent, *Commentaries*, 2: 282. [64] *Pierson*, 182 (emphasis added).

By the time Kent wrote the *Commentaries*, the New York Supreme Court case had decided a subsequent case, *Buster v. Newkirk* (1822), in which the Court said it was following *Pierson*.[65] This was not a case of hot pursuit, or at least not straightforwardly; indeed, it seemed to be marked by the lack of continued or at least vigorous pursuit by the first hunter when a second hunter encountered the wild animal (this time a deer) after the original hunter had abandoned it. The original hunter (Newkirk) wounded the deer but not so badly it could not still run. Newkirk gave up the chase and went home overnight (presumably because it was dark) and the deer ran six miles near to the house of the second hunter (Buster). When Newkirk returned the following morning to follow the blood of the wounded animal, he ended up at Buster's house and learned that the previous evening Buster had killed the deer. A wrinkle in the story is that Newkirk's dog participated in the kill, making it arguably at least a case of lukewarm pursuit; even though Newkirk went home, he left his animal to pursue the hunt and the dog was his property. Perhaps in recognition of this or the initial wounding – it is not said – Buster offered Newkirk the meat of the deer. However, Buster refused to hand over the skin, which became the subject of Newkirk's suit, and for which he was awarded 75¢ by a jury. Despite the wounding, presumably because it was not a mortal wounding and because Newkirk suspended the pursuit (at least in his own physical person), the New York Supreme Court said that his occupancy was insufficient, that the animal had not been deprived of its natural liberty and brought within the power and control of the original pursuer. As such, Buster was free to take it (even though it was with the help of Newkirk's dog).

Kent referred to *Buster v. Newkirk* in his discussion of *Pierson* in the *Commentaries*, noting that "mere pursuit [...] did not create a property [...] and the same doctrine was afterwards declared in *Buster v. Newkirk*."[66] This was an odd use of that authority, for *Buster v. Newkirk* involved wounding and continued pursuit at least by Newkirk's dog. It was hardly a case of *mere* pursuit, even if it did not qualify as vigorous and continued pursuit. Although Newkirk had returned home, the dog at least had followed, waiting for the deer to fall. The wounding alone made the case significantly different from *Pierson*. However, Kent was obviously keen when writing the *Commentaries* to use the few New York authorities he had at his

65 *Buster v. Newkirk*, 20 Johns. Rep. 75 (N.Y. Sup. Ct., 1822).
66 Kent, *Commentaries*, 2: 283.

fingertips so that they built on one another and were mutually reinforcing. If this could not be made to work for these hunting conflict cases, which were not that complicated, it would be difficult to keep alive faith in use of the common law as a system for more difficult scenarios.[67] Omitting the "reach" from (what was probably) the earlier annotation ("the reach or power of the pursuer") meant keeping out a word that would carry with it some of the flavor of hot pursuit that Livingston had seen in *Pierson* (quite legitimately as it was at Post's lawyer behest) and that Barbeyrac and Pothier had thought was in the law. Kent was keen to edit it out and leave out the name of the great jurist Pothier. We are not sure what the minimum amount of control was that worked in order to secure the property right (evidently as per *Buster v. Newkirk* inconclusive wounding was not enough if pursuit was abandoned overnight) but pursuit alone (even with wounding and leaving a dog in place) was not enough.

We will see that subsequent commentators forgot Kent's careful parsing of the issue – an actual taking was not required; what *was* required was power or control – and interpreted the majority's position as Justinian's, namely, that actual capture was what was needed to establish occupancy. Yet truly, Kent was careful at least in the initial paragraph of his discussion of *Pierson* and *Buster v. Newkirk* to stay within the bounds established by Pothier, namely, that what was key was the power or control of the pursuer (and a dog was insufficient to maintain that, as in *Buster v. Newkirk*). The power and control was what was required. So even if there was wounding (as in *Buster v. Newkirk*) it might not be mortal; even if there were traps, they might not be inescapable (as in some of the later nineteenth-century fish net cases such as *Young v. Hitchens*); and even if there was close persistent pursuit (as in *Pierson*) the animal had to be within the pursuer's power and not just within reach, as Barbeyrac and Livingston held – or perhaps being within reach brought it within one's power. Actual irreversible capture (e.g. killing the animal) would certainly qualify, but, technically speaking, Barbeyrac was correct that an actual taking was not required.

[67] Kent was not sitting on the New York Supreme Court when it decided *Buster v. Newkirk* and even if he saw that it was a stretch to say that case was a case of mere pursuit, the decision stated that "[t]he principle decided in the case of *Pierson v. Post*, 3 Cai 175, are applicable here" and occupancy in a wild animal "is sufficient if the animal is deprived of his natural liberty, by wounding or otherwise, so that he is brought within the power and control of the pursuer." *Buster v. Newkirk*, 75.

How then did the majority come to stand for the capture rule/actual taking via Kent's *Commentaries*? Well, after discussing *Pierson* and *Buster v. Newkirk*, Kent started a new paragraph with the following words: "The civil law contained the same principle as that which the Supreme Court adopted."[68] He then wrote immediately after this, citing to the *Institutes* (Chapters 12 and 13) and the *Digest* passage on wounding, that "[i]t was a question in the Roman law, whether a wild beast belonged to him who had wounded it so that it might easily be taken. The civilians differed on the question; but Justinian adopted the opinion, that the property in the wounded wild beast did not attach until the beast was actually taken."[69] This sounds very much like Kent wanted to argue that Justinian's rule on actual taking had made it into the civil law and was then adopted by the New York Supreme Court in *Pierson* and *Buster v. Newkirk*. Or at least this is how Kent was understood to argue by Oliver Wendell Holmes Jr. Holmes who edited the twelfth edition of Kent's *Commentaries* and said in his famous *Common Law* lecture on possession that "[t]he Roman and the common law agree that, in general, fresh pursuit of wild animals does not give the pursuer the rights of possession. *Until escape has been made impossible* by some means, another may step in and kill or catch and carry off the game if he can."[70] Here Holmes described *Pierson* and cited to Kent's discussion of the case and *Buster v. Newkirk* in the *Commentaries*.[71]

The lecture or chapter in Kent's *Commentaries* in which *Pierson* is discussed is titled "Of the Nature and Various Kinds of Personal Property," and the discussion starts with the moveable/immovable distinction, explaining the historic importance of the distinction between real and personal property in the common law.[72] "[T]he law of chattels, once so unimportant," Kent wrote, "has grown into a system, which, by its magnitude, overshadows [...] the learning of real estates."[73] Kent then presented the distinction between absolute and qualified property, relying on Justinian's *Institutes* to discuss air, light, and water, things which, by their nature, are "the subject of a qualified property by occupancy."[74] He highlighted animals *ferae naturae*, exploring problems distinguishing wild from tame animals and explaining that tame or domestic animals and

[68] Kent, *Commentaries*, 2: 283. [69] Ibid.

[70] Oliver Wendell Holmes Jr., *The Common Law* (Boston, MA: Little, Brown, 1881), 217 (emphasis added).

[71] Ibid., 217, 217 n. 1. [72] See Kent, *Commentaries*, 2: 277. [73] Ibid., 2: 278.

[74] Ibid., 2: 281.

those that have an *animus revertendi*, or habit of returning, are owned absolutely, whereas animals that are "wild by nature" are qualified property until they can no longer escape.[75] Kent presented the majority ruling in *Pierson* with no reference to Livingston's dissent or any hint that the case might have actually been a situation of hot pursuit rather than mere pursuit, noting only that the majority rule and mere pursuit interpretation had been followed in *Buster v. Newkirk*.[76] This even though the *mere* in *Pierson* (no wounding) was different than the *mere* in *Buster v. Newkirk* (not hot enough). *Buster v. Newkirk* then certainly added to the sense subsequent legal scholars had that what had been rejected in it (and looking back in *Pierson*) was the hot pursuit rule, and what had been accepted and set out as the common law position in both cases was the capture rule.

TEXT, SOURCES, AND ARGUMENT: AN OPENING CLAIM

Kent's *Commentaries* were part of what John Langbein has termed Kent's "struggle for learned law."[77] They were intended to be the equivalent of Blackstone's *Commentaries* for the United States, and were received as such. Like other works in the "institute" tradition from Gaius and the Roman law, the *Commentaries* were to provide a centralizing and unifying role for a sovereign nation state in the same way that a Civil Code did for civil law countries like France, Germany, and Spain.[78] They were, therefore, an extremely important legal/political project in the early American period. It was of especial importance to Federalists like Kent, who were in the process of losing their direct political power, as the process of the systematic displacement of Federalists and their

[75] Ibid. [76] Ibid., 2: 283.

[77] Langbein, "Chancellor Kent and the History of Legal Literature," 566–70 (section entitled "The Struggle for Learned Law").

[78] See John W. Cairns, "Blackstone, an English Institutist: Legal Literature and the Rise of the Nation State," 4 *Oxford Journal of Legal Studies* (1984): 318–60, 322 (France and Spain lacked a unified legal system, laws varied from region to region, and both had monarchs who wanted to centralize government and unify the realm. In both countries, "the monarchy played an important role in creating national law, first, by fostering a sense of national identity, and by centering rule on the king, ignoring local structural political differences, secondly, by providing royal legislation valid for the whole kingdom, and thirdly, by promoting the study of national law in the universities"). On Gaius and the Institutes structure, see Donald R. Kelley, "Gaius Noster: Substructures of Western Social Thought," 84 *The American Historical Review* (1979): 619–48, 620 ("Gaius formulated (if he did not create) one of the most distinctive and enduring systems of thought in Western history").

replacement by Republicans increased in the first third of the nineteenth century.[79] Didactic works that helped establish a common law for the United States became an extremely important part of efforts by conservatives taking the position that legislatively enacted codes, which they feared would come under too much popular or democratic influence, were unnecessary.[80] Admittedly, cases like *Pierson* and *Buster v. Newkirk* were strictly New York law, but New York law was influential then (as now) not just in other states but in other countries. Just as Blackstone traveled so influentially to the United States, Kent's *Commentaries* also traveled widely, used and relied upon in other jurisdictions (as we shall see in Chapter 7). The mere pursuit interpretation of *Pierson* and its apparent support in a subsequent case like *Buster v. Newkirk* was just the kind of serious law-building through a common law use of cases that Kent was keen to promote when he was on the bench, and then promulgate in his *Commentaries*. As if addressing an uncertain audience who needed convincing, Kent's message was "see, it works."[81]

Kent clearly knew there was a contrary view – Livingston's – but, no doubt he thought it better to ignore the dissent in *Pierson*, which we will see was an inherently unstable text, and instead highlight and promote *Pierson* as a serious working precedent on mere pursuit, its value as such proven in subsequent cases like *Buster v. Newkirk*. In so doing, Kent lay

[79] See Daniel J. Hulsebosch, *Constituting Empire: New York and the Transformation of Constitutionalism in the Atlantic World, 1664–1830* (Chapel Hill: University of North Carolina Press, 2005), 278–79 (emphasizing the way that "Federalists turned to the nonlegislative dimensions of law and legal training, the areas of legal culture that were beyond the reach of electoral politics [...] [I]f they could not control decision making directly, they could try to control the raw material on which decisions were made: the reports, treatises, handbooks, and educational institutions that inculcated law's purpose [...] [resulting in the] painstaking acculturation of lawyers and judges in a supposedly nonpartisan legal culture").

[80] See ibid., 299 ("in practice the codification controversy was a conflict between two groups of lawyers: those who wanted to unify American law through treatises and legal education, and those who wanted to do so as delegates of state legislatures"); 280 ("Kent and other Federalist heirs resisted most codification efforts because they arose at the *state* rather than the national level. The federal government lacked the power to enact a private-law code"). See also Robert W. Gordon, "Book Review [of *The American Codification Movement: A Study of Antebellum Legal Reform* by C.M. Cook]," 36 *Vanderbilt Law Review* (1983): 431–58 (explaining how codes are usually elite and therefore fairly technical and conservative legal projects even when undertaken by legislatures).

[81] An important question is whether without the massaging of treatise writers and other legal scholars the common law system does work as a way to produce and refine legal doctrine.

down the track or set the tone for how *Pierson* was treated until the middle of the twentieth century when Livingston's dissent (for better or worse) reasserted itself, the very definition of an irrepressible or fugitive piece of American legal culture. As we shall see, the dissent was then once more tamed, this time by those looking for a clear (and allegedly obviously inferior) contrast to the bright line rule "he who kills takes."

Kent's discussion in the *Commentaries* of the degree of control necessary to establish possession in a wild animal reproduced a traditional (and very serious) philosophical rhythm for American property law: property moves or does not move; the immovable kind can be owned absolutely; the movable kind is subject to a qualified property right in which possession must be perfected by occupation; wild animals are the quintessential form of this kind of movable property and are distinguished from tame or domestic animals, which cannot regain their freedom through escape and generally have an *animus revertendi* or habit of returning.[82] Kent featured *Pierson* prominently, asking and answering the classic question relating to wild animals for an American audience: mere pursuit of a wild animal was insufficient to credit the first occupant; even if an actual taking was not required, the animal had to come within the power or control of the pursuer in order for there to be occupancy of it. This was a subtle point that quickly degenerated into the requirement of an actual taking.[83] The *Commentaries* then made that answer readily available to others throughout the English-speaking common law world with a theoretical or legal intellectual bent, including jurists in both the United Kingdom and Canada.[84]

TEXT, SOURCES, AND ARGUMENT: FIRST OBSERVATIONS, AND A TALE OF DISCOVERY

The appellate case report that law students regularly read, often in the first few days of their property class, records the lawyers and judges in *Pierson* wrestling with old learned authorities. These texts were a standard part of an

[82] Kent, *Commentaries*, 2: 277–81. [83] See ibid., 2: 282–83.

[84] Chapter 7 will explore transportation of *Pierson* from the United States to England through Oliver Wendell Homes Jr. to Frederick Pollock. This chapter also explains the transmission of *Pierson* to the Supreme Court of Canada through a case called the *Gerring* in 1897 through a textbook edition of Kent's *Commentaries* and a Canadian lawyer for the Crown, William Bruce Almon Ritchie, who attended Harvard Law School in 1881–82, and cited to the work in his factum before the court. It inspired one of the judges on that court to write an opinion even more elaborate and learned than *Pierson* itself.

elite lawyer's education in the eighteenth- and early nineteenth centuries. We will see that they were connected to serious and lucrative areas of legal practice, giving lawyers every incentive to learn how to work with them. In short, what appear as arcane and antique texts to students and lawyers today were entirely familiar and instrumentally useful to the lawyers of the early republic. Justinian's *Institutes* served as a kind of first-year law text, invaluable – just as Blackstone's *Commentaries* themselves were – in an apprenticeship environment in the United States where there were few formal law schools and a scarcity of readable common-law treatises.[85] Modern-day students, who go nowhere near the *Institutes*, may never have heard of Blackstone, and probably have next to no exposure to thinkers like Pufendorf, regularly tell me when we study the larger context of *Pierson* in their later years of law school that they find all of the case's references and learned discussion utterly bewildering. If the first encounter with *Pierson* occurs early in a student's legal education, which is more likely than not, given that the course "Property" is often taught in the first semester of first year, and *Pierson* is so often used as an introduction to the concept of property, it may throw students into a panic (I can't understand anything – there is a lot of Latin in the judgment that may go untranslated in their casebook) or despair (Is this what law school is going to be like? This is not at all what I imagined).[86]

Many students nevertheless respond well to *Pierson*, so much so that I am told by some property professors who have tried to remove it from their course that students are upset and ask why they are not studying the famous fox case. It is one of the few cases practicing lawyers will remember from law school, especially if it is taught in a mocking or humorous way by a teacher who does something unusual and memorable, like bringing in a stuffed fox and re-

[85] See Watson, "Introduction to Law for Second-year Students," 437 n. 26 (noting the long history of the *Institutes* as a textbook for first-year students). See also Coquillette, "Justinian in Braintree," 399 n. 7 (on the importance of civil law treatises in an early American environment). See Daniel J. Boorstin, *The Mysterious Science of the Law: An Essay on Blackstone's Commentaries showing how Blackstone, Employing Eighteenth-Century Ideas of Science, Religion, History, Aesthetics, and Philosophy, made of the Law at once a Conservative and a Mysterious Science* (Boston, MA: Beacon Press, 1958) (on Blackstone in America).

[86] See e.g. Alfred Connor Bowman, Book Review of *The Right of Hot Pursuit in International Law* by Nicholas M. Poulantzas and A. W. Sijthoff (1969) in "Books for Lawyers," 59 *American Bar Association Journal* (1973): 237–38, 237 (referring to *Pierson* as "the classic law school casebook problem involving the fox" that "[m]ost of us will remember, painfully").

enacting the hunting scene.[87] The pompousness of the legal argument, its learnedness, invites such treatment, as does the seemingly trivial value of the object of dispute, a fox killed so many years ago.

I did not study *Pierson* as a law student and so did not experience it, as so many do, as a rite of passage in first- or second-year law school.[88] Instead, I became intrigued by the case as a matter of legal history when I encountered it as a junior law teacher at a conference in 2005.[89] It sounded so contrived – the beach, the warring litigants, the near-hysteria about imperiled chickens in Livingston's dissent, where he refers to the fox as a *hostem humani generis* or enemy of humankind.[90] It was almost like a hunting-themed fairy tale. Could it have been true? Had it

[87] See e.g. "Dedication in Remembrance: Barry L. Zaretsky," 63 *Brooklyn Law Review* (1997): i–xxxvii, specifically remarks by Professor William S. Jordan III, University of Akron School of Law, xvi–xviii, xvi (remembering a law school classmate who died, noting that he "was a star in law school from the very beginning [...] Because his name came last in the alphabet, Barry was chosen to play the fox in the famous Property case *Pierson v.* Post [...] At the beginning of our first Property class, he ran across the front of the classroom carrying a stuffed fox, which someone else shot from the back of the room. For some of us, it is the only thing we remember from law school"). I must add here the correction of a common misperception, which is that the fox was shot by Pierson; it was clubbed to death, as local legend later had it, with "a broken rail," i.e. a piece of fence railing. See H.P. Hedges, "Pierson vs. Post" (Thursday October 24, 1895) *Sag-Harbor Express*, Suffolk County, NY. There are problems relying on an account so long after the fact but none of the original sources mention a gun/shooting.

[88] The case is, however, taught in Canadian law schools. See e.g. Mary Jane Mossman and Philip Girard, *Property Law: Cases and Commentary*, 3rd ed. (Toronto: Emond Montgomery Publications, 2014), 99–111 (not reproducing the case but excerpting from Carol Rose's discussion of it in "Possession as the Origin of Property," Patricia Williams's *The Alchemy of Race and Rights*, Angela Fernandez responding to Rose and Ziff on seals in a new section entitled "Rethinking *Pierson v. Post*"); Bruce Ziff et al., *A Property Reader: Cases, Questions, and Commentary*, 3rd ed. (Toronto: Thomson Carswell, 2012), 303–304 nn. 6 and 7 (excerpting from the majority and the dissent and asking about the relative costs of each approach); Bruce Ziff, *Principles of Property Law*, 6th ed. (Toronto: Thomson Carswell, 2014), 137 n. 18 (footnote to the case in the context of a discussion of wild animals and providing citations to more recent work on the case, including my own). Canadian law teachers often use their own mimeographed materials in addition to or instead of a published casebook and at my institution, the University of Toronto, at least four of my colleagues teach *Pierson* from its full text (Lisa Austin, Abraham Drassinower, Douglas Sanderson, and Larissa Katz).

[89] American Society for Legal History meeting, Annual Meeting, Cincinnati, Ohio, November 12, 2005. The panel was entitled "Case Microhistories" and the paper was by Andrea McDowell, "*Pierson v. Post* and the Rules of Foxhunting." McDowell later published her piece as "Legal Fictions in *Pierson v. Post*," 105 *Michigan Law Review* (2006–2007): 735–77. I agree with what McDowell said in her piece, important aspects of which have been confirmed in the discovered Judgment Roll. See Chapter 5, specifically on the new element of malice and the structure of the case as a tort case.

[90] *Pierson*, 180.

really happened? As Andrea McDowell put it in her presentation at that conference, the case had a surreal feel. On any number of levels it did not seem to make sense. I soon learned that in addition to McDowell another legal scholar, Bethany Berger, was working on the case. The three of us – McDowell, Berger, and myself – constituted a kind of cottage industry with a new focus on *Pierson*. We were engaged in the creation of a new kind of legal literature that sought to reconstruct the case both in its local context and its later pedagogical trajectory.[91]

Kent's annotations on his copy of *Pierson* intrigued me further (see Figure I.1).[92] Kent was the first person to put *Pierson* into serious scholarly circulation. I became convinced that he had somehow played a role in engineering its peculiarly learned and academic tone. McDowell had located a record of a similar dispute over a fox from Connecticut that was handled in a much more rough-and-ready way, and this seemed to bring home the special nature of the New York case.[93] Curious, I decided I needed to try to get to the bottom of the matter. I was looking for (and hoping to find) direct evidence of Kent's involvement, but I was still also half-thinking and wondering whether there ever had been an actual case at all, a reaction I often get when I describe the case to people who did not learn it at law school, either because they are Canadian and were not taught it or they are not lawyers. I also had my doubts about the capture rule; I was starting to think that Livingston might have been right to advocate hot pursuit when it came to hunting. This is the rule that the New York legislature later adopted to govern the hunting of deer.[94] And

91 For instance, in July 2006 the three of us appeared together on a panel at the Annual Meeting of the Law and Society Association (Baltimore, MD) moderated by Debora Threedy. Berger published her piece as Bethany R. Berger, "It's Not About the Fox: The Untold History of *Pierson v. Post*," 55 *Duke Law Journal* (2005–2006): 1089–1143. We are often cited and discussed together. See e.g. Stuart Banner, "21st Century Fox: *Pierson v. Post*, Then and Now" Comment in "Forum, *Pierson v. Post*: Capturing New Facts about the Fox," 27 *Law and History Review* (2009): 145–94, 185–88, 185 n. 2; Jesse Dukeminier, James E. Krier, Gregory S. Alexander, Michael H. Schill, Lior Jacob Strahilevitz, 8th ed., *Property* (New York: Aspen Law and Business, 2014), 23–24 n. 1.

92 I read about this annotated copy of the case in Donald M. Roper, "The New York Supreme Court and Economic Development, 1798–1823" in Glenn Porter and William H. Mulligan, Jr. eds., *Working Papers from the Regional Economic History Research Center; Law and Economic Development: Papers from the Fall 1979 Regional Economic History Conference* (Wilmington, DE: Greenville, 1980), 82 n. 31, which I located through Langbein, "Chancellor Kent and the History of Legal Literature," 562 n. 75.

93 This Connecticut case is reproduced from McDowell's article in Appendix D, *Sharpe v. Sabin*.

94 Discussed in more detail in Chapter 1.

through the annotations I learned that Pothier also wrote in support of the hot pursuit rule, which had some uptake in Canada.[95]

Law and economics scholars who entertained the query I raised about the capture rule at an event bringing junior and senior scholars together in 2007 did not quite know what to do with my suggestion that the hot pursuit rule might be superior. To them I think it seemed obvious that the bright line rule must be the right one.[96] Indeed, Carol Rose had written a very famous article in 1985 to advance a "clear act" argument using *Pierson* as her touchstone.[97] This argument, combined with a general idea about cost and efficiency, namely, which rule is more costly (less efficient) and more likely to incite litigants to sue, tends to augur in favor of Pierson. The idea is that Pierson's actual taking of the animal was clearer than Post's pursuit and that the clearer rule will (we speculate) lead to less litigation when the situation arises in the future in similar circumstances. Unclear, however, is what is *not clear* about Post's signaling of his intention to take the animal. The facts of the case have always said that Pierson *knew* of Post's intention to take the fox: "Pierson, well knowing the fox was so hunted and pursued, did in the sight of Post, to prevent his catching the same, kill and carry it off."[98] Given that, *Pierson* simply cannot stand as a good example of the clear-act theory. This response to and use of *Pierson* looks to be a product of a particular moment in the 1980s (which continues today to some extent) when at least some law professors were very keen on promoting clear rules that they believed would maximize efficiency or increase competition, and seizing on historical examples that, they claimed, proved the common law had always been dedicated to efficiency. Such claims and ambitions, which strike a historian as wildly acontextual, have translated into a belief that more clarity was always better even when it was not needed or, as in the *Pierson* case, was literally overkill.

On history's side of the aisle, other legal historians were skeptical that anything more could be discovered about the case. People have looked,

95 In Canada there is some support in the case law for the hot pursuit rule, not surprisingly given Pothier's position on this, in Québec. See *Charlebois v. Richmond*, 12 *The Lower Canada Jurist-Collection des décisions du bas-Canada* (Montreal: John Lovell, 1868), 55–56 (rejecting Roman law and Justinian's requirement that the wild animal (a bear) must be taken, choosing instead what is termed the French law in which following the animal gave the pursuer possession of it against an interloper who killed and took it).

96 Stanford-Yale Junior Faculty Forum, Stanford Law School, May 19, 2007.

97 Carol M. Rose, "Possession as the Origin of Property," 52 *University of Chicago Law Review* (1985): 73–88.

98 *Pierson*, 175.

I was told. There was talk about records consumed in fires. McDowell, I remember, said keep looking. Members of the Toronto Legal History Group agreed. I kept at it and discovered a Judgment Roll for the *Pierson* (or as it was spelled there, "Peirson") case in New York City in the New York County Clerk's Office, Division of Old Records. I had searched so many places where documentation relating to the case might have been located that I recall thinking, "Well if there is nothing at a place called 'the Division of Old Records,' I will have to accept defeat." Luckily this office had recently reorganized the filing system used to search the Judgment Rolls in old cases and was able to locate and send me a photocopy of the Judgment Roll in the case. One page is reproduced in Figure B.1; a full transcript is reproduced in Appendix B; and the transcript plus scans of each page of the photocopy of the handwritten text has been posted through the University of Toronto (https://dataverse.scholarsportal.info/dataset.xhtml?persistentId=doi:10.5683/SP/3HJKJ7). These last will be important to future students of *Pierson*, as the original has gone missing from the County Clerk's Office, lost (or perhaps stolen) after the discovery of its existence was publicized in 2009. This is an unfortunate turn of events, for it to have been discovered and then lost again so quickly.

The Judgment Roll, or "the lost record" in *Post v. Pierson* (as it originally was), provided much hitherto unknown information about the case – the amount that was awarded by a jury to Post (75¢), the costs Pierson was ordered to pay after losing the jury trial ($5), the names of the jury members (economic information on them based on old tax records is provided in Appendix C), the date of the incident (December 2, 1802), the time, date, and place of trial (December 30, 1802 at 2 p.m. at the house of Hugh Gelston Jr.), confirmation of the names of the lawyers, and the amount of money Post was ordered to pay ($126.37).[99] It also revealed that Post originally alleged malice against Pierson, in other words that Pierson not only knew he was in pursuit of the fox but that Pierson took it in order to spoil his fun.[100] This new piece of information is relevant, as we will see in Chapter 5, to understanding

[99] I originally reported the amount Post was ordered to pay as $121.37, which is what the Judgment Roll recorded. See Judgment Roll, p. 19, Appendix B. However, I have since located another record of the *Pierson* case, which records the amount of "Damages and Costs" at $126.37. See "Archival Note" at the end of this Introduction. The difference is presumably the $5 award to Post from the court below, which he now had to reimburse to Pierson along with the $121.37 incurred on appeal.

[100] See Judgment Roll, p. 5, Appendix B.

Pierson as a case that had its origins in tort law rather than property, a slightly embarrassing situation for such a famous property law case. It was, as McDowell had suspected and wrote before it was confirmed by the lost record, "a defective torts case."[101] We also learn that there were seven witnesses at the jury trial.[102]

Alfred Brophy organized a forum on my discovery of the Judgment Roll in *Law and History Review* in 2009, where he compared it to the unearthing of a long-lost Beatles recording for law students and law professors.[103] I reported on and explained what I had discovered.[104] A group of property law scholars responded. Charles Donahue who had previously written extensively about *Pierson,* concluded that what I had found squared up with what he had been saying for many years.[105] Stuart Banner provided an overview of the extensive scholarship on *Pierson*, noting that "[t]he case is so famous [. . .] it has become an object of study in its own right [. . .] it is one of the few cases that everyone in the profession knows."[106] James Krier criticized the legal historian's penchant for accumulating factual information. He reiterated what has become since the 1980s the classic law and economics analysis of the case: one that demonstrates the superiority of bright line rules to allegedly fuzzy standards.[107]

Still unable to corroborate Kent's involvement, I published another article floating the theory that Kent would have had an interest in encouraging junior members of the bar and bench to treat the case in the elaborate and learned way that they did in order to produce the kind of precedent

101 McDowell, "Legal Fictions in *Pierson v. Post*," 735.

102 See Judgment Roll, p. 10, Appendix B.

103 See Alfred L. Brophy, "Introduction: A Famous Fox, a Surfacing Whale, and the Forgotten Slave" in "Forum, *Pierson v. Post*: Capturing New Facts about the Fox," 27 *Law and History Review* (2009): 145–94, 145–47, 145–46 (although "not quite a lost Beatles recording, for law students and property professors, it may be close").

104 Angela Fernandez, "The Lost Record of *Pierson v. Post*, the Famous Fox Case" in "Forum, *Pierson v. Post*: Capturing New Facts about the Fox," 27 *Law and History Review* (2009): 145–94, 149–78.

105 Charles Donahue Jr., "Papyrology and 3 Caines 175" Comment in "Forum, *Pierson v. Post*: Capturing New Facts about the Fox," 27 *Law and History Review* (2009): 145–94, 179–84.

106 Banner, "21st Century Fox: *Pierson v. Post*, Then and Now," 188.

107 See James E. Krier, "Facts, Information, and the Newly Discovered Record in *Pierson v. Post*" Comment in "Forum, *Pierson v. Post*: Capturing New Facts about the Fox," 27 *Law and History Review* (2009): 145–94, 189–94, 193. In response, see Angela Fernandez, "Fuzzy Rules and Clear Enough Standards: The Uses and Abuses of *Pierson v. Post*" in Focus Feature "Foxes, Seals, Whales and the Rule of Capture: Animals in the Law and Legal History," 63 *University of Toronto Law Journal* (2013): 30–137, 97–125.

New York Supreme Court

Jesse Pierson vs. Lodowick Post

Record

Sanford atty.

Filed Septemr 10th. 1805

FIGURE 1.2 Judgment Roll, Sanford Filing, originally filed as Law Judgment #1805 P-33. Division of Old Records, New York County Clerk's Office, New York City, NY. Now available as a download as "Pierson-Post-20.jpg" (https://dataverse.scholarsportal.info/dataset.xhtml?persistentId=doi:10.5683/SP/3HJKJ7).

that would be worthy of and usable in a work like the *Commentaries*.[108] I still believe Kent would have had that interest; however, it is a difficult thesis either to prove or disprove, and I have been driven to confess and accept that there simply is no evidence of any special engineering of the case on his part.[109] I console myself with the point that it is important enough that Kent's discussion of the case in his *Commentaries* helped it become as famous as it did. He reappears therefore in this work in the last part of the book where the uptake or reception story of *Pierson* is told (Chapter 7). I have located a new document showing that Kent was present on the day that *Pierson* was probably argued.[110] And Kent massaged the decision in the way described above. However, he could not have controlled the way Livingston dealt with the case or its later reporting by George Caines (as we will examine in Chapter 6).

I have come to believe that after all the digging, chasing and hunting, records lost, found, and lost again, the most important thing about the *Pierson* decision was not in fact something hidden and mysterious that properly speaking ever needed to be uncovered or discovered. It was actually always there, hiding in plain sight: Livingston's dissent. This book therefore takes that dissent as its starting point, asking why an eminent judge like Brockholst Livingston, who went on to sit on the United States Supreme Court and wrote scores of serious judgments, would write a flippant (and, we will see, as McDowell first pointed out, an ultimately quite confused) opinion for one of the state's highest courts, the New York Supreme Court? Why did he think it was appropriate to use the legal decision as an opportunity for what I call here legal "solemn foolery"?[111] The answer relates to how others involved in the dispute, both lay and professional, behaved, as well as the subject matter of the case, an animal that was not thought to be intrinsically very important – morally, legally, or economically. Essentially, an argument over a spoiled

[108] See Angela Fernandez, "*Pierson v. Post*: A Great Debate, James Kent, and the Project of Building a Learned Law for New York State," 34:2 *Law and Social Inquiry* (2009): 301–36.

[109] I accept Dan Ernst's characterization of the theory about Kent's involvement in the case as "the dog that didn't bark." See Daniel R. Ernst, "*Pierson v. Post*: The New Learning," 13 *Green Bag 2d* (2009): 31–42, 41.

[110] See "Archival Note" at the end of the Introduction.

[111] I adopt this phrase from Philip J. Finkelpearl, *John Marston of the Middle Temple: An Elizabethan Dramatist in His Social Setting* (Cambridge, MA: Harvard University Press, 1969), 37.

hunt provided the perfect opportunity for the display of some sporting wit, which Livingston provided in spades.

This case was in origin a squabble between two wealthy and stubborn young men in their 20s over an animal a jury decided was worth a mere 75¢ (or the wrong of interfering with its taking was valued at a mere 75¢). Yet push on the two men did for more than two years (or at least Pierson pushed on to appeal the original decision, leaving Post no choice but to defend his jury award). The involvement of fancy and expensive professionals arguing the case on the basis of exotic authorities certainly upped the ante in terms of time and money, as compared with, say, the no-nonsense Connecticut case, *Sharpe v. Sabin* (reproduced in Appendix D). We will see that there is evidence that the $126.37 Post was ultimately forced to pay created hardship for him. We will also see that the New York legislature capped the amount of costs that could be awarded in small claims cases, an explicit recognition that what happened to Post, having to pay such a large amount of costs when so small an amount was actually in dispute was not fair. So much time and attention had been lavished on the fox case – by the parties, by the lawyers, by Tompkins J. in his majority decision – that Livingston took things to the next level, responding to a situation already out of hand, extending that excessiveness in what we will see was a classic instance of Rabelaisian play of gargantuan and perhaps even Shakespearean proportions.[112] Livingston was providing a capstone of extravagant high drama to the original jousting over the quarry carried on in the same stubborn and overblown way by the other legal professionals involved. Indeed, the book's central argument is that the case should be viewed as (a playful) product of early nineteenth-century American legal professionalization. Legal professionals got involved in the *Pierson* case and blew it entirely out of proportion. Livingston simply seized an opportunity to write in a fun and witty way about a situation that had an inherent humor about it, a long and protracted legal fight over a long-dead and never-thought-to-be-very-valuable fox.

However, the exercise of fun and wit does not mean that the playfulness did not (and does not continue to) do serious ideological work. As was the case with Rabelais's work itself, the momentary transgression – in this

[112] See François Rabelais, *Gargantua and Pantagruel*, M.A. Screech trans. (London, New York, Toronto et al.: Penguin Classics, 2006). Gargantua was "the large-mouthed voracious giant in Rabelais." See *Oxford English Dictionary*, s.v. "Gargantua."

case, injecting foolery into what would ordinarily be a serious law report – operates to affirm that which is abiding, namely, a position on the proper relationship of non-human animals to human animals and the important role of (a very masculine) professionalized law. Mocking the learnedness, as Livingston did, effectively communicates how secure and superior the legal professionals involved in the case took themselves to be.

First, the lawyers gave themselves license to treat the case in the elaborate way they did at the litigants' risk and ultimately at the great expense to one of them penalized under the British rule of costs used by the small claims statute in which the loser pays. Secondly, Livingston, who arguably made the whole situation worse, considered himself free and entitled to make fun or at least indirectly criticize the lawyers, his colleagues, the parties, and the approach taken to the case. And all of this could be expressed with impunity. The legal professionals were acting as if the case belonged to them and not to the litigants, and this was not considered to be improper, at least by them.

Indeed, *propriety* itself is another way of thinking about property and its entitlements, namely, the stuff toward which one can *properly* consider oneself to be behaving in a (socially and legally) acceptable way (excluding others, selling, leasing, and subjecting to various forms of transfer and use).[113] Public offices have a long history of being thought of as property, alienable and heritable in some cases.[114] Judicial positions in New York were not very different than other forms of patronage routinely distributed in a turbulent and factious political environment, although office holders did not turn over with each change in power as they would in appointments to the post office

113 See Gregory S. Alexander, *Commodity and Propriety: Competing Visions of Property in American Legal Thought, 1776–1970* (Chicago: University of Chicago Press, 1997), 1–4, who takes the phrase "property as propriety" from Carol M. Rose, "'Takings' and the Practices of Property: Property as Wealth, Property as 'Propriety'" in *Property and Persuasion: Essays on the History, Theory, and Rhetoric of Ownership* (Boulder, CO: Westview Press, 1994), 58–65 (in which "propriety" is understood in the sense of a "proper" ordering of social and political life, which Rose associates with governing authority with hierarchical characteristics, including monarchical forms of government and the family and a relationship of trust and responsibility to the larger community as in *noblesse oblige*). Alexander contrasts the civic idea of property-as-propriety with the negative liberty in property-as-commodity, arguing that in the former, "proper society is more than just what emerges from market relations," and that liberty is best examined through the historical dialectic between propriety and commodity.

114 See Rose, "Property as Wealth, Property as 'Propriety,'" 60 (giving the examples of eighteenth-century France and its judicial magistracies and seventeenth- and eighteenth-century England).

or customs house.[115] Caines too would have seen his office as *his* in a strong sense (including its products, the reports) as we will examine in Chapter 6. This sense of office as property – including the opportunity to play with the case in elaborate ways – probably informed the behavior of the legal professionals involved in *Pierson*, for better or for worse. We will see in Chapter 2 that *Pierson* also fits within literary traditions of treating animals in this way as well as within legal traditions of solemn foolery.

Livingston's text then is a complicated one. It should be thought of as much literature as law – rather like Herman Melville's disquisition on the law of capture in *Moby Dick*, it was never meant to be taken literally, at least not in all its aspects. Hence, my choice to use an excerpt from *Moby Dick* to preside over all of the chapters.[116] Modern legal scholars who understand Livingston's dissent as a straightforward statement of policy have been taken in by his solemn foolery. They have perceived as policy what is in fact a multifaceted piece of literature, some parts serious, some parts not, a text that itself subverts any attempt to establish an authoritative meaning or to turn a necessarily fluid and multifaceted artifact into a hard object. This book is about trying to recover that original non-policy oriented understanding of the dissent, and by extension the rest of the case, and, in doing so, to come to a better understanding of the important historical and cultural category of lawyerly solemn foolery and how it operated in the context of early nineteenth-century American legal professionalization. This is behavior that actually looks quite *un*professional to us today – think of where it ends up leaving a litigant who must pay for the expense of a juridical romp all out of proportion to what was at stake in the case. In this case the loser was Post, who ended up, much like a person at the end of a long night of eating and drinking, stuck with the bill for everyone else's fun. Indeed the partying, albeit of a more serious scholarly sort, continued and has gone on to the present day, and the range of ideological work done by the playing has multiplied in various ways.

[115] Indeed, those who sat on the New York Supreme Court tended to sit in their judicial positions (they were appointed not elected) until the time was ripe for them to enter a more rough and tumble political stage and attempt to secure positions such as Governor of New York (e.g. Morgan Lewis and Daniel Tompkins were both successful at this, Tompkins going on to become the vice president of the United States).

[116] For further comment on and discussion of the mistaken reliance on *Moby Dick* as a serious text by legal scholars, see Christopher Tomlins, "Animals Accurs'd: *Ferae Naturae* and the Law of Property in Nineteenth-Century North America" in Focus Feature "Foxes, Seals, Whales and the Rule of Capture: Animals in the Law and Legal History," 63 *University of Toronto Law Journal* (2013): 30–137, 35–52, 36–40.

I am conscious that this book itself is a contribution to that ongoing scholarly partying. Still, it has a serious purpose. Joseph Singer has written eloquently about the way in which a "critical" or "relational" approach to first-year property and first-possession cases such as *Pierson* (and the American Indian lands case *Johnson* v. *M'Intosh*) help draw "students' attention to issues that are problematic to the basic assumptions underlying possession and labor as true and legitimate original sources of property."[117] Legal history has long been one way of engaging in a critical legal approach and the focus on *Pierson* taken here is relational – the relation between these two young men in their time and place, the relationship to the hunted animal, and the profession's ongoing relationship with this case – in order to demonstrate a wide array of attitudes about property, animals, and the law.[118]

This book uses Livingston's dissent as a point of entry into the question of American professional legal culture as seen through the many faces of *Pierson* v. *Post*. It employs three disciplinary perspectives. Part I uses, among other approaches, the lens of *Law and Literature* in order to situate and understand Livingston's dissent. Chapter 1 begins by explaining the problems and confusions in the dissent and why it is a mistake to read it as a serious legal text rather than as a piece of legal solemn foolery. Chapter 2 outlines how the dissent fits into a category of contemporary playful judicial behavior and a historical lawyerly literary tradition of hunting and fishing-themed sporting wit. This is the dissent understood as an example of domestic American Rabelaisian humor, wrapped up in a (disturbing) Shakespearean twist. Part II shifts into a different mode, one that can be helpfully thought of as *Legal History as Social History*. Chapter 3 explains the Justice of the Peace proceedings at the jury level, providing economic information about the jurors through the use of sources like local tax records, and a description of the trial, and its locale. Chapter 4 focuses on Pierson's lawyer, Nathan Sanford, and the role he played in the appeal of this case and others like it, in which the amounts at issues were greatly exceeded by costs accrued, and which took an inordinate amount of time to decide. Chapter 5 explores issues relating to the status of the land on which the fox was caught and the description of that land as wasteland, the categorization of the fox as an animal *ferae naturae*, and the significance of arguing the case in trespass-on-the-case rather than trespass to its origins as a tort or property case. Part III takes yet

[117] Joseph William Singer, "Starting Property," 46 *Saint Louis University Law Journal* (2002): 565–80, 570.

[118] Jennifer Nedelsky, *Law's Relations: A Relational Theory of Self, Autonomy, and Law* (New York: Oxford University Press, 2011).

another turn toward *Legal History as Intellectual History*. Chapter 6 examines the important role of the reporter in *Pierson*, a man named George Caines, his bad relationship with James Kent, and the generally underacknowledged and underappreciated role of the reporter in law-making, so important a precondition of the launch of a leading case like *Pierson* to legal fame. Finally, Chapter 7 examines the scholarly and pedagogical trajectory of *Pierson*, tracing it through Kent, Holmes, and Pollock to twentieth-century casebooks and academic scholarly literature written by the New Mandarins, often with some kind of law and economics perspective.[119]

This final chapter traces the reductionist turn the case took in the later twentieth century, specifically how it was turned into a parsed down (and misleading) lesson about the alleged superiority of clear rules (the capture rule) to fuzzy standards (the hot pursuit rule). Livingston's hot pursuit rule was always a live alternative to the capture rule, a rule that we now know has created some very serious problems, not just for the issue of who owns wild animals but as the rule applies to other shared natural resources such as oil and gas, and water, including groundwater. I trace the use of *Pierson* in a selection of important law review articles and law school casebooks in order to historicize what the case has come to mean in the American legal profession. The claim here is that at least one corner of legal scholars have tried to cannibalize the case, sucking it of its lifeblood, turning it into a thoroughly serious affair and losing sight of its playful and literary character. A crude policy perspective in other words has thoroughly overshadowed what can be known from a more nuanced law and humanities perspective. A lot more interesting, I argue, than a rules versus standards debate is to appreciate the case as an instance of solemn foolery and an extended lesson in some of the follies of professionalization, both in the early nineteenth century, when the case took place, and in later waves of legal academic professionalization to the present day.

Like "The Foxe to the Huntesman," the poem with which the book begins – a plea for mercy from a fox (sympathetic to the fox) difficult to

[119] Bob Gordon wrote in his famous "Critical Legal Histories" about the "mandarin materials" that those who are legally trained know and are comfortable handling. See Robert W. Gordon, "Critical Legal Histories," 36 *Stanford Law Review* (1984): 57–125, 120–22. See also Robert W. Gordon, "Simpson's Leading Cases [Review of *Leading Cases in the Common Law* by A. W. B. Simpson]," 95 *Michigan Law Review* (1997): 2044–2054, 2047 (referring to "the high theoretical mandarins of the law," which include Langdellian doctrinal scientists, modern jurisprudential thinkers like Ronald Dworkin, and law and economics theorists such as Ronald Coase).

reconcile with its inclusion in a hunting manual (a how-to book, not generally directed to or expected to elicit mercy or sympathy for the hunted animal) – this book's tone toggles between the solemn and the slightly silly or mock.[120] I have hunted down a great deal of serious information relating to the original circumstances of *Pierson*. I have carefully explained the animal *ferae naturae* arguments and parsed the fine distinctions between trespass and trespass-on-the case, property, and tort. In these aspects of the book, I am treating *Pierson* as a fit object of serious study in the same way Kent or any other latter-day legal mandarin or "High Boffin" would.[121] However, there is also a lot of fun in the book, fun I had researching and writing it that (I hope) comes through the text as written; as, for example, when explaining in its early chapters other examples of the playful literature in which Livingston's dissent fits. I think it is important for both of these modes – the serious and the silly – to be present in the book, for I see them as appropriate to the object under inspection, the *Pierson* case, which itself straddles both worlds to which readers have related and responded, historically and currently.

Yet I am aware that fun and play can often come at someone's expense. Here, ultimately, it seems to me to come at the animal's, the fox's, expense. Hence the book's dedication "to poor Reynard" and my attempt to address the (often gendered) issue of violence as it arises in a project I never thought of as particularly related to either gender or violence but has come to seem more so to me over time. This aspect became more insistent after I realized, while using a local census to find out more information about the jurors and other individuals in the case, just how much slave-owning there was on early nineteenth-century Long Island (there was a lot, see Chapter 3). The Roman law roots of capture-justified slavery and first-taker occupation of land played an important role in early nineteenth-century legal and political life. Given the importance of slavery as a mode of property ownership and the expansion of the nation and its imperialistic aspirations, it becomes difficult to ignore those larger dimensions of first-possession ownership through occupation and the importance of Justinian to early Americans. Given the reality of slaveholding and expansionism in the United States in the antebellum period, no legal treatment of the concepts of ownership and first-possession through

120 The dual perspectives on the poem in *The Noble Arte of Venerie* are discussed in more detail in Chapter 2.

121 Gordon, "Simpson's Leading Cases," 2049, 2054 (referring to the "High Boffins").

occupation, especially a treatment relying on Roman law, was ever innocuous. Yet *Pierson* has come down to us as an innocuous and even funny case about a morally and economically unimportant animal. This looks different when seen from the perspective of slavery and colonialism – a point brought home by Patricia Williams in connecting the fox in *Pierson* with her formerly enslaved great-great-grandmother.[122] And then there is the connection to the gendered violence of the hunt via *Titus Andronicus* and the phrase "saucy intruder" (see Chapter 2).

I do not see the connections and topics I have explored here as at all eccentric, although I am aware that there is a risk of being seen in that way, as if I am taking far too seriously something that is flippant by design. This is the risk of overlaboring to explain a joke, long said to be among the most tiresome of exercises.[123] Yet *Pierson* is a joke to which our adherence tells us much about ourselves. As Alfred Brophy asked in the *Law and History Review* forum, why do "we choose this case to have so much 'fun'"?[124] We might eventually live in a world in which it would *not* go without saying that the hunting down and bludgeoning of a fox is an occasion for pomp and fuss with a comical twist. Sadly, that is not the world that produced this case or that has received and reproduced it over and over again. At least not to date. What of the point that the lawyers professionalized this case beyond all recognition, leaving the litigants and the actual original dispute far behind? Well some might say that this is the triumph in a long tug-of-war between professional and lay justice in which professionalized justice won. However, at the time, lay conceptions pushed back – the case came to be remembered years later as a lesson in why it was a mistake to go to a lawyer, and the legislature put caps on the costs that could be incurred in small claims cases. It is not true then that

[122] See Patricia J. Williams, *The Alchemy of Race and Rights* (Cambridge, MA: Harvard University Press, 1991), 156–57. This powerful description of Williams's great-great grandmother is reproduced in Chapter 2. It is widely referred to on writing on law and literature, legal education, and feminist legal theory. See e.g. Nancy L. Cook, "Outside the Tradition: Literature as Legal Scholarship," 63 *University of Cincinnati Law Review* (1994–95): 95–164, 143 n. 321; Clark D. Cunningham, "Learning from Law Students: A Socratic Approach to Law and Literature?," 63 *University of Cincinnati Law Review* (1994–95): 195–220, 213 n. 41; Carrie Menkel-Meadow, "Mainstreaming Feminist Legal Theory," 23 *Pacific Law Journal* (1991–92): 1493–1542, 1512 n. 99.

[123] This is Cicero's point that a joke explained is a joke lost. See Mary Beard, *Laughter in Ancient Rome: On Joking, Tickling, and Cracking Up* (Berkeley; Los Angeles; London: University of California Press, 2014), 12.

[124] Brophy, "Introduction: A Famous Fox, a Surfacing Whale, and the Forgotten Slave," 146.

everyone at the time agreed with the way the case went, in terms of outcome or costs.

Readers of the book most interested in Livingston's dissent and the solemn foolery thesis and its literary and social dimensions will find Chapters 1 and 2 most on point. If you are a lawyer picking up this book because you remember studying *Pierson* in law school and you want to find out more about the original case, the best chapters for you will be 1, 3, and 4 on the local Long Island context, the lawyers, and the participants in the original dispute. If you are interested in the ideological implications of the decision, the first two chapters are important, and then if you are up for a fairly significant amount of utterly serious legal doctrinal information, Chapter 5 will be where you next want to go. Both Chapter 6 on the reporter and Chapter 7 on the academic trajectory of the case relate to the canonization of the case and its mandarization. They are most closely tied into the argument about a potentially problematic professionalization at work in *Pierson*'s many incarnations.

The point of this organization is to offer something for a range of interests and curiosities. My aim in amassing all of this information and presenting it through the lens of Livingston's dissent and solemn foolery and the professionalization thesis is not to discredit *Pierson*. I have (for better or worse) become very attached to *Pierson*, having worked on it now for over ten years. I am not trying to have it excised from the canon, assuming that anything short of a bomb blast could make that happen. I do think, however, that some of what I argue for in the book should make readers of the text question whether they should keep teaching it, and if the decision is "yes, it is such an important (and well-loved) installment in the canon of law school cases," to think about how to do it in a way that attends to the criticisms that this intense study of the case has revealed: the viability of a hot pursuit rule (in a hunting context) and the problems with a capture rule for wild animals (and natural resources more generally); how legal professionals turned a simple dispute into something unrecognizable and out of proportion to what was at stake, producing a winner and leaving a loser to pay excessive costs for what a jury thought at least was a valid claim (and whether that was a *proper* use of their positions); the animal itself and the disregard expressed toward it as an insignificant object of lethal occupation; Roman law occupation and its connection to slavery and the colonization of what is conceptualized as *res nullius* (empty things) and *terre nullius* (empty lands) in terms of first possession; and the way that all of these issues come wrapped up in a playful package in Livingston's dissent, which erases or hides from sight many of these important issues, unless of course they are unpacked and given attention.

It might be that we will see *Pierson* fall into disrepute and join the ranks of cases such as *Plessy v. Ferguson* (giving constitutional blessing to Jim Crow), *Dred Scott* (upholding the extension of slavery in new territories of the United States), *Korematsu* (justifying the internment of Japanese-Americans during World War II), and *Buck v. Bell* (a collusive case upholding the constitutionality of a forced sterilization statute).[125] Banner points to *Johnson v. M'Intosh*, another seminal property case that began to displace *Pierson* for first-case property casebook status in the 1970s, which has come to be seen as discredited, given sympathetic views toward Native Americans.[126] In that case, Chief Justice Marshall of the United States Supreme Court justified the expropriation of Indigenous lands through the idea that Europeans had discovered America and thereby obtained sovereignty. Banner argues that American Indians owned the land, had property rights unaffected by sovereignty, and colonists recognized that ownership by purchasing that land as opposed to seizing it.[127] Those land purchases often transpired under morally suspect circumstances.[128] And later colonists increasingly took over uncultivated land in appropriations that were illegal under Indigenous and English law.[129] However, the conquest by discovery was not the way white

[125] See J. M. Balkin and Sanford Levinson, "Legal Canons: An Introduction" in J.M. Balkin and Sanford Levinson eds., *Legal Canons* (New York: New York University Press, 2000), 3–44, 13 (including *Plessy* v. *Ferguson* as the quintessentially unjust case included in the law school constitutional canon), 9 (naming *Dred Scott, United States* v. *Debs*, Korematsu v. *United States*, and *The Chinese Exclusion Case* as those that might be included in the constitutional law canon in order to provide cultural literary to law students as citizens in a democracy). I add *Buck* v. *Bell* based on Paul Lombardo's demonstration that it was a morally bankrupt test case. See Paul A. Lombardo, *Three Generations, No Imbeciles: Eugenics, the Supreme Court, and Buck v. Bell* (Baltimore: Johns Hopkins University Press, 2008).

[126] *Johnson* v. *M'Intosh*, 21 U.S. (8 Wheat.) 543 (U.S. Sup. Ct., 1823); Stuart Banner, *How the Indians Lost Their Land: Land and Power on the Frontier* (Cambridge, MA: Belknap Press of Harvard University Press, 2005), 11 (using the idea of "an anti-canon").

[127] See ibid., 26 (the amount of land acquired by wars was small and much more was purchased in the colonial period); 26–28 (pointing to evidence in the form of large numbers of surviving deed, statutes regulating the purchasing process, and cases in which American Indians were recognized as owners of their land).

[128] Price paid is certainly a striking issue. See e.g. Chapter 2 (where Banner explains the purchase of Manhattan for $24 dollars), 25 (describing the purchase of great tracts of land for small sums as "bargain hunting" rather than conquest). On other kinds of pressure, see ibid., 49–56.

[129] See ibid., 35.

Europeans thought of their relationship to American Indians and their land. Disagreements arose over uncultivated land (including hunting grounds) that might or might not have been seen as vacant by Europeans, but farm land (and American Indians farmed) was to be purchased. To do otherwise was robbery.[130]

Being a member of the anti-canon means becoming a case that law students are taught to criticize, thereby turning from famous to infamous. This is already happening with *Pierson* to some extent in some law school classrooms, in which casebook materials contrast the case with custom, or draw out the parallel to oil and gas, and other fugitive resources, and now even connect it to animal or nonhuman rights.[131] This book will provide further opportunity to engage with *Pierson* in the relational and critical ways that Singer described on a range of issues, though it by no means exhausts those approaches.

In addition to reconstructing the context of *Pierson* itself, much of the book is concerned to demonstrate how *Pierson* assumed the position in the legal profession it has occupied for the last two hundred years. I see it as an object lesson in professional American legal culture in-the-making. Its story is a microhistory of legal professionalization in the nineteenth century, how that happened, at whose expense and at what cost, followed by a very particular kind of twentieth century academic professionalization. It should cause us to ask ourselves, by extension, what we are doing when we use a case like *Pierson* to professionalize law students today.[132] The explanation "well, it has always been there," does not suffice. Livingston would agree.

Many policy or economics-oriented legal scholars would say that the actual facts and histories of the individual cases used in a case method or precedent-based system are irrelevant. After all, and legal historians would agree, the cases mean what we, legal professionals, have collectively come to say they stand for. They continue to have that status and meaning only as long as we continue to imbue them with it. Brian

[130] See ibid., 45. Banner notes that repeated land sale drove American Indians farther west and deeper into poverty. See ibid., 48. For more on *Johnson v. M'Intosh* see Lindsay G. Robertson, *Conquest by Law: How the Discovery of America Dispossessed Indigenous Peoples of Their Lands* (Oxford; New York: Oxford University Press, 2005).

[131] See French and Korngold eds., *Cases and Text on Property*, 6th ed. (2015), 80 n. 4 (referring to the work of Steven Wise and the Nonhuman Rights Project amongst others working on animal rights).

[132] See generally Elizabeth Mertz, *Language of Law School: Learning to "Think like a Lawyer"* (New York; Oxford: Oxford University Press, 2007) and Christopher Tomlins discussion of her work in the *Pierson* context. Tomlins, "Animals Accurs'd," 49.

Simpson, who pioneered the brand of legal historical scholarship I employ here, "legal archaeology," called the process in which a legal case becomes a leading case the "continued reception" of a case in a common-law system.[133] Yet the actual facts and histories when revealed in a process of archaeological retrieval will come to influence that collective meaning. It is right and proper that they do so. The law is full of fictions. It probably could not operate without them. However, there is a place where fiction meets historical fact, as best as we can make it out. Those facts, at least in *Pierson*, are premised on a good dose of fictional or literary nuance that has, by and large, gone underappreciated, or not appreciated at all. This book reclaims that space, complete with the nuance and contradiction it contains, for one of the legal profession's most (in)famous cases.

Archival Note: Since the 2009 reporting on my discovery of the Judgment Roll in *Pierson*, I have found two other sources in the Albany

[133] A. W. B. Simpson, "The Common Law and Legal Theory" in A. W. B. Simpson ed., *Oxford Essays in Jurisprudence* (Oxford: Clarendon Press, 1973), 77–99, 86. See also Angela Fernandez and Markus D. Dubber eds., *Law Books in Action: Essays on the Anglo-American Legal Treatise* (Oxford; Portland Oregon: Hart Publishing, 2012), a book dedicated to Simpson, on the role of the legal treatise in this process of authoritative transmission, given his important work on the legal treatise, specifically, "The Rise and Fall of the Legal Treatise: Legal Principles and the Forms of Legal Literature," 48 *University of Chicago Law Review* (1981): 632–79 and "Innovation in Nineteenth Century Contract Law" first published in 91 *Law Quarterly Review* (1975): 247–78 and republished in A. W. B. Simpson ed., *Legal Theory and Legal History: Essays on the Common Law* (London; Ronceverte, WV: Hambledon Press, 1987), 171–202. Simpson explained in "The Study of Cases" in *Leading Cases in the Common Law* (Oxford: Clarendon Press, 1995), 1–12, 12, that he was tempted to call this style of legal scholarship "legal archeology" but refrained from doing so. The field, however, has overtaken the preference he expressed to refrain from using the phrase. See e.g. Debora L. Threedy, "Legal Archaeology: Excavating Cases, Reconstructing Context," 80 *Tulane Law Review* (2005–2006): 1197–1238, providing a discussion of the history of the field, starting with Richard Danzig's *The Capability Problem in Contract Law: Further Readings on Well-Known Cases* (Mineola, NY: Foundation Press, 1978) (2nd ed. 2004), laying out different categories of case-in-context studies (e.g. those that deal with inequality of resources or lawyers' errors such as Judith Maute's study of the *Peevyhouse* decision, problems with so-called found facts that turn out to be incorrect such as Threedy's own study of *Alaska Packers'*, and the collusive case as explored in Paul Lombardo's work on *Buck v. Bell*), and offering guidelines for pursuing and evaluating such studies. See Judith L. Maute, "*Peevyhouse v. Garland Coal & Mining Co.* Revisited: The Ballad of Willie and Lucille," 89 *Northwestern University Law Review* (1994–95): 1341–1486; Debora L. Threedy, "A Fish Story: *Alaska Packers' Association v. Domenico*," *Utah Law Review* (2000): 185–221; Lombardo, *Three Generations, No Imbeciles*. Simpson retired from the University of Michigan in 2009 and died on January 10, 2011. See www.theguardian .com/law/2011/feb/01/brian-simpson-obituary.

archives where the case was recorded, one of which provides a correction on the amount of costs Post was ordered to pay (adding $5 to the originally reported $121.37 to make a total of $126.37).[134] The other source places Kent at the hearing of the *Pierson* case and provides what was probably the hearing date: August 7, 1805.[135] Sadly, as noted above, the Judgment Roll itself has disappeared from the New York County Clerk's Office in New York City. Luckily, there was an opportunity to create a transcript of that document from a photocopy of the original before it disappeared. That transcript, which I originally prepared along with the forum for the *Law and History Review* website, is reproduced in Appendix B for the use of future scholars and researchers. I have not included the photocopy of the manuscript pages as the handwriting of the Judgment Roll would not reproduce well in a book. The link to the transcript and photocopied Judgment Roll manuscript pages was lost in the changeover to *Cambridge Journals Online* a number of years ago. At the suggestion of the former editor of *Law and History Review* Elizabeth Dale, I have created a new home for the handwritten text at the University of Toronto, Faculty of Law: website, https://dataverse.scholarsportal.info/dataset.xhtml?persistentId=doi:10.5683/SP/3HJKJ7. I have also provided the County Clerk's Office in New York City with a photocopy of the photocopy in case that link also proves to be impermanent. Perhaps eventually the original document will be found. See also Appendix E, "Corrections to Secondary Sources," for a collection of errors, my own, and others that have been made regarding this oh so slippery or foxy of cases.

[134] Supreme Court of Judicature (NY), Docket of Judgments, J0131-82, vol. 4, New York State Archives, Albany, NY, which records the amount of "Damages and Costs" as $126.37 (as opposed to the $121.37 I originally reported). Pierson is spelled the usual way here (as opposed to the "Peirson" that appears in the Judgment Roll, Appendix B) and Pierson's lawyer, Sandford, is spelled here with the "d," when it usually appears without the "d" (see e.g. Figure I.2 above).

[135] Supreme Court of Judicature (NY), General and Special Term Minute Books, J0130-82, New York State Archives, Albany, NY. This record lists the judges who were present on the day the case came before the court, Wednesday August 7, 1805, starting with Chief Justice Kent, Justices Livingston, Thompson, Spencer, and Tompkins. Tompkins signed the judgment on September 10, 1805. See Judgment Roll, p. 20, Appendix B and Figure B.1. The September date is also given in the Docket of Judgments ibid.

PART I

THE LITERARY HISTORY OF *PIERSON*

LIVINGSTON, J.[1]: My opinion differs from that of the court. Of six exceptions, taken to the proceedings below, all are abandoned except the third, which reduces the controversy to a single question.

Whether a person, who with his own hounds, starts and hunts a fox, on waste and uninhabited ground, and is on the point of seizing his prey, acquires such an interest in the animal, as to have a right of action against another, who in view of the huntsman and his dogs in full pursuit, and with knowledge of the chase, shall kill and carry him away?

This is a knotty point, and should have been submitted to the arbitration of sportsmen, without poring over *Justinian, Fleta, Bracton, Puffendorf, Locke, Barbeyrac* or *Blackstone*, all of whom have been cited; they would have had no difficulty in coming to a prompt and correct conclusion. In a court, thus constituted, the skin and carcas[s] of poor *Reynard* would have been properly disposed of, and a precedent set, interfering with no usage or custom which the experience of ages has sanctioned, and which must be so well known to every votary of *Diana*. But the parties have referred the question to our judgment, and we must dispose of it as well as we can, from the partial lights we possess, leaving to a higher tribunal, the correction of any mistake which we may be so unfortunate as to make. By the pleadings it is admitted, that a fox is a "wild and noxious beast." Both parties have regarded him, as the law of nations does a pirate "*hostem*

[1] The reproduction of Livingston's dissent provided here was created with the text of *Pierson* v. *Post* in George Caines, *New-York term reports of cases argued and determined in the Supreme Court of that state*, vol. 3 (New York: I. Riley, 1806), 180–82, translations of Latin maxims added.

humani generis,"[2] and although "*de mortuis nil nisi bonum*,"[3] be a maxim of our profession, the memory of the deceased has not been spared. His depredations on farmers and on barn-yards, have not been forgotten; and to put him to death, wherever found, is allowed to be meritorious, and of public benefit. Hence it follows, that our decision should have in view the greatest possible encouragement to the destruction of an animal, so cunning and ruthless in his career. But who would keep a pack of hounds; or what gentleman, at the sound of the horn, and at peep of day, would mount his steed, and for hours together, "*sub jove frigido*,"[4] or a vertical sun, pursue the windings of this wily quadruped, if, just as night came on, and his stratagems and strength were nearly exhausted, a saucy intruder, who had not shared in the honors or labours of the chase, were permitted to come in at the death, and bear away in triumph the object of pursuit? Whatever *Justinian* may have thought of the matter, it must be recollected that his code was compiled many hundred years ago, and it would be very hard indeed, at the distance of so many centuries, not to have a right to establish a rule for ourselves. In this day, we read of no order of men, who made it a business, in the language of the declaration in this cause, "with hounds and dogs to find, start, pursue, hunt and chase," these animals, and that too, without any other motive, than the preservation of *Roman* poultry; if this diversion had been then in fashion, the lawyers who composed his institutes, would have taken care not to pass it by, without suitable encouragement. If anything therefore, in the digests or pandects shall appear to militate against the defendant in error, who, on this occasion, was the foxhunter, we have only to say *tempora mutantur*;[5] and if men themselves change with the times, why should not laws also undergo an alteration?

It may be expected, however, by the learned counsel, that more particular notice be taken of their authorities. I have examined them all, and feel great difficulty in determining, whether to acquire dominion over a thing, before in common, it be sufficient that we barely see it, or know where it is, or wish for it, or make a declaration of our will respecting it; or whether, in the case of wild beasts, setting a trap, or lying in wait, or starting, or pursuing, be enough; or if an actual wounding, or killing, or bodily tact and occupation be necessary. Writers on general law, who have favored us

[2] "Enemy of humankind."

[3] This proverb is usually taken to mean "never speak ill of the dead."

[4] A phrase from Horace that literally means "under cold Jupiter" but is usually taken to mean something more like "in the cold air" or "braving the cold."

[5] "Times change."

with their speculations on these points, differ on them all; but, great as is the diversity of sentiment among them, some conclusion must be adopted on the question immediately before us. After mature deliberation, I embrace that of *Barbeyrac*, as the most rational, and least liable to objection. If at liberty, we might imitate the courtesy of a certain Emperor, who, to avoid giving offence to the advocates of any of these different doctrines, adopted a middle course, and by ingenious distinctions, rendered it difficult to say (as often happens after a fierce and angry contest) to whom the palm of victory belonged. He ordained, that if a beast be followed with *large dogs and hounds*, he shall belong to the hunter, not to the chance occupant; and in like manner, if he be killed or wounded with a lance or sword; but if chased with *beagles only*, then he passed to the captor, not to the first pursuer. If slain with a dart, a sling or a bow, he fell to the hunter, if still in chase, and not to him who might afterwards find and seize him.

Now, as we are without any municipal regulations of our own, and the pursuit here, for aught that appears on the case, being with dogs and hounds of *imperial stature*, we are at liberty to adopt one of the provisions just cited, which comports also with the learned conclusion of *Barbeyrac*, that property in animals *feræ naturæ*, may be acquired without bodily touch or manucaption, provided the pursuer be within reach, or have a *reasonable* prospect (which certainly existed here) of taking, what he has *thus* discovered an intention of converting to his own use.

When we reflect also that the interest of our husbandmen, the most useful of men in any community, will be advanced by the destruction of a beast so pernicious and incorrigible, we cannot greatly err, in saying, that a pursuit like the present, through waste and unoccupied lands, and which must inevitably and speedily have terminated in corporal possession, or bodily *seisin*, confers such a right to the object of it, as to make any one a wrong doer, who shall interfere and shoulder the spoil. The *justice's* judgment ought, therefore, in my opinion, to be affirmed.

FIGURE 1.1 The Honorable Justice Livingston reproduced from item affixed to p. [viii] of Kent's copy of William Johnson, vol. 1, *Reports of Cases Argued and Determined in the Supreme Court of Judicature and in the Court for the Trial of Impeachments and Correction of Errors in the State of New York* (New York: I. Riley, 1807) [Spine title: Johnson's Reports]. New York State Library, Manuscripts and Special Collections, Albany, NY.

1

Solemn Foolery

A large whale's case generally yields about five hundred gallons of sperm, though from unavoidable circumstances, considerable of it is spilled, leaks, and dribbles away, or is otherwise irrevocably lost in the ticklish business of securing what you can.

Herman Melville, *Moby-Dick, or the Whale* (1851)[1]

Livingston has a fine Roman face; an aquiline nose, high forehead, bold head, and projecting chin [...] He evidently thinks with great solidity and seizes on the strong points of argument [...] In private society he is accessible and easy, and enjoys with great good humor the vivacities, if I may coin a word, of the wit and the moralist.

Judge Joseph Story in *The Life and Letters of Joseph Story* (1851)[2]

Brockholst Livingston's dissent in *Pierson* v. *Post* is written in an unusual style, a clear departure from the way that he usually wrote legal opinions either at the New York Supreme Court or later at the United States Supreme Court. There is a tradition of "burlesque" law reports that it might be said to fit, "humorous reports, designed to amuse and perhaps to appeal to literary tastes."[3] Livingston's opinion has been described as an

[1] Quote from p. 372.

[2] At p. 167, quoted in Gerald T. Dunne, "Brockholst Livingston" in Leon Friedman and Fred L. Israel eds., vol. 1, *The Justices of the United States Supreme Court, 1789–1969: Their Lives and Major Opinions* (New York: Chelsea House and Bowker, 1969): 386–403, 391. On the Story-Livingston friendship (where the passage is also quoted), see Gerald T. Dunne, "The Story-Livingston Correspondence (1812–1822)," 10 *American Journal of Legal History* (1966): 224–36, 224.

[3] See Erwin C. Surrency, *A History of American Law Publishing* (New York: Oceana Publications, 1990), 49.

instance of "judicial wit," and as an example of the way in which his writing style was, "occasionally, delightful."[4]

It must be noted that the dissent was not universally well received at the time of its publication. The editors of the serious and high-minded journal *The Monthly Anthology, and Boston Review* wrote in a review of the 1805 collection of reports in which the decision appeared that they "were sorry to observe in Vol. III. p. 180, in the opinion of Justice Livingston, so much pleasantry at the expense of dignity and decorum. Humour is a very good thing, but it no more becomes the legal robe upon the bench, than the sacerdotal at the altar."[5] It was not appropriate, in other words, for a judge to horse around in this fashion any more than it would suit a priest to do so in the pulpit. However, the decision earned Livingston plaudits in other corners, including the following comparison to Charles Lamb, an English essayist and popularizer of Shakespeare:

> Those who would like to see a sample of his general learning and wit will find an extraordinary opinion which he delivered from the bench of the Supreme Court of New York, in the adjudged case of Pierson *versus* Post, by referring to 3 Caines's Reports, 175. The question before the court related to the rights of a hunter in the game he had started, and after long chase nearly captured, as against an interloper who, chancing to come by at the eleventh hour, killed and appropriated the animal. The decision of the court, resting upon strict law, was adverse to the meritorious Nimrod's [Post's] claim for redress. Judge Livingston took the occasion to express his dissent from the conclusions of his brethren, where his dissent could do no harm, in an opinion of considerable length, in which the gravity of the ermine laboriously treads the verge of refined drollery. It is such an opinion as Charles Lamb might have prepared for hypothetical delivery upon the same state of facts, unhampered by any judicial responsibility.[6]

A similar favorable nod came from a Common Pleas judge in Livingston County in the 1830s, who apparently liked to refer to *Pierson* as "containing the most genuine legal witticism in our language."[7] The dissent was included in the early 1870s in a book entitled *Curiosities of the Law*

[4] See Dunne, "Brockholst Livingston," 399, 394. This biographical entry reproduces *Pierson*, 399–401, noting that it is the only decision by Livingston included in modern-day casebooks.

[5] "The Boston Review: Article 29 *New-York Term Reports of cases argued* ... " by George Caines in *The Monthly Anthology and Boston Review Containing Sketches and Reports of Philosophy, Religion, History, Arts and Manners* (July 1 1806): 367–69, 369. See also Peter S. Field, "The Birth of Secular High Culture: *The Monthly Anthology and Boston Review* and its Critics," 17:4 *Journal of the Early Republic* (1997): 575–609.

[6] Charles Havens Hunt, *Life of Edward Livingston* (New York: D. Appleton, 1864), 53.

[7] "Samuel H. Fitzhugh" in L.B. Proctor, vol. 1, *The Bench and Bar of New York* (New York: Diossy and Co., 1870), 514.

Reporters.[8] Reports generally were more literary in the nineteenth century than we think of them today, a point that will be explored in more detail in Chapter 6. Yet the decision was unusual even for the time, as these comments indicate.

THE SCENE

To take the dissent seriously will lead the reader into a thicket of problems. First, as previous writers on the case have pointed out, Livingston's understanding of foxhunting left much to be desired, as he may (or may not) have been aware.[9] The Romans did indeed hunt foxes.[10] Moreover, the popularity of English-style foxhunting usually results in more rather than fewer foxes.[11] While it is true that a successful foxhunt will result in one less fox in a neighborhood's fox population when that animal is killed, the introduction of English-style foxhunting into a predominately rural and agricultural environment like early nineteenth-century Long Island would have meant an aggregate *increase* in the fox population because those who engaged in hunting as sport required the animals to be available in the area for their big game to take place. Gentry living in places in which this kind of foxhunting was undertaken in England took steps to encourage healthy fox populations, going so far as to breed litters themselves, much to the consternation of farmers vexed by the efforts they would have to expend in trying to keep their poultry alive, to say nothing of the inconveniences of the hunt itself – fences damaged, fields trampled.[12] Livingston's support for Post on the grounds that foxhunting was doing a service for chickens (and the farming interest) was

[8] Franklin Fiske Heard, *Curiosities of the Law Reporters* (Boston, MA: Printed for W.S. Bartlett by Lee and Shepard, 1871), 158–62.

[9] Notably Watson, "Introduction to Law for Second-Year Law Students"; McDowell, "Legal Fictions in *Pierson* v. *Post*."

[10] See Watson, ibid., 442 ("the Romans did keep and breed dogs for hunting, a pastime passionately pursued even by emperors").

[11] See ibid., 441 ("The great increase of foxes [in England] in the nineteenth century was due to the sportsmen. They wanted there to be foxes! Indeed, as is made plain time and again in Anthony Trollope's novels, the gentleman was expected 'to preserve foxes,' as the phrase was. Woe – social woe – to the farmer who shot the fox devouring his chickens, instead of preserving it for the hunt. Poisoning or shooting foxes could be described as 'vulpicide' or 'murder' by the hunting fraternity").

[12] See McDowell, "Legal Fictions in *Pierson* v. *Post*," 738 ("In practice, foxhunters of the eighteenth century did not seek to eradicate foxes but actually went to great lengths to maintain the population by protecting their breeding areas and, when there was a scarcity in one location, by bringing in foxes from another"). See also 748–52.

fundamentally confused.[13] A vote for the farming interest would have been a vote for Pierson, not Post.

A second set of issues relates to custom. Livingston's suggestion that the dispute ought to have been "submitted to the arbitration of sportsmen" rather than to his own and his colleagues' "partial lights" is often understood to be a call to decide the dispute according to hunting custom. Law school casebooks, for instance, will sometimes follow *Pierson* v. *Post* with a whaling case called *Ghen* v. *Rich* in which a Massachusetts court followed a custom in Cape Cod that vested ownership of a whale killed at sea in its original hunter and allowed a salvage fee to the party who discovered it dead on the beach.[14] Allowing a finder's fee probably encouraged the prompt removal of large soon-to be-rotting carcasses from beaches while preserving the value of the first hunter's labor. No one would hunt whales in the manner followed in this case, using a bomb-lance that caused the animal to sink at once and resurface in one to three days, unless that original labor was protected. The pedagogical lesson is to set a case in which a court refused to follow the hunting custom, *Pierson* v. *Post*, against another in which custom is followed.[15]

There is some evidence that the "hot pursuit" rule Livingston advocated in *Pierson* did represent a hunting custom. We know, for instance, that the New York legislature reversed *Pierson* v. *Post* in Suffolk County (where the case took place) and neighboring Queen's County in 1844 in a statute making continued pursuit sufficient in deer hunting.[16] Deer hunting was probably more prevalent and more important to more sportsmen in these areas than foxhunting. A person can, after all, eat the deer meat and use the skin, neither of which one can do with a hunted fox, which will be destroyed by the dogs, at least in an English-style hunt. The need to reverse the capture rule for deer, so close to home, suggests Livingston was on to something in thinking there was a hunting custom of respecting the hot pursuit of an original hunter. However, we need to be careful, for there are many examples of lawyers and courts inventing

[13] Livingston wrote that the fox's "depredations on farmers and on barn-yards, have not been forgotten." *Pierson*, 180.

[14] *Ghen v. Rich*, 8 F. 159 (MA: D.C., 1881).

[15] See e.g. Dukeminier, Krier et al., 8th ed. *Property* (2014), 26–30, especially note 5 on p. 26 and note 2 on pp. 29–30.

[16] *Laws of New York*, April 1, 1844, ch. 109, N.Y.S.R.S. 3rd ed., vol. 1, 883, noted in James Kent, vol. 2, *Commentaries on American Law*, 6th ed. (New York: W. Kent, 1848), 348–49 n. e ("any person who starts and pursues such game, shall be deemed in possession of the same, *so long as he continues in fresh pursuit* thereof") (emphasis in the original).

customs like this in animal-hunting contexts. It was common, it seems, to refer to one practice or custom as the dominant one, when actually the lawyers or judges were in those very cases actively engaged in the process of choosing one custom over another, elevating its status over competing, perhaps equally long-standing and customary practices.[17] Making something look old or traditional, when in fact it is not, but is being reconstructed as such in order to give it legitimacy and attractiveness, is a powerful tool of social, cultural, and legal persuasion.[18]

Even if we could determine that hunters' custom in the area was indeed to respect another hunter who was in hot pursuit of an animal, only Post was a hunter in the requisite sense. It is true that Pierson killed the fox and so hunted it in that sense. However, Pierson was not *out hunting* for foxes as Post was. Local tradition had it that Pierson saw Post and his friends pursuing the fox and knowing they were in hot pursuit clubbed the fox with a broken rail or piece of fence railing.[19] We learned from the Judgment Roll that seven witnesses testified at the trial.[20] Presumably some of these were Post's friends who were out on the hunt with him. According to Henry Hedges, who added the information about the fence railing, writing about the case for a local newspaper, the *Sag-Harbor Express*, in 1895, Pierson was walking on his way home from his job as a school teacher in a nearby village when he saw the commotion, swooped in, and spoiled the fun by taking the fox.[21]

[17] See Bruce Ziff, "The Law of Capture, Newfoundland-Style" in Focus Feature "Foxes, Seals, Whales and the Rule of Capture: Animals in the Law and Legal History," 63 *University of Toronto Law Journal* (2013): 30–137, 53–72; Robert Deal, *The Law of the Whale Hunt: Dispute Resolution, Property Law, and American Whalers, 1780–1880* (New York: Cambridge University Press, 2016), earlier portions of which appeared in Robert Deal, "The Judicial Invention of Property Norms: Ellickson's Whalemen Revisited" in Focus Feature "Foxes, Seals, Whales and the Rule of Capture: Animals in the Law and Legal History," 63 *University of Toronto Law Journal* (2013): 30–137, 73–96 and Robert C. Deal, "Fast-Fish, Loose-Fish: How Whalemen, Lawyers, and Judges Created the British Property Law of Whaling," 37 *Ecology Law Quarterly* (2010): 199–236.

[18] See Stephen Nissenbaum, *The Battle for Christmas* (New York: Vintage Books; Random House, 1996) (on how old Carnival traditions became a festival of domesticity and consumerism that we know as Christmas only in the nineteenth century). See generally Eric Hobsbawm and Terence Ranger eds., *The Invention of Tradition* (Cambridge; New York; Melbourne: Cambridge University Press, 1983). See Tomlins, "Animals Accurs'd," 40–41 (commenting on Deal's work in the above Focus Feature on lawyers and judges inventing and elevating competing customs and bringing in the work of Martin Chanock, *Law, Custom, and Social Order: The Colonial Experience in Malawi and Zambia* [Cambridge UK; Cambridge University Press, 1985]).

[19] Hedges, "Pierson vs. Post," *Sag-Harbor Express* (1895).

[20] See Judgment Roll, p. 10, Appendix B.

[21] Hedges, "Pierson vs. Post," *Sag-Harbor Express* (1895).

Jesse Pierson was a member of a large local farming family who owned a lot of land in the community called Sagaponack next to the beach where the hunt took place. Pierson was said to have clubbed the fox with a broken rail when it took refuge "in an old shoal well near Peter's pond, not far from the ocean shore and some mile or less east of Sag Street."[22] (See Figure 1.2, from "[a]bout the year 1800," which marks Peter's Pond to the east of Sag Street.)

Now Jesse was a schoolteacher and not of substantial or independent means at the time of the case.[23] However, as we can see in Figure 1.2, his house was on the southern end of Sagg Street at the end of a long strip of Pierson family properties in Sagaponack. "By purchase and exchange and inheritance, the Piersons became the largest land owners in the place."[24] Despite his relative youth (twenty-two at the time of the case) and his lack of independent wealth, Jesse would "[b]y family background alone [...] possess substantial social status."[25] And he would presumably have been at one with the interests of his family, to whom foxes were a nuisance. In doing what he did, Jesse was acting to protect chickens (and farmers' fences and fields). He was actually doing what Livingston advocated, namely, viewing the fox as a pirate to be put to death wherever and whenever possible. Pierson refused to defer to a sporting hunt in which the hunted animal might well get away. He was grabbing an opportunity to rid the area of a fox that he and his family would have considered a nuisance. This was less hunting than pest extermination. To him the fox was vermin, not a valuable object of recreational pursuit.[26]

Jesse Pierson may have had a second motive in acting in the ungentlemanly way that he did, namely, in order to let Post and his friends know how he and his family felt about the introduction of English-style foxhunting into their neighborhood. The Judgment Roll in the case records the

[22] Ibid.

[23] Jesse does not appear on the 1801 list for tax assessment purposes. He is on both the 1803 and 1806 lists at $100 of personal property. He appears on the 1818 list with his father David at $2,000 of real property. Copies of Tax Assessment Rolls for 1801, 1803, 1806, and 1818 provided by former Southampton Town Historian Henry Moëller, located in Southampton Town Hall, Southampton, New York.

[24] James Truslow Adams, *Memorials of Old Bridgehampton* (Bridgehampton, NY: Privately Printed, 1916), 76.

[25] Ann Sandford, "Rural Wealth and American Property Law: The Sagaponack and Bridgehampton Connections 1802 and 1805" (Summer 2011) *The Bridge: Annual Magazine of the Bridgehampton Historical Society*, 18–21, 20.

[26] McDowell, "Legal Fictions in *Pierson* v. *Post*," 762 ("foxhunting was pest control to some and an elite sport to others").

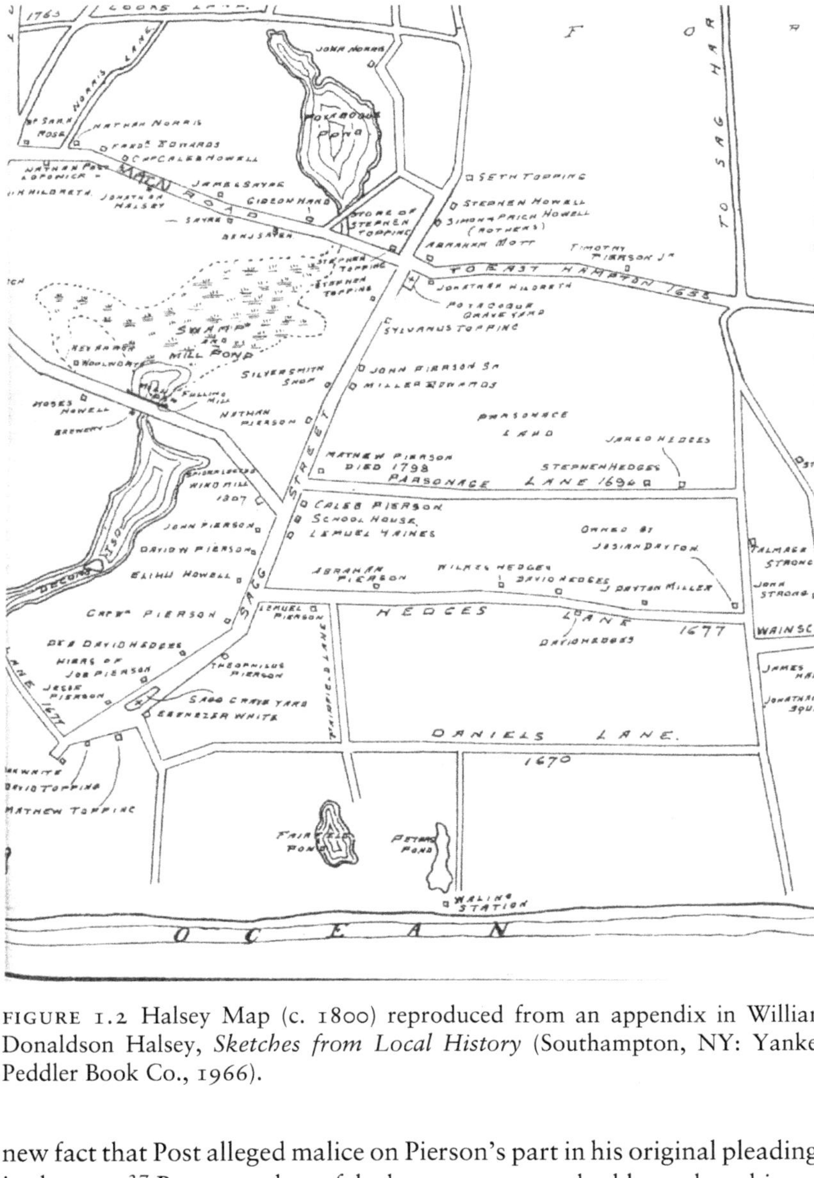

FIGURE 1.2 Halsey Map (c. 1800) reproduced from an appendix in William Donaldson Halsey, *Sketches from Local History* (Southampton, NY: Yankee Peddler Book Co., 1966).

new fact that Post alleged malice on Pierson's part in his original pleadings in the case.[27] Post must have felt that some wrong had been done him, at

[27] See Judgment Roll, pp. 4–5 (Post alleged that Jesse, "*with intention to injure him*[,] the said Lodowick[,] and to prevent the said hounds and dogs from catching and taking the said Fox and with intention to hinder the said Lodowick from having the said Fox

least in Pierson's intent, going beyond merely taking the animal he considered his by virtue of his hot pursuit. Perhaps, unlike Livingston, Pierson actually did understand what the introduction of the sport into the community meant. He might have been trying to actively communicate to Post and his friends how unwelcome the activity was in his and his family's eyes. Or if he did not have the environmental consciousness to know what serious foxhunting would mean to the fox population in Sagaponack, it might have been a general expression of disapproval toward the activity.

Both the Piersons and the Posts were wealthy families. Nathan Post and his son Lodowick were listed together on a tax assessment roll from 1801 at $2,900 worth of property, compared against David Pierson's $2,460.[28] In 1803, the Posts were still ahead with $2,800 compared to David Pierson's $2,360.[29] Both families had been in the community since its earliest days of settlement.[30] Both Nathan Post and David Pierson were town trustees in 1796, so it would be fair to conclude that both were men of substance and influence.[31] However, they lived in different areas and their wealth came from different sources, which helps explain the friction over the fox.[32]

Nathan Post almost certainly owned farmland and cattle and so he would not have been tone-deaf to the Piersons' farming

did [...] *maliciously* kill the said Fox"); p. 5 (Post and the dogs and hounds chasing the fox were "in the view of the said Jesse [...] [who] did then and there *maliciously* take and carry away the said Fox"), Appendix B (emphasis added).

[28] The Posts list real property only. David Pierson's was broken down into $2,200 in real property and $260 in personal property. See Tax Assessment Roll, 1801.

[29] Again the Posts' listing was for real property only and David Pierson had $2,100 in real property and $260 in personal property. See Tax Assessment Roll, 1803.

[30] See Frederic Gregory Mather, *The Refugees of 1776 from Long Island to Connecticut* (Albany, NY: J.B. Lyon Co., 1913), 505 (giving the genealogy of David Pierson), 511 (giving the genealogy of Richard Post, whose great-great grandson was Captain Nathan Post). See also 512 (listing Nathan with his two brothers, Joseph and Jeremiah). Both Henry Pierson and Richard Post are listed in the November 1, 1676 patent ("A Patent or Confirmation Granted to the Inhabitants of the Towne of South Hampton"). They are both also listed in the later confirming "Dongan Patent" in 1686. Handwritten copies of both of these are located in Series 12943, Letters Patent, the first at Book 4, pp. 100–102 and the second at Book 6, pp. 35–45. Copies of these documents provided by the New York State Library, Albany, NY.

[31] See *Town Records*, vol. 3: 348.

[32] Bethany Berger claimed that Nathan Post was not descended from the original town inhabitant Richard Post. See Berger, "It's Not About the Fox," 1125–26. However, this was an error, explained in greater detail in Chapter 5 where I discuss Berger's larger thesis.

perspective on the fox.[33] However, his wealth was derived primarily from seafaring pursuits, as the title "Captain" in his name indicates. He was among the refugees that fled the British occupation of Long Island during the Revolutionary War.[34] During this time he was a privateer and the captain of an armed sloop named *Revenge*.[35] During the 1790s he assumed part ownership of a brig that engaged in trade in the West Indies.[36] He owned one slave.[37] The Post house stood on the main road closer to Sagaponack than Sag Harbor, just east of the village of Bridgehampton.[38] It was said that in addition to wainscoting in the dining room, there was a slave whipping post in the kitchen.[39] Post is identified among the revolutionary era residents of Sag Harbor and described as a mariner and later master of a ship that sailed from that port to the West Indies.[40]

Sag Harbor is on the north shore of the South Fork of Long Island, sheltered by Peconic Bay and the North Fork of Long Island, which is itself sheltered by Long Island Sound and mainland Connecticut (see Figure 1.3). It stands out in the region as a village that "never fit the agrarian pattern" of Southampton,[41] the pattern certainly found south of the main road in Sagaponack where the Piersons owned so much land (see Figure 1.2). Coastal and foreign trade gave Sag Harbor a vibrant commercial life, much of it related to the high traffic in its harbor created by the whaling industry. Indeed, "[b]y 1789 its port was busier than New York City's."[42] Wealth in Sag Harbor was "fueled by maritime

[33] See Sandford, "Rural Wealth and American Property Law," 20 (on the farming point); (listing Nathan Post as having bought four cattle).

[34] Mather, *The Refugees of 1776*, 254. [35] Ibid., 512.

[36] Sandford, "Rural Wealth and American Property Law," 6.

[37] See *Heads of Families at the First Census of the United States Taken in the Year 1790, New York* (Washington, DC: Government Printing Office, 1908), 167.

[38] See Geoffrey K. Fleming, *Images of America: Bridgehampton* (Charleston, SC: Arcadia Publishing, 2003), 54 (for a photograph of the house c. 1880 then known as "Sayrelands"). It is still standing on the main road, Montauk Highway.

[39] Hedges, "Pierson vs. Post," *Sag-Harbor Express* (1895).

[40] Dorothy Ingersoll Zaykowski, *Sag Harbor: The Story of an American Beauty* (Sag Harbor, NY: Sag Harbor Historical Society, 1991), 188.

[41] Mary Cummings, "Introduction" to *Images of America: Southampton* (Charleston, SC; Chicago, IL; Portsmouth, NH; San Francisco, CA: Arcadia Publishing, 1996), 7.

[42] Ibid., 7–8.

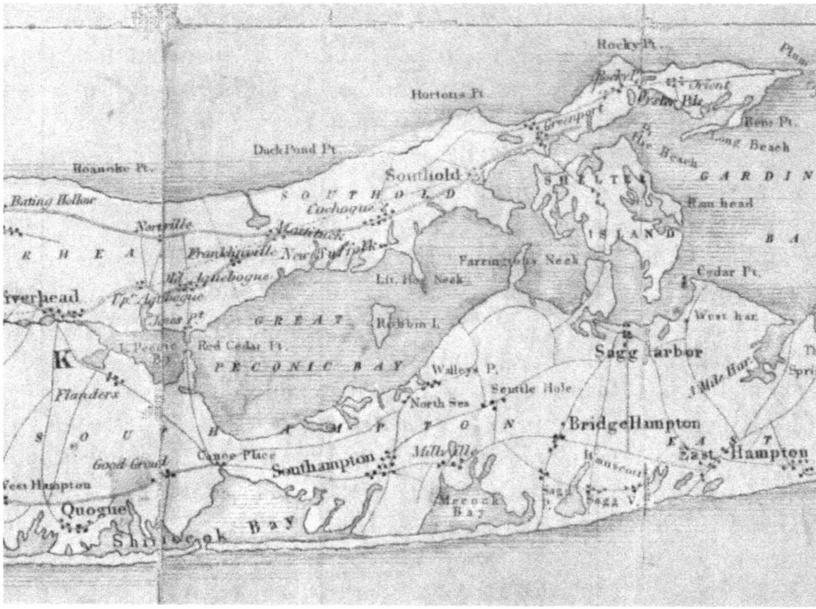

FIGURE 1.3 "Traveller's Map of Long Island" (1843) by Joseph Hutchins Colton. New York Public Library, NY.

trade and whaling, and their spin-off industries, shipbuilding and rope-making."[43]

Sag Harbor was a fishing, whaling, seafaring, and sea trading place, which to this day has a very distinct feel from the Hamptons (Bridgehampton, Southampton, and East Hampton). The Hamptons were primarily rural, not ritzy, as we think of them today, and the English towns, as they were known on the South Shore, were settled by people who came from Connecticut. They brought with them Congregational and Presbyterian forms of religion and a Puritan culture in which the fox would have been seen as vermin and English-style foxhunting as wasteful and extravagant. Foxhunting in Connecticut, for example, could consist in something as unsportsmanlike as laying out fish heads at night and shooting as many animals as possible under a full moon.[44] Sag Harbor, on the other hand, was more New York than Connecticut, more urban, more

[43] Ann H. Sandford, "Rural Connections: Early Republic Bridgehampton and Its Wider World, 1790–1805," 15 *Long Island Historical Journal* (2002/2003): 1–22, 6.

[44] See McDowell, "Legal Fictions in *Pierson* v. *Post*," 764–65.

cosmopolitan, and more boisterous in the way that often characterizes seagoing communities. The eastern end of Long Island, particularly the Hamptons, had long been involved in a push and pull between Connecticut (across the water) and New York (by way of land attachment).[45] As McDowell put it, two very different views of foxes and foxhunting – "hunting in style versus hunting to kill" – pulled in the different directions of the two regions and their respective cultures.[46] The Piersons would likely have seen Post's foxhunt as anti-Puritan, anti-Connecticut, too New York, and too ostentatious. Hence, spoiling the hunt was not just a way to protect their own interests, which would have been threatened by English-style fox hunting, but also to register their disapproval of a different way of being wealthy in their community.

This kind of nuanced conflict between competing social interests in a relatively small geographic region, one agrarian and the other up-and-coming mercantile, has been identified with remarkable events in American history, notably the Salem witch trials in Massachusetts in the late seventeenth century.[47] It is not so difficult to believe that the Pierson and Post families cared enough about their competing views of the fox and their competing positions in the community, agrarian wealth versus shipping and trade wealth, that they were quite willing to use the law to fight to vindicate their respective conceptions of the neighborhood's custom.

[45] See William Donaldson Halsey, *Sketches from Local History* (Southampton, NY: Yankee Peddler Book Company, 1966), 9–12. Connecticut was reached easily by water, whereas crossing the ninety miles to Manhattan took more than two days by stagecoach. Cummings, "Introduction" to *Images of America: Southampton*, 7; see also Adams, *Memorials of Old Bridgehampton*, 164 (packet lines ran between Sag Harbor and Middleton, Connecticut, as well as Sag Harbor and New London, three times a week).

[46] McDowell, "Legal Fictions in *Pierson* v. *Post*," 765.

[47] Noted by Christopher Tomlins, *Freedom Bound: Law, Labor, and Civic Identity in Colonizing English America, 1580–1865* (New York: Cambridge University Press, 2010), 307 n. 35. See Paul Boyer and Stephen Nissenbaum, *Salem Possessed: The Social Origin of Witchcraft* (Cambridge, MA: Harvard University Press, 1974). These two well-respected colonial historians argued that the Salem witch trials in Massachusetts in the seventeenth century were a product of a clash between individuals associated with one community oriented around agrarian life in Salem Village, who turned on those connected to the mercantile and prosperous Salem Town. Salem Town had long refused to give Salem Village the control over its own affairs that it wanted: its own minister, its own school, exemption from paying taxes to Salem Town, and its own town status. The people who lived in Salem Village (the agrarian group) blamed Salem Town (the mercantile group) for their decline and witchcraft for their troubles. The family names in the Salem witch trial conflict also started with "P"s – the Putnams were the farming family to whom many of the persecutors were connected and the targeted rising mercantile family were the Porters.

Indeed, no one who has read E.P. Thompson's classic *Whigs and Hunters* can doubt the tremendous social significance that can readily attach to hunted deer, hunting dogs, stolen horses, and poached rabbits.[48]

There are obviously tremendous differences between eighteenth-century England and nineteenth-century America on issues relating to hunting, perhaps the most significant of which is that hunting in America (especially as a food source) was premised on the antithesis of the English system, where hunting was a form of aristocratic privilege, defined precisely by its non-inclusiveness. As one historian of hunting in America has put it, "backwoods farmers of the colonial era regarded hunting not as a privilege but as a right; to be American was to take game without the hindrance of aristocratic game laws."[49] More to the Thompson point, "[c]olonists killed game for food, for market, for bounties, and for an escape from the drudgery of farming. Few hunted to create or to renew a traditional social hierarchy; hence few adhered to English nomenclature or codes of sportsmanship."[50] This would certainly describe Pierson, who did not respect Post's signaling of his intention to take the fox by pursuing it with a group of friends with hounds. Post was probably aping gentlemanly stature rather than faithfully reproducing it: his pursuit was not on horseback or in scarlet coat. Nevertheless, Post's hunt, with "dogs and hounds," and Pierson's response – remember the alleged malice – did seem to be about social hierarchy.[51] This is true even if Pierson did not have the ecological consciousness to understand what the introduction of foxhunting would mean to farmers in terms of an increase in fox populations and even if he did not know a lot about what introduction of the sport would mean for farmers' fences and fields. Pierson was not motivated to do what he did because he wanted to eat the fox, or sell it, or turn it in for a bounty. So far as Post was concerned, Pierson intervened to spoil his fun, a form of amusement that Pierson may have understood that, if it accelerated, would conflict with his family's interests.

On the South Fork of Long Island in the early 1800s, the very well-connected Piersons were probably experiencing some frustration at their inability to outpace the fast-charging Nathan Post, who had moved south of Sag Harbor, closer to their lands, literally on the border of Sagaponack

[48] See E.P. Thompson, *Whigs and Hunters: The Origin of the Black Act* (New York: Pantheon Books, 1975).

[49] Daniel Justin Herman, *Hunting and the American Imagination* (Washington: Smithsonian Institution Press, 2001), 45.

[50] Ibid., 23. [51] *Pierson*, 175.

on the main road outside Bridgehampton, and up in the world in terms of money he made. In Thompson's account, "the new rich," "bringing money from outside the community, became targets of poaching at the hands of "Blacks" who belonged to a "declining gentry and yeoman class," frustrated by the newcomers' increasing disregard for customary use and neighborhood opinion.[52] The Piersons could certainly be viewed as declining gentry, seeking to express the point that in their community foxes were vermin to be killed whenever and wherever possible and that English-style fox hunting was unwelcome. Post took them to law for Jesse Pierson's bold and undoubtedly rude assertion of that point of view. However, it bears noticing that once Post took to law, the Pierson response was not to turn to black face paint and other "extra-legal" means, which in Thompson's account elicited the infamously harsh *Black Act*, backing up a long process of enclosing public or common land and protecting privatized forms of property. Thompson's (controversial) point at the end of *Whigs and Hunters* was that there was a kind of "rule of law" in the seemingly lawless behavior of the resisting rebels and their blackened faces and law could, in addition to being a bourgeois right, be a powerful customary right.[53] What is important to see for present purposes is that the Piersons used the "rule of law" on its face, the clear *Black Act* kind of rule of law. Specifically, they took steps to out-legal Post: they hired an excellent lawyer with ties to the area and to their family, who raised a variety of process-related points on appeal and killed Post with costs. It is difficult to see Pierson as a defender of the commons or upholding customary rights, as was true in Thompson's famous case. *Pierson* v. *Post* was a conflict that played itself out in a thoroughly and uncontroversial legal way. Unlike the eighteenth-century English case, it was saturated in formal state law from start to finish.

THE DISSENT

With some of this background understanding of what was at issue in *Pierson* v. *Post* and why these two families were fighting over a fox, we return to Livingston's dissent. Livingston preferred a decision for Post and

[52] See Thompson, *Whigs and Hunters*, 108–15.

[53] See Robert W. Gordon, "E.P. Thompson's Legacies" in *Taming the Past: Essays on Law in History and History in Law* (Cambridge UK; New York: Cambridge University Press, 2017), 149–55, 151 (providing the quotation from Thompson that "law did not keep politely to a 'level' but was at every bloody level").

the hot pursuit rule. However, his characterization of the fox as a pirate to be killed whenever and wherever possible was actually consistent with what Pierson did in the case, kill the fox when he had a chance because, after all, in an English-style foxhunt the fox could, and often did, get away – the point captured in the Court's interpretation of Justinian's *Institutes*. Post, on the other hand, viewed the fox as a valuable object of recreational pursuit (even if the description of the fox as a "wild and noxious beast" came from his pleadings).[54] This kind of clash of custom, two different ways of viewing the fox and foxhunting, could not be resolved by "the arbitration of sportsmen" who would have immediately sympathized and agreed with Post over Pierson, the "saucy intruder," as Livingston memorably described him.[55]

Livingston came from a wealthy and near-aristocratic background. James Kent noted in the flyleaf of one of his books opposite the image of Livingston he pasted in the book (reproduced in Figure 1.1) that when Livingston died at age 66 in Washington in 1823 "[t]he public were surprised by the Discovery of the extent of his property." Livingston's real estate was worth $70,000 and he had $300,000 of personal estate "well funded in Stock, Bonds and Mortgages. His annual income (exclusive of his salary) was $21,600!" Livingston's total wealth amounted to a tremendous amount of money for the time and well worth Kent's exclamation point. It put Livingston in a completely different league than even ordinarily elite Americans we are used to reading about in American history. It should probably be noted that the present-day Bush family (of presidentially associated fame – George H.W., George W., and most recent aspirant Jeb Bush) is descended from the Livingston family.[56] Yet simply being very rich would not necessarily have made Livingston familiar with foxhunting.

English-style foxhunting was much more prevalent in the Southern and Middle states than the North, where pursuit, usually of the red fox, was ordinarily done on foot, not on horseback. One sportsman explained that foxes were never followed on horseback in the North given the rugged and mountainous ground and the damage that pursuit on horseback would cause to farmland and fences. Consequently the fox would often get away, resulting in a disappointed hunt. In the South, the target of the hunt was the gray fox, rather than the red fox. The gray fox was easier to catch and tended to run its course through woods and uncultivated land, so the chase caused little damage to plantation owners and was therefore

[54] *Pierson*, 180. [55] Ibid., 180, 181.
[56] See http://en.wikipedia.org/wiki/Livingston_family.

tolerated by them.[57] Accounts of foxhunting from sportsmen in the Northern states tend to confirm that the type of foxhunting undertaken there was a more rustic and less gentlemanly affair than common in the South. One hunter from Western New York described a rather ungentlemanly practice of getting the dogs to rouse the fox and crouching by a wall to wait and shoot it.[58] Another from New Jersey acknowledged that the men involved in the hunt were "not gentlemen, it is true" and that the country was so rough horses could not travel over it.[59]

There was an English-style hunt on Western Long Island in Hempstead introduced by one John Evers in 1768. Evers was an Englishman who began to hunt with dogs, horses, and huntsmen imported from the British Isles and "[t]he descendants of these hounds were used in the nineteenth century to form the Meadow Brook Hounds."[60] The Hempstead operation included George Washington among its subscribers, perhaps "the best-known [American] foxhunter of all time."[61] He learned about the sport and practiced it enthusiastically before the Revolutionary War in his native Virginia, where riding conditions made pursuit in the English style, i.e. on horseback, more feasible.[62] It is true that Meadow Brook was later quite a famous hunt club.[63] However, it was not established in that form until late in the nineteenth century (1880).[64] The Revolutionary War put an end to the Hempstead operation as it did to the Gloucester Foxhunting Club outside Philadelphia.[65] Members of this club actually did most of their hunting in New Jersey, where Livingston was from.[66] A survey of American hunt club history notes that what followed was "a

[57] See "Fox-Hunting in America," *Spirit of the Times: A Chronicle of the Turf, Agriculture, Field Sports, Literature and the Stage* (September 13, 1856), 363.

[58] See "Fox-Hunting in Western New York," *Spirit of the Times* (February 28, 1857), 25.

[59] "Fox-Hunting in New Jersey," *Spirit of the Times* (January 30, 1858), 606.

[60] See Caroline Jones, "Fox Hunting in America," *American Heritage* 24:6 (1973): 62–101, 68.

[61] A. Henry Higginson and Julian Ingersoll Chamberlain, *Hunting in the United States and Canada: Being an illustrated history of each of the hunt clubs and individual packs on the North American Continent, and presenting first-hand information of early colonial fox hunting, hitherto unpublished, as well as reproductions of portraits of early celebrities the existence of which has not been known to hunting men* (London: William Heinemann Ltd., 1928), 100 (noting Washington's subscription); Jones, "Fox Hunting in America," 67 (describing Washington as "the best-known foxhunter of all time").

[62] Jones, "Fox Hunting in America," 67.

[63] See ibid., 101, depicting avid hunter Theodore Roosevelt with horses and hounds, noting he was a member of Meadow Brook Hounds, and his home at Oyster Bay was an assembly point for the club's meet in 1885.

[64] See Higginson and Chamberlain, *Hunting in the United States and Canada*, 103.

[65] Ibid., 100. [66] See Herman, *Hunting and the American Imagination*, 71.

period of inactivity," not surprising given the strong English associations with the sport and the locations of British occupation during the Revolutionary War.[67] This survey states that "[t]here was little or no hunting around New York City until 1874."[68] In much of the North, foxhunting "became a neglected art in the Jacksonian and antebellum eras and remained so until a new elite rediscovered it in the Gilded Age."[69] The Middle and Southern states were different. In the antebellum period, "foxes were hunted quite regularly by wealthy landowners in Pennsylvania, Maryland, and Virginia. A pack of hounds became as integral a part of a gentleman's assets as his 'horses, slaves and guns.'"[70]

We do not know what exposure Livingston had to American variations of foxhunting. He certainly seems to have had in mind the English-style hunt on horseback when he wrote about the "gentleman, [who] at the sound of the horn, and at peep of day [...] mount[s] his steed."[71] His knowledge of the sport was probably the same as other "elite colonists who read British literature [...] and who sought to build personae and estates comparable to those of the English gentry."[72] There is no reason to suppose that knowledge extended to what exactly one required of a fox population in order to sustain a reliably successful hunt. Indeed, Livingstone's mistake that a finding for Post rather than Pierson would actually result in a decrease in the area's fox population suggests he did not have more than a general knowledge of the hunt, since the introduction of more organized forms of the sport would increase foxes at the direct expense of farmers and landowners like the Piersons. The kind of catch-it-and-kill-it-if-you-can style of hunting Pierson was engaged in was actually the kind that would result in the reduction of the fox population and the protection of chickens. So much of what Livingston said in his dissent is just plain silly that trying to make serious sense of it seems like a fool's errand. As McDowell put it, Livingston probably "did not entirely believe his own argument" and so "we should not try too hard to make sense of the internal contradictions."[73] It is full of "spurious and disconnected" policy arguments that result in a "rather surreal" feel.[74]

Yet there was seriousness mixed in with the silliness. So it is worth asking what we should take seriously, and why. For instance, the dissent

67 Higginson and Chamberlain, *Hunting in the United States and Canada*, 100.

68 Ibid., 101. 69 Herman, *Hunting and the American Imagination*, 72.

70 Jones, "Fox Hunting in America," 65. 71 *Pierson*, 180.

72 Herman, *Hunting and the American Imagination*, 68. That literature did not, however, include Trollope, as his books came later in the nineteenth century.

73 McDowell, "Legal Fictions in *Pierson* v. *Post*," 742. 74 Ibid., 765.

contains a serious point about the perils of relying on foreign authorities (Roman, civilian, and even British) to decide homegrown adjudicated disputes. First, there was considerable disagreement among those authorities. Second, American conditions might augur in favor of a different rule or solution. Livingston wrote in *Pierson*: "Writers on general law, who have favored us with their speculations on these points, differ on them all; but, great as is the diversity of sentiment among them, some conclusion must be adopted on the question immediately before us."[75] There was a need for practical action and one could not simply rely on foreign authorities if they were not in agreement. Given that diversity of sentiment, Americans would need to think for themselves what the best rule for their circumstances would be: "Whatever *Justinian* may have thought of the matter, it must be recollected that his code was compiled many hundred years ago, and it would be very hard indeed, at the distance of so many centuries, not to have a right to establish a rule for ourselves."[76] Dismissing Pierson's lawyer's reliance on Justinian, Livingston asserted that "[i]f any thing [...] in the digests or pandects shall appear to militate against" Post, then "we have only to say *tempora mutantur*," times change, "and if men themselves change with the times, why should not laws also undergo an alteration?"[77]

We know the concerns Livingston expressed in these passages of *Pierson* were real. There are a number of other cases from the New York Supreme Court from the same period in which he makes similar points. One year earlier, for instance, we find him noting in the marine insurance case *Lawrence* v. *Sebor* that: "The French law has been referred to as settling this point [...] but on looking into Emerignon and Valin, we shall find them at variance."[78] Earlier that year, in a case of the capture of a New York ship by the British, *Leavenworth* v. *Delafield*, Livingston, struggling with how to apportion recovery of the crew's wages for the four-month delay in delivery as between the insurers of the vessel and the insurers of the freight, referred to a diverse range of writers – the Dutch jurist Ricard, the English writer Beawes's book on *Lex Mercatoria* or the law merchant, Emerignon, and Pothier's treatise on maritime contracts or charter parties.[79] Noting that the English rule was not exactly on point, Livingston wrote, "we are at liberty to make one for ourselves."[80]

[75] *Pierson*, 181. [76] Ibid. [77] Ibid.
[78] *Lawrence* v. *Sebor*, 2 Cai. R. 203, 207 (N.Y. Sup. Ct., 1804).
[79] *Leavenworth* v. *Delafield*, 1 Cai. R. 573, 577–79 (N.Y. Sup. Ct., 1804).
[80] Ibid., 579.

In a case a year later and in the same volume of reported cases as *Pierson*, Livingston distinguished *Leavenworth* v. *Delafield* and the case of capture from a situation of embargo, where unlike capture, the crew was not retained to preserve the ship's cargo and prevent total loss. In an embargo "the sovereign [...] neither claims the ship or cargo, but only for political reasons prevents their immediate departure."[81] In that situation, Livingston thought that neither insurer should cover the loss. He relied on Ricard to make the distinction between capture and embargo, rejected what Pothier had to say, and noted that Emerignon taught that there was "a diversity of opinion among" the "foreign writers."[82] Livingston wrote that he would follow the English rule, "not on the ground of authority [...] but as the most reasonable; the most comfortable to the understanding of different classes of underwriters; the best calculated to prevent confusion and embarrassment, and the most likely to throw upon each the loss which the particular subject insured by him has sustained."[83] Here, then, we encounter the same points that *Pierson* treats humorously – about inconclusive disagreement amongst the foreign writers, the need to feel free to make an indigenous rule "for ourselves," and the call to think things through, independently of authority, from first principles and in keeping with current needs and conditions.

Marine insurance fell within a more general area of mercantile quasi-international private law known as the law merchant, "the *jus gentium*, or common private law of all nations," relied on when disputes arose between merchants from different countries.[84] It had "a strong continental bias," given the trading power of the Dutch and other civil law countries such as France, Spain, Portugal, and Italy, whose scholars helped shape it.[85] In England, the law merchant was first used for foreign merchants, offering rules favorable to them as a way to entice them to set up shop there. The law merchant was originally administered by the High Court of Admiralty, as so many of the commercial disputes arose in a maritime context over business matters relating to shipping (promissory notes, bills of exchange, commercial agents, and insurance contracts). Common-law courts laid claim to the jurisdiction by virtue of an

[81] *Penny and Scribner* v. *The New York Insurance Company*, 3 Cai. R. 155, 159 (N.Y. Sup. Ct., 1805).

[82] Ibid., 159–60. [83] Ibid., 160.

[84] Herbert Alan Johnson, *The Law Merchant and Negotiable Instruments in Colonial New York, 1664 to 1730* (Chicago, IL: Loyola University Press, 1963), 20.

[85] Ibid., 17.

irrefutable pleading fiction that deemed the venue of the dispute to be in England. This made the law merchant part of English common law.[86]

The law merchant was a very important area of law in both colonial and early America, especially for legal communities whose economies were intimately tied to maritime trade, places like New York City, Boston, and Philadelphia. Indeed, it has been said that "marine insurance cases laid the foundation for New York law."[87] Conflict between England, France, and Spain after the French Revolution afforded great opportunities for American traders, given the new country's neutral status amid these rival nations seeking to defend and expand their overseas empires.[88] Attention focused on French and British possessions in the West Indies, where American trade was permitted with the French and carried on via smuggling with the British and other foreign colonies.[89] Risk capital moved "[a]lmost overnight" from land speculation to "the newly promising field of marine insurance."[90] In the 1790s, "the neutral Americans became the carriers for the world."[91] Hence, the importance of this area of the law for early Americans.[92]

Kent and Livingston would go toe-to-toe on law merchant points of law during the time they shared the bench at the New York Supreme Court. Both men learned how to use continental sources at the knee of Alexander Hamilton, who did a great deal of legal business after the revolution arguing commercial law and maritime insurance cases specifically.[93]

Kent famously wrote about his habit of presenting his ideas of what would be best for New York law accompanied by a Roman or continental law authority, calling this his "plan" for the erection of a "temple of our

[86] See ibid., 18–19. Johnson describes the law merchant in colonial New York (pp. 22–27) and explains (see p. 27) that law merchant work was concentrated in the New York City Mayor's Court, which used the same British venue system based on fictitious pleadings, noting the advanced state of the law merchant's reception into the common law by that time.

[87] See Julius Goebel Jr., vol. 2, *The Law Practice of Alexander Hamilton: Documents and Commentary* (New York: Columbia University Press, 1969), "Preface," ix.

[88] Ibid., viii. [89] Ibid., 34. [90] Ibid., ix. [91] Ibid., 42.

[92] We will see in Chapter 6 that both George Caines, reporter for the New York Supreme Court at the time of *Pierson*, and his successor, William Johnson, published books on the law merchant and maritime law respectively.

[93] William Kent, *Memoirs and Letters of James Kent, LL.D.: Late Chancellor of the State of New York, Author of "Commentaries on American Law," etc. by his great-grandson William Kent of the New York Bar* (Boston, MA: Little, Brown, 1898), 317–18. See also Goebel, *The Law Practice of Alexander Hamilton*, 2: 391–778 (on New York maritime law and Hamilton's practice, including full texts of his marine insurance cases).

jurisprudence."[94] And he identified Livingston as the only judge among his "brethren" on the New York Supreme Court whom he could not "rout and carry" by waving his "mysterious wand of French and civil law."[95] In a marine insurance case called *Walden* v. *Leroy*, for example, Livingston vigorously dissented from Kent's ruling that as between the owners of a ship and the merchants of the ship's goods, the merchants' insurance ought to cover losses arising from repair of the ship. Kent relied on Ricard, Beawes (who endorsed Ricard), Emerignon, and pointed to an established rule in the commercial court of Pisa.[96] Livingston's dissent was based on the idea that shipowners should not be encouraged to wait until they have cargo on board to do ship repairs that the merchant's insurance would then cover. His view, which seems much more compelling than Kent's, was that merchants do not pay for repairs to the ship if they happen before the voyage and they should not be made responsible for them simply because they have arisen after their goods are on board. Livingston criticized Kent's heavy reliance on Ricard, writing that this novel claim had been unsuccessful in England. "[A] channel, which leaves no doubt of the information being correct," indicated that the merchants' insurance would not cover the loss in that country.[97] Livingston apologized for the length of his opinion but stated that he viewed its length as justified by "the importance of the question, than which few can occur more interesting to the mercantile world."[98]

In *Pierson*, intense debate over foreign authorities looks esoteric and strange, given the lack of a significant economic context that would explain and render understandable expending so much energy on such a minor dispute, a squabble between neighbors (albeit rich ones), from Long Island over a 75¢ jury award. However, once one sees the kinds of commercial contexts in which these authorities could be so powerfully deployed, the effort taken in their research and learning makes more sense. Knowledge and familiarity with these sources, along with skill in their forensic use, were part of an apprenticeship-oriented legal education.

Because foreign authorities were useful and directly applicable to important and lucrative areas of legal practice at the time, a demonstrated capacity to handle them provided a clear line of separation between the run-of-the-mill lawyer, the pettifogger, and the profession's well-paid elite – the Ciceronian lawyer-statesmen who displayed

[94] Kent, *Memoirs*, 117. [95] Ibid.
[96] *Walden* v. *LeRoy*, 2 Cai. R. 263, 265–66 (N.Y. Sup. Ct., 1805). [97] Ibid., 269.
[98] Ibid., 273.

their worth by demonstrating familiarity with and a working command of classical texts.[99] It was genuinely difficult to employ these sources. Their use required study, application of a certain kind of attention, literacy in languages other than English (Latin and/or French), and, importantly, access to copies of the books, usually (at least at first) from the personal library of a more senior member of the profession, the senior person in an apprenticeship arrangement or a more informal mentoring relationship.[100] There is sense here, not nonsense or exoticism for exoticism's sake, even though that is how it may at first appear.

The importance of economic gain and loss in other cases helps explain, for instance, why we see the same passages of Justinian's *Institutes* relied on in John Adams's eighteenth-century Boston whaling case and *Pierson* v. *Post*'s early nineteenth-century New York. Daniel Coquillette has shown how the young Adams wanted to use Chapters 12 and 13 of the *Institutes* (the same passages Pierson's lawyer relied on) in a Boston whaling dispute in 1768.[101] Two whalers were arguing over who was the rightful owner of a harpooned whale – the one who first sighted it and harpooned it but then lost it, or the one who succeeded in bringing it in. Unlike Post's lawyer, Adams had access to the parallel text in the *Digest*. His notes indicate that in preparing the case Adams cross-referenced the

99 On the centrality of the Ciceronian model of the lawyer-statesman with classical learning in early America, see Robert A. Ferguson, *Law and Letters in American Culture* (Cambridge, MA: Harvard University Press, 1984). I draw extensively on Ferguson's book in the next chapter.

100 An apprenticeship arrangement – the primary form of legal education in the United States until late in the nineteenth century – often involved an exchange between the senior lawyer and junior student, of the latter paying for their position and performing clerical tasks (copying and filling in the lawyer's forms) for access to the senior lawyer's books and, if fortunate, some guidance in reading them, which ones and what to make sure they understood from them. A work like *Hoffman's Course of Legal Study* was a way to try and standardize what lawyers were getting lawyers-in-training to read in these apprenticeship arrangements. It could also operate as a booklist, what classic and standard texts should be in a personal law library or a city or county bar association library. For a description of the apprenticeship system and examples of the course of readings in the offices of various famous lawyers, see Jenni Parrish, "Law Books and Legal Publishing in America, 1760–1840," 72 *Law Library Journal* (1979): 355–452, 356–58. On late eighteenth and early nineteenth-century lawyers' libraries, see the symposium convened and presided over by Morris L. Cohen, "Historical Development of the American Lawyer's Library," 61 *Law Library Journal* (1968): 440–62. See also Morris L. Cohen, "Thomas Jefferson Recommends a Course of Law Study," 119 *University of Pennsylvania Law Review* (1971): 823–44. See generally on apprenticeship and law book lists, Charles Warren, *A History of the American Bar* (Boston, MA: Little, Brown, 1911), 161–87.

101 See Coquillette, "Justinian in Braintree," 384–85.

Institutes with the *Digest* and appreciated the Trebatius disagreement. There is no indication that Adams's classical learning was ever brought to bear on the case. Robert Deal explains that the case ultimately went to arbitration and was decided in favor of the second striker probably on the grounds that the harpoon or iron of the first ship was not attached when the second one struck.[102] The point is we see Adams struggling with the same sources in arguments over an animal of obviously great economic consequence in an important New England industry.

One year later the same passages from the *Institutes* pop up again in an important British copyright case, *Miller* v. *Taylor* (1769), where the publication of a literary work was compared to the voluntary freeing of a bird. Mr. Justice Aston wrote there that "[t]he quotation from the *Institutes* relating to wild animals is very applicable in this case. They [the birds or the works of art] are yours, while they continue in your possession, but no longer."[103] It was, in other words, truly a transatlantic piece of text, the importance of which resonated on both sides of the Atlantic Ocean, as well as the American Revolution.[104]

Whales were economically important all along the east coast of the United States. There were certainly lots of disputes involving whales – even if they were not regularly litigated.[105] Foxes, however, would raise an eyebrow. Really how important were foxes to the economy of New York or New England? Not very. Yet the same sources, just like these widely-known passages from Justinian's *Institutes*, could still be

[102] See Deal, *The Law of the Whale Hunt*, 68–69.

[103] Sir James Burrow, *Reports of Cases argued and adjudged in the Court of King's Bench, during the time Lord Mansfield presided in that Court, from Michelmas Term 1756 to Easter Term 1772, in five volumes*, vol. 4 (1766–1770) 3rd ed. (London: Printed for W. Clark and J. Butterworth, 1812), 2363.

[104] Chapters 12 and 13, appeared in the first five pages of the popular George Harris (1761) British edition of an English translation of the *Institutes*, widely used and relied on until an 1812 American edition appeared. See Thomas Cooper, *The Institutes of Justinian: with notes* (Philadelphia, PA: P. Byrne, 1812).

[105] See Deal, "Fast-Fish, Loose-Fish" (making the point in the paper's abstract that litigation was rare and violence even more so). See also Deal, "The Judicial Invention of Property Norms," 95 (the reasons for cases rarely coming to court included the high cost of litigation – in terms of both money and time, which made compromise an option that made good economic and business sense. Also whalemen had a long history of sharing or "mateship" and of going halves when disputes arose). See generally, Deal, *The Law of the Whale Hunt* and review by Angela Fernandez, "'Coke-Upon-Littleton of the Fist': Law, Customs, and Complications," *Legal History: JOTWELL (The Journal of Things We Like (Lots))* (January 2017), (https://legalhist.jotwell.com/coke-upon-littleton-of-the-fist-law-custom-and-complications/).

trotted out by lawyers trained in their use, and sure enough this is what happened in *Pierson*. Livingston's turn to comic relief would be both invited and justified by the minor importance of the fox, economically speaking, in a world where the authorities so ingeniously mobilized were otherwise connected to very serious business. These were authorities relevant and used in disputes relating to animals in hunting or resource extraction, industries of high economic importance (e.g. whales, seals, or fish), or they were loosely connected to economically significant areas of the law such as the law merchant with its weighty concentration on such matters as risk allocation in marine insurance, promissory notes, and other negotiable lending instruments (e.g. bills of exchange).[106] These were, indeed, some of the most important legal issues of the day, issues with which Livingston was intimately familiar.

Livingston specialized in commercial law and maritime law when he went on to sit on the United States Supreme Court.[107] No one would say that the use of the law merchant and other continentally-influenced sources were unimportant or a joke to him. American legal historians have doubted how much civil law was used to come to conclusions at variance with the answers that would have been given under the common law; they have noted that the law merchant came to be thoroughly incorporated into the common law. Yet there is no question that Kent relied heavily on civil law and continental sources in both his judicial opinion and in his *Commentaries*, even if those references were often ornamental rather than substantial and "mere window dressing."[108]

[106] See Daniel R. Coquillette, "Legal Ideology and Incorporation IV: The Nature of Civilian Influence on Modern Anglo-American Commercial Law," 67 *Boston University Law Review* (1987): 877–970, 881–920 (on bills of exchange).

[107] See Robert E. Cushman, "Henry Brockholst Livingston," *Dictionary of American Biography* (noting that Livingston wrote only thirty-eight majority opinions when he was on the United State Supreme Court, none of which dealt with a constitutional issue – "they deal rather with questions of maritime and commercial law in which he was deeply interested and highly trained").

[108] Watson, "Chancellor Kent's Use of Foreign Law," 49. Similar conclusions have been made about the use of civil law sources by Joseph Story. See M. H. Hoeflich, "John Austin and Joseph Story: Two Nineteenth Century Perspectives on the Utility of the Civil Law for the Common Law Lawyer," 29 *American Journal of Legal History* (1985): 36–77, reproduced in M. H. Hoeflich, *Roman and Civil Law and the Development of Anglo-American Jurisprudence in the Nineteenth Century* (Athens; London: University of Georgia Press, 1997), 9–49. Looking at the period between 1790 and 1820, Dick Helmholtz found forensic use of the civil law in all fourteen states surveyed, noting that this use was not "an isolated phenomenon" or peculiar to a particular region and that citation was "regular" but "comparatively infrequent" when compared to the use of common law sources. See Richard H. Helmholtz, "Use of the Civil Law in

Kent's personal library contained "Malyne[']s *Lex Mercatoria*,"[109] works on maritime law such as M. D. A. Azuni's treatise *The Maritime Law of Europe* and the "Admiralty Cases in Hopkins,"[110] as well as many books on international law and the law of nations.[111] He created a nearly one-hundred-page abridgement of Emerigon's two-volume treatise on maritime insurance in 1804 and proceeded to cite to and rely on Emerignon in some of the cases discussed that year, and again, much later, in Volume 3 of the *Commentaries*, where his lectures relating to maritime law appear.[112] In short, use and reliance on foreign sources was serious business for both Kent and Livingston, just as they were generally for elite lawyers in New York in this period.

All that said, there is no question that Livingston was amusing himself in *Pierson* by taking some kind of ironic distance from those sources. Consider the point in the dissent when Livingston, rather dramatically, declares that as between Justinian (Pierson) and Barbeyrac (Post), his choice, "[a]fter mature deliberation," will be to "embrace" Barbeyrac.[113] Here Livingston pretends to be deciding the case, rather slavishly, on the authority of the eminent Barbeyrac, who was no mere commentator. However, the point is immediately followed by some decidedly whimsical musings about choosing Barbeyrac (hot pursuit) based on the type and size of dog Post was using. At this point in the text, Livingston purports to be relying on the writings of "a certain Emperor," the twelfth-century Holy Roman Emperor Frederick I, who gave the hunter (here that would be Post) the animal if pursued "with large dogs and hounds" but sided with the interloper (i.e. Pierson) "if chased with beagles only."[114] This cannot be taken seriously: Livingston had no access to any information about Post's dogs, what kind they were or what size they were. However, there is a seriousness in it, for precisely this point about

Post-Revolutionary American Jurisprudence," 66 *Tulane Law Review* (1991–92): 1649–84, 1653. See also Peter Stein, "The Attraction of the Civil Law in Post-Revolutionary America," 52 *Virginia Law Review* (1966): 403–34.

[109] See *Kent Family Papers*, vol. 8: 88. [110] Ibid., 116, 110.

[111] See ibid., 112 ("Vattel"); 60, 111 ("Wheaton on International Law" and "Wheaton's History of the Law of Nations"); 112 ("Ward's History of the Law of Nations, 2 vols"); 54 ("Gardener on International Law"); 89 ("Chitty's Law of Nations"). On the transatlantic nature of Kent's law library, see Daniel Hulsebosch, "An Empire of Law: Chancellor Kent and the Revolution in Books in the Early Republic," 60 *Alabama Law Review* (2008–2009): 377–424.

[112] See Charles E. Shields III, "Chancellor Kent's Abridgment of Emerignon's Maritime Insurance," 108 *Pennsylvania State Law Review* (2003–2004): 1123–1247, 1165–1179.

[113] *Pierson*, 181. [114] Ibid., 182.

Emperor Frederick is made in Pufendorf's text some half-dozen pages away from the first occupant passages and the contentious adverse note on the text by Barbeyrac.[115]

The kind and size-of-dog discussion reinforces what I take to be Livingston's general (and serious) point; namely that an overly-slavish reliance on foreign authorities was not going to necessarily give appropriate (or at least not automatically appropriate) guidance on what rule to choose. Those authorities might be helpful in thinking through a problem on which there was not yet a homegrown pronouncement; but they could not be relied on in a robotic or automatic way, as if they could simply be cited authoritatively as one would reference Biblical chapter and verse to settle a matter, as the behavior of the lawyers (and Tompkins also) seemed to suggest. On that point, Livingston *dissented* from the rest of the bench who were much more content to let (a certain interpretation of) Justinian's *Institutes* decide the matter, without discussion or comment on that technique of legal argumentation, the decisive or conclusive argument from authority. Had Pothier's property treatise been wheeled out by Post's lawyer – had an English translation been available as there was for his other books or had the lawyer been fluent in French and a copy been accessible – it might have won against Justinian and we would have seen a hot pursuit rule prevail. The serendipity is striking.

Another serious point raised in the dissent, embedded again in a witty package, was the issue of Pierson's wrongful interference with Post's expectation that he would be compensated for his labor. Livingston was the only judge or lawyer to include Locke in the list of authorities who had weighed in on the point about occupation of a wild animal by a first taker – the "knotty point [...] should have been submitted to the

[115] The first occupant passages and the note are in Book 4, Chapter 6, section 2 and the later discussion of Emperor Frederick is in section 10. I originally wrote about this that Livingston's point seemed to be that "one might as well flip through the pages of a law book and go with whatever one's finger happened to alight upon if one was going to refuse to think the problem through independent of authority, however eminent." Fernandez, "*Pierson* v. *Post*: A Great Debate," 307. However, that precise passage in the Pufendorf text actually corresponds to one of the citations Post's lawyer, Cadwallader David Colden, originally gave to section 10, referring to a point in Barbeyrac's note there (a point about a "false notion of possession"). See *Pierson*, 177; Pufendorf, *Law of Nature and Nations*, Book 4, Chapter 6, Section 10. Livingston wrote that of the authorities referred to by the "learned counsel" he had "examined them all." *Pierson*, 181. So it was not random. It seems likely that Livingston was directed to this spot in Pufendorf's text by Colden and rather than relying on a point in the note by Barbeyrac, he was struck by and reproduced the kind and size-of-dog business in Pufendorf's principal text.

arbitration of sportsmen, without poring over Justinian, Fleta, Bracton, Puffendorf, *Locke*, Barbeyrac or Blackstone," Livingston wrote.[116]

Livingston's choice of Post and the hot pursuit rule was Lockean, favoring Post's initial investment in his hunt and his labors, for "who would keep a pack of hounds" and chase a fox around all day "if, just as night came on, and his stratagems and strength were nearly exhausted, a saucy intruder, *who had not shared in the honors or labours of the chase*, were permitted to come in at the death, and bear away in triumph the object of pursuit?"[117] What resources had Pierson committed to the endeavor, coming along out of nowhere and clubbing the fox "without outlay or effort worth naming"?[118] As Locke wrote in the *Second Treatise*:

> the hare that anyone is hunting, is thought his who pursues her during the chase. For being a beast that is still looked upon as common, [. . .] whoever has employed so much labor about any of that kind, as to find and pursue her, has thereby removed her from a state of nature, wherein she was common, and hath begun a property.[119]

The effort involved in starting and pursuing the animal was, according to Locke, a form of labor – the starting of "a property" – and, as such, it deserved legal protection. Indeed, the court's rejection of the Lockean solution to the problem of the hunted animal is perplexing in light of the importance of Locke's philosophy to early Americans.[120]

There are certainly serious aspects to the dissent. First, its insistence on the early American Lockean theory of the transformative power of labor. Second, its support for the hot pursuit rule, which, as we have seen, was a perfectly legitimate and time-honored way in which to establish ownership of a wild animal. Third, its concern that early American lawyers and judges think for themselves on important first-principle legal issues, which was of general concern to Livingston and discussed by him in

116 *Pierson*, 180 (emphasis added). Again Livingston might have been reading around the passages cited by the lawyers, which he claims to have examined. See ibid. Pierson's lawyer's reference to *Blackstone's Commentaries* was to p. 403 and Locke is discussed on p. 405. See *Blackstone's Commentaries*, 2: 405.

117 *Pierson*, 180–81 [emphasis added].

118 Hedges, "Pierson vs. Post," *Sag-Harbor Express* (1895).

119 Krier, "Facts, Information, and the Newly Discovered Record," 192 n. 9 (quoting from Locke to support the point that Livingston's dissent is Lockean).

120 Donahue, "*Animalia Ferae Naturae*," 61 (the choice of "the Hobbesian Puffendorf over the Lockean Barbeyrac [. . .] is perhaps the strangest part of a strange case. Why did the court reject the teachings of a follower of Locke, a thinker whose views were much more consonant with prevailing ideology than those of Hobbes?").

other cases. Fourth, perhaps even support for following custom where that can be ascertained with some degree of reliability: it might well be that the 1844 deer-hunting statute reversing *Pierson* for this part of Long Island acknowledged a local norm of respect for hot pursuit in the hunting of an animal on land (as opposed to whales or fish in the water), a norm that local people probably cared about applied to an animal much more widely hunted (for meat and hide) than foxes ever were, especially before the end of the nineteenth century and before any serious widespread presence of English-style foxhunting.

But there is so much else in the dissent which is either inaccurate or misleading or, worse, fundamentally confused. One can go round and round in circles trying to make sense of those confusions. What did Livingston know, what did he not know about English-style foxhunting and fox populations? What might he have known about Post's dogs? Which parts of what he wrote were serious and which silly? Probably one should simply accept that Livingston decided to abandon ordinary judgment-writing norms and engaged instead in a kind of delightful self-indulgent romp. The dissent does not hang together or make perfect sense, and we should not ask it to. It does not conform to the genre of "legal decision." Rather, it is a piece of legal solemn foolery. Like Melville's exegesis on whale hunting in *Moby-Dick*, it is a mistake to read it as a straightforward text.[121]

It is unusual but not unheard of for a legal judgment to be written in this way. When a judge does it, we want to know why. The historian who thought the dissent could have been issued from the pen of Charles Lamb, the satirist who wrote "[l]awyers I suppose, were children once," thought it was relevant that Livingston could see that "his dissent could do no harm."[122] In other words, it was banal or neutral vis-à-vis the law; it would not have an impact on what the law was, what the case would stand for, as lawyers like to say. And so, Kent, for instance, could (and did) later safely ignore it.

Yet innocuousness does not explain why Livingston did what he did. Why did he choose this case to make his queer mixture of serious and silly points? He did not do it in any other case that we know about. A large part

[121] See Tomlins, "Animals Accurs'd," 36–40.

[122] Hunt, *Life of Edward Livingston*, 53. The quote is located in Charles Lamb, "The Old Benchers of the Inner Temple" in E. V. Lucas ed., *The Works of Charles and Mary Lamb*, vol. 2, *Elia and the Last Essays of Elia* (London: Metheun; New York: AMS Press, 1903), 82–91, 84.

of the answer I think is to be found in the bare fact that *Pierson* was about a spoiled hunt in pursuit of an animal that was not thought to be very valuable, economically or morally. Fox hunting was not an economically important industry like whaling or fishing. The fox was not valued as a live animal or a being in its own right as it might currently be. The actions of Post, if allowed to go to their completion, would have resulted in the death of the fox as surely as Pierson's clubbing. And even Post admitted in his pleadings that the fox was "a wild and noxious animal."[123] Nor did the dead fox have much value as property. The allegation of malice shows that Post was suing over the affront of Pierson's interference in his sport, not over property in the animal itself. The 75¢ jury award, such a trivial or insignificant amount, brought home the point about lack of value. The animal's worthlessness justified flippant treatment of its hunt and death and that worthlessness was in turn reinforced by that flippant treatment.

The lawyers on appeal treated the dispute in an overblown and bombastic way, citing the forms of legal authority they had been taught were considered authoritative, discussing them elaborately in a kind of sport of words that mirrored the sport the dispute was about, the sparring between the two litigants over the fox. Here the lawyers took their lead from the texts that were available and familiar to them, especially as they fancied themselves to be up-and-coming lawyers – elite lawyers, not pettifoggers. Their approach was learned. It was expensive. They were participating in what I have called elsewhere, "a great debate."[124]

The lawyers slotted the fox into the category of an animal *ferae naturae* and engaged with the old and well-known arguments and discussions about occupation of a wild animal by a first taker on unowned land in a very particular set of legal and philosophical texts – texts they were familiar with that happen to have become quite foreign to us. We will see in Chapter 5 that their approach made for something of a forced argument in terms of the way that the animal was characterized and how the land on which is was caught was understood. Tompkins reacted seriously to this exercise or debate, taking the lawyers' arguments at face value, and writing what was an unusually long opinion for him.[125] Livingston responded with his own form of sporting wit, upping the ante on the

[123] *Pierson*, 180. [124] See Fernandez, ""*Pierson* v. *Post*: A Great Debate."

[125] Tompkins heard 258 cases before *Pierson*, writing only eleven times. Three of these were a one-line decisions "I agree" and the other eight in 1805 were short compared to *Pierson*. The three cases after *Pierson* in 1805 returned to his laconic style and the same is generally true of the sixteen others he produced before the end of his judicial

case as a fit object of sport. We will see in the next chapter that this kind of behavior fell into a recognizable lawyerly literary tradition of dealing with animals in a witty or sporting way. In it we will see a range of legal cases in which humor or wit is used to make a point and literary examples in which animals and hunting figure in comic prose with legal themes. I argue there that seen against this background, Livingston's decision is helpfully understood as an early American instance of Rabelaisian play, a literary rather than purely (or even primarily) legal text.

career in 1807. For a breakdown of Tompkins's cases with citations, see Fernandez, "*Pierson* v. *Post*: A Great Debate," 308–9.

2

Rabelaisian Play

> *There are certain queer times and occasions in this strange mixed affair we call life when a man takes this whole universe for a vast practical joke, though the wit thereof he but dimly discerns, and more than suspects that the joke is at nobody's expense but his own [. . .] as for small difficulties and worryings, prospects of sudden disaster, peril of life and limb; all these, and death itself, seem to him only sly, good-natured hits, and jolly punches in the side bestowed by the unseen and unaccountable old joker [. . .] There is nothing like the perils of whaling to breed this free and easy sort of genial, desperado philosophy; and with it I now regarded this whole voyage of the Pequod, and the great White Whale its object.*
>
> Herman Melville, *Moby-Dick, or the Whale* (1851)[1]

The previous chapter argued that Livingston's dissent, while containing some serious points, should not be approached as a straightforward legal text. It is wily and foxy, a piece of solemn foolery. In the first part of the current chapter, I seek to establish that Livingston would have seen *Pierson* as a suitable opportunity for creating just such a playful text by exploring the associations that exist between nonhuman animals and legal literariness. Specifically I examine a collection of modern legal cases in which judges have taken a playful approach (a form of "law *as* literature") and nineteenth-century works of literature with animal-related legal themes ("law *in* literature").[2]

[1] Quote from p. 247.

[2] See Robert Weisberg, Austin Sarat, Cathrine O. Frank, and Matthew Anderson eds., Law, Literature, and Cultural Unity: Between Celebration and Lament" in *Teaching Law and Literature* (New York: Modern Language Association of America, 2011), 86–97, 88. For a recent example of the analysis of the rhetorical style in modern legal decisions through the

MODERN SOLEMN FOOLERY

We begin this inquiry by examining a number of modern-day examples of solemn foolery. Livingston's behavior is no purely nineteenth-century phenomenon. Consider the case of the judge who embedded a code in a copyright dispute involving Dan Brown's uber-popular thriller, *The Da Vinci Code*.[3] Peter Goodrich has analyzed this case and pointed out that there is "a species of onomatopoeia" in making the language of expression in a judgment mirror the content of the decision.[4] In a case where the two books (an earlier non-fictional work of historical speculation and Dan Brown's novel, which acknowledged the earlier work but went beyond it) were about codes, riddles, and the like, "the style of the judgment," embedding a code in it, "reflect[ed] the subject matter of the case." The style of the judgment reproduced what the judge had been required by the case to determine, i.e. decode whether the novel was an original work or one that infringed the copyright of the earlier book.[5] Goodrich calls the judge's decision to embed the code an example of *serio ludere* or "serious play."[6] *Pierson* v. *Post* can be understood in a similar way. The style of argument and judgment-writing reflected the decision (at least by Livingston) to treat the case as an occasion for some sporting fun and sporting wit, a decision that made sense in the same onomatopoeic way given that it was a dispute over who owned a hunted fox, an object of the sport of hunting. The dispute was transformed by the legal professionals into a "sport of words" or a "sport of wit" in the sense of "sport" as "a piece of intellectual or literary playfulness."[7]

Like hunting, fishing seems to bring out the playful literariness of some judges. Consider another modern case from Mississippi, *Dycus* v. *Sillers* (1990).[8] This was a dispute over "a fishin' hole."[9] The judgment cites

lens of "law *as* literature," see Greig Henderson, *Creating Legal Worlds: Story and Style in a Culture of Argument* (Toronto: University of Toronto Press, 2015). See also review of Henderson's book by Angela Fernandez, "Law and Literature for Legal Historians," *Legal History: JOTWELL (The Journal of Things We Like (Lots))* (March 22, 2016), available at http://legalhist.jotwell.com/law-and-literature-for-legal-historians/.

3 *The Da Vinci Code* (New York: Random House, 2003).

4 Peter Goodrich, "Legal Enigmas – Antonio de Nebrija, The Da Vinci Code and the Emendation of Law," *Oxford Journal of Legal Studies* 30 (2010): 71–99, 90.

5 Ibid. The judge's name was Mr. Justice Peter Smith and the Code was cracked due to the hints sent by the judge in emails to a lawyer who writes for the *Guardian*. For an explanation of the embedded code see https://en.wikipedia.org/wiki/Smithy_code.

6 Goodrich, "Legal Enigmas," 93.

7 *Oxford English Dictionary*, s.v. "Sport" 2c.

8 *Dycus et al.* v. *Sillers et al.*, 55 So. 2d 486 (Miss. Sup. Ct., 1990).

9 Ibid., 487; repeated, 492.

Pierson, which is how I came upon it.[10] It begins with a long exegesis on hunting and fishing (mostly fishing), using the same kind of onomatopoeic echo of a sport as an occasion for sporting fun. It draws on writers as diverse as William Faulkner, Mark Twain, and John Grisham.[11] It also includes local reminiscences, obscure poetry, short stories and novels (obscure at least to a non-Southerner and I suspect also to a Southerner), encyclopedia excerpts, and collections of naturalists' observations. The Chief Justice of the Mississippi Supreme Court felt the need to distance himself from his colleague's flight of fancy, writing that "the first twelve pages of the majority opinion would best have been left unsaid, or relegated to a work of prose or fiction."[12] Why? In his opinion, "[t]he Bench and Bar have much law and many opinions to read and digest and should be permitted to choose when and where to read for pleasure."[13] However, the majority-writing judge obviously could not resist.

Post's hunt in *Pierson* falls into the same category of fun or playful activities such as recreational fishing or reading a thriller novel for pleasure. These activities are valueless from an economic perspective but extremely valuable and enjoyable to those who do and love them. So the idea would be that someone interested in recreational fishing would enjoy the judge's jaunt in *Dycus* v. *Sillers* or a person really absorbed by *The Da Vinci Code*, as many people were a number of years ago, would be thrilled to think they saw – and lo and behold to actually find – a code embedded in the legal text about the copyright dispute.

There are other examples of judges seizing upon opportunities to express themselves outside the range of orthodox legal expression, adopting a kind of literary voice, thereby constituting what one might think of as moments of breaking away from the ordinarily dry and formal tone of most reported decisions. Recent Canadian jurisprudence seems to have its fair share of such examples. Three instances are best understood as judges pointedly telling litigants to refrain from wasting a court's time with certain kinds of arguments and/or chastising litigants for engaging in bad or misguided behavior. It is as if a pact or understanding about appropriate behavior has been violated, the party or parties do it first in some way, and the judge feels he can and should follow suit. In other words, the initial break with the ordinary justifies further judicial deviation

[10] Ibid., 502. [11] Ibid., 488 (Faulkner); 490 (Twain); 491, 492 (Grisham).
[12] Ibid., 508–509. [13] Ibid., 509.

from the ordinary. Or, as the editors of one collection of examples of judicial humor put it, the judge is faced with a case of such absurdity that it fairly demands an equally absurd or amusing response.[14] It is, of course, debatable whether judges ought to be permitting themselves this kind of literary license.[15]

[14] John B. McClay and Wendy L. Matthews eds., *Corpus Juris Humorous in Brief: A Compilation of Humorous, Extraordinary, Outrageous, Unusual, Infamous, and Witty Opinions from 1256 A.D. to the Present* (New York: Barnes and Noble, 1994).

[15] See e.g. Mary Kate Kearney, "The Propriety of Poetry in Judicial Opinions," 12 *Widener Law Journal* (2003): 597–617 (arguing, using a decision in verse from the Superior Court of Pennsylvania, that judicial humor can be well-done, i.e. not ridicule a litigant and be good poetry); Susan K. Rushing, "Is Judicial Humor Judicious?" 1 *Scribes Journal of Legal Writing* (1990): 125–42 (arguing that the success or failure of judicial humor depends on whether it helps or hinders a judge composing an effective opinion and arguing that some types of judicial humor detract from the effective presentation of legal rules, especially if it confuses the reader); George Rose Smith, "A Critique of Judicial Humor," 43 *Arkansas Law Review* (1990): 1–26 (providing two controlling principles for the successful use of judicial humor: (i) that it be brief; and (ii) that it be genuinely relevant to the legal analysis); Steven Lubet, "Bullying from the Bench," 5 *Green Bag* 2d (2001): 11–15 (arguing that a particular Texas judge's attempts at judicial humor resulted in an abuse of discretion, constituting public shaming that is cruel and counterproductive).

These sources are taken from a website on Judicial Humor compiled by the Gallagher Law Library at the University of Washington School of Law (https://lib.law.uw.edu/ref/judhumor.html).

This website also lists and categorizes examples of judicial humor, the largest one of which is Parody and Verse in Opinions, divided into Federal and State court examples. There are a surprisingly large number, over twenty. The next category is Veiled References, followed by Animals in Opinions, Humorous Plaintiffs, Extraordinary Circumstances, and, of course, Miscellaneous. Collections of legal wit are apt to use the word "miscellany" in their title. See e.g. R. Megarry, *Miscellany-at-law: A Diversion for Lawyers and Others* (London: Stevens, 1955). "Doggerel," or comic verse in irregular rhythm, is another oft-used phrase that occurs in these writings. All of these writings can be thought of as fragments with an ephemeral quality given the way that they transcend legal subject areas and are not readily findable using ordinary search mechanisms. See also Thomas E. Baker, "A Compendium of Clever and Amusing Law Review Writings: An Idiosyncratic Bibliography of Miscellany with in kind annotations intended as a humorous diversion for the gentle reader," 51 *Drake Law Review* (2002–2003): 105–149.

Pierson is itself the subject of much mock-humor. See e.g. Ridgely Schlockverse III, "Mad Dogs and Englishmen: *Pierson* v. *Post*– a Ditty Dedicated to Freshman Law Students, Confused on the Merits," 17 *Nova Law Review* (1992–93): 857–65. This article appears in a volume entitled "Symposium: Nova (Humor in the) Law Review." *Pierson* also made an appearance in the parody of the American Law Institute Restatement projects. See Gretchen Craft Rubin and Jamie G. Heller, "Restatement of Love: Tentative Draft," 104 *Yale Law Journal* (1994–95): 707–730, 715 n. 24 (noting that "[t]he classic case of *Pierson* v. *Post* [...] established that 'mere pursuit' does not confer possession. In love, however, pursuit may in certain situations grant a temporary

Often "[j]udicial humor is neither judicial nor humorous."[16]

The first example is a sad family-law case, *Bruni* v. *Bruni* (2010), in which the mother of one of the children caught up in a difficult divorce so comprehensively alienated her daughter from the father that the then-thirteen-year old girl wanted nothing to do with him.[17] The judge Justice J.W. Quinn ordered the mother's spousal support (or alimony) award to be set at $1 a month.[18] The decision begins:

> Paging Dr. Freud. Paging Dr. Freud. This is yet another case that reveals the ineffectiveness of Family Court in a bitter custody/access dispute, where the parties require therapeutic intervention rather than legal attention. Here, a husband and wife have been marinating in a mutual hatred so intense as to surely amount to a personality disorder requiring treatment.[19]

The bad behavior in this case included death threats and an attempt by the ex-wife to run the ex-husband over with her van. The judgment's sardonic footnote to this point reads: "This is always a telltale sign that a husband and wife are drifting apart."[20] Fourteen times in the preceding eighteen months the parties brought the police into their "petty disagreements."[21] The judge recounts many examples of public and private name-calling, the creation of a false Facebook account on which the ex-husband posted derogatory comments to make it appear

right, albeit one that is not clearly defined. This right is subject to a reasonable statute of limitations"); 715 n. 25 (quoting the passage from Livingston's dissent on the "saucy intruder" swooping in and bearing away "the object of pursuit" in order to support the point that ill will can result from one person succeeding in establishing a relationship where another failed to do so and feels a strong though unrequited attachment). See also David H. Vernon, "A Week to Remember: Of Pregnant Cows, Slipped Horses, Sterile Bulls, Chickens, Heifers, and the Human Animal," 32 *Journal of Legal Education* (1982): 403–12, 403 (arguing that contracts should, like property, use a succession of animal cases in its first week, noting *Pierson* was the first case in the property casebook by Casner and Leach and the first week was spent "worrying about foxes, ducks, fish, and whales"); Lawrence Savell, "Law Review: A Love Story," written by a New York lawyer appearing in *California Lawyer* (February 2003), *Vermont Bar Journal* (March 2003), *Nebraska Lawyer* (April 2003), *New Jersey Lawyer* (June 2003) (where the first footnote goes to *Pierson* in reference to the "vixenish allure" of an old girlfriend the protagonist first met in property class at the University of Michigan and hopes to see at a law school reunion).

[16] George Rose Smith, "A Primer of Opinion Writing, for Four New Judges," 21 *Arkansas Law Review* (1967–68): 197–212, 210, quoted in *Corpus Juris Humorous*, 1.

[17] *Bruni* v. *Bruni*, 2010 ONSC 6568 (Can LII) http://canlii.ca/t/2dnn1.

[18] Ibid., para. 212. [19] Ibid., paras. 1–2.

[20] Ibid., para. 18 n. 6. The rhetorical device is called "meiosis," a form of deliberate understatement.

[21] Ibid., para. 70.

as if they had been authored by the ex-wife, and insulting and insensitive text messages. The judge notes:

> In recent years, the evidence in family law trials typically includes reams of text messages between the parties, helpfully laying bare their true characters. Assessing credibility is not nearly as difficult as it was before the use of e-mails and text messages became prolific. Parties are not shy about splattering their spleens throughout cyberspace.[22]

The judge's condemnation of bad behavior expanded to include the new common-law partners of each of the parties.[23] The parties were unresponsive to the judge's prompting that they refrain from belittling each other in front of the children and therapy was considered by him to be hopeless given their track record. "The function of a Family Court is not to change people," he wrote, "but to dispose of their disputes at a given point in time. I preside over a court, not a church."[24] The judge repeatedly described the father as engaging in inept parenting and described the wife's parental alienation behavior as "evil."[25] In his own words, as "the parties repeatedly have shown that they are immune to reason [...] I have tried ridicule as a last resort."[26]

In the second case, *R. v. Duncan* (2013), the judge recounts his experience with a self-represented litigant, who used an internet-based "freemen of the land" style of argument (denying, for example, the court's jurisdiction over him).[27] Mr. Justice Fergus O'Donnell described how:

> Mr. Duncan provided me with an "affidavit of truth," a rather substantial volume that appeared to me to be the result of somebody doing a Google search for terms like "jurisdiction" and the like and then cobbling them together in such a way that it makes James Joyce's *Ulysses* look like an easy read. This hodgepodge of irrelevancies relied upon by Mr. Duncan was one of the misbegotten fruits of the internet. Finding it was a waste of Mr. Duncan's time; printing it was a waste of trees and my reading it was a waste of my time and public money.[28]

Policemen in the case had arrested Mr. Duncan for resisting arrest after failing to signal a right-hand turn and then refusing to identify himself when he was stopped and questioned. The judge's autobiographical account of his encounter with Mr. Duncan ranged over references like the above to James Joyce's *Ulysses*, William Shakespeare, Joseph Conrad,

[22] Ibid., n. 23. "[S]plattering [...] spleens" is an example of the rhetorical device of "consonance," a species of alliteration (a repetition of the same consonant), more specifically "sibilance" when it happens with the letter "s" or letters "sh."

[23] Ibid., paras. 74–86. [24] Ibid., para. 131. [25] Ibid. para. 210. [26] Ibid., para. 213.

[27] *R. v. Duncan*, 2013 ONCJ 160 (CanLII) http://canlii.ca/t/fwsmo. [28] Ibid., para. 9.

John Donne's famous line that "no man is an island, entire of itself," and Lewis Carroll's *Alice in Wonderland*.[29] This last was in reference to the "silly path he [Mr. Duncan] wanted to go down,"[30] rather than simply pointing out that the *Highway Traffic Act* does not make it illegal to turn right without signaling unless it is unsafe to do so – without the commission of an underlying offence, Duncan's resistance to the arrest was legitimate. O'Donnell J. ended the decision with the following very explicit words of chastisement: "Mr. Duncan did not strike me as a fool and individual acts seldom define people, but the [...] 'affidavit of truth' [and other documents] he offered to me in court were regrettable descents into foolishness and Mr. Duncan would be well-advised to be more discriminating [about] what parts of the internet he models himself upon in the future."[31]

The third case, written by a former colleague of mine who established the law and literature program at the University of Toronto, has something of a *Pierson* v. *Post* feel in the sense that it was a squabble between two rich neighbors in a wealthy area of Toronto – Forest Hill is not quite the Hamptons but not too far off, at least in Canadian terms.[32] These litigants were fighting over various minor poop-and-scoop dog feces and dog urination issues they had with each other, parking their (expensive) cars (legally) in front of one another's houses, as well as more serious concerns relating to video and cell phone surveillance of each other. The Defendants were taking pictures of the Plaintiffs' house and trying to make voice recordings of things the Plaintiffs would yell at them from their house (often it seems the defendants were only pretending to take photos and make recordings just to infuriate the Plaintiffs) and the Plaintiffs had the Defendants' house under 24/7 video surveillance.[33]

[29] Ibid., n. 3 (Shakespeare and Conrad); Donne quote in para. 31 (Donne).

[30] Ibid., para. 30.

[31] Ibid., para. 31. There are so many cases of this kind of internet-based "freeman of the land" style of argument that there is now an acronym for such litigants in Canada: "OPCA" or litigants who use "Organized Pseudolegal Commercial Argument" concepts and schemes, often based on materials adopted and adapted from American "gurus." For a comprehensive explanation of the situation, especially in the province of Alberta, see *Meads* v. *Meads*, 543 A.R. 215 (2012); 2012 ABQB 571 (CanLII) http://canlii.ca/t/fsvjq.

[32] *Morland-Jones* v. *Taerk*, 2014 ONSC 3061 (CanLII) http://canlii.ca/t/g6wvd.

[33] Ibid., paras. 4-5 (Two cameras are aimed directly at the Defendants' front door and driveway. They "record, 24/7/365, every movement in and out of the Defendants' home. The Plaintiffs can see when Ms. Taerk leaves to go shopping, they can study what the Defendants are wearing every morning when they pick up their newspaper on the front step, they have a videotaped record of when Mr. Taerk goes to work or walks his dog, etc. Nothing that the Defendants do escapes the Plaintiffs' video camera lens").

Justice Edward Morgan wrote the following, chastising both parties for not being able to settle their differences without coming to court:

> In my view, the parties do not need a judge; what they need is a rather stern kindergarten teacher. I say this with the greatest of respect, as both the Plaintiffs and the Defendants are educated professionals who are successful in their work lives and are otherwise productive members of the community. Despite their many advantages in life, however, they are acting like children.[34]

The problem in the case was that there was nothing in the Plaintiffs' claim beyond the "allegation that the Defendants have been misbehaving and disturbing their peaceful life in this leafy corner of paradise."[35] Morgan J. pointed out that "a court cannot order the Defendants to be nice to the Plaintiffs. Litigation must focus on legal wrongs and legal rights – commodities which are in remarkably short supply in this action."[36] To give a remedy in the case would only encourage litigiousness amongst neighbors. Citing a 2001 New York case which denied giving damages for emotional distress over the death of a family pet,[37] Morgan J. wrote:

> What is true regarding the death of a family pet is certainly true regarding the scatology of a family pet. There is no claim for pooping and scooping into the neighbour's garbage can, and there is no claim for letting Rover water the neighbour's hedge. Likewise, there is no claim for looking at the neighbour's pretty house, parking a car legally but with malintent, engaging in faux photography on a public street, [. . .] walking on the sidewalk with dictaphone in hand, or just plain thinking badly of a person who lives nearby.[38]

The claim was dismissed and each side was ordered to pay its own tens of thousands of dollars in legal fees – where the ordinary Ontario rule would be to have the loser pay the winner's costs in addition to their own (here what would have resulted was the Plaintiffs paying the costs of the fake-stalking Defendants, which did not seem quite right).

All of the Canadian judges employ a deviation from ordinary judicial tone to underline the frivolity of the litigation before them and/or the bad or misguided behavior of the litigants. A certain amount of their tone can be attributed to frustration with self-represented litigants.[39] That is

[34] Ibid., para. 23. [35] Ibid., para. 3. [36] Ibid., para. 24.

[37] Ibid., para. 25, citing and quoting from *Johnson* v. *Douglas*, 734 NYS 2d 847, 187 Misc 2d 509 (2001).

[38] *Morland-Jones* v. *Taerk*, para. 26.

[39] See Nicholas Bala and Rachel Birnbaum, "The Rise of the Self-Represented Litigant and the Challenges for Family Lawyers," *The Family Way* (October 2012), Newsletter of the National Family Law Section of the Canadian Bar Association.

certainly the case in *R.* v. *Duncan*, where the fact that Mr. Duncan was self-represented was so important, but it is also present in *Bruni* v. *Bruni*, where the husband and wife had lawyers early on and for the pleadings but came to trial unrepresented.[40] Evident also is a frustration with use of the court system to resolve conflicts that should find their resolution elsewhere – at the knee of a kindergarten teacher in *Morland-Jones* v. *Taerk* or on the couch of Dr. Freud in *Bruni* v. *Bruni*. One sees in these cases the point that the legal system cannot provide plaintiffs with what they are looking for if there are no legal rights corresponding to the wrongs about which they are complaining. Morgan J. in *Morland-Jones* v. *Taerk* observes that a "remarkable short supply" of "legal wrongs and legal rights" characterizes the action. A court is simply not in a position to force neighbors to be nice or to think nice thoughts about each other.[41] The judge in *Bruni* v. *Bruni* noted that the cause of the discord between husband and wife was hatred – "a hardened, harmful, high-octane hatred" and "[c]onsequently, the likelihood of an amicable resolution is laughable (hatred devours reason); and a satisfactory legal solution is impossible (hatred has no legal remedy)."[42] One finds the same sentiment in *Pierson*, in Justice Tompkins's point that Pierson's behavior might have been "uncourteous or unkind" but was productive of no legal wrong.[43] "[H]atred has no legal remedy."[44]

These modern examples demonstrate that the judicial turn to a kind of literary playfulness – solemn foolery – is by no means always connected explicitly to an animal context, and that there is often a serious point at

[40] See *Bruni* v. *Bruni*, para. 69. The frustration of the judge is evident at para. 7 where he writes: "Presiding over a family trial [...] where the parties are self-represented [...] is a solitary and unfulfilling experience. What evidence was not brought forward because the parties failed to perceive its relevance? What evidence that was introduced would have been recast under a skillful cross-examination? With whom do I play devil's advocate on questions of law?" But see *The Hearing Clinic (Niagara Falls) Inc. v. 866073 Ontario Limited, et al*, 2014 ONSC 5831 (CanLII) http://canlii.ca/t/gdtz2 (where the same judge uses a similar kind of judicial humor in a case where the litigants were skillfully represented). See para. 10 (describing the three-year fraud trial as being akin to "a physical deformity that one, eventually, accepts as a permanent condition" saved only by "the unrelenting civility of counsel and their unceasing mastery of the evidence, all under difficult circumstances") and para. 1500 (expressing appreciation to all counsel and complimenting one of the defendant's lawyers for "conducting some of the most effective cross-examination that I have ever witnessed").

[41] *Morland-Jones* v. *Taerk*, para. 24.

[42] *Bruni* v. *Bruni*, para. 10. "[H]ardened, harmful, high-octane hatred" is another example of the use of the rhetorical device of "consonance."

[43] *Pierson*, 179-80.

[44] *Bruni* v. *Bruni*, para. 10.

issue. The judges use ridicule to make the point, whether it be to discourage certain kinds of litigation (where no fitting legal remedy exists) or to criticize misguided or bad behavior (easily on display in the case of the *pro se* or self-represented litigant). In another noteworthy example, a California judge makes use of *Star Trek* terminology and references in the course of publicly chastising lawyers involved in a predatory "porno trolling" scheme.[45] However, there is an animal connection in *Morland-Jones* v. *Taerk* worth mentioning. Morgan J. describes how the trial began with video footage of the "dog feces incident," mocking it as "a high point of this claim."[46] It and the "dog urination issue" are explained in detail at the outset of the decision.[47] These become the source of later references to "the scatology of a family pet" and "Rover water[ing] the neighbor's hedge," presented clearly as issues of the most minor significance, about which these two neighbors ought not be in court at all.[48]

In *Pierson*, Reynard is treated with a dignity that rises above the level of Rover's waste. Indeed, no one in *Pierson* suggests that there is anything inappropriate or strange about trying a case of such minor economic significance in such a serious and elaborate way and at such a high level of court jurisdiction – at least not explicitly. However, it is possible to read the mocking tone Livingston takes in his dissent as an indication that, actually, he did have a problem with expending so much energy at the state Supreme Court level on a petty dispute over what all would have

[45] See *Ingenuity 13 LLC* v. *John Doe*, 2013 WL 1898633 (U.S. D.C., C.D. California).

[46] *Morland-Jones* v. *Taerk*, para. 8. [47] See ibid., paras. 6-8.

[48] It is worth noting that the first chapter of *Corpus Juris Humorous* are nonhuman animal cases. See pp. 1-51. The animals represented include the dog, horse, cat, mouse, pig, mule, wasp, fish, deer, bed bug, and butterfly. The dog cases stand out: *Aetna Insurance Company* v. *Sachs* (a 1960 Missouri court held that a French poodle named André, whose owners did not prevent him from urinating on their expensive rug and other furnishings could not then claim for the damage he caused); *Wiley* v. *Slater* (the New York Supreme Court in 1856 decided a case of dog fighting referring to its *code duello*); *Roos* v. *Loeser* (an innocent and expensive Pomeranian was killed by a known-to-be-vicious and off-leash Airedale, with the Californian court noting that dogs were once of no intrinsic value, kept by the whim or caprice of the owner and not a subject of larceny according to Blackstone, but the law now recognizes they are of pecuniary value, granting $1,000 for the Pomeranian in 1919); *Montgomery* v. *Maryland Casualty* (an ode to the dog throughout history and in literature).The Yale Law Library's Rare Book exhibition curated by Mark S. Weiner, *Woof, Moo, & Grr: A Carnival of Animals in Law Books* (February 1–May 31, 2017) displayed an assortment of humorous depictions of nonhuman animals in law books.

agreed was a (virtually) worthless animal. The mocking tone taken to the whole affair may have been his way of saying making that point indirectly.

Livingston held that the appeal should not have been allowed – "the justice's judgment ought to be affirmed."[49] If we think about it practically, to do otherwise would reward Pierson for making so much out of an issue that one might think he actually ought to have let go with the 75¢ jury award. It was of course his technical right to appeal and attempt to win in order to have Post pay all costs, including the $5 from the jury trial for which Pierson was liable. However, one must wonder if part of the reason why Livingston took the tone he did was to highlight – ironically by pouring things on even more thickly – what a waste of resources, time, and energy it was to take the case so seriously. The wit was then a kind of expression of annoyance at Pierson, the "saucy intruder" for pressing on as he did.

The thing to notice is that Livingston's criticism, if indeed it was criticism, was not directly and explicitly made, and so contrasts nicely with the moderns, who make the point explicitly in a way that cannot be missed. In *Morland-Jones* v. *Taerk* Morgan J. comments that "the courts as public institutions are already bursting at the seams with all manner of claims. To add to that public burden the type of exchanges that these parties have engaged in would be to let the litigious society stray without a leash – or perhaps without a *lis*."[50] There is an animal reference in the pun on a dog's leash. Here also is direct criticism and judgment of the parties, including reference to concerns about litigiousness and wasting the court's time and thereby public money, as there was also in *R.* v. *Duncan*. If the parties press on with a small petty claim against each other they open themselves up to ridicule and a judge who will (or may) feel justified in treating their irrational persistence as license to strut his stuff in the likeness of a Benjamin Cardozo.[51]

Such a decision will be much more widely read than the usual staid judgment, given its irreverent and playful tone. *Moorland-Jones* v. *Taerk*

[49] *Pierson*, 182. [50] *Morland-Jones* v. *Taerk*, para. 25.

[51] Cardozo's work from the 1920s and 1930s is generally taken to be an important foundation of the law and literature movement. See the prefaces to *Cardozo Studies in Law and Literature* 1 (1989): v–xviii. Livingston and Cardozo are explicitly compared in the short preface to a reproduction of *Pierson* in which the author describes *Pierson* as a work of "judicial wit" and claims that both men left their best work in the New York reports rather than in those of the United States Supreme Court. See Dunne, "Brockholst Livingston," 399.

was covered by both the *Toronto Star* and the *Globe and Mail* at the time it was released, both of which focused on the part of the decision stating the parties' need for a stern kindergarten teacher.[52] The case was also discussed in a forum for lawyers, the *Law Times*, on a blog where members of the legal community weighed in on what they thought about judges speaking out using this kind of voice.[53] The case is also now used as the first case all first-year law students at the University of Toronto read in a summer preparatory course on Legal Methods.[54] As one of the course creators and instructors, Martha Shaffer, puts it, *Morland-Jones* v. *Taerk* "is an amusing introduction to case law and illustrates that not all 'wrongs' are legal wrongs with legal remedies."[55] In addition to being grounded in local and recent events in the city in which these students are studying, *Morland-Jones* v. *Taerk* also offers an entertaining package. In that sense, it operates very much like the traditional first-place use of *Pierson* in American property law casebooks, a phenomenon we will explore in more detail in Chapter 7.

It might even be that modern judges, like the judge in the "porno trolling" case, whose references to *Star Trek* do not seem to bear any relationship to the case at hand, are invoking the literary (or just plain unusual speech) precisely in order to increase the circulation of the decision, especially relevant in a case which involves lawyerly misconduct, as this one did. Here we encounter lawyers engaging in fraud and identity theft in order to pressure the individuals they have accused of copyright violations (on their shell company's pornographic internet videos) to settle rather than risk public exposure as consumers of pornography. Targeted individuals would be sent an offer to settle each copyright infringement for about $4,000, which many of them paid, resulting in ill-gotten gains of millions of dollars to the lawyers. The judge stated that for targeted individuals "resistance is futile" and he described one of the front men in the deceptive scheme as "just a redshirt" (i.e. an expendable *Star Trek* character), as well as opening the decision with a quote from *Star Trek II:*

[52] See e.g. *Globe and Mail* (www.theglobeandmail.com/report-on-business/top-business-stories/judge-scolds-warring-rich-neighbours-for-kindergarten-antics-in-torontos-tony-forest-hill/article18771751/).

[53] See e.g. Yamri Taddese, "Judge's Actions in Forest Hill Neighbor Dispute Debated," *Law Times* (June 2, 2014).

[54] "Legal Methods Intensive Course," University of Toronto, Faculty of Law (August 24–September 3, 2015).

[55] Email to the author, October 26, 2015.

The Wrath of Khan: "The needs of the many outweigh the needs of the few."[56] However, those references fall away after the first paragraph of the decision, which goes on to describe the fraud and identity theft and to publicly chastise the lawyers for "borrow[ing] the authority of the Court to pressure settlement."[57] And it was a "defraud[ing] [of] the Court" to use the presumption that that the Court would "blindly approve" their early discovery requests to push on with more high-pressure settlement tactics.[58] The *Star Trek* references, then, seem to be nothing more than a way to capture more readers than such a case would ordinarily receive, to speak directly to lawyers to convince them to refrain from engaging in such shenanigans (at the risk of being publicly shamed, fittingly as they threatened to shame the targets of their scheme), and perhaps even to alert other courts to the possibility of similar abuse in their own court systems.

It would be fair to say that the irreverent, unusual, or playful tone in all of these modern cases is taken up with what looks to be a pedagogical or didactic aim, namely, to *teach* readers of the text something important about the role of the court, the proper way to appear before it and the role of lawyers in it. When any of these norms are violated – parties appear without counsel with far-out arguments (what we might think of as the foolish solemnity used by litigants using "freemen of the land"-style arguments accompanied by seals and thumbprints),[59] parties or their lawyers enter claims for which no remedy can be given, or parties or lawyers abuse the authority of the court system in some way – the judge feels entitled to deviate from ordinary serious tone in order to teach the lesson to others: do not do this. The break in ordinary legal speech has in a sense been authorized by the parties themselves, who decided to go on the energy and time-wasting adventure or frolic, and the judge is reacting to this with more of the same or one of his own.

We might helpfully think of what is going on in the modern cases as a legal turn to literariness to make some kind of serious point playfully. The literariness of Livingston's dissent must also be set against examples of works of literature with legal themes and connections, especially those that deal expressly with animal and hunting themes and are closer in time

[56] *Ingenuity 13 LLC* v. *John Doe*, para. 1. [57] Ibid., para. 3. [58] Ibid., para. 4.

[59] See *Meads* v. *Meads* for many examples of such foolish solemnity sorted into different OPCA litigant categories.

and space to the *Pierson* case. We will consider some here in the balance of this part of the chapter.

SPORTING WIT, LEGAL AND LITERARY

Consider first an early American lawyer-writer named William Post Hawes. Hawes was a native of Long Island who wrote short stories for a variety of New York literary magazines in the first half of the nineteenth century. He specialized in the tall tale. A collection of his pieces, *Sporting Scenes and Sundry Sketches*, published posthumously, exhibits a kind of playfulness not unlike the writing in Livingston's dissent.[60] Hawes was writing for the general public. However, he littered his prose with lawyerly references. In one story, for example, he made reference to a hunting god's "fee-simple foot-hold among the stars" and noted that such a property interest could not be found in any mortal land title registry.[61] In a story involving a controversy about the categorizations Hawes's pseudonymous character J. Cypress Jr. used in an article about quail and partridge, Cypress responded to his critics by asking for "leave to amend – as the lawyers say – 'on payment of costs.'"[62] One of his critics charged him with having been misled in this ornithological matter by his "Law Latin."[63] Another of Hawes's bird descriptions speaks about the ability to "bring an action of trespass and recover damages" from the animal.[64]

Hunting gods, anthropomorphized animals, and Law Latin: this is all very reminiscent of elements of Livingston's dissent. Hawes wrote a short piece on the Latin phrase *tempora mutantor*, a phrase that Livingston happened to use.[65] One of the Cypress stories contains a footnote to Blackstone on the point that the pursuing and taking of "all beasts of chase" in England were subject to the rights of the King "or to such only as were authorized under him."[66] In America, Cypress wrote, "[t]hank God! [W]e have equal rights, in matters of venation, here. No puny-face spawn of a title, King or Queen, Duke or Squire" shall take away our game.[67] The sentiment as it relates to American independence is very similar to Livingston's call "to establish a rule for ourselves."[68] I do not mean to claim that Hawes was copying *Pierson* v. *Post* in his fictional writing,

[60] *Sporting Scenes and Sundry Sketches: Being the Miscellaneous writings of J. Cypress, Jr.*, 2 vols., Frank Forester [a.k.a. Henry William Herbert] ed. (New York: Gould, Banks and Co., 1842).

[61] See *Sporting Scenes and Sundry Sketches*, vol. 1: 161. [62] Ibid., 123. [63] Ibid., 136.

[64] Ibid., 183. [65] See *Sporting Scenes and Sundry Sketches*, vol. 2: 142; *Pierson*, 180.

[66] *Sporting Scenes and Sundry Sketches*, vol. 1: 176. [67] Ibid. [68] *Pierson*, 181.

although he might well have known the case being himself a lawyer from Long Island. I wish rather to call attention to the similarity in style and to certain themes that Hawes's work shares with Livingston's dissent, notably those relating to hunting and a masculine world of sporting and lawyerly literariness, a variety of sporting wit.

In another section of Hawes's work an impromptu "Court of Dover" is summoned and held among a group of men, hunting buddies, enjoying their evening around a fire on the beach drinking after a day's hunting. The original Court of Dover after which this spontaneous event was named (and others like it, including more stable fraternal societies) took place in Kent, England. It heard disputes relating to Dover Castle and the famous port of Dover, and was famous for being troublesome and overreaching its authority.[69] However, by the mid-nineteenth century, the term had become a generic way to refer to a debate or social club, often specifically a "Judge and Jury Club," which the *New-York Herald* in 1845 announced would be established in New York "[a]fter the manner of the celebrated Club of that name in London."[70] This was a kind of theatrical performance that a tourist to London might visit for entertainment, in which he or she would find a room set up in the manner of Westminster Hall, with actors dressed as judges and lawyers in wig and robes, who put on a mock trial.[71] The trials were "humorous, and the mock gravity constitute[d] much of the fun – yet they contain[ed] matter sufficiently grave for the exercise of serious eloquence."[72]

There seem to have been many groups calling themselves "Courts of Dover" in nineteenth-century New York. The 1845 club described itself as organized for gentlemen "desirous of practicing as debaters, or obtaining experience as controversialists," promising sessions that would be "much more attractive, entertaining, and instructive than those of any Court of

[69] As early as the fourteenth century, the Court of Dover was seen as "a troublespot [...] a source of irritation, discontent, and controversy" due to the way in which it routinely exceeded its authority. See John Smith Roskill, *The Impeachment of Michael de la Poele, Earl of Suffolk in 1336: In the Context of the Reign of Richard II* (UK: Manchester University Press, 1984), 89–91. A 1451 Parliamentary petition claimed that "the Officers of the Court of Dover, in Kent, vex and arrest Men, in all Parts of the Country, upon untrue Actions, and require great Fees of them for their Deliverance." See vol. 2, *The Parliamentary or Constitutional History of England: Being a faithful account of all the most remarkable transactions in Parliament, from the earliest times* (Printed and sold by T. Osborne and W. Sandby, 1751), 265.

[70] See "Multiple Classified Advertisements," *The New-York Herald*, (April 17, 1845), column F.

[71] See " Etchings in England, by a Cosmopolitan, Letter X," *Atlas* (Boston) (January 9, 1846), column B.

[72] Ibid.

FIGURE 2.1 "The Court of Dover in Full Session" by William Charles reproduced from the frontispiece to *The American Magazine of Wit, a Collection of Anecdotes, Stories, and Narratives, Humorous, Marvelous, Witty, Queer, Remarkable, and Interesting, Partly Selected and Partly Original by a Judge of the Convivial Court of Dover aided by a Jury of Odd Fellows* (New York: Printed by H. C. Southwick, 1808), 331.

Dover, which has ever been known in this city."[73] The same year, another group, which described itself as combining merry "wit, wine, fun and good humor," included a magic trick involving an automated chess box.[74] Yet another convivial version, a picture of which is reproduced in Figure 2.1, traced itself back to 1763 and met in the city to drink and socialize – play games, tell stories and jokes, recite poems, and sing songs. Members were required to have "a sound constitution, be of a social turn, and an admirer of women, roast beef, and porter."[75] Initiation involved a lot of drinking from "the book," "usually a quarter pot of porter" (see the mug with "The Book" written on it in Figure 2.1).

[73] *The New-York Herald* (April 17, 1845).

[74] " How It Was Done and Who Did It – A Chess Story," *Frank Leslie's Illustrated Newspaper (N.Y.)* (March 3, 1869), 217, column B (describing a chess match held at a "Court of Dover" in 1845).

[75] *The American Magazine of Wit, a Collection of Anecdotes, Stories, and Narratives, Humorous, Marvelous, Witty, Queer, Remarkable, and Interesting, Partly Selected and Partly Original by a Judge of the Convivial Court of Dover aided by a Jury of Odd Fellows* (New York: Printed by H. C. Southwick, 1808), 331.

An 1808 newspaper advertised a special session of a Court of Dover that was to be convened at the wedding of its "high-sheriff," where "the laws" would be executed "against a certain round of beef, two gammons, sundry bottles of wine, and several other articles which will then be brought forward for trial."[76]

Courts of Dover were amalgams of fun, entertainment, drinking, and some degree of literariness or seriousness, wrapped up in legal trappings. In Hawes's story, the court was called to order to settle a point that had become contentious among the (drunken) men as to the relative superiority of dogs to cats or cats to dogs. The dispute grew out of a sexual joke, and one man's insult to the masculinity of another.[77] It escalated into claims of citations to "the statutes of the Beach" and a reference to the protagonist's co-counsel, his hunted fox, which he threw up during his argument in a dramatic flourish by the leg.[78] The fox played an important role in the following (nonsensical) winning argument: "a dog runs on four feet; and so a cat is like a fox, and a dog is like a fox, and things that are equal to the same are equal to one another; and so a cat is a dog, and a dog is a cat."[79] Nonhuman animals here are firmly in the world of playful *things*. The free white adult men of the court – at the time, the only category of truly free *persons*, taking part in these groups,

[76] "Court of Dover," *New York Commercial Advertiser* (June 13, 1808).

[77] The character Ned Locus is trying to tell of his exotic travels to "the Lanjan Empire" and being entertained by "the sister of the governor [of Suez], Julia Kleokatrina" and he mentions as part of his detail in the story-telling a Siberian puppy dog that sat on her lap. He is interrupted by the men falling asleep, i.e. passing out. When he takes up the story the next night, he asks the men where he was and he is told "when you got [to] sleep in Julia [...] Kleokatrina's lap." Ned says "No, that was the Siberian puppy dog." His interlocutor, Cypress, the main protagonist in these stories, says it must have been Ned, who fell asleep in her lap, as he likes to take his comfort [...] and Ned then utters a Greek aphorism, which the editor's note says is about a cat liking fish but being afraid to wet its feet. The inference being that Ned would have liked to have been the cat in Julia Kleokatrina's lap but lacked the nerve to curl up there. Ned gets angry, calls for a Court of Dover, charging Cypress with "quot[ing] Heathen languages wrongly or appositvely," and declaring it "highly ridiculous" to state a quotation about cats when they were speaking of dogs. Ned further accuses Cypress of "having bored us with a pretended illustration of his weak wit [...] and has substituted the effeminacy of lazy cats, for [...] high spirited, hard-working pointers." Ned appears to be objecting to Cypress's inference that he, Ned, was a pussy (as in a wimp), where he wants to be thought of in his story to the other men as having pursued Kleokatrina as bravely and manly as a hunting dog, as a dog would pursue a cat, or in her case a *kat* (Kelo*kat*rina). See *Sporting Scenes and Sundry Sketches*, vol. 1: 80–90.

[78] See ibid., 91–92. [79] Ibid., 92.

probably readings texts like Hawes's – were clearly on the other side of the *thing/person* divide.[80]

Members of these groups were bringing a lawyerly and quasi-literary solemn foolery to amuse themselves but probably also to further professional goals. One Court of Dover operating in New York City appointed a prosecutor for a mock trial the group was conducting (circa 1834), went on to become a prosecutor for the state government in New York.[81] An Irish-American lawyer named John McKeon eventually became District Attorney for the City of New York in 1847. The records of this group were mailed to Deputy Collector of the Custom House, George Davis, from England sometime between 1841 and 1849.[82] Davis was the president of the group in 1834. The records include a long speech delivered by him justifying a change to the group's Constitution (which he says had not been amended for three centuries) in order to allow non-members to participate in its proceedings, for example to act as witnesses. There is a lot of "mumbo jumbo" in these records, including a striking page of text in the ancient Christian language of Syriac, complete with red wax seals and signatures (see Figure 2.2).[83] Yet one is struck by the seriousness with which this particular example of legal solemn foolery (or quasi-legal foolish solemnity) was executed. Davis's handwritten speech, for instance, is edited, suggesting that it was prepared for actual presentation at a meeting of the group.

"The Moot" in New York, established in 1770, debated legal questions sent to it from the official state Supreme Court. It sent its determinations

[80] The insult in Hawes's story turned on a Greek aphorism, which means it is likely that female readers of the text would not have understood it, as women did not generally receive education in the classics, including Latin and Greek. This reproduces the female exclusion of the hunting trip itself, a thoroughly male space in which animals are treated as mere playthings.

[81] See Angela Fernandez, "The Ancient and Honorable Court of Dover: Serious Mock, Solemn Foolery, and Sporting Wit in Nineteenth-Century New York State," 2012 *Australian and New Zealand Law and History E-Journal*, Referred paper No. 7, 194-239, 211–13, (http://www.austlii.edu.au/cgi-bin/viewdoc/au/journals/ANZLawHisteJl//2012/7).html, explaining the documents related to this Court of Dover located in the papers of Pierson's lawyer, Nathan Sanford. See "Records of the Honorable and Ancient Court of Dover," Nathan Sanford Papers SC14054, Folder 5, Manuscripts and Special Collections, New York State Library, Albany, NY.

[82] The appointment letter is reproduced in color in Fernandez, "The Ancient and Honorable Court of Dover," 212. See also 201–202.

[83] Jerome Mushkat, *Tammany: The Evolution of a Political Machine, 1789–1865* (Syracuse, NY: Syracuse University Press, 1971), 8 (describing the Tammany Society as a purely fraternal order, complete with "mystical mumbo jumbo [...] secret handshakes, outlandish costumes, and grandiloquent titles").

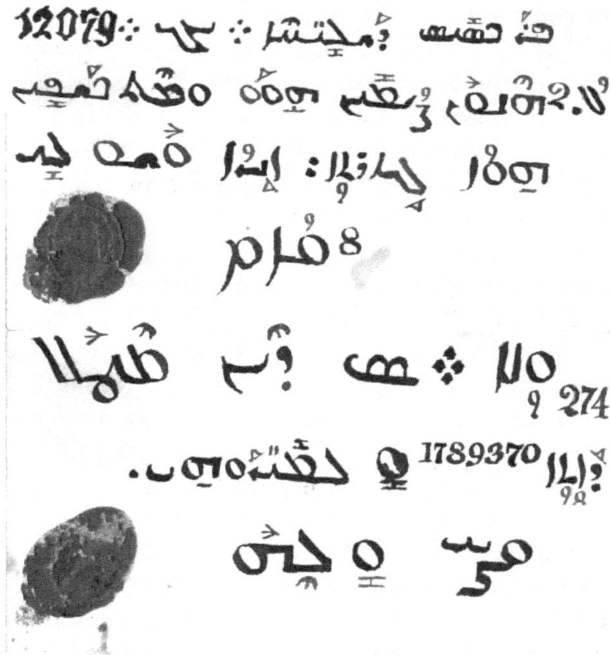

FIGURE 2.2 Syriac Text of 1834 "Honorable and Ancient Court of Dover," Nathan Sanford Papers SC14054, Folder 5. NY State Library, Manuscripts and Special Collections, Albany, NY.

back to that Court in the form of the opinions of the group of distinguished lawyers who came to the meetings, argued the issue, and voted on the result.[84] Its practice of conducting debates which were then written up with accompanying authorities in the group's minutes can be thought of as the first law reports in the jurisdiction, or at least a mock law report.[85]

[84] See Theodore Sedgwick, *A Memoir of the Life of William Livingston* (New York: J. and J. Harper, 1833), 151 (this was a question connected to the taxation of costs Sedgwick found sent to the Moot by the Chief Justice of the Supreme Court for their opinion). Herbert Johnson finds a second question in which the Moot was again asked for its opinion by Chief Justice Daniel Horsmanden, relating to the regulation of juries taken from the courtroom to view lands for the purpose of valuation. See Herbert Alan Johnson, "John Jay: Lawyer in a Time of Transition, 1764–1775," 124 *University of Pennsylvania Law Review* (1975–76): 1260–92, 1285.

[85] Hamlin, who up until recently had written the most extensively on the Moot (along perhaps with Herbert Johnson), did not consider the minutes to be reports, noting that

Much of what the Moot debated in the 1770s had to do with issues that would directly engage the liability of lawyers and in which they had a direct and pressing interest. The issues would have been taken up for the same reasons such issues are of interest to present-day bar associations and other groups of practicing lawyers. For example, the Moot debated whether lawyers should advance expenses such as sheriff's fees on behalf of litigating clients (decided in the negative); how an executor (many of whom were of course lawyers) ought to behave in terms of the order in which to satisfy creditors so as to avoid engaging their own personal liability (they struggled in a number of sessions to arrive at clarity on this point); whether an executor in New Jersey could be sued in a New York court (decided in the affirmative); whether real property in New York was available to satisfy judgment against an executor (emphatically determined in the negative, though without providing much in the way of argument, reasons, or authorities).[86]

The group also served a more general educative role in the way that a law school might. This was important in an environment where no formal legal education existed beyond apprenticeship, constituting what Paul Hamlin has called "a graduate school for the study of legal problems."[87] Indeed, many mentor/mentee relationships existed among the members, which included a quarter to a third of the New York bar over its almost five-year history from 1770 to 1775.[88] Many of the Moot's debates involved hypotheticals very much like those used in exercises at

three members of that group were meant to attend regular sessions of the Supreme Court and make reports of its proceedings. He says they would have been the first reporters but "[w]hatever reports there were, if any, have not been discovered." See Paul Hamlin, *Legal Education in Colonial New York* (New York: Da Capo Press, 1970), 104 n. 12. However, given that the minutes contain authorities allowing reconstruction of the arguments made and a record of who voted for what, they would appear to be themselves like proto-reports or mock reports. I would, however, not have thought of them as such before reading Michael R. Lazerwitz, "The Moot: A Colonial New York Lawyers' Club in the Early 1770s," 56 *American Journal of Legal History* (2016): 265-97, which carefully reconstructs each of the debates leaving one with the impression that at least some of the essential elements of a reported case (e.g. reasons and authorities) were often (although certainly not always) included, although as hypotheticals they obviously did not involve factual scenarios or real litigants and determinations which bound them (or bound later regular courts).

86 For a review and explanation of each of these debates, see Lazerwitz, "The Moot: A Colonial New York Lawyers' Club in the Early 1770s," 278–90.

87 Hamlin, *Legal Education in Colonial New York*, 97.

88 See Lazerwitz, "The Moot: A Colonial New York Lawyers' Club in the Early 1770s," 271.

English Inns of Court. The group had a lot of connections to the Inns, especially Gray's Inn.

The group's first president, none other than Brockholst Livingston's father, William Livingston, was admitted to the Middle Temple.[89] Two of his mentors, James Alexander and William Smith, had attended Gray's Inn.[90] The Chief Justice of the Supreme Court, who was sending points for the group to determine, Daniel Horsemanden, attended both the Inner Temple and Middle Temple.[91] The Moot itself was "named after the well-known debating society at Gray's Inn" and is said to have been modeled on it.[92] One of the sons of William Smith, loyalist William Smith Jr., was a co-founder of the group with Livingston, and, initially at least, his rival as leader of it.[93] Hence both of the group's leaders, Smith and Livingston, had an important paternal and quasi-paternal connections to Gray's Inn. However, William Livingston (aged forty-seven in 1770) was the most senior member.[94] Livingston was "clubbical," as it is sometimes put,

89 Hamlin, *Legal Education in Colonial New York*, 149 (providing lists of members of the New York Bar who attended British Inns of Court). See also C. E. A. Bedwell, "American Middle Templars," 25 *American Historical Review* (1920): 680–89, 681, 683; E. Alfred Jones, "William Livingston," *American Members of the Inns of Court* (London: Saint Catherine Press, 1924), 134–35. Jones writes: "Five members of the Livingston family were students at the Inns of Court. As early as 1706 Robert Livingston, son of the first Lord of the Manor of Livingston, joined the Middle Temple. Two other Livingstons were Middle Templars. The most conspicuous was William Livingston, the future Governor of New Jersey." See "Introduction," *American Members of the Inns of Court*, xix. Middle Temple was the most popular of the Inns for Americans. See "Introduction," xxviii.

90 Jones, "William Livingston," 134; "James Alexander," 2; "William Smith," 201.

91 Hamlin, *Legal Education in Colonial New York*, 148–49.

92 Jones, "William Livingston," 135; Hamlin, *Legal Education in Colonial New York*, 97.

93 See Hamlin, *Legal Education in Colonial New York*, 203 (recording that at the initial vote Livingston obtained five votes and Smith three, whereby Livingston was unanimously declared president and Smith vice president.

William Smith Sr. trained at least two other founding members of the Moot in his law office in addition to William Smith Jr. and William Livingston, namely, William Livingston's younger kinsman Robert R. Livingston, and William Smith's younger brother, Thomas Smith. See the biographies in Appendix A of Lazerwitz, "The Moot: A Colonial New York Lawyers' Club in the Early 1770s," 294–97.

William Smith Jr.'s loyalty to the Crown during the Revolution resulted in an appointment as Chief Justice of Québec. See Jones, "William Smith," 202. Smith Jr. is cast as one of the leading moderates trying to restore civilian (rather than military) rule of New York City during its occupation during the Revolutionary War in Ruma Chopra, *Unnatural Rebellion: Loyalists in New York City during the Revolution* (Charlottesville, VA; London: University of Virginia Press, 2011).

94 Lazerwitz, "The Moot: A Colonial New York Lawyers' Club in the Early 1770s," 271.

having founded in 1750, when he was a younger man, a group called "the Whig Club," which held meetings weekly at the "King's Arms."[95]

In the activities of the Moot we can see seriousness growing out of or intimately associated with and connected to a range of attitudes on decorum, conviviality, silliness, and so on. Even the Moot, organized originally by lawyers reacting to the "riotousness" of other New York City clubs for young men, met in the evenings at local taverns during which food and drink were consumed (although it was stated that they be paid for by 10:00 p.m.).[96] And while it certainly fell on the more serious side of such groups, even the Moot debated a hypothetical relating to whether a writ of right could be prosecuted in the colony "for Want of Knights."[97] The whimsy that would accompany such an inquiry is of the kind that would be present in a Court of Dover debate, presenting a humorous matter with "mock gravity" containing "matter sufficiently grave for the exercise of serious eloquence."[98] The knight requirement would have been a live question at some point in England, as the authorities referred to by the New York Moot members indicate. However, there were not (as far as I know) any knights in the colony of New York and this reality would presumably have added to the fun of the debate, which became an exercise of parsing and presenting the authorities in order to arrive at a solution to the problem and reassurance that knights were not in fact necessary in order to prosecute a writ of right.

It is probably a feature of *our* tendency to see professionalism as steadfastly excluding the whimsical or the silly that inclines us to dismiss the importance of quasi-formal gatherings of lawyers as places where professional work of all kind was going on. It is this same tendency that I believe contributed to the overly serious reception of Livingston's dissent in *Pierson* that we will examine in Chapter 7. Groups like the 1834 Court of Dover (that admittedly included quite a lot of foolish solemnity or solemn foolery) would, like a more serious counterpart such as the

95 Jones, "William Livingston," *American Members of the Inns of Court*, 134. The Moot minutes designated the King's Arms Tavern or Bardin's for their first Friday of the month monthly meeting, where they held their first meeting in 1770. However, by a majority of the members they were authorized to choose a different location, which they did for their second meeting, the Queen's Head Tavern run by Samuel Francis. Meetings in 1771 took place at the Province Arms Tavern or New York Arms Tavern run by Richard Bolton. See Lazerwitz, "The Moot: A Colonial New York Lawyers' Club in the Early 1770s," 274.

96 See Lazerwitz, "The Moot: A Colonial New York Lawyers' Club in the Early 1770s," 274.

97 Ibid., 286–87.

98 "Etchings in England, by a Cosmopolitan, Letter X."

Moot, have been serving the role of creating and cementing important professional and social bonds, enacting homosociality in the way all-male groups do, and operating like modern-day networking.[99] Networking, socializing, and debating were all valuable activities for lawyers and other professionals keen to demonstrate their powers of persuasion and fitness for all manner of social, legal, and political positions.[100]

The modern-day law school includes practices that echo the kind of ribaldry we find in both the New York Moot and the New York Court of Dover. Consider moot court competitions, which are serious (often solemn and well-attended public) occasions, in which law students work hard writing a factum and arguing from it in competition with each other and against students from other schools. Moot court competitions might, in the case of a showcase annual moot, be presided over by judges who are alumni or are otherwise connected to the school. The moot problem sometimes includes a jurisdiction-granting legal fiction to make it clear (in a mock way) that the pretend court may indeed preside over the matter to be adjudicated by stipulating it is to be heard by "the Court of X," where X is the name of the building housing the moot court room or "the law of Y," where Y is the name of the school.

From 2004 to 2007, McGill University ran the Shakespeare Moot Court in which law students were paired with students in the English department to prepare a factum and argue one side of a legal problem such as same-sex marriage or the trial of Holocaust concentration camp guards. They were to use the works of Shakespeare as the sole "codex, Digest, and Institutes" of the court, called the Court of Shakespeare, where judgments were written by the presiding professor-judges, one

99 Homosociality, social but not necessarily romantic or sexual relationships between men (or between women), is often identified with the work of Eve Sedgwick, who focused specifically on male homosexuality. See Eve Kosofsky Sedgwick, *Between Men: English Literature and Male Homosocial Desire* (New York: Columbia University Press, 1985); *Epistemology of the Closet* (Berkeley: University of California Press, 1990).

100 See Jessica Winston, *Lawyers at Play: Literature, Law, and Politics at the Early Modern Inns of Court, 1558–1581* (Oxford UK: Oxford University Press, 2016). Winston's argument is that the Inns of Court came to be literary centers due to a generation of young men in the 1560s who used forms like poetry and drama to participate in and comment on social and political life and, through their demonstrated skill in those areas, recommend themselves for positions of government in Elizabethan England's "legal magistracy," i.e. as worthy of positions of governance in the growing administrative state (as lawyers, justices of the peace, town recorders and other civic office holders, as well as gentlemen landholders managing legal disputes on their estates) as the need for personnel (especially lawyers or those with at least some legal training) for these roles increased and career opportunities in the church diminished.

a law professor and the other a Shakespeare scholar.[101] The University of Toronto runs a "Literary Moot," a public event in which law professors (including the Dean) participate and (to great fun) assume the roles of literary characters in the trials of literary characters taken from *The Great Gatsby* (2014), *Oliver Twist* (2015), and Shakespeare's *Othello* (2016).[102]

Another example, different again, is *Popov* v. *Hyashi*, a case between two men claiming to be the owners of a record-setting Barry Bonds home-run baseball. Part of the trial was held at Hastings College of Law, so students could learn from and professors participate in this *Pierson*-like case on first possession.[103] Who owns a baseball when it is hit into the stands? Is it analogous to a wild animal (i.e. is it free and open to ownership by capture)? What degree of control is required to constitute possession of it? Here the original catcher of the ball lost control of it in the scrum and violence that the landing of the ball created.[104]

101 See Desmond Manderson, "In the *Tout Court* of Shakespeare: Interdisciplinary Pedagogy in Law," 54 *Journal of Legal Education* (2004): 283–301; Desmond Manderson and Paul Yachnin, "Love on Trial: Nature, Law, and Same-Sex Marriage in the Court of Shakespeare," 49 *McGill Law Journal* (2004): 475–511. For archived material on the project, see www.mcgill.ca/shakespearemoot/. For historical studies of cases in Courts of Love, see Peter Goodrich, *Law in the Courts of Love: Literature and Other Minor Jurisprudences* (London; New York: Routledge, 1996); Peter Goodrich, *The Laws of Love: A Brief Historical and Practical Manual* (Basingstoke, Hampshire; New York: Palgrave Macmillan, 2006).

102 The 2016 event, "Iago on Trial," focused on whether Iago could be convicted under the *Criminal Code* for counseling the murder of Desdemona in Shakespeare's *Othello*. The proceeds of the University of Toronto Literary Moot go toward providing free liberal arts classes through "University in the Community," an organization that provides free university-level liberal arts classes to adults who have experienced barriers to higher education. See (www.law.utoronto.ca/events/iago-trial-university-toronto-literary-moot).

103 *Popov* v. *Hayashi*, 2002 WL 31833731 (Cal. Sup. Ct., San Francisco County, 2002).

104 *Popov* v. *Hyashi* was an "unpublished" case, which even though it is publicly available means it has an uncertain precedential value, even in California, where it was decided. This status is further complicated by the fact that it is a decision of a trial court, which, when unpublished, are explicitly excluded by a rule of practice from being binding authority. The "pre-possessory" or qualified legal interest it created, which forced the two litigants to share ownership of the record-setting 73rd Barry Bonds home run ball, strikes one as less in keeping with the law, at least as it was before the case, and more like the right thing to do in the circumstances. Popov could not show he would have retained control of the ball had the crowd not interfered with him and Hyashi did nothing wrong in picking it up in the chaos that the hit and catch created. It is probably what the two men should have agreed to without going to court and spending a lot of money on lawyers, actions that ultimately tainted the value of the ball, which ultimately sold at auction for $450,000, much less than the $1–2 million that was anticipated. See the

At the more convivial end of the continuum is the annual law school review or Follies, as we call them at my school, where students sing songs with juridical rhymes in place of the actual lyrics, and act in skits that poke fun at their professors and call attention to grievances or express anxiety over such things as feeling pressured to take a soul-sucking job at a large law firm (or worse wanting one and not being offered one). These events are classic invocations of Rabelais and "the world turned upside down" in action, where there is an enactment of the spirit and idea of Bakhtin's "carnival," a "temporary licensed suspension and reversal of order, the time when the low shall be high and the high, low, the moment of upturning."[105] It involves the disruption of formal polite speech and behavior and the temporary privileging of lower orders (the equivalent of the popular, the people of the institution, the students) and lower (often explicitly genital) zones.[106] In a law school context, it is a way for students to showcase otherwise hidden talents (dancing, singing, and acting) and to blow off steam over being on the powerless end of decisions related to grading, rising tuition, the state of the economy, and tight job markets, a way of expressing frustration in the face of powerlessness and lack of control. However, on that one night the students are in control, specifically of what they choose to make fun of and how.

The Inns of Court staged masques or revels, from which the modern-day examples are loosely descended. One of these, held at Gray's Inn at Christmas time 1595–96, for instance, included a production of Shakespeare's *Comedy of Errors*.[107] Philip Finkelpearl, from whom

documentary *Up for Grabs: The ~~Historical~~ Hysterical Battle for the Bonds Ball*, directed by Michael Wranovics (2005) DVD, which includes the video of Popov's catch and Hyashi's retrieval, interviews with witnesses and sports journalists covering the event, the opinions of citizens of San Francisco on who should have the ball, the judge who rendered the decision, Kevin M. McCarthy, the Hastings College of Law part of the trial (complete with disagreeing professors' testimony), and the sorry aftermath of attempts to manipulate media coverage and auction to raise (or attempt to preserve) the value of the ball, which had become associated with the legal fight rather than a great sports achievement.

105 Stuart Hall, "For Allon White: Metaphors of Transformation" in David Morley and Kuan-Hsing Chen eds., *Stuart Hall: Critical Dialogues in Cultural Studies* (London; New York: Routledge, 1996): 286–306, 290.

106 Ibid. ("The 'carnivalesque' includes [... language ...] in which the genital zones, 'the material bodily lower strata,' and all that belongs to them are exalted and the formal, polite forms of conduct and discourse dethroned," quoting Stallybrass and White, *The Politics and Poetics of Transgression*).

107 A record of the revels was printed as *Gesta Grayorum: or, the History of the High and mighty Prince, Henry Prince of Purpoole, Arch-Duke of Stapulia and Bernardia, Duke of High and Nether Holborn, Marquis of St. Giles and Tottenham, Count Palatine of*

I borrow the phrase "solemn foolery," explains that a severe housing shortage in London resulted in the residency of many young men at the Inns who were either not very interested in studying the law or who were but found their talents lay elsewhere, often in a more literary direction, or who simply got distracted by the wealth of fun and sin of Elizabethan London. This situation created an association between the Inns and sophisticated literary activity, and resulted in some of the best and liveliest society in the London of its day, including residencies by the poet John Donne, and playwrights William Shakespeare and, the subject of Finkelpearl's book, John Marston.[108]

Less literary, though noteworthy was "the Basoche," a fifteenth- and sixteenth-century French society for law clerks, which created "a miniature kingdom, with all the administrative and judicial machinery that a kingdom required. It even had its own system of coinage."[109] It had a King, Chancellor, courts, attorneys-general, corporation counsel, court clerks, registrars, prothonotaries, and even its own prison. The Court of the Basoche heard cases involving civil suits brought by one clerk against another or for claims brought against law clerks by merchants and tailors. This court also tried assault and battery and dispensed fines or short sentences in the Basoche prison. There were appeals in certain cases, taken before the *Grande Conseil*. The proceedings were formulated by the clerks but arguments were undertaken by practicing lawyers. The clerks also tried imaginary lawsuits, as well as burlesque lawsuits given at carnival time, called *causes grasses* (or *cause solennelle*). Here

Bloomsbury and Clerkenwell, Great Lord of the Cantons of Islington, Kentish Town, Paddington and Knightsbridge, Knight of the Most Heroical Order of the Helmet, and Sovereign of the Same, Who Reigned and Died, A.D. 1594. Together with a Masque, as it was presented (by His Highness's Command) for the Entertainment of Q. Elizabeth; who, with the Nobles of both Courts, was present thereat (London, 1688) (Printed for the Malone Society by Frederick Hall at the Oxford University Press, 1914), 22 ("a Comedy of Errors [...] was played by the Players"). Purpoole was a variation on "Portpool," the area of London where Gray's Inn is located, and the next two regions are based on the locations of two of the Inns of Chancery associated with Gray's Inn: Staple Inn and Barnard's Inn. See Winston, *Lawyers at Play*, 42 n. 100.

108 See Finkelpearl, *John Marston*, 17. See also Winston, *Lawyers at Play*, who provides a very rigorous understanding of how the more well-known work of the 1590s and 1600s by figures like Marston and Shakespeare grew out of an earlier generation of writers in the 1560s who produced a wide range of "literature," often on seemingly less literary works such as translations of classical texts. See Chapters 4 and 6.

109 Howard Graham Harvey, *The Theatre of the Basoche: The Contribution of Law Societies to French Mediaeval Comedy* (Cambridge, MA: Harvard University Press, 1941), 18.

the case was likely to be scandalous or ridiculous, sometimes involving a real-life scandal with which the regular lawyers and judges in the audience would be familiar, or a person well-known to the audience would be given a mock trial.[110] The problems treated as the *causes grasses* often focused on sex – adultery or infidelity, or the legitimacy of children. What was satirized was less the administration of justice or the officers of the court and more the people who were responsible for the situation, the folly of the litigants.

Finkelpearl notes that no one has investigated whether the revels at the Inns of Court in the sixteenth century in England were influenced by the Basoche and the highly developed ceremonies of the law clerks in France. There certainly are striking parallels – "the formation of a mock court, fictitious arrangements, concentration on sexual jokes, the formulation of satiric laws and regulations for their Kingdom."[111] The revels recorded in *Gesta Grayorum* included a mock trial of the "Sorcerer" or "Conjurer" responsible for the "Night of Errors" and putting on the play, for which a jury of twenty-four was impaneled to give a verdict. They acquitted the prisoner "[a]nd this was the end of [their] Law-Sports, concerning the Night of Errors."[112] "Law-Sports" or Law Games are often organized between rival law schools reminiscent of, although of course very different than, the Christmastime frolic underway on the night of the performance of *A Comedy of Errors* between those resident at Gray's Inn and those who were visiting from the Inner Temple. Indeed, the trial on that occasion stemmed from a "charge" that the "Templarians" should not have been offered anything other than dancing and reveling and were disappointed that a play was proffered.[113] Funny to think that a play with the sophistication of Shakespeare's *A Comedy of Errors* could be the subject of complaint in this way; one must wonder if the "Sorcerer" or "Conjurer" may have been Shakespeare himself, and whether the funniness or oddness of the charge was part of the absurdity and reversals so essential to a good night of revels.[114]

Even fact patterns on law school exams can be a strange kind of creative outlet, this time for law professors. For example, a torts professor might construct a fact pattern in which three little bears are walking down the street. One slips and falls. The property is owned by the big bad wolf, who has failed to clear the snow from his sidewalk. And on it goes, painting a far-

[110] Ibid., 19–20. [111] Finkelpearl, *John Marston*, 35 n. 2. [112] *Gesta Greyorum*, 24.

[113] Ibid., 22.

[114] Ibid., 23 (the "Sorcerer or Conjurer" "caused the Stage to be built, and Scaffolds to be reared [. . .] caused divers Ladies and Gentlewomen [. . .] to be invited to our Sports [. . .] [and] the State of *Templaria*, to be disgraced [. . .] that he had foisted a Company of base and common Fellows, to make up our Disorders with a Play of Errors and Confusions").

fetched fantastical or fairy-tale-like scenario designed to trigger the student into identifying or flagging issues that correspond to doctrine and principles in legal cases covered in the course.

I raise these modern-day law school examples (and some of their older antecedents) – some admittedly more literary than others – to illustrate that what might seem like old (and defunct) lawyerly solemn foolery is alive and well in present-day environments of professionals-in-the-making, performing and reenacting new versions of old rituals. Some of the foolery we find in the historical sources should not be difficult for us to understand and enjoy, at least for lawyers and others who have been through professional training and who have been exposed to and experienced or participated in (or, depending on your view, been subjected to) some of these practices. The degree of seriousness or silliness is surprisingly variable in each of the cultural forms and this tells us something important about professionalism – we think of it as the antithesis of silliness. It is serious business. A law school, like a medical school, requires a lot of study and hard work. It is expensive to attend. And it is engaged in the business of producing practitioners with serious public duties and professional responsibilities to manage and control power of various kinds – their own personal economic power, the power of their clients, which can include state power.

However, that serious business, and those serious responsibilities, exist alongside – and are indeed often grown inside – some very creative cultural practices, with important social dimensions that are thoroughly humanistic. They often pass without comment, or at least academic scrutiny or historical/theoretical contextualization. And, indeed, as universities, and especially professional schools like law schools, are pressed to become more and more purveyors of technical rule rather than places for intellectual investigation, we are increasingly unable to recognize (let alone talk about and problematize) such practices and what they mean for issues like the role of law and lawyers in creating a more just world or challenges relating to gender and other forms of diversity in the profession. Like the dissent in *Pierson* itself, which makes reference to many things that are difficult for students and lawyers today to understand (Latin phrases, long-dead philosophers, literary or allusive references like "saucy intruder"), we are reproducing legal culture, and, in the process, producing law, in ways we do not fully understand or appreciate. Like cultural references at any time, multiple meanings generated by creative deployment would have been a lot easier for contemporary audiences or readers of these texts to grasp and appreciate. In other words, contemporaries would know and understand what was going on; those meanings are much easier for later audiences to lose. And then these later audiences make their own new meanings.

REYNARD THE FOX

Consider next an early American writer, Pennsylvania lawyer and judge Hugh Henry Brackenridge.[115] Brackenridge wrote a popular novel modeled on *Don Quixote* called *Modern Chivalry*, which was published in 1797.[116] In one episode in the book, the sidekick Sancho Panza character, Teague O'Reagan, is mistaken for an animal and put on trial using the laws of *ferae naturae*.[117]

At the beginning of the chapter, Teague, who has been tarred and feathered, takes refuge in a forest. He climbs a tree in order to avoid being eaten by wolves and is discovered by some hunters, who mistake him for an unknown species of animal. He is then taken in by individuals who put him on display as a rare and exotic beast. Opinion among those who have paid a quarter to see him is divided as to whether he is a true bird/beast or just a man. Some philosophers in a scientific society take an interest in him and want to buy him for closer examination, having concluded from their preliminary examination that he was "an animal of a species wholly new, and of a middle nature between a bird and a beast; yet so wildly differing from a bat, as not to be classed with it."[118] Teague fears dissection and pleads with his keepers not to sell him. A writ of *habeas corpus* is issued to his keepers, who defend themselves by alleging property by caption. Their lawyer argues, citing Blackstone, that Teague is "an animal in which there can be no property absolute or qualified, being *ferae naturae*, or of an untamed nature, such as a panther or a buffalo; of which it is laid down that no larceny can be committed, as not being the subject of property."[119] The other lawyer responds that Teague is an animal that could serve as food and so the passage does not apply.[120] Whether Teague is man or beast is put to a jury. His keepers' lawyers argue that half the jury should be composed of beasts. They are overruled and the issue arises whether the philosophers' expert opinion should be admitted as one would admit evidence of commercial practice in a court. The medieval text of the tales of a particularly wily fox, *The History*

[115] Discussed by Ferguson, *Law and Letters in American Culture*, 119–28.

[116] H. H. Brackenridge, *Modern Chivalry: Containing the Adventures of Captain John Farrago, and Teague O'Regan, his servant*, vol. 4 (Philadelphia, PA: John M'Culloch, 1797).

[117] See ibid., 139–57. [118] Ibid., 146. [119] Ibid., 152. [120] Ibid., 153.

of Reynard the Fox, is produced to prove that beasts could, like Teague, speak English. and this is decisive in gaining dismissal of the writ.[121] Teague stays with his keepers, who promptly sell him to the philosophers. He is shipped off to a foreign society for further examination, at which point he manages to escape.

Modern Chivalry's account of Teague's trial and of the lawyers' arguments might well have referred to *Pierson* v. *Post* had it been written in the nineteenth century rather than the late eighteenth century. It demonstrates that a playful attitude toward the intersection of animals and the law was an established trope that created manifold opportunities for wit, humor, and literary drama in early American lawyerly literary writing.[122] The reference to the medieval text, *Reynard the Fox*, is especially interesting. In this book, Reynard is brought before the Lion King to answer to complaints made by other animals that he has tricked, by grieving family members whose relatives (notably chickens) he has slain, and by all those upon whom he has generally wreaked havoc. He is tried and sentenced to death but eludes the gallows with his honey-coated tongue, convincing the Queen on multiple occasions to intercede on his behalf. The fact that Brackenridge could refer to the book without explanation suggests that contemporary readers would have understood, at least generally, its relevance and significance.

Partly due to the influence of *Reynard the Fox*, "Reynard" came to be understood as a word for a fox, chiefly in literature, either as a proper name or occasionally as a common noun.[123] Hawes named one of the characters in his hunting and fishing trip stories "Raynor."[124] Apparently, an eighteenth-century German professor drew attention to the value of *Reynard the Fox* for the interpretation of old German law, which helps us understand why this work and its influence would have been known to early American lawyer-writers like Brackenridge.[125] Its more immediate impact could be felt in another medieval text that shortly followed *Reynard the Fox*, in which foxes were categorized with the "stenchy"

[121] Ibid., 155–56. For a modern edition, see Donald D. Sands, *The History of Reynard the Fox, Translated and Printed by William Caxton in 1481* (Cambridge, MA: Harvard University Press, 1960).

[122] The other example Ferguson explores (less humor and more drama) is an incident in James Fenimore Cooper's novel *The Pioneers* in which the novel's hero, Natty Bumppo, is prosecuted by his future father-in-law, Justice Templeton, for a breach of the judge's game laws for shooting a deer out of season. See Ferguson, *Law and Letters in American Culture*, 299–300.

[123] See *Oxford English Dictionary*, s.v. "Reynard" 1 (Oxford University Press, 2016).

[124] See e.g. *Sporting Scenes and Sundry Sketches*, vol. 1: 100.

[125] See Murray, *Lawyers' Merriments*, 28.

(as opposed to "sweet") beasts, noted for their "evil physiognomy" and a nature that is "deceitful and tricky above all other beasts and exceedingly malicious."[126] Aesop's fables bring us an even older fox – the trickster in *The Fox and the Crow* and the grump justifying his malcontent in *The Fox and the Grapes.*[127]

In short, Livingston drew upon an old and well-established literary tradition when he referred to the fox in *Pierson* as "Renard" and anthropomorphized the animal as "him."[128] Texts like *Reynard the Fox*, Aesop's fables, and their influence are not far in the background when Livingston spoke of the fox as a "pirate, *'hostem humani generis,'*" an enemy of all mankind, whose "depredations on farmers and on barnyards, have not been forgotten" and whose career has been "so cunning and ruthless."[129] Nor was Livingston's an isolated invocation. Consider the following story from Baltimore published in 1840 in the sporting magazine *Spirit of the Times*. The narrator and his friends were pursuing a bagged fox that they purchased and let loose for their chase. They lost its scent and came upon a man, who spoke no English having recently arrived in the country from San Domingo.

> "Have you seen the fox?" enquired one of our party. "Fox?" was the reply. "Yes," said the gentleman, "have you seen the fox?" "Quel est fox?" said the man. Now it happened that one of the hunt was a little of a French scholar and asked the man if he had seen Reynard. "Reynard! Oui – voil[à]" said he, pointing with his left thumb over his shoulder [to his knapsack] – "voil[à]," said he, and sure enough there he was – his hind feet peeping from the bag. Great God he had shot our fox and bagged him.[130]

[126] Edward P. Evans, *The Criminal Prosecution and Capital Punishment of Animals* (London: William Heinemann, 1906), 55–57 (quoting from a 1486 book *Le Livre du Roy Modus et de la Reyne Racio*, i.e. *The Book of King Mode and Queen Reason).*

[127] There are at least ten other fables featuring the fox. See *A History of the Life of Aesop according to Sir Robert L'Estrange* (Portsmith, NH: S. Sewall, 1808), 75-76 (*The Fox that lost his tail*), 79 (*The Fox and the Carved Head*), 83–84 (*The Fox and the Bramble*), 86-87 (*The Fox and the Countryman*), 87 (*The Boar and the Fox*), 99–100 (*The Cock and the Fox*), 104 (*The Fox and the Cock*), 104–05 (*The Lion, the Ass, and the Fox*), 108–9 (*The Lion, the Bear, and the Fox*), 117 (*The Fox and the Wolf*).

[128] *Pierson*, 180 ("Renard" reference); 180 (uses of "him"). In the version of the case in the second edition of Caines's Reports the original capitalization is removed and the spelling is changed to "reynard." See George Caines, *New-York Term Reports of Cases Argued and Determined in the Supreme Court of that State*, 2nd ed., vol. 3 (New York: Van Winkle and Wiley Printers, 1814), 175-81, 179.

[129] *Pierson*, 180.

[130] "Fox-Hunting: A Chase Long Since," *Spirit of the Times* (January 25, 1840), 559.

In this story, the anthropomorphized "Reynard" was an internationally recognized word for a fox. Unlike Pierson, who defiantly stood by his claim to the animal, having knowingly taken it, the inadvertent interloper in this story was apologetic when confronted by the angry crowd, "more than twenty enraged horsemen cursing him in tones and cadences from the screech owl down to the under-notes of a bull frog." Once he was made to understand "the extent of the injury he had done us. Poor Devil, he now hopped from side to side like a caged bird always tendering the dead fox to the last loud speaker. After heaping a whirlwind of abuse upon him he was permitted to depart."[131]

What do we know about the connections between those involved in *Pierson* v. *Post* and this kind of sporting lawyerly literary humor, specifically Livingston? Well, Livingston was quite closely connected to a figure who is generally taken to be the father of the Knickerbocker style of writing in New York in the first half of the nineteenth century, Washington Irving. Irving actually worked as a law clerk in the New York law offices of Henry Masterton, Brockholst Livingston, and Josiah Ogden Hoffman over a ten-year period (1799–1809).[132] Irving passed the bar in 1806,[133] but the law was not his passion. During this same period of his life he was writing two of his most important early works: *Salmagundi; or, the Whim-whams and Opinions of Lancelot*

[131] Ibid. The man's race or color is not mentioned. However, the superiority/inferiority embedded in the narrative and the fact that he had recently arrived from San Domingo, i.e. the Caribbean, suggests that he was black or of mixed race. If he was, he was presumably a free man and not a slave, as he is described as carrying a gun. "San Domingo" in 1840, would have referred to both the Spanish Santo Domingo (that became fully independent in 1844 as the Dominican Republic) and the French San Domingue (that became Haiti in the successful slave rebellion of 1804). The two parts of the island were united from 1822–1844, and so would have been considered "one and indivisible" in 1840 despite the long-standing rivalry that existed (and continues to exist). See Laisco Lancer, "The Conflict Between Haiti and the Dominican Republic" available at All Empires, Online Historical Community (www.allempires.com/article/index.php?q=conflict_haiti_dominican). However, if it was an old story, it might have been originally about a person with white, black, or of mixed-race origins coming to the United States after the Revolution in Haiti, which produced a large influx of immigrants and whose free/slave status (if not white) was unclear given the formal abolition of slavery in San Domingue in 1794. See David Patrick Geggus and Norman Fiering eds., *The World of the Haitian Revolution* (Bloomington: Indiana University Press, 2009), referred to by Rebecca J. Scott, "Social Facts, Legal Fictions, and the Attribution of Slave Status: The Puzzle of Prescription," 35 *Law and History Review* (2017): 9–30, 16 n. 14.

[132] Ferguson, *Law and Letters in American Culture*, 151.

[133] William L. Hedges, *Washington Irving: An American Study, 1802–1832* (Baltimore, MD: Johns Hopkins Press, 1965), 44 (describing his pass as "more through courtesy than dessert, for I scarcely answered a single question correctly").

Langstaff, Esq. and Others (1807–1808); and *Diedrich Knickerbocker's A History of New York* (1809).[134] It is unclear how much contact he and Livingston would have had once Livingston was appointed to the New York Supreme Court in 1802.[135] And, indeed, the famous Knickerbocker mock history was produced in secret.[136] However, Irving and his co-authors of *Salmagundi* were part of a literary club called the Calliopean Club.[137] This was exactly the type of literary activity that would have been near and dear to Livingston's own heart. Livingston was credited with publishing *Democracy: An Epic Poem* under the pseudonym Aquiline Nimble-Chops in 1794.[138] Another epic poem followed the next year under the pseudonym De Bellarm Superbos.[139] His own father, the governor of New Jersey, William Livingston, was an extraordinarily prolific polemicist for the revolutionary cause, writing more than a hundred propaganda pieces under at least twenty pseudonyms, and, as discussed above, he helped found and served as the first president of the New York Moot.[140] A biographical note on Brockholst Livingston's life in a collection on United States Supreme Court Justices notes that his "genial and ebullient personality [...] helped make the Marshall Court a 'band of brothers.'"[141]

Playful lawyerly and political literariness were thus firmly part of Brockholst Livingston's world. His dissent in *Pierson* was of a piece with that. In fact it is an example of the Rabelaisian humor that later came to dominate the domestic American literary market in the first half of the nineteenth century. The Rabelaisian style was a vein of humor inspired by

134 Ferguson, *Law and Letters in American Culture*, 151.

135 See Hedges, *Washington Irving*, 60 (noting that Irving switched from Livingston to Josiah Ogden Hoffman, Livingston's partner, when Livingston was appointed).

136 See ibid., 10.

137 See Evert A. Duyckinck, Editor's Preface, *Salmagundi; or, the Whim-whams and Opinions of Lancelot Langstaff, Esq. and Others* (1807–1808) (New York: Putnam, 1860), vii–ix. Duychinck advocated a home-grown American literature, starting a movement called "Young America" that did battle with more conservative Whig literary critics who were English-oriented like Lewis Gaylord Clark of the *Knickerbocker*. This was an extremely high-pitched and prolonged political battle that took place between Whigs and Democrats in New York City from about 1830 to 1860. See Perry Miller, *The Raven and the Whale: The War of Words and Wits in the Era of Poe and Melville* (New York: Harcourt, Brace and Company, 1956).

138 Michael B. Dougan, "Livingston, Brockholst" *American National Biography Online*.

139 *Aristocracy: An Epic Poem* (Philadelphia, PA, 1795).

140 See Carl E. Prince, "Livingston, William," *American National Biography Online*.

141 Dunne, "Brockholst Livingston," 395.

Irving but perfected by a group of writers called the Knickerbockers.[142] Its starting point was a rejection of New England transcendentalism and austere Puritanism.[143] The editor of the *Knickerbocker*, Lewis Gaylord Clark, defined the Rabelaisian style as "one in which learning flows as spontaneously as exhaustless humor."[144] He selected Charles Gotfrey Leland, an American humorist and folklorist from Philadelphia, as its representative, describing the style, in the following way: first, there is an "extraordinary display of universal learning"; second, a "minute exactness of quotation"; next, an "extravagant spirit of fun"; followed by a "capricious and provoking love of digression"; and, finally, the "upsetting of admitted ideas, by which trifles are seriously descanted upon, and bolstered up with endless authorities, until they expand into gigantic proportions, while time-honored truths are shuffled by with the most whimsical contempt."[145] Livingston's dissent fits all these elements – display of learning, a spirit of fun, a love of digression, blowing trifles like a 75¢ jury award up into gigantic or gargantuan proportions – like a glove.

Robert Ferguson has written extensively about the lost world of the literary lawyer, describing a time in early America when the lawyer "was, in fact, professionally dependent upon a fusion of law and literature."[146] Lawyers wrote literature (poems and plays) in order to display their wit and skill, not just as a general matter but as a specific demonstration of their mastery of what was considered a species of lawyerly expertise. "Until 1830," Ferguson claims, "the centrality of the courtroom speech made eloquence and extensive learning more important than a knowledge of technical law."[147] General erudition was considered much more significant than technical expertise gained from working with cases and statutes.[148] In that context, classical learning was a touchstone and a standard of professionalism.[149] However, humor was also important. It actually "represented the cardinal achievement of the lawyer in post-Revolutionary literature."[150] Humor tempered "[t]he solemnity of the Founding Fathers"

[142] See Miller, *The Raven and the Whale*, 67–68.

[143] Many of the early writers were from New England originally and were keen to prove that they were not "Bostonian prudes." Ibid., 17. See also 18 (describing the phenomenon of New Englanders who escaped to Manhattan and "conscientiously divested themselves of Puritan austerity and gave themselves up, if not exactly to riot, then to the delights of that existence which in New York was proclaimed to be 'Rabelaisian'").

[144] Ibid., 260. [145] Quoted in ibid.

[146] Ferguson, *Law and Letters in American Culture*, 6. [147] Ibid., 70.

[148] See ibid., 66. [149] Ibid., 27. [150] Ibid., 99.

and "furnished an acceptable means of escape."[151] Yet humor was also more than escape. Ferguson writes that as the Founders' perspective faded in relevance and "[a]s the premises of republicanism shifted in the light of experience, humor often became a fresher and more comfortable reality."[152]

The rift between law and the humanities has intensified so much that it is difficult for us to imagine a time when the law was integrally bound up not just with politics and economics, as it is today, but also with literature, rhetoric, history, philosophy, and humor. Our current divide simply did not exist for early Americans, who were connected to an older world in which law figured as one of the humanistic studies. As one of the characters in Sir Walter Scott's famous novel *Guy Mannering* (1815) put it: "A lawyer without history or literature is a mechanic, a mere working mason; if he possesses some knowledge of these, he may venture to call himself an architect."[153] Elite lawyers in colonial and early America took a view like this very seriously, building large and impressive libraries and priding themselves on the extent of their non-legal learning.[154] Yet there was also always a light or playful side to "the

[151] Ibid. [152] Ibid.

[153] Quoted in David Murray, *Lawyers' Merriments* (Glasgow: J. MacLehose and Sons, 1912), 262.

[154] It is true that lawyers' libraries tended to contain an overwhelming proportion of legal treatises and reports. See e.g. Joseph Towne Wheeler, "Reading Interests of the Professional Classes in Colonial Maryland, 1700–1776," 36 *Maryland Historical Magazine* (1941): 281–301, 289. However, they often also contained non-legal books. This was the case for Litchfield Law School owner and operator, Tapping Reeve, whose list of books at his death contained a separation between "Books in the House" or what is later referred to as "the Family library" and "Law Library," the former of which was much longer and included a wide variety of works of philosophy, history, religion, and literature, including Shakespeare's works, *Clarissa* by Samuel Richardson, and Homer's *Iliad*. Typescript of "Tapping Reeve's Inventory, 1824," Litchfield Historical Society, Litchfield, CT. For arguments about the important role of literature, particularly fiction, to the worlds of law and politics and the building of national public life for second-generation statesmen such as Joseph Story and John Marshall and Story's admiration for Jane Austen, see Alison L. LaCroix, "The Lawyers' Library in the Early American Republic" in Alison L. LaCroix and Martha Nussbaum eds. *Subversion and Sympathy: Gender, Law, and the British Novel* (New York: Oxford University Press, 2013), 251–73. See also Alison L. LaCroix, "The Founders' Fiction: Reading Eighteenth-Century Novels in Company with the American Revolutionaries," 9:3 *Common-Place: The Journal of Early American Life* (April 2009) (www.common-place-archives.org/vol-09/no-03/lacroix/), emphasizing the proportion of novels in Thomas Jefferson's category of the "Fine Arts" (along with numerous plays and collections of poems) that he recommended to his brother-in-law as the basis of a good library and highlighting novels discussed by contemporaries such as John Adams and Aaron Burr.

high-minded bombast of republican culture," which found ways to express itself.[155]

THE FOX, A SAUCY INTRUDER

The display of universal learning in the Rabelaisian style is arguably present in *Pierson* in some striking parallels between Livingston's dissent and Shakespeare's great tragedy *Titus Andronicus*.[156] The play features an important hunting scene in which something very close to Livingston's phrase "saucy intruder" is used. References to Rome, where *Titus Andronicus* is set, permeate Livingston's text. Two sets of brothers offer parallels to Pierson and Post, and the raped and mutilated daughter of Titus – Lavinia – resembles the hunted fox, although we will see that the animal to which she is repeatedly compared is a deer.

Unlike the time "when men of letters argued before a bench of scholars," as Robert Ferguson has elegantly put it of republican lawyers in the antebellum period, it is probably fair to say that most of us do not "read quite literally with everything in mind." Nor can we assume "the same versatility and scope in others."[157] Bodies of knowledge, including literary knowledge, and perhaps especially classical knowledge (or the kind of self-conscious allusion or plays on Rome that we find in Shakespeare) are no longer part of a common shared world, even for academics – and perhaps especially for them, for bodies of knowledge and training in different fields have become more and more specialized. This connection to *Titus Andronicus* leaped off the page for literature scholar Mary Nyquist, who pointed it out to me when she read the case along with manuscript chapters of this book in a working group that I organize "Animals in the Law and Humanities." By and large, *Pierson* has not been understood as a literary text by lawyers and in that sense we have failed to understand an important dimension – and as we will see an important gendered dimension – of the case.

Livingston may not have had *Titus Andronicus* explicitly in mind when he used the phrase "saucy intruder" to describe Jesse Pierson and we will see Shakespeare did not use the exact phrase. Still, the phrase is such

[155] Ferguson, *Law and Letters in America*, 95.

[156] William Shakespeare, *Titus Andronicus*, Barbara A. Mowat and Paul Werstine eds. (New York; London; Toronto; Sydney: Simon and Schuster Paperbacks, The Folger Shakespeare Library, 2005). I will provide the act, scene, and line number citations in these footnotes, along with the page numbers to this edition.

[157] Ferguson, *Law and Letters in America*, 67.

a striking and memorable part of *Pierson* – and especially evocative of the dissent and its literary dimensions. This is true even if Livingston did not have the play specifically in mind. Recovery of the case's historical and literary context is important for *us* sitting downstream as at least one relevant "interpretive community."[158] We are recipients of the case as a text, but we are highly unlikely to recognize its many allusions. When law students play on the phrase, as some of my students did a few years ago at Halloween, one dressed up as the hunter Post, another as the fox, and a third as a bottle of Heinz tomato ketchup (sauce), they had been struck by the vividness of the phrase but undertook a distinctly *modern* representation of what it meant.

Titus Andronicus opens with Titus returning to Rome, victorious after a ten-year fight against the Goths. He brings with him as prisoner Tamora, Queen of the Goths, her three sons, and Tamora's lover, Aaron the Moor. Titus orders the ritual death of Tamora's eldest son, Alarbus. She vows revenge. Titus declines an invitation to take up the position of Emperor and gives the throne to Saturninus, the eldest of the two sons of the previous Emperor, who has been vying for the position with his younger brother Bassianus. Titus offers Saturninus "Rome's rich ornament," his daughter Lavinia, who is, rather inconveniently, already betrothed to Bassianus.[159] Bassianus and other members of the family who feel the betrothal ought to be honored take Lavinia away and Titus kills one of his own sons in the quarrel that ensues. In a surprising turn, Saturninus takes a fancy to Tamora and decides to make her Empress, creating a reversal of fortune for Tamora, freeing her (along with her two surviving sons and Aaron) and giving her the power to enact her revenge on Titus.

Saturninus and Tamora are wed. Lavinia and Bassianus are wed. A hunting expedition is planned to celebrate both marriages. Meanwhile, Tamora's two surviving sons, Demetrius and Chiron, argue over which of them loves Lavinia more and whether one of them will be able to seduce her. As Demetrius puts it: "She is a woman, therefore may be wooed; / She is a woman, therefore may be won; / She is Lavinia, therefore must be loved."[160] He goes on to compare this process of wooing a woman to hunting a deer. "What, hast not thou full often struck a doe," Demetrius asks Chiron, "And borne her cleanly by the keeper's nose?"[161] Aaron

[158] See Stanley Fish, *Is There a Text in This Class?: The Authority of Interpretive Communities* (Cambridge, MA: Harvard University Press, 1980).

[159] *Titus Andronicus*, 1. 1. 52; p. 11.

[160] Ibid., 2. 1. 86–88; p. 55.

[161] Ibid., 2. 2. 98; p. 55.

makes a decisive intervention by suggesting that the two should not fight but they should "be friends, and join for that you jar."[162] They both may win, he suggests, by taking Lavinia by force on the hunting expedition. And in laying out this plan, Aaron makes it plain that Lavinia is the hunted deer:

> My lords, a solemn hunting is in hand [. . .]
> The forest walks are wide and spacious,
> And many unfrequented plots there are,
> Fitted by kind for rape and villainy.
> Single you thither then this dainty doe,
> And strike her home by force, if not by words.[163]

Aaron then devises a further plan. He will have Tamora entice the boys to rape and mutilate Lavina. In this they follow and one-up King Tereus in Ovid's *Metamorphoses* who attempts to cover up his rape of his sister-in-law Philomela by cutting out her tongue, Demetrius and Chiron cut out Lavinia's tongue and cut off her hands so she can neither name nor write the names of her attackers.[164] Aaron also wants them to murder Bassianus and he devises a plan to frame two of Titus's sons for this crime.

Titus, oblivious of the danger to come to his daughter and the rest of his family, turns up the morning after the marriages and proclaims in much the same spirit as informs Livingston's text: "The hunt is up, the moon is bright and gray, / The fields are fragrant, and the woods are green."[165] Saturninus, equally oblivious, chimes in "And to our sport," and to Tamora, "Madam, now shall you see / Our Roman hunting."[166] They plan to pursue panther and hart, which are male red deer six years or older.[167] Demetrius says in an aside to Chiron "we hunt not, we, with horse nor hound, / But hope to pluck a dainty doe to ground."[168] The female deer they refer to is of course Lavinia.

The newly wedded Lavinia and Bassianus come upon Aaron and Tamora alone in the woods. Aaron tells Tamora to pick a quarrel with them and he will go and fetch Demetrius and Chiron. Bassianus asks

162 Ibid., 2. 1. 110; p. 55. 163 Ibid., 2. 1. 119–25; p. 57.

164 See ibid., 62 n. 43 and "Appendix: Ovid's Tale of Philomela," reproduced from Ovid's *Metamorphoses* (1597), ibid., 225–39.

165 Ibid., 2. 2. 1–2; p. 59.

166 Ibid., 2. 2. 20-22; p. 59. Apparently hunting for Romans did not have the mythic and ceremonial importance it did for the Greeks and it was not a traditional Roman pastime. It came to Rome "as a rich man's affectation" in which "Romans with pretensions to Greek culture" took it up in much the same way as some American Anglophiles took up British fox hunting. See Matt Cartmill, *A View to a Death in the Morning: Hunting and Nature through History* (Cambridge, MA: Harvard University Press, 1993), 42.

167 *Titus Andronicus*, 1. 1. 503; p. 45. 168 Ibid., 2. 3. 29–30; p. 61.

"Who have we here? Rome's royal empress [. . .] Or is it Dian, habited like her[?]"[169] Livingston of course also refers to Diana, the goddess of hunting.[170] She is also the goddess of chastity, an irony here as Tamora who has just been wed to Saturninus and crowned Empress of Rome has in the previous scene been trying to have sex with Aaron, who is too preoccupied with his vengeful plan to comply.[171] Now Bassianus has called Tamora Diana, not something immediately insulting, at least given that they are all out hunting. However, following Aaron's direction to pick a quarrel, Tamora retorts:

> Saucy controller of my private steps,
> Had I the power that some say Dian had,
> Thy temples should be planted presently
> With horns, as was Acteon's, and the hounds
> Should drive upon thy new-transformèd limbs,
> Unmannerly intruder as thou art.[172]

Acteon was turned into a deer by the goddess Diana when he saw her bathing and for this she had him torn apart by hounds.[173] Tamora wishes a similar fate upon Bassianus who has interrupted her with her lover. Most notably, she has called Bassianus a "[s]aucy controller" of her "private steps" and an "[u]nmannerly intruder," something very close to the phrase Livingston used to characterize Pierson: "a saucy intruder."[174] Bassianus asks Tamora:

> Why are you sequestered from all your train,
> Dismounted from your snow-white goodly steed,
> And wandered hither to an obscure plot,
> Accompanied but with a barbarous Moor,
> If foul desire had not conducted you?[175]

So Bassianus calling Tamora Diana, the goddess of chastity, might have been a pointed reference after all. Lavinia adds: "And being intercepted in your sport, / Great reason that my noble lord [Bassianus] be rated / For sauciness."[176]

[169] Ibid., 2. 3. 55–57; p. 65. [170] *Pierson*, 180.
[171] *Titus Andronicus*, 2.3. 10–50; pp. 61–63. See also p. 64 n. 57, identifying Diana as the goddess of chastity and the hunt, and p. 70 for a picture of her.
[172] *Titus Andronicus*, 2. 3. 60–65; p. 65.
[173] See ibid., p. 64 n. 62–64; see also p. 80 for a picture of the transformed Acteon attacked by his hounds.
[174] *Pierson*, 181. [175] *Titus Andronicus*, 2. 3. 75–79; pp. 65–67.
[176] Ibid., 2. 3. 80-83; p. 67.

As this scene makes plain, the intrusion, alleged by the one party (Tamora) to be "saucy," denied to be so by the other faction (Bassianus and Lavinia), is on a sexual encounter and the "sport," as Lavinia terms it, is sexual sport.[177] The saucy intrusion happens in the context of a Roman hunt. The references to the violence that will be done to both Bassianus and Lavinia are plain. They are the prey. As the plotters and instigators of these deeds, Aaron and Tamora are the ravenous tigers.[178] Titus's brother Marcus finds Lavinia "straying in the park, / Seeking to hide herself as doth the deer / That hath received some unrecuring wound."[179] Titus continues with the deer trope, interchanging it with "my dear": "It was my dear, and he that wounded her / Hath hurt me more than had he killed me dead [...] dear Lavinia, dearer than my soul."[180] The "dear/deer" juxtaposition is used frequently throughout Shakespeare's plays, eight of which include hunting scenes or episodes. Hunting imagery recurs throughout the canon.[181] Deer in particular were highly symbolic of the innocent, the graceful, and the beautiful – "stereotypically perfect, magical animals."[182]

There are many references to Rome in Livingston's dissent – Roman law, hunting, gods and goddesses. We would expect to see Roman law, specifically Justinian, in an early American discussion of the question of

177 Later in the play, Tamora gives birth to a mixed-race baby, whom she orders killed, as its color will give away her infidelity to the Emperor. Aaron, however, saves the baby. Its fate is unknown at the play's end. Julie Taymor's movie adaptation of the play aims for a redemptive note lacking in Shakespeare's original by providing an alternate ending in which Titus's grandson walks out of the Roman Coliseum holding the baby into the dawning of a new day. The boy as witness frames many of the scenes and his innocence serves to temper despair as all the revenge and counterrevenge unfolds. *Titus*, directed by Julie Taymor (1999), DVD.

178 *Titus Andronicus*, 5. 3. 5; p. 191 (referring to Aaron as "[t]his ravenous tiger, this accursèd devil"); 5. 3. 197; p. 207 (a reference to "that ravenous tiger, Tamora"); and 3. 1. 55-57; p. 95 (Titus declaring Rome to be "but a wilderness of tigers [...] / Tigers must prey, and Rome affords no prey / But me and mine").

179 Ibid., 3. 1. 90–92; p. 97.

180 Ibid., 3. 1. 93–94, 104; p. 97.

181 See Edward Berry, *Shakespeare and the Hunt: A Cultural and Social Study* (Cambridge, UK: Cambridge University Press, 2001), 34, 14.

182 Cartmill, *A View to a Death in the Morning*, 159. The best modern example of a deer standing for innocence and beauty is *Bambi* and the tremendous influence it has had on rhetoric and political speech in the twentieth century. Indeed, Cartmill mentions in his excellent chapter on *Bambi* that it seems to be on its way to becoming "a lower-case generic noun." See p. 183. He also notes that George H.W. Bush (along with boxer George Foreman) have spoken of their reluctance to hunt and kill deer due to the awe they command. See 274 n. 72. Cartmill explains on p. 68 that the Greeks saw deer as cowardly; but in the medieval period, "deer began for the first time to be invested with an aura of nobility and even of supernatural awe."

how one acquires possession in wild animals. However, we also get a nod in the dissent to "Roman poultry" and what the Romans did and did not hunt.[183] There is the whimsical reference to dogs of "imperial stature" and what that meant to one Emperor who was dearly devoted to hunting.[184] In addition to Diana, goddess of the hunt, Livingston even includes an oblique reference to the chief Roman god Jove or Jupiter, the equivalent of the Greek god Zeus.[185] Titus describes Philomela as "[r]avished and wronged [. . .] [f]orced in the ruthless, vast, and gloomy woods."[186] The term "vast" in this context means "waste, uninhabited, deserted."[187] It echoes in Livingston's description of the beach where the fox was hunted as "waste and uninhabited ground."[188] "O, had we never, never hunted there!" laments Titus.[189] One can see why Livingston was compared to Charles Lamb, given the role that Lamb played bringing Shakespeare to Americans. Livingston, if indeed he had *Titus Andronicus* in mind, was giving the scuffle between Pierson and Post Shakespearean proportions.

There is an echo here in Livingston's own physiognomy, which was often described as Roman. Joseph Story, for instance, commented on Livingston's "fine Roman face" and "aquiline nose."[190] The nose again was described by a contemporary as "a regular Roman triumph." See Figure 1.1 at the beginning of Chapter 1.[191] Livingston was also described as having an "explosive temprement [sic] and rambunctious sense of humor."[192] A serial duelist (at least one of Livingston's duels resulted

183 *Pierson*, 181.

184 The decision refers to "a certain Emperor." Ibid., 181. However, the point that is discussed at this place in Pufendorf's text, differentiating between the two owners on the basis of the size and type of dog used, identifies that Emperor as Frederic. See Pufendorf, *Law of Nature and Nations*, Book 4, Chapter 6, section 10.

185 Livingston wrote "at the sound of the horn, and at peep of day, [the hunting gentleman] would mount his steed, and for hours together, '*sub jove frigido*,' or a vertical sun, pursue the windings of this wily quadruped." *Pierson*, 180–81. I have translated *sub jove frigido*, a phrase from Horace, as "in the cold air." However, it literally means "under cold Jupiter." Lavinia also referred to Jove or Jupiter in the saucy intruder scene. She refers to the fact that Saturninus is to be made a cuckold with horns by Tamora and Aaron and she says: "Jove shield your husband from his hounds today! 'Tis pity they should take him for a stag" (*Titus Andronicus*, 2. 3. 70–71; p. 65). In the latter, its use is the equivalent of "by Jove."

186 *Titus Andronicus*, 4. 1. 54–55; p. 125. 187 See ibid. 124 n. 55.

188 *Pierson*, 180. This differs from the language the majority used to describe the beach: "wild and uninhabited, unpossessed and waste land." *Pierson*, 175. We will see in Chapter 5 that this language came from Post's declaration.

189 *Titus Andronicus*, 4. 1. 57; p. 125.

190 Quoted in Dunne, "Brockholst Livingston," 391. 191 Ibid., 396. 192 Ibid.

from what he had written about the man who challenged him), his escapades caused one biographical note to record rather ominously that "[o]vertones of violence tincture much of his career."[193] This included an attempt to assassinate him in 1785; in 1798, he killed a man in a duel. He was known in the family for having a propensity toward dueling. In 1803, Livingston issued a bench warrant, eliciting from two warring newspapermen, one of them William Coleman, the first (unofficial) Reporter in New York before he went on to become the Federalist editor of the *New York Evening Post*, a promise to refrain from dueling and keep their battle to pen and paper.[194] Pen and paper were, in other words, vivid to Livingston. They were a way to control violence and condemn it, as with the warring newspapermen. Or, on the other hand, pen and paper might condone violence, as in the case of the fox by reducing its suffering and death to a joke.

Now Livingston's use of the phrase "saucy intruder" was not necessarily an allusion to Shakespeare. The phrase was in circulation in a variety of contexts by the time he wrote his text in the early nineteenth century. It appears to have been used not infrequently in a sexual context, especially in the eighteenth century. For example, one Monsieur de Voiture wrote the following in a letter to a friend about one of his love affairs:

> But here I will stop my Narration, for what need I trouble my self to send every Particular to you, who are old enough to imagine 'em of your self. Only this I will add, That we strove all Night long, which of us should express their Love in the most Emphatical Manner; and that that sawcy Intruder, sleep, found us too well employ'd to offer to interrupt us.[195]

Here sleep is the saucy intruder. In another instance, an Italian woman, angered at being interrupted with the lover whom she favored by a would-be lover she did not favor at all, calls for her husband to catch the unfavored lover and punish him, calling him "the saucy Intruder."[196]

[193] Ibid.

[194] See Allan Nevins, *The Evening Post: A Century of Journalism* (New York: Russell and Russell, 1968), 47–48.

[195] Monsieur de Voiture, *Familiar and courtly letters written by Monsieur Voiture to persons of the greatest honour, wit, and quality of both sexes in the court of France; made English by Mr. Dryden* ... (London: Printed for Sam Briscoe, 1700), 102.

[196] Charles Gildon, vol. 2, *The New Metamorphosis; or, pleasant transformation of the Golden ass of Lucius Apuleius of Medaura. Also the golden spy* ... *Written in Italian by Carlo Monte Socio* (London: Printed for Sam Briscoe, 1724), 171.

This is much like Tamora being angered (or feigning it) at having been interrupted with Aaron and sending for her sons to punish Bassianus (the saucy intruder) and Lavinia.[197] In yet another usage, the saucy intruder is a young woman named Emily who has run away with another man, escaping the romantic intentions of a gentleman who was keen on her and has now found himself caught in the embarrassing seduction of one of his tenant's daughters.[198] His friend writes to him, advising him to forget the farmer's daughter and to find Emily "and take what revenge on her thou think'st best [...] Spare no pains to get her into your power again [...] Revenge is the word."[199] The phrase also turns up in a hunting context, specifically an account of an elephant hunting expedition in South Africa. Here the hunter writes of the hunted elephant who came upon him unexpectedly, "[i]t may be thought, indeed, that, out of revenge at least, I ought to have fired my piece at this saucy intruder."[200]

Now these sexual and hunting contexts might well be connected to Shakespeare's influence or it may be that Shakespeare's own use of the ideas ("saucy controller," "[u]nmannerly intruder," "sauciness") stemmed from some common idea or set of ideas around "saucy intruder." The idea of encroachment seems important.[201] And in at least some of these instances, including Shakespeare's, encroachment is used to justify a violent response of some kind – catching out the unwelcome lover, shooting the elephant, punishing Emily in some way ("serv[ing] her in the manner she deserves").[202] Their intrusion is Tamora's excuse for turning on Lavinia and Bassianus, who can now (dangerously for Tamora) report her adultery to the Emperor. The phrase was also used in a religious

[197] This woman, her name is Biancha, gets the unfavored lover to hide by hanging outside her window by a rope both ends of which were tied to the bars of the window. She turns him in to the husband. Upon hearing this, the unfortunate lover cuts the rope and falls into a canal outside the window. He is rescued by a gondola but becomes ill and dies on his way from Venice to Ferrara. See ibid., 170–71.

[198] Ann Emelinda Skinn, vol. 1, *The Old Maid; or, History of Miss Ravensworth. In a Series of Letters. By Mrs. Skinn, Late Miss Masterman, of York* (Dublin: Printed by J. Potts, 1771), 145.

[199] Ibid, 146.

[200] Anders Sparrman, *A Voyage to the Cape of Good Hope: Towards the Antarctic Polar Circle, and Round the World: But Chiefly into the Country of the Hottentots and Caffres, from the Year 1772, to 1776* (Cape of Good Hope, South Africa: G. G. J. and J. Robinson, 1785), 324.

[201] See John Taylor, *The world runnes on vveles: or oddes, betwixt carts and coaches* (1635), 3 ("For the word Encroach I think that best befits it [the coach], for I think neuer such an impudent, prowd sawcie Intruder or Encroacher came into the world as a Coach is").

[202] *The Old Maid*, 145.

context to refer to outsiders, non-believers, and intruders.[203] This too suggests an implicit justification of force or exclusion against the impertinent interloper.[204] In other words, there is an important general cultural connection and context surrounding the use of the phrase "saucy intruder" that we can see existed and would have been there for Livingston as well even if he did not have the play explicitly in mind.

As offensive as it is to equate Lavinia with a hunted (and in the legal case, killed) animal, this is clearly what is done in Shakespeare's play. Indeed, when Titus kills Lavinia at the end of the play he asks Saturninus whether the Roman centurion Virginius did right to kill his daughter who was raped. He says yes, she "should not survive her shame, / [a]nd by her presence still renew his sorrows."[205] Here as modern readers we feel what one commentator has called "the weight of the patriarchal society" in which Lavinia is but a pawn and upset at the view that her rape makes her life not worth living.[206] Rape was seen as a fate worse than death.[207] This is also one of the few explicitly legal moments in the play when Titus refers to the actions of Virginius as "[a] pattern, precedent, and lively warrant."[208] Living as he did in the early nineteenth century, Livingston would almost certainly have identified with that patriarchal structure, even if he did not agree with the Virginius precedent. Did Livingston have Lavinia in mind when he wrote "Poor Reynard"? This raises a challenging issue, which is that "Poor Reynard" is clearly also embedded in the witticism and humor of Livingston's dissent.

As indicated above, *Titus Andronicus* is full of dreadful deeds done in the name of sport, humor, and jest. Aaron describes the attack on Lavinia

[203] See e.g. Antony Fawkner, *The widowes petition delivered in a sermon before the judges at the assises held at Northampton, July 25, 1633* [...] (Oxford: Printed by John Lichfield, 1635), 4 ("A light that illumines the humble back-standers, and a light that dazels the saucy intruders. The disciples could see [...] The multitudes could not see"); William Bowman, *The imposture of Methodism display'd* [...] *Occasion'd by The Rise of a certain Modern sect of Enthusiasts (among them) call'd Methodists* (London: Printed for Joseph Lord, 1740), 85.

[204] In the Methodist example above, it was exclusion of Methodists from the use of Church of England pulpits. Ibid. ("I know of no Law [...] that obliges any Incumbent whatsoever to leave his Pulpit open to every saucy intruder, or to let it out as a Stage for Mountebanks and Jack-puddings, to play their tricks upon, and from then to propagate their Impostures and Delusions").

[205] *Titus Andronicus*, 5. 3. 41–42; p. 195.

[206] Alexander Leggatt, "*Titus Andronicus*: A Modern Perspective" in *Titus Andronicus*, 241–50, 247.

[207] Berry, *Shakespeare and the Hunt*, 85.

[208] *Titus Andronicus*, 5.3. 44; p. 195.

as "[t]rim sport" for Demetrius and Chiron.[209] Aaron tricks Titus into cutting off his own hand in the hope of having the two sons Aaron framed for murdering Bassianus returned to him. The hand is sent back with the heads of both sons and Titus is told his grief is his enemies "sports."[210] Aaron's account of the trick emphasizes his own enjoyment at perpetrating it. He recounts spying through a crevice in the wall at the moment when Titus receives the heads and the returned hand:

> [I] laughed so heartily
> That both mine eyes were rainy like to his.
> And when I told the Empress of this sport,
> She sounded [swooned] almost at my pleasing tale,
> And for my tidings gave me twenty kisses.[211]

Titus says that his hand was cut off "and made a merry jest."[212] There is nothing funny about any of these cruel and sadistic jokes and tricks and the violence they entail. Indeed, the play is carefully constructed to make its audience feel horror – mounting horror – at each of the games as they are played, and as Titus, caught in the grip of his revenge, counter-plays. This reaches its climax when Titus kills Tamora's two surviving sons, Demetrius and Chiron, the ones who raped and mutilated Lavina, bakes them into pies, and feeds them to their mother, who is told she is eating her children.[213] This is a literal enactment of the Philomela tale in Ovid's *Metamorphoses*, as Philomela's sister punishes her husband Tereus the rapist by killing their son and baking him into a pie.[214]

One of Seneca's plays, *Thyestes*, also provides a story of two brothers who feud over the throne, and here the subsequent revenge of one over the other is to have his nephews killed and fed to their father. Translations of Seneca's plays were very popular among Oxford and Cambridge men who later attended the Inns of Court or were connected to the same social circles as those who did.[215] According to one scholar, Shakespeare was

[209] Ibid., 5. 1. 97; p. 171. [210] Ibid., 3. 1. 243; p. 107. [211] Ibid., 5. 1. 118–22; p. 173.

[212] Ibid., 5. 2. 178; p. 189.

[213] Ibid., 5. 3. 61-63; p. 197 ("Why, there they are, both bakèd in this pie, / Whereof their mother daintily hath fed, / Eating the flesh that she herself hath bred"). Taymor puts Titus in a white chef's toque and smock during this banquet scene in the movie *Titus*, creating a very striking maniacal effect.

[214] See "Ovid's Tale of Philomela" in Titus Andronicus, 235-38. In the story, Tereus's wife Progne takes their small son Itys and with Philomela kills him and feeds him to Tereus who "swallowed down the selfsame flesh that of his bowels [loins] bred" (p. 238).

[215] See Winston, *Lawyers at Play*, Chapter 6, 155–57 (on *Thyestes* specifically).

reading Ovid through Seneca, particularly in relationship to the reference in *Titus* to "the ruthless, vast, and gloomy woods [...] where we did hunt."[216]

Both Ovid and Seneca's works influenced Shakespeare. And both would have been recognizable to the audiences of *Titus*. The commonly shared feature of revenge cannibalism in all three works, tricking a parent into eating their own child or children, is so dramatic.

The pies or "pasties" featured in *Titus* were ordinarily made of venison or deer meat.[217] Hence Titus avenges the hunting, rape, and dismemberment of his "dear" Lavinia by reducing her attackers to an analogue of dismembered deer meat, cooked up and presented to their mother as a delicacy.[218]

The director of a modern film adaptation of the play, *Titus* (1999), Julie Taymor, says that the play might be the "greatest dissertation [...] ever written on violence."[219] In it Shakespeare touched on every kind of violence there is. First, "war (which we condone)." His conquest of the Goths in war is what gives Titus the glory to reenter Rome and leads to the invitation to become Emperor; in refusing the invitation on the grounds of old age, he sets up the deadly rivalry between Bassianus and Saturninus. Second, "ritual violence and religion," on display in the opening ritual sacrifice of Tamora's eldest son upon Titus's arrival in Rome. This is the event that causes Tamora to swear vengeance on Titus and thus begin the cycle of revenge and counter-revenge. Third, "a kind of domestic violence," which occurs when Titus slays one of his own sons in a fit of passion when that son disobeys him by refusing to retreat from his support of the union between Lavinia and Bassianus. Fourth, the "lust and rape" of Lavinia and her mutilation. And, finally, fifth, the "nihilism" of Tamora's lover Aaron, who dies regretting only that he did not do more evil.[220]

Unlike *Titus Andronicus*, where we are painfully aware of the ever-escalating violence, the humor and the wit in Livingston's dissent act as a cover for the violence that has taken place in the case in the first place,

[216] See Michael Pincombe, "Classical and Contemporary Sources of the 'Gloomy Woods' of *Titus Andronicus*: Ovid, Seneca, Spenser" in John Batchelor, Tom Cain, and Claire Lamont eds., *Shakespearean Essays in Honour of E.A.J. Honigmann* (United Kingdom: Macmillan Press; New York: St. Martin's Press, 1997), 40–55.

[217] Berry, *Shakespeare and the Hunt*, 81.

[218] See ibid., 85.

[219] See "Julie Taymor at Columbia University" (February 25, 2000) on Disc 2 of *Titus*.

[220] *Titus Andronicus*, 5. 1. 143–46; p. 175 ("I have done a thousand dreadful things / As willingly as one would kill a fly, / And nothing grieves me heartily indeed / But that I cannot do ten thousand more").

namely, the killing of the fox. The cavalier tone and the layers or levels of lawyerly professionalization erase very effectively that original violence, put it out from view.

THE FOX, A PIRATE AND ENEMY OF HUMANKIND

Privateers in Time of War are a Nursery of Pyrates against a Peace
Daniel Defoe, *A General History of the Pyrates* (1724)

It is certainly true that the following important premise is shared by all the antagonists in *Pierson*: there is nothing wrong with killing the fox. Both Pierson and Post were committed to its death. Pierson simply beat Post to it. Neither judge openly questions it. Nonetheless, Livingston felt the need to provide a justification for its killing – the laudable yet laugh-worthy general safety of chickens. The fox is a predator and is therefore outside the law. As Livingston puts it, "[b]oth parties have regarded him, as the law of nations does a pirate '*hostem humani generis*,' an enemy of humankind."[221] As a pirate, the fox is stateless and force against him by anyone is justified. The fox – whose "depredations on farmers and on barn-yards, have not been forgotten" and whose "career" has been "so cunning and ruthless" – is like a pirate to be put to death wherever found.[222]

Yet it is significant that Livingston felt he needed to provide a justification for hunting and killing the fox. In other words, it did not simply go without saying that it was permissible. Criticisms of hunting and the killing of non-human animals certainly existed amongst British eighteenth-century writers and thinkers that would have been known in the United States in the early nineteenth century.[223] Jonathan Swift, for example, noted that butchers could not be jurors on British capital cases, as they were thought to have become desensitized to killing the innocent.[224] And while philosophers and thinkers such as Benjamin Franklin, Voltaire, and Rousseau

[221] *Pierson*, 180. [222] Ibid.

[223] For example, both Alexander Pope and Samuel Johnson criticized hunting in their writings. Pope described chasing deer to the death as what one modern commentator called "a sort of lynching on horseback" and Johnson, who came later and was influenced by Pope, wrote "[i]t is very strange, and very melancholy, that the paucity of human pleasures should persuade us ever to call hunting one of them." See Cartmill, *A View to a Death in the Morning*, 107.

[224] Ibid., 108.

criticized eating nonhuman animals but could not bring themselves to give it up, they "saw meat eating as a questionable habit that needed to be given some sort of moral justification."[225] Hence, the idea that some justification was required for killing the innocent fox (or for hunting generally) would have been grounded in the thoughts and discussions of Livingston's day. No, Livingston insists, the fox was not innocent; he was a pirate, an enemy of all humankind, a predator and justifiably the target of anyone (Pierson or Post) in a kind of open season or war against hostile animals, supported in and by the law of nations in which all civilized people participated.

Jody Greene has described the way that *hostis humani generis* has long operated as "an endlessly generative fiction," in which the pirate, the person who poses an international threat (traditionally to commerce), can be hunted down and treated as if outside the law.[226] She argues that the person in the role of the pirate changes over time; our own modern day pirate is the terrorist in the "the war on terror" fought by Western nations against Islamic extremism since 9/11, a figure, according to at least some members of the former George W. Bush administration, excluded from the ordinary legal process and human rights protections that would, for instance, prohibit torture.[227] Greene surveys writers in the traditional canon of international law such as Grotius and concludes that the pirate is playing an extremely important role in their thought, operating as what she calls "the constitutive exception," "the extralegal figure without whom that body of legal thinking would not have been able to delimit itself in the first place."[228] The pirate is a perpetual other,

[225] Ibid. Cartmill describes how "ethical vegetarianism" ("abstention from meat on the theory that it is wrong to kill animals for food") was very unusual, with the exception of a few eccentrics such as Leonardo da Vinci, until the late 1600s when it began to be widely discussed and books on it began to appear. The arguments also seemed – as many of them are today – to be based on health. Alexander Pope and Jeremy Bentham concluded that killing animals for food was only morally justified if the animal felt no pain. Cartmill notes that "ancient vegetarianism" came from "eccentric minority doctrines about ritual pollution or reincarnation, not in any belief in the value of animal life." Ibid., 40.

[226] See Jody Greene, "*Hostis Humani Generis*," 34 *Critical Inquiry* (2008): 683-705, 696. Providing the Defoe quote reproduced above at 688.

[227] Ibid., 699, 687. See "Coda," 703–705 (on one of the infamous John Yoo Department of Justice memos on whether interrogation methods used on al Queda operatives constituted torture under international law, reproduced from Karen J. Greenberg and Joshua L. Dratel eds., *The Torture Papers: The Road to Abu Ghraib* (New York: Cambridge University Press, 2005), 218–22).

[228] Greene, "*Hostis Humani Generis*," 695.

needed to establish (and continuously reestablish) what normal or non-other is.[229]

Greene also points out that *hostis humani generis* was treated by lawyers as a sort of comical exaggeration, a kind of "rhetorical invective." She describes a group of Irish seafarers who purported to be legitimate privateers who were tried (and some of them executed) as pirates in late seventeenth-century England.[230] The lawyers assembled for this trial, known as the Golding trial, made it clear "through their knowing smiles" that the phrase "*hostis humani generis*" was never meant to be taken literally.[231] It was impossible that one person could be an enemy of *all* humankind, or at war with *the whole world*. The phrase, then, had a tendency toward exaggeration.[232] Matthew Tindall, who attended the Golding trial, saw and noted the smiles of the lawyers in response to use of the phrase. He wrote that "*Hostis Humani Generis*, is neither a Definition, or as much a Description of a Pirat, but a Rhetorical Invective to shew the Odiousness of that Crime."[233] Though the phrase carried the power of life and death, it was, at the same time, a fiction, an object of lawyerly amusement, a kind of inside joke that provoked laughter and knowing smiles in a way that it seems unlikely a non-lawyer would have understood.

The pursuit and prosecution of pirates echoed and reinforced the idea that there was an insider and an outsider (British/Irish; legitimate privateer/illegitimate pirate) and that lawyers and judges policed the line, smiling from their safe professional positions about their inside information. The use of arcane and elaborate legal terminology, often in Latin or Law French, operated to keep specialized legal knowledge from becoming widely available. The traditionally oral and highly memorial nature of the common law, or the common law as custom developing among a small "gerontocratic" group of English lawyers and judges, helped ensure that legal knowledge remained a restricted expertise, and the lawyers who knew it (or had access to the books like law reports and legal treatises in which it came to be, albeit imperfectly, contained) valuable.[234] Law

[229] The perpetual exotic Eastern other has long been associated with the work of Edward W. Said, *Orientalism* (New York: Pantheon Books, 1978).

[230] See Greene, "*Hostis Humani Generis*," 685–86. [231] Ibid., 700. [232] Ibid., 691.

[233] Ibid., 683 (quoting from Matthew Tindall, *An Essay Concerning the Law of Nations* [1694]).

[234] Richard J. Ross, "The Memorial Culture of Early Modern English Lawyers: Memory as Keyword, Shelter, and Identity, 1560–1640," 10 *Yale Journal of Law and Humanities* (1998): 229–326; Simpson, "The Common Law and Legal Theory," 95 ("The organization

schools continue to serve that kind of cartel function, although they have of course in subsequent centuries vastly extended who is in the know in terms of both gender and race, and the legal information is much more accessible.

A version of this expert legal knowledge was certainly on display in *Pierson*, both in the learned Roman and civil law authorities discussed by the lawyers and taken up by the judges. The majority decision of Tompkins J. reproduces long passages from the cited authorities in Latin, much to the chagrin of modern-day law students.[235] Livingston's dissent makes use of the following Latin phrases: *hostes humani generis* [enemy of humankind]; *de mortuis nil nisi bonum* [never speak ill of the dead]; *sub jove frigido* [in the cold air]; and *tempora mutantur* [times change].[236] These phrases seem to be for him part of the joke and of his literary effort, making fun of the learned seriousness with which both Tompkins and the two lawyers present the case: Reynard the Fox, *the enemy of humankind*, of whom, now that he has been killed, *we ought not speak ill*, pursued bravely by Post *in the cold air*, whose capture by the "saucy intruder" Pierson ought to be governed by a rule "of our own," not Justinian's from ancient Rome, for *times change* and have changed since that day.

We can see a mock version of legal expertise performed in the colorful seals and red Syriac text used in the 1834 New York Court of Dover documents, which I found in the papers of Pierson's lawyer Nathan Sanford.[237] Here the court is engaged in amending its constitution and prosecuting one of its number.

Syriac was an ancient language, not widely known, probably used to suggest the existence of a kind of insider code, a way to connote the "ancient and honorable" character of the group and its rituals.

Yet another version of this insider knowledge is on display in the elaborate rituals and terminology involved in an English-style aristocratic deer hunt: special terms for different kinds of deer droppings, different antler configurations and hoof prints; particular ways of describing different hunting dogs, their movement and behavior.[238] The aristocratic hunter was also required to learn a set of signals (including cries and horn

of the profession was gerontocratic [...] and promotion depended on approval by the senior members of the profession").

[235] See e.g. *Pierson*, 179 (quoting Grotius). [236] Ibid., 180–81.

[237] See Fernandez, "The Ancient and Honorable Court of Dover."

[238] Cartmill, *A View to a Death in the Morning*, 64.

calls) for both fellow hunters and dogs, "together with hundreds of other details of terminology, etiquette, and ceremony."[239] The most complicated part of this kind of high hunt was the "breaking of the stag," "the ceremonial gutting and butchering of the slain deer," with different parts given to different participants in the hunt in hierarchical order.[240] Like the punishment that might be inflicted in a Court of Dover, hunters who used the wrong terminology in an Aristocratic English hunt were subjected to "[a] public spanking with the flat of a hunting knife."[241]

So what is the significance of Livingston's feeling that he needed to provide a justification for hunting and killing the fox? His justification signals that it did not simply go without saying that the hunt was (morally or legally) permissible. Yet because that justification was given in a humorous way, in keeping it seems with a tradition associated with *hostis humani generis*, in a text dripping with lawyerly solemn foolery, we may assume it was not intended, and I hazard to guess has seldom been received, as a serious message.

No justification really was required, the bottom-line message seems to be. Indeed, the arguably obvious permissibility is exactly what made it appropriate to deal with the dispute in a witty or sporting way in the first place. There is transgression in Livingston's text. That is why *The Monthly Anthology, and Boston Review* criticized him for impropriety, essentially confusing the categories of high (law) and low (humor), choosing pleasantry at the expense of the "dignity and decorum" due to "the legal robe upon the bench."[242] However, Livingston's transgression confirms and reinforces the underlying basic norm that it is perfectly permissible to kill nonhuman animals that conflict with or are useful for human interests, including the whimsical or pleasurable activity of hunting. The hunted fox creates an opportunity for play or sport. The fox *per se* is an essentially worthless creature whose significance and importance has been blown out of proportion. Livingston is descanting on the basic melody (who first acquired possession of the fox), adding levels or layers that constitute an instance of transgressive play.[243] His dissent makes no difference to the outcome of the case (as the commentator who compared Livingston to Charles Lamb pointed out); it is an opportunity to exercise his literary talents, while at the same time signaling a serious message about the fit and proper place of the human animal to

[239] Ibid. [240] Ibid. [241] Ibid., 65. [242] "The Boston Review" (July 1, 1806), 369.

[243] See Peter Stallybrass and Allon White, *The Politics and Poetics of Transgression* (London: Methuen, 1986).

other animals.[244] The humor makes that very serious point feel like it could never really be questioned, something that went without saying. But there was of course *saying* in the whole performance, an indication that this *saying* did indeed need to be *said*, or at least Livingston thought it did. And the play was not, as play very rarely is, mere play.[245]

To anthropomorphize the fox in an ordinary case might lead one to identify with it.[246] In Livingston's dissent, however, the humor signals to the reader that even though the text happens to include a serious message that the killing of this animal is justified, all of this is not really serious. The solemn foolery itself, taking the opportunity to create more sport or play from the dispute over the hunt and possession of the animal, confirms that the fox is not on par with the (white male) human being. Rather disturbingly, if the allusions to *Titus Andronicus* were in Livingston's mind, the fox might be equated with a hunted and tortured woman (Lavinia). However, the fox is clearly below the secure and privileged male participating in these legal proceedings, so clearly it is a fit opportunity for fun and games. This is true whether the men are using the law in an attempt to vindicate their rights (Pierson and Post) or acting in their professional role as lawyer or judge, arguing, writing, deciding, doing that important and usually very serious work. The transgression and affirmation then is also of the legal rights of private parties and the work of legal professionals in seeing (finally) to their vindication (however crippled one party will be by exorbitant costs). In other words, there is implicitly an affirmation of the importance of professionalized (one might say uber-professionalized) formal state law. Hence we have a departure in this one case, an instance of solemn foolery, that actually confirms the ordinary work of law in all its serious cases. Like all transgression, Livingston's transgression ultimately affirms that which it has turned on its head. The fox is in all this just a thing, a mere play thing, a piece of contested property, as its canonization in property law casebooks and classrooms confirms year after year.[247]

244 Hunt, *Life of Edward Livingston*, 53.

245 When Michel Bakhtin wrote about Rabelais in his famous book *Rabelais and his World* (1968), it was arguably Bakhtin's central insight to insist that as a historical, cultural and political phenomenon, play was rarely mere play. See p. 43 ("play [...] is rarely mere play: it articulates cultural and political meanings").

246 See e.g. Joseph Wharton Lippincott, *Red Ben: The Fox of Oak Ridge* (Philadelphia, PA: Penn Publishing, 1919).

247 On the legal "thinghood" of nonhuman animals, see Steven M. Wise, "The Legal Thinghood of Nonhuman Animals," 23 *Boston College Environmental Affairs Law Review* (1995–96): 471–546.

Some modern-day readers of *Pierson* have reacted to the killing of the fox in an empathetic way. In her book *The Alchemy of Race and Rights* (1991), Patricia Williams compared the fox in *Pierson* with her great-great -grandmother, who was a slave:

> [S]he and the fox shared a common lot, were either owned or unowned, never the owner. And whether owned or unowned, rights over them never filtered down to them; rights to their persons were never vested in them. When owned, issues of physical, mental, and emotional abuse or cruelty were assigned by the law to the private tolerance, whimsy, or insanity of an external master. And when unowned – free, freed, or escaped – again their situation was uncontrollably precarious, for as objects *to be* owned, they and the game of their conquest were seen only as potential enhancements to some other self.[248]

Conventional treatment of the case leaves intact a base line set of assumptions about the superiority of human whim/desire over animal life. As Williams put it, both the fox and her great-great-grandmother were imagined as "fair game from the perspective of those who had rights; but from their own point of view, they were objects of a murderous hunt."[249] In much the same way that nineteenth-century men would have thought nothing about the sexist dimensions of their thought or their deeply held racial prejudices, we might do well to think about the general tendency that many of us share with our nineteenth-century contemporaries to care not one whit about the fox. Those other categories (female, black) are – or at least were – markings of being on the outside, of not being human, or at least not fully human, partaking in the animal. As consciousness shifts, as seems likely, on the morality of an unabashedly utilitarian approach to nonhuman animals and the unquestioned superiority of the human animal to all the rest, it may be that it will come to be viewed as inappropriate for both the fox and a female slave to be made participants in a "game of their conquest."[250] It may even be that we will come to identify the fox with Lavinia in what must be one of Shakespeare's most violent plays, a woman who has been

[248] See Williams, *The Alchemy of Race and Rights: Diary of a Law Professor*, 156–57. This passage first appeared in Patricia J. Williams, "Alchemical Notes: Reconstructing Ideals from Deconstructed Rights *Minority Critiques of the Critical Legal Studies Movement*," 22 *Harvard Civil Rights-Civil Liberties Law Review* (1987): 401–33, 420–21. Williams provided more information on her great, great grandmother Sophie there. Sophie Miller was bought as a child by a white lawyer named Arthur Miller who impregnated her with a child named Mary, who served as a domestic servant in his house to Miller's white wife and white children. See 418–19.

[249] Williams, *The Alchemy of Race and Rights*, 157. [250] Ibid.

reduced to utter powerlessness, subjected to extreme violence, deprived of the power to communicate.

Some property-law professors approach the case unconventionally, putting the fox at the center of the debate in a thoughtful way. My colleague Abraham Drassinower speaks about "the silence of the fox" in *Pierson* and the connection between that silence and the personhood required by a bearer of legal rights, including a property right. Drassinower writes:

> The silence of the fox [. . .] signifies its exclusion from the community of entities whose voice is recognized as a voice that counts, whose acts are worthy of respect. When the fox screams because a hunter mortally wounds it, we do not ask it to tell us its story. But when a hunter screams because another hunter snaps up a prey about to be captured, then [. . .] [we] ask both hunters to tell their stories. The point is simply that persons, not animals, have standing as owners, as entities capable of claiming entitlements through their acts, as beings whose stories get a hearing [. . .] Neither of the parties can be treated as a mere fox. Neither of the parties can be silenced [. . .] As far as the law of property is concerned, the fox is a mere object of desire, a mere thing whose claim to be a part of the legal story is that two persons want it simultaneously.[251]

This simultaneous desire is key to what happens to Lavinia in *Titus*. First she is wanted by both of the brothers who would be Emperor (Saturninus and Bassianus), who quarrel over her and one of whom wins (Bassianus). Then she is wanted by the two rapists, also brothers (Demetrius and Chiron), who find a way both can win what they want in a "love" that turns at Aaron's instigation so quickly and easily into violence. She too is a "mere object of desire," unable to tell her story until she realizes she can draw her family's attention to the account of Philomela's rape in a copy of Ovid's *Metamorphoses* and scratches the names of the attackers in the dirt with a stick in her mouth.[252] Legal personhood is used to decide who can be a storyteller and who cannot.[253]

[251] Abraham Drassinower, "Capturing Ideas: Copyright and the Law of First Possession," 54 *Cleveland State Law Review* (2006): 191–204, 193–94.

[252] *Titus Andronicus*, 4. 1. 30-80; pp. 123–27.

[253] But see Steven M. Wise, *Rattling the Cage: Towards Legal Rights for Animals* (Boston, MA: De Capo Press, 2000; 2nd ed. 2014), arguing for legal personhood for certain non-human animals. Sue Donaldson and Will Kymlicka explore the citizenship possibility in *Zoopolis: A Political Theory of Animal Rights* (Oxford: Oxford University Press, 2011). The Anthropocene has made it difficult to continue to believe in the story of human superiority to the environment and other animals, as the work of those like Bruno Latour and Jane Bennett have demonstrated and as is evident in the shift in the humanities from

Alfred Brophy has written that what interests him "about *Pierson* is not so much what's going on it, but why we choose this case to have so much 'fun.'"[254] It is the context of the original "fun" and how well that translates over time that raises a difficult question here. Brophy says he stopped teaching *Pierson* years ago: "where once foxes crossed the terrain of my class, I now start with slaves and Native Americans."[255]

Christopher Tomlins has written the following about what the future of *Pierson* might be:

> Perhaps one in which the currency of *a priori* reasoning or the construction of seamless rule systems has been undone by historicist contingency; or in which the counter-position that prefers firm fixed rules to fuzzy standards has dissolved under the impress of our acknowledgement that, in fact, we shuttle back and forth between them depending opportunistically on our position relative to the objective. Perhaps it will be one in which *Pierson* has been altogether liberated from doctrine – in which legal education's current turn towards lawyerly practice treasures the case for its performative display of argumentation; or in which law school courses on the legal profession turn to it to study professional culture and acculturation; or in which the ever-rising numbers of women in law schools use it to problematize the bar's masculinity and to probe its formative rituals. Perhaps it will be one in which state decentralization has reintroduced the salience of the local, the particular, and the inconsistent, to the resolution of disputes. Perhaps, even, it will be one in which animals rights consciousness has moved *Pierson* v. *Post* [and the other cases dealing with seals and whales] into the realm of crimes against sentient life: an object lesson, not in how to parse relations between *people* and *possession*, but instead in the morals attending slaughter for play or profit.[256]

Like the whale in *Moby-Dick*, Tomlins notes that the fox is silent.[257] He also wrote: "It seems only fitting, then, to end [a symposium on foxes, seals, and whales] penitently, to pay homage to the ghosts of all the whales and seals and foxes and others whose capture and death has been the occasion for all the human argument and merriment, commerce and law" that has been exposed in the papers of the event.[258] And he gives the fox a voice, a curse to those that hunted him down.[259]

traditional humanism to post-humanism. See e.g. Bruno Latour, "Agency at the Time of the Anthropocene," 45:1 *New Literary History* (2014): 1–18; Jane Bennett, *Vibrant Matter: A Political Ecology of Things* (Durham: Duke University Press, 2010). See also Simon L. Lewis and Mark A. Maslin, *The Human Planet: How We Created the Anthropocene* (New Haven, CT: Yale University Press, 2018).

254 Brophy, "Introduction: A Famous Fox, a Surfacing Whale, and the Forgotten Slave," 146.

255 Ibid., 147. 256 Tomlins, "Animals Accurs'd," 50. 257 Ibid., 51. 258 Ibid.

259 Ibid., 52 (quoting from a ballad *D'ye Ken John Peel* in which "that fox, with his last breath / Curs'd them all as he died in the morning").

The poem provided at the outset of the book, "The Foxe to the Huntesman," by George Gascoigne from his *The Noble Arte of Venerie* (1575) provides a set of arguments beyond a curse for the fox. We hear him (or her) assert his (or her) right "to plead at barre." The argument is essentially that it is hypocritical for humans to blame, hate, and hunt the fox when humans are themselves guilty of many more crimes:

> I sigh (yet smyle) to see, that man (yea master man)
> Can play his part in pollicie, as well as Raynard can.
> And yet forsoth the Foxe is he that beares the blame
> But two leged Foxes eate the ducks, when foure legs beare the name.

Yes, the fox admits, there is some chicken-thieving that goes on. But man, the two-legged fox, "can spoyle, more profit in an houre,/ Than Raynard rifles in a yere, when he doth most deuoure." And while the fox is the one that bears the blame, "[M]an yea master man)/ Can play his part in pollicie, as well as Raynard can." In addition to hypocrisy, the fox charges humans with vanity:

> But wherto serue these sundry sports, these chases manyfold?
> Forsoth to feede their thoughts, with drags of vaine delight [. . .]
> They must haue newfound games, to make the laugh their fill,
> They must have foules, they must haue beasts, to bayt, to hunt, to kyll.
> And all (when all is done) is nothing else but vayne,
> So Salomon the wiseman sayd, and so says Raynerd playne.

The fox also points out that the "subtletie and wit" that foxes are known for are qualities that "I never yet saw day,/ But euvery town had two or three, which Rainards parts could play."

The poem is perfect for *Pierson* for at least three reasons. First, its understanding makes Livingston rather than Raynard the fox, for exercise and expression of his "subtletie and wit," a designation utterly appropriate in the circumstances. Second, the emphasis in the poem on the all-too-human quality of vanity and vain-seeking behavior is especially apt when one thinks on the vanity that was driving the behavior of those involved in the case from start to finish – the litigants, the lawyers, and the judges. And, third, and interestingly, scholars, it turns out, disagree (or at least debate) whether this poem by Gascoigne is a serious plea for sympathy toward the fox or itself a kind of joke.

The Noble Arte of Venerie was a hunting manual, something that one would not expect to see putting forward any kind of critical perspective on the activity. Edward Berry, the author of *Shakespeare and the Hunt*, explains that the book suddenly shifts from technical descriptions of how to hunt (including directions on such points as dismemberment of a carcass) to the sympathetic perspectives of four of the hunted animals (the hart, hare, fox, and otter).[260] "This is strange stuff to find in a handbook for hunters," Matt Cartmill writes.[261] It might be that "all the poetic weeping and cursing of the game animals" in this book was actually meant to be funny.[262] Berry thinks the poems by the animals are placed there to challenge readers to think about the morality of hunting and that this was connected to Gascoigne's ambiguous social position and cynicism toward war.[263]

The need to train men to participate in war was often used as a justification for hunting, specifically for men to learn how to use a gun and kill an animal, deal with the blood and shock of taking away life, so that it would be easier for them to shift from killing nonhuman animals to the human animal in wartime killing.[264] Cartmill ultimately concludes that "there is not much to smile at" in these speeches by the animals.[265] He sees them as examples of criticism of hunting that emerged in the Renaissance period in Western Europe after an overwhelmingly positive attitude toward the activity in the Medieval period. He believes this shift occurred due to increased class conflict (animosity toward hunting as an aristocratic activity) and new skepticism about the place of humans in the world (specifically doubts about the special status of the human being and its superiority to other animals).[266]

Gascoigne is one of Jessica Winston's inns-of-court men of the 1560s. He attended Gray's Inn in 1655 and returned in the mid-1560s.[267] The *Noble Arte of Venerie* seems to have been employing the same kind of doublespeak that Winston explains so often characterized the literary work produced by those at the Inns of Court in this period. Many of these plays, poems, and translations were operating as advice guides to noblemen ("counsel literature"), literary products that facilitated the building

[260] See Berry, *Shakespeare and the Hunt*, 28.

[261] Cartmill, *A View to a Death in the Morning*, 83.

[262] Ibid.

[263] See Berry, *Shakespeare and the Hunt*, 28.

[264] See Cartmill, *A View to a Death in the Morning*, 30 (hunting has long been regarded as a kind of "war game, the first step in a young man's combat training"; "Hunting and war require similar weapons, skills and inner qualities"; the strategy of the hunt corresponds to military tactics on the battlefield); 135 ("the Great White Hunter" takes on a racialized significance in the big-game hunting European aristocrats viewed "as a sort of war game," important "as a symbol of the whole imperial enterprise," specifically to express dominion over native land, animals, and people in places like colonial Africa and India).

[265] See ibid., 83.

[266] See ibid., 84–91.

[267] Winston, *Lawyers at Play*, 94.

of a distinctive social and political professional identity for the Inns and those who attended and remained affiliated with them.[268] Winston explains that the writing often involved a severe moralism wrapped up in a package that would not risk giving too much offence. Why? Well, the authors were using literary demonstrations to seek preferment and career advancement, and upright moral comportment was an indication of the author's suitability for taking on one of the many public offices in the growing Elizabethan administration.

It is true that the day-to-day work of a Justice of the Peace did not involve much poetry writing. However, involvement with literary works that discussed virtue were taken as a demonstration of virtue, thereby, as Winston puts it, closing "the gap between ideology and practice at the heart of humanist theory."[269] So, for instance, writing poetry that rejected romantic love as dangerous and extoled the virtues of public service demonstrated that the author had at least thought about what kind of virtue made one fit for public office.[270]

Winston explains that currying favor was not something at which Gasoigne excelled. So, for example, he turned the versification assignment given to him by his fellow Innsmen when he returned to Gray's Inn into a joke.[271] He may well have been doing the same in *The Noble Arte of Venerie*, writing on a topic that was of interest to noblemen from the serious perspective of a hunting manual but ultimately in a scornful or disdainful way that was evidently characteristic of him.[272] It was unlikely to be well received by his intended audience, providing as it did empathetic views from the hunted animals' perspectives. Gascoigne might also have genuinely believed in the moral position, namely, being against causing unnecessary harm and cruelty to animals and the book was a literary space in which to express that view.[273]

[268] Ibid., 158. [269] Ibid., 54. [270] See ibid., Chapter 3. [271] See ibid., 94–97.
[272] Ibid., 95.
[273] The treatment of animals is not a topic Winston canvasses. However, she notes that the strict moralism in the writings of inns-of-court men took the form of the dangers of love and lust, ironically expressed in verse. See ibid., Chapter 3. The *Magistrate's Mirror*, a work that Winston treats extensively in the book, is a collection of tragedies warning of the vices leaders and Kings and Queens (for Queen Elizabeth) can fall into unless they exercise good moral sense, e.g. falling prey to flatterers, over-reaching in terms of absolute rule and tyranny, or becoming overly ambitious or prideful. See ibid., 127–33. Overkill, in terms of blood sports and blood lust amongst nobles engaged in hunting in the King or Queen's name, could certainly be one such vice, especially when peasants or the middling sort, who might actually use those animals for food and clothing, were prevented from doing so by Royal prerogative.

It was quite typical for writing in this genre to provide contrasting perspectives on controversial political issues, for example, having the voices of different characters in a play express different views or rival truths about controversial issues.[274] Such a device was especially important when one of the truths being voiced, say in a play, was a challenge to the monarch's authority, as any criticism of hunting would be. However, if it is also a joke, then this insulates the author from the charges of crossing the line and keeps him in the good books of those reading the text or hearing the play.

The mixture of solemn and silly is, in other words, a way of communicating criticism and voicing dissent but in a polite and deferential way compatible with future preferment within the establishment, the members of which are meant to be impressed enough by the author's humanist dexterity to recommend him for a position that will ultimately have little to do with composing poems or translating plays. Being able to maintain this polite but critical distance from court and Crown and inhabit it successfully was essential to the role the Inns played as semiautonomous spaces. Although not expressly part of Winston's thesis, it stands to reason that this role was, in turn, key to the development of the common law lawyer's professional identity in which independence played (and continues to play) such a key role. Winston teaches us that it was literature which facilitated the process of a semiautonomous professional identity for lawyers in sixteenth-century England. Literature, especially drama, allowed those at the Inns of Court to enter into controversial political discussion "in a protected way, under the cover of fiction."[275] "[A]t the

[274] See ibid., 156 (discussing criticism of King Thyestes put in the mouth of his servant and the chorus also expressing laudable ideals which the play does not put forward as accurate or true). See also ibid., 204 (explaining how one of Gascoigne's plays *Supposes* "does not follow through on or respond to the political and social issue it raises," i.e. a concern about whether magistrates are reliable and acting for the public good).

[275] Ibid., 188. The question Winston focuses on that was of grave concern in the 1560s relating to Queen Elizabeth's status as a single person without an heir. It was dangerous to weigh in on this issue – Should she marry or was chastity better for a queen than marriage? If she should marry, whom should she marry? An Englishman or would a foreigner be acceptable? Edmund Plowden wrote a treatise on the succession issue but kept it a closely guarded manuscript given the danger he felt that it created for him. See ibid., 191, 196. The issues were ones inns-of-court men could comment on, at least for a time, "under the cover of fiction" a play provided but a treatise could not. In the 1670s one innsman's treatise on Elizabeth's would-be husband cost him his right hand, which she ordered be publicly chopped off. That man, John Stubbe "wrote as an individual, rather than as part of a collective; he authored a treatise, instead of historical

Inns of Court literary play was the unacknowledged but ever-present associate to the common law in the history of early modern legal professionalization."[276]

The ambiguity in Gascoigne's book – is the fox's perspective serious or is it a joke? – is nicely echoed in *Pierson*. Given the placement of the poem in a hunting manual, is the voice of the fox really meant to elicit sympathy for the fox? We have a similar question to ask of Livingston's dissent: Given its nonsensical dimensions and its attempt to be humorous and entertaining, was it meant to be taken seriously? There is no doubt that the hot pursuit rule was a serious (and viable) legal rule on how to acquire possession in wild animals. Yet it is a mistake, I have argued in these first two chapters, to reduce the dissent to a policy position (an allegedly fuzzy standard) and ignore the literary dimensions of the text if one is to understand the case in its time and place. It is also a mistake to ignore the important ideological work the argument/narrative in the dissent was doing (and continues to do) with respect to the justification of violence toward nonhuman animals. In this, Livingston was acting very much like a two-legged fox, seeming to be doing one thing but really, slyly, doing another. The love many hunters express toward nonhuman animals, which often amounts to reverence toward them, is a true paradox in human-animal relationships.[277] It is also often importantly gendered.[278] Ships also have been gendered female, and in prize cases, where courts of admiralty ruled on the seizure of ships by privateers legally empowered to plunder the high seas, the vessel being pursued was "the chase" (from *la chasse* or "the hunt" in French).[279]

Now the saucy intruder in *Pierson* was not the fox, whose death was justified (given the slaughtered chickens) as a form of revenge of human animals against foxes, killing them wherever and whenever possible.

fiction; he disseminated in print, instead of performance [...] Stubbe was the wrong person counselling Elizabeth in the wrong way at the wrong time." Ibid., 227.

276 Ibid., 225.

277 See Erika Ritter, *The Dog by the Cradle, the Serpent Beneath: Some Paradoxes of Human-Animal Relationships* (Toronto: Key Porter Books, 2009).

278 The female here often stands in for the hunted animal, penetrated by arrow, spear, or gun, a kind of symbolic rape. The male is learning to inure oneself to the pain of death, killing with kindness, as a way to kill the love we feel for animals that might be learning to kill kindness in ourselves. See Ritter, ibid., 42–45. Ritter describes the way that stories and movies like *The Yearling* and *Old Yeller* depict a boy "matriculating to manhood" by killing his beloved pet, securing the approval of his father through this all-important act of slaughter. See ibid., 33–37.

279 Donald A. Petrie, *The Prize Game: Lawful Looting on the High Seas in the Days of Fighting Sail* (Annapolis, MD: Naval Institute Press, 1999), 4.

We might recall that Nathan Post's revolutionary war ship was called the *Revenge*. His son, Lodowick, was the first mover in the action, using the law to express his anger at having his sport interrupted, resentment directed toward Pierson, whom Post argued was motivated by malice.[280] Indeed, channeling his desire for revenge against Pierson through the legal process was a way for Post to legitimize that anger, wash it clean of any taint of impropriety that would accompany self-help, black face paint, or any other extralegal means. In other words, Lodowick Post did what he was supposed to do. He went to the legal system to get the wrong against him redressed in a small claims court before a jury of his peers at what was supposed to be a low cost. In that he acted more like a privateer than a pirate – both plundered, but the key distinction between the two was that the privateer was authorized by one nation to attack the ships of enemy nations and so was doing it by legal rather than illegal means. Once the conflict ends, the privateer must decide whether to turn pirate or become a legitimate merchant.[281] Nathan Post went legitimate after he fought against the British who were occupying Long Island along with New York City during the Revolutionary War and from whom he fled and worked against as a privateer. Yet, his way of being wealthy seemed to rub the traditional landowners in the area, the Piersons, the wrong way. These neighbors may have thought of him (and his son) (along with their wealth) as more pirate than not, even if smuggling was thought to define a patriot and had been a long and widely followed practice.

Livingston wrote as if to vindicate Post – Post was not the pirate, the fox was the pirate; and the saucy intruder was Pierson. So, in keeping with the use of that phrase, was there violence then against Pierson that would have been justified in Livingston's eyes for Pierson's encroachment?

[280] See Judgment Roll, p. 5, Appendix B.

[281] Greene, "*Hostis Humani Generis*," 688 ("Privateers in wartime carried letters of marque or other commissioning documents authorizing them to attack or capture ships belonging to enemy nations, take those aboard ship prisoner, and expropriate any property deemed valuable or useful, including, where desirable the ship itself. When the immediate conflict came to a close, those letters or other authenticating documents were considered null and void, leaving those who held them either to turn pirate or to enter the ranks of legal merchant-adventurers"). See also Petrie, *The Prize Game*, 69 (emphasizing that where a pirate was a person "at war with all the world" and attacking at sea any vessel that could be victimized, the hostilities of privateers "were directed solely against the declared enemies of the sovereign whose commission they held or, subject to the control of a prize court, neutral vessels carrying troops of cargo in aid of such enemies").

Today we might think of something like Robert Cover's understanding of the law itself as inescapably violent, that is to say, imposing a state of affairs (imprisonment or money judgment) against the will of the losing party.[282] In this situation, it would be upholding Post's jury verdict (his 75¢ fox and $5 in costs) and dismissing Pierson's appeal, in which case Pierson would lose not just the $5.75 from the first trial but also the much larger costs after the appeal, amounting to $126.37. Yet this is not what happened. Pierson hired Nathan Sanford, who raised a variety of procedural points on appeal. The case dragged on for over two years. And ultimately, because the New York Supreme Court chose Justinian over other competing authorities on how possession in a wild animals was established, it would be Post who was on the hook for $126.37.

How did all this happen? How did this case go from relatively simple and straightforward jury trial with a 75¢ award to an elaborately argued and expensive affair that lasted well over two years? The next two chapters explore these questions and in the process examine other local dimensions of the case. More specifically, Chapter 3 explains the first level of the jury trial, examining among other things where the trial took place, who the jurors were, and how the process worked. Chapter 4 analyzes the lawyerization of the case on appeal, focusing especially on Pierson's lawyer Nathan Sanford. We do not know when exactly lawyers became involved in *Pierson*. However, their involvement certainly helps account for how the case developed, specifically how it got blown so out of proportion – for taking as long as it did and costing so much, but also for taking the elaborate turn it took, a turn that gave Livingston fodder for his imaginative play.

[282] See Robert M. Cover, "Violence and the Word," 95 *Yale Law Journal* (1986): 1601–30, 1601 ("Legal interpretation takes place in a field of pain and death. This is true in several senses. Legal interpretive acts signal and occasion the imposition of violence upon others: A judge articulates her understanding of a text, and as a result, somebody loses his freedom, his property, his children, even his life. Interpretations in law also constitute justifications for violence which has already occurred or which is about to occur. When interpreters have finished their work, they frequently leave behind victims whose lives have been torn apart by these organized, social practices of violence. Neither legal interpretation nor the violence it occasions may be properly understood apart from one another").

PART II

THE SOCIAL HISTORY OF *PIERSON*

3

Local Justice

Two enormous wooden pots painted black, and suspended by asses' ears, swung from the cross-trees of an old top-mast, planted in front of an old doorway [of the Nantucket inn]. The horns of the cross-trees were sawed off on the other side, so that this old top-mast looked not a little like a gallows. Perhaps I was over sensitive to such impressions at the time, but I could not help staring at this gallows with a vague misgiving. A sort of crick was in my neck as I gazed up to the two remaining horns: yes, two of them, one for Queequeg, and one for me.

Herman Melville, *Moby-Dick, or the Whale* (1851)[1]

In this chapter, we examine the local aspects of the *Pierson v. Post* case, where the trial took place, who the jurors were, and how the trial was run under the small claims process in early nineteenth-century New York under the *Twenty-Five Dollar Act*. This statute was used for cases where the amount at issue was less than $25, the statute which replaced the older *Ten Pound Act*.[2] If the suggestion made in Chapter 1 is correct, and part of the friction between Pierson and Post and their families was grounded in local geography, specifically, seafaring Sag Harbor versus agrarian Bridgehampton/Sagaponack, it is worth noting that both the Justice of

[1] Quote taken from pp. 72–73.

[2] *An act for the more speedy recovery of debts, to the value of twenty-five dollars*, passed April 7, 1801 (Albany: Charles R. and George Webster, 1802) (hereafter *Twenty-Five Dollar Act*). The *Ten Pound Act* was originally passed in 1787 and added to in 1795. See *The Ten Pound Act: that is to say, an act for the more speedy recovery of debts to the value of ten pounds ... enacted ... the 17th day of April, in the year of our Lord 1787 ... and the additional act thereto, passed the 9th day of April, 1795, entitled, "An act to amend an act for the more speedy recovery of debts to the value of ten pounds ... "* (Lansingburgh, NY: Silvester Tiffany, 1795) (hereafter *Ten Pound Act*).

the Peace in the case and a majority of the members of the local jury who sat on it were residents of Sag Harbor. One might have thought that would bode well for Post who was a member of this community, and it did in the sense that he technically won his case and was awarded the highest amount of costs permissible under the statute, $5. However, the jury went nowhere near their maximum allowance in money damages, $25, awarding Post a mere 75¢ for the loss of the fox.

Juries of course do not give reasons for their decisions. This jury may have been expressing a rejection of Post's contention that it was wrong to interfere with his hunt *with malice*. No, the jury seemed to be saying through the 75¢ award, Post would only receive a nominal or token sum for what was in their view not a serious wrong even if it was with malice. However, it is worth noting that 75¢ was about what would be awarded for a fox caught as bounty, which in 1791 at least was 4 shillings or 48 pence, and so the jury might have thought of themselves as giving that amount for what was in effect Pierson's theft of Post's fox.[3] Whether the jury valued the fox at its bounty price or simply assigned a token amount as an expression of their disagreement with (or low regard for) the weightiness of Post's slight, they were not giving Post very much for his claim. It could hardly be called a big win for Post or a validation of his view (and claim) that foxhunting should not be subject to intentional or malicious interference.

So even a jury that would have had a geographic preference for or identification with Post was not able to endorse his view of the fox as a valuable object of recreational pursuit. That view likely had more to do with wealth and class than geographical region: we will see that, on the whole, the jury members chosen (and the Justice of the Peace) were substantially less wealthy than either Pierson or Post. If the claim was less about the fox itself and more about seeking redress against Pierson's malicious interference with Post's hunt, one might expect to see Post's Sag Harbor neighbors support him in that. Yet again this would seem to be more about wealth and class than region. It seems entirely plausible that a wealthy person from Sag Harbor would have a different conception of what was a slight worthy of high compensation than a person of more modest means from either Sag Harbor or Bridgehampton, wealth or class background thereby trumping regional affiliation.

[3] *Town Records*, vol. 3: 332 ("a bounty of four shillings [be given] on every fox taken between the twentieth day of March and the twentieth day of June following"). With a shilling at twelve pence, this would make the bounty forty-eight pence.

The Justice of the Peace who tried the case was a man named John N. Fordham. The Fordhams were one of the original families to settle Sag Harbor around 1730 and their family name is prominent in descriptions of the place.[4] A Nathan Fordham, Jr., son of a large landowner Nathan Fordham Esq., was involved in construction of a wharf there in 1761.[5] Wharves played an important role in the offshore whaling industry in which sloops cruised near the shore and brought captured whale bone and blubber back into the harbor.[6] The household of Nathan Fordham Esq. included six slaves – the largest number of slaves in one household in Southampton Town in 1790.[7] Nathan Fordham Esq. had another son, John Nathan Fordham, probably our "John N. Fordham," and he kept a tavern in Sag Harbor.[8] There is reference to a "Captain John N. Fordham" from 1795, suggesting that at one time he was also involved in whaling or shipping.[9] There is also a "John N. Fordham & Son" listed as a grocery business in the business directory from 1804–1810.[10]

John N. Fordham was very active in town government. He is listed as an assessor and a trustee in 1796, an assessor in 1797 and 1799, an overseer of the highway in 1800 and 1807, a trustee in 1801, and a supervisor in 1806.[11] Town records list Fordham among those given the right to make a connection between an inland pond (known as Otter Pond) and the sea to make a fish pond. Apparently, each person who helped with the work in 1783 received a barrel of New England rum.[12] Those rights to the pond were then transferred to another party to make

[4] See H.P. Hedges, "Early Sag-Harbor" in *Tracing the Past: Writings of Henry P. Hedges, 1817–1911, Relating to the History of the East End, Including East Hampton, Southampton, Sag Harbor, Bridgehampton, and Southold in Suffolk County, New York*, Tom Twomey ed. (New York: Newmarket Press, 2000), 178–211, 200–201, 181–87.

[5] Ibid., 181, 183. See Zaykowski, *Sag Harbor*, 18–19 (for more on the wharf), 333 (listing Nathan Fordham among "Early Inhabitants" taken from a Sag Harbor village census in 1775).

[6] Hedges, "Early Sag-Harbor" in *Tracing the Past*, 183.

[7] There are two listings for Nathan Fordham. The one with the six slaves is probably Nathan Fordham Esq., as he would have had more time to develop the large household described there (two free white males sixteen and above, one free white male under the age of sixteen, five free white females and three other free persons). The other Nathan Fordham has no slaves, no servants, a free white female (likely his wife), and three free white males under sixteen years. See *First Census of the United States Taken in the Year 1790*, 168.

[8] Hedges, "Early Sag-Harbor" in *Tracing the Past*, 202. [9] Zaykowski, *Sag Harbor*, 12.

[10] Ibid., 351. [11] *Town Records*, vol. 3: 348, 350, 356, 358, 381, 359, 375.

[12] Hedges, "Early Sag Harbor" in *Tracing the Past*, 180.

a mill stream in 1793.[13] He is listed in one tax assessment at what looks to be $575 of real property and $300 of personal property for a total of $875 in 1801.[14] This means that he was not nearly as wealthy as either David Pierson (listed at $2,460 worth of property in 1801) or Nathan and Lodowick Post (listed at $2,900 in 1801).[15] The average amount of real and personal property for the jurors in 1803 was $1,209.[16] However, Fordham was later wealthy enough to own slaves, perhaps through inheritance from his father.

Fordham manumitted a slave named Jude in 1806 and another on February 16, 1808, just two years before his own death.[17] Some years later, two of the slaves belonging to his estate with the surname Jupiter applied for manumission and certificates from the Overseers of the Poor – Isaac Jupiter on December 7, 1813, and Lois Jupiter on July 12, 1819.[18] Lois was twenty-two in 1819, which would have made her about eleven at the time Fordham died. The point of the certificate from the Overseers of the Poor seemed to be to make it clear that her manumission "exonerate[d] the estate of her late master and his representatives from her future support," as per a statute that was passed in April of that year.[19] The Overseers stated that "she [Lois] is now twenty-two years old," hence no longer a child, and "appears to be well and hearty, and as capable of supporting herself as any other person of color of the like age."[20] In other words, the positive support to which she had been entitled by virtue of her slave status was no longer available to her and she was required to fend for herself. Although she had been a child in his household, Fordham's relatives were not about to let her become a tax on his estate.

Fordham was clearly busy on many fronts, running a tavern, captaining a ship, and later operating a grocery store with his son. In other words, he was by no means a full-time judge. He was prominent in town governance and decently propertied, as would befit a Justice of the Peace, probably respected more for his place in the community than for any detailed knowledge of the law. Justices of the Peace, one source noted, like the suitors of the magistrate's court themselves, were "presumed [...] to be plain people, unacquainted with legal learning, pursuing [or adjudicating] a right in matters of

[13] *Town Records*, vol. 3: 338–39. [14] See Tax Assessment Roll, 1801. [15] Ibid.
[16] This figure is based on the figures for 1803 from "Jury Tax Table" in Appendix C.
[17] *Town Records*, vol. 3: 375. See also Index to Deaths, 36, Long Island Collection, East Hampton Library, East Hampton, NY; Van Buren Will Index, Liber B., p. 79.
[18] See *Town Records*, vol. 4: 12–13, 36 (spelling her last name "Jubiter," likely a typo).
[19] Ibid., 36. [20] Ibid.

a small concern."[21] It was this lack of legal learning that made the cases tried in a magistrate's court so vulnerable to reversal. The professionals – lawyers in particular – would justify pushing for those reversals by pointing to the informality and lack of legal propriety in proceedings before Justices of the Peace (see e.g. Figure 3.1). Those same professionals (and other state legal actors) were the direct beneficiaries of the new business opportunities this kind of management and supervision of magistrates' courts generated. In Post's case, Pierson's lawyer, Nathan Sanford, challenged a variety of procedural issues.[22] Fordham was then commanded to explain in the writ of *certiorari* everything he had done in the case, which he dutifully did.

This back-and-forth between Sanford's challenges and Fordham's reply is captured in the Judgment Roll reproduced in Appendix B. Livingston had said in the reported case that there were six exceptions taken but the case was going to focus on the third exception, which amounted to the question whether at law Post had a legally protected interest in the fox.[23] Prior to discovery of the Judgment Roll there was no way of knowing what the other five exceptions were. The Judgment Roll tells us, describing each of the six alleged "manifest errors" in turn.

First, Sanford objected that Pierson's summons did not authorize a specific Constable to serve it. It was made out to "any of the Constables of the County of Suffolk."[24] Second, Sanford objected to the serving of the summons, alleging it violated the minimum six days of notice to appear.[25] Third, he claimed that that there an insufficiency "in law" for Post "to have[,] maintain[,] or support his [...] action against [...] Peirson and therefore the said judgment [...] rendered and given is vicious[,] erroneous[,] and void in law."[26] Fourth, the jury venire did not specify the purpose for which the twelve freeholders were summoned.[27] Fifth, the Justice of the Peace tallied the costs in the case, whereas that task was for the jury to perform.[28] And, finally, sixth, in what would appear to be generic or just-in-case piece of pleading, Sanford alleged that there was "great and manifest error" in the judgment being awarded to Post when, "by the law of the land," judgment ought to have been given for Pierson.[29]

[21] Esek Cowen, *A Treatise on the Civil Jurisdiction of a Justice of the Peace, in the State of New York* (Albany, NY: W.M. Gould 1821), 320.
[22] See Judgment Roll, pp. 11–14, Appendix B. [23] *Pierson*, 180.
[24] Judgment Roll, p. 11, Appendix B. [25] See ibid., pp. 11–12. [26] Ibid., p. 12.
[27] Ibid., pp. 12–13. [28] Ibid., p. 13. [29] Ibid., p. 14.

FIGURE 3.1 "Justice's Court in the Backwoods" (1850) by Thompkins Harrison Matteson; oil on canvass, H: 31¾ x W: 44 in. Fenimore Art Museum, Cooperstown, New York, Gift of Stephen C. Clark, N0411.1955. Photograph by Richard Walker.

None of the procedural objections – how the Constable was deputized, how the service to Pierson was executed, how the jury venire omitted why they were to appear, and that the judge rather than the jury itself tallied the costs – were weighty or important enough to result in a reversal. Service might well have been, and when I first wrote about this, I thought that it had been violated and that it was odd that Sanford had agreed to reduce the case only to the third objection. However, the record indicates that service was indeed properly executed.[30] And we will see below that for the judge rather than the jury to tally costs had become a moot point by the time *Pierson* was decided. Presumably, failure to nominate a particular constable was not considered an

[30] I thought that Pierson had not been properly served based on some difficult-to-read handwriting on p. 9 of the Judgment Roll, Appendix B, which I thought was "Jesey Larson." Charles Donahue was correct to say that text should be read as "Jesse Peirson," in which case it would appear that Pierson was served within the six-day notice period, that is on December 22. See Fernandez, "The Lost Record," 173; Donahue, "Papyrology," 183–84.

egregious error, nor was the failure to explain on the jury venire why potential jurors were being summoned. Livingston wrote that "[o]f six exceptions, taken to the proceedings below, all are abandoned except the third, which reduces the controversy to a single question," whether Post had acquired an interest in the fox so as to have a right of action against Pierson, who "in view of the huntsman and his dogs in full pursuit, and with knowledge of the chase," killed and carried the fox away.[31] So, the lawyers agreed, including Pierson's lawyer who had raised all the procedural points, that they would be abandoned and the focus would be on the fox and whether actual capture was required for its possession or whether a chase (which Livingston assumed was a hot chase) would be enough.

As Captain Nathan Post was, like Fordham, intimately connected to Sag Harbor (later Posts and Fordhams appear side-by-side in the business directory of Main Street of Sag Harbor[32]) one might have thought Post would have done better to have had his case heard by Fordham alone rather than by a jury. However, either a plaintiff or a defendant could request a jury under the *Twenty-Five Dollar Act*.[33] And here, Post (perhaps unwisely as things turned out) chose a jury to hear his case.[34] His decision to do so probably reflects the strength of popular feeling about the right to trial by jury.[35] Trial by jury likely had an important legitimating effect, both for the way Post himself saw what had been won (or lost), and for how the result would have been viewed in the eyes of his neighbors.

The Judgment Roll gave us another piece of new information, namely, that there were seven witnesses at the jury trial.[36] Perhaps these were the "companions" of Post, as one account put it, out hunting with him with the "dogs and hounds."[37] If that was the case, Post may well have deemed it socially necessary to vindicate – via a jury of his peers – the very public insult Pierson had delivered for all those seven sets of eyes to see (see

[31] *Pierson*, 180. [32] See Zaykowski, *Sag Harbor*, 326.

[33] See s. 12, *Twenty-Five Dollar Act*.

[34] Fordham wrote that Post "did demand of me[,] the said John N. Fordham[,] that the said action should be tried by a jury." Judgment Roll, p. 5, Appendix B.

[35] See Goebel, *The Law Practice of Alexander Hamilton*, 2: 15 (noting that the New York Constitution of 1777 guaranteed that "trial by jury, in all cases, in which it hath heretofore been used in the colony of New-York, shall be established, and remain inviolate forever").

[36] Judgment Roll, p. 10, Appendix B.

[37] Hedges, "Pierson vs. Post," *Sag-Harbor Express* (1895); *Pierson*, 175.

Figure 4.1 for the kind of attention the capture of a fox might cause in Southampton Town).

Sanford objected to Fordham rather than the jury tallying the costs in the case.[38] Inspecting Fordham's list of charges, one can see that there were items that Fordham should not have included. He also overcharged for certain things.[39] These excessive charges totaled 53.5¢ – not a great deal of money, perhaps a feature of the relaxed style of justice in a magistrate's court. However, one gets the impression that Fordham was trying hard to reach the $5 maximum allowed to him under the *Twenty-Five Dollar Act* – he was forced to round his total down, from $5.04 to $5. Fordham might have been motivated to do this by the jury's own low money damages award, just 75¢, which he could not amend. His friendly feeling toward Post was probably based on a number of factors including their shared connections to Sag Harbor through Lodowick's father Nathan.

Unlike Nathan Post, who was living on the edge of Sagaponack, where the Pierson family was from, and seemed to have his feet in both the rural Bridgehampton/Sagaponack and commercial Sag Harbor worlds, Fordham was firmly located in Sag Harbor. He would have little reason to identify with the Pierson family's agricultural interests and their view of the fox as vermin (to be killed wherever and whenever possible) and (if they had the requisite knowledge and ecological consciousness) their view of English-style foxhunting as a threat to farmers' chickens and fences. We have seen that the taking of the fox by one of the younger Pierson family members, Jesse, was probably an attempt to put the Posts in their place – Lodowick for putting on airs by being out hunting with "dogs and hounds"[40] and the elder Nathan for bringing his different (and seemingly more successful) way of being wealthy to the doorstep of the Piersons in a way they did not appreciate (especially if he was outpacing them). This political (familial, regional, and economic) tension was unlikely to have been lost on Fordham and indeed the jurors. However, unlike the Sag Harbor jurors, who we will see did not identify with Post's slight, Fordham might well have felt more pull toward Post. Why?

[38] See Judgment Roll, p. 13, Appendix B.

[39] Fordham was not supposed to charge the 6¢ he did for swearing the Constable nor was the 42¢ he charged for swearing the evidence authorized by s. 21 of the *Twenty-Five Dollar Act*. He overcharged for a number of items – 37.5¢ rather than 36¢ for jurors who attended but were not sworn and 9.5¢ rather than 9¢ for the summons.

[40] *Pierson*, 175.

Nathan Post was also a magistrate and it seems likely that he played a key role in encouraging his son Lodowick to sue in order to obtain justice from a fellow Justice of the Peace.[41] Fordham was staffing a legal system, albeit in a part-time way, that was supposed to be and had in the past been very successful at providing cheap, fast, and informal justice. Fordham then would have had an interest (in the way a jury member would not) in seeing the young man who turned to this legal process (and his father, who also helped staff the system) prevail in order to obtain compensation for the very public insult he received. And, to put it bluntly, the 75¢ that the jury gave was not much of a vindication.

It is possible that the jury saw the 75¢ as a kind of compromise, giving Post something (if not much) but technically Pierson loses (and must pay the costs). So in the wake of the case, when people in these close knits communities discussed, as they certainly did, the all-important question "Who won the fox fight?" there was something in it for everyone, some face-saving for Post and his family against the Pierson slight but by no means a resounding victory for Post. 75¢ was a way to acknowledge, yes, Pierson had done Post wrong by taking "his" fox valued at about the bounty price. However, Post had misread his audience if he thought that they would be sympathetic to the aspect of intentional interference or malice as a slight to an up-and-coming gentleman from a wealthy family worthy of significant compensation. There was no appetite for hitting the Pierson family with that expression of disapprobation or that support of Post's lifestyle choice, hunting foxes with "dogs and hounds."[42]

Sanford was correct to object that the judge rather than the jury had tallied the costs: the point was not clear in the statute and had not been adjudicated. However, in the period between Sanford's command for the writ of *certiorari* from Fordham in early 1803 and the New York Supreme Court's determination in August or September of 1805, the issue was settled in another case Sanford argued called *Brown v. Smith*.[43] There the New York Supreme Court rejected his argument and held that a Justice of the Peace was permitted to tally the costs in a jury trial under *The Twenty-Five Dollar Act*.

[41] Hedges wrote that the fathers of both young men were spurring them on. See Hedges, "Pierson vs. Post," *Sag-Harbor Express* (1895). The gravestone recorded in Adams, *Memorials of Old Bridgehampton*, 334, sets out that Nathan Post Esq. was "a respectable Magistrate."

[42] *Pierson*, 175. [43] See *Brown* v. *Smith*, 3 Caines Rep. 81 (N.Y. Sup. Ct., 1805).

The Constable in Post's case was man named Thomas L. Harris. Town records show him serving in that role in 1799–1802, 1807, and 1808–1809.[44] Hence, Harris was relatively seasoned when Post brought his claim in 1802. The 1801 tax roll shows Harris listed no personal property and real property worth $300, $250 in 1803, $200 in 1806, and $400 in 1818.[45] In other words, Harris was of relatively modest means, owning less than Fordham, less than the average person in the jury pool and much less than either father of Pierson or Post. Harris's household in 1790 consisted of himself, two free white females, and no slaves.[46] The Constable was the enforcement arm of the court.[47] The job was "difficult" and "unpopular," since carrying out the orders of the court after a trial "could mean, in a criminal case, administering punishment or, in a civil suit, presenting an execution."[48] The Constable was the court official with the least amount of power and prestige.[49] However, he had important roles to play in the small claims jury trial, one of which was summoning the venire of twelve men from which the jury of six in a case like this would be chosen.

How did a jury trial work in New York in this period? The Sheriff in each county kept a book of persons qualified to serve as jurors, with their places of abode. The Sheriff or his "under officer" (e.g. the clerk in his office) was responsible for creating the "array" or venire of jurors in the panel from which the final members were chosen by ballot.[50]

The *Twenty-Five Dollar Act* does not specify how the venire of twelve was chosen. It was probably up to the Constable to choose whomever he thought fit and was available from the Sheriff's list or his own similar list. Fordham says in his account that he issued a "Venire" to Harris, "commanding him to summon twelve good and lawful men being freeholders of the town of Southampton [...] who should in no wise be of kin" to either party "nor [be] interested in the said cause."[51] Harris "then and there," that is on December 30, the day of the trial, made "due return of the said

44 *Town Records*, vol. 3: 356, 358, 359, 360. 382, 384 and vol. 4: 1.

45 See Tax Assessment Rolls, 1801, 1803, 1806, 1818.

46 See *First Census of the United States Taken in the Year 1790*, 168.

47 See Martha J. McNamara, *From Tavern to Courthouse: Architecture and Ritual in American Law, 1658–1860* (Baltimore, London: Johns Hopkins University Press, 2004), 60.

48 Ibid., 42. 49 Ibid., 60.

50 See Wyche, *Treatise on the Practice of the New York Supreme Court of Judicature of the State of New York*, 141 (identifying a 1765 practice rule requiring this for jury trials).

51 See Judgment Roll, pp. 5–6, Appendix B.

Venire and annexed a pannel thereto containing the names of twelve freeholders whom he had duly summoned."[52]

The statute was clear that the six jurors were to be selected by the Constable who rolled up the ballots "all as near as may be, in one and the same manner, and put [them] together in a box, or some convenient thing."[53] Fordham recorded that this ballot-box procedure was followed:

> [T]he names of the persons so impannelled were severally written on several and distinct pieces of paper as nearly of one size as could be and were delivered to me[,] the said John N. Fordham[,] (by the said Constable who returned the said panel) rolled up by him all as nearly as could be in one and the same manner and put together into a box and thereupon the said John N. Fordham did draw out six of the said papers one after another on which the following persons were named and who being respectively called did appear and were not challenged and being approved of by me[,] the said Justice[,] as indifferent [. . .] to try the said cause and were severally sworn well and truly to try the matter in [in]difference between Lodowick Post Plaintiff and Jesse Peirson Defendant.[54]

The statute required that jurors "should in no wise be of kin" to either the plaintiff or the defendant.[55] This might have been raised as a problem in relationship to James Sayre, who was selected for the jury of six. Lodowick Post's wife, Elizabeth, was a Sayre.[56] One would have thought that this would have disqualified her relation, James Sayre, from the jury venire and as a serving juror in the case. Apparently, however, Sayre was "not challenged" by Pierson and was "approved" by Fordham "as indifferent [. . .] to try the said cause."[57] This oversight may again have been a feature of the informal nature of Justice of the Peace proceedings. However, it was also a symptom of how close-knit early nineteenth century localities were. Pierson's lawyer did not raise the matter on appeal.

The twelve men summoned for the venire were: Thomas Beebe, Theophilus Cook, Charles Douglas, William R. Halsey, John F. Havens, Silas Havens, Isaac Jessup, John Norris, Zacheus Payne, Stephen Satterly, James Sayre, and Abraham Topping.[58] Five of these men were, like

[52] Ibid., p. 6. [53] S. 12, *Twenty-Five Dollar Act*.

[54] Judgment Roll, pp. 6–7, Appendix B. [55] Ibid., p. 5, Appendix B.

[56] See Adams, *Memorials of Old Bridgehampton*, 334 (listing Lodowick Post, 1777–1842, and his wife, Elizabeth Sayre, 1775–1831, along with their children, all buried in the Poxabogue Cemetery).

[57] Judgment Roll, p. 6, Appendix B.

[58] Listed names in alphabetical order and in some cases changed name spelling from what appears on p. 11 of the Judgment Roll in Appendix B. See also Appendix C, where each is listed in a chart with the property that they were taxed on for years that were available

Fordham, from Sag Harbor (Beebe, Douglas, John F. Havens, Silas Havens, and Satterly). The other seven were from Bridgehampton (Cook, Halsey, Jessup, Norris, Payne, Sayre, and Topping). This initial list reflected more of a tilt toward Bridgehampton than Sag Harbor by 7:5. However, of these twelve, the following six were chosen by ballot – that is, by chance: Douglas, John F. Havens, Silas Havens, Payne, Satterly, and Sayre. The jury was therefore ultimately more of a Sag Harbor jury (four members) than a Bridgehampton jury (two).

As noted above, the average amount of real and personal property for the eleven of the twelve potential jurors in 1803 was $1,209.[59] This average, while higher than Fordham's $875 in 1801, was much lower than both David Pierson's total of $2,460 and Nathan and Lodowick's $2,900 in the same year.[60] The potential juror with the largest amount of property was Theophilus Cook at $3,000 in house and land and $1,000 in personal property for a total of $4,000. He was wealthier than anyone else involved in the case, including the litigants, but he did not make it onto the jury of six. The lowest property-owning juror was Zacheus Payne at $160 of real property and no personal property. Of the other jurors, Thomas Beebe was closest to Cook at a total of $2,600; then came Abraham Topping at $1,200, James Sayre at $1,170, and William R. Halsey at $1,050. Six of the eleven (and seven of twelve if we count John F. Havens, who is not listed for 1803, but who is in 1801) had total property taxed at less than $1,000. They are, in order from most to least, John F. Havens, $900 in 1801, Isaac Jessup at $820, Silas Havens at $650, Charles Douglas at $600, Stephen Satterly at $550, and John Norris at $496. Jonathan Havens was the only member of the group who owned a slave, at least in 1790.[61]

Of the over $1,000 group, only one, James Sayre, Post's wife's relative, made it on to the jury of six chosen from this panel of twelve. The two richest potential jurors, Cook and Beebe, did not. Thomas Beebe was the person most likely to identify with Post, hailing also from Sag Harbor with a similar property owning profile. Indeed, Beebe was the only person in

from local tax records. The chart also puts the names of the six that were chosen for the jury in bold and underlined.

59 Calculation based on the numbers in the chart at Appendix C.

60 Tax Assessment Roll, 1801.

61 See *First Census of the United States Taken in the Year 1790*, 167–68. Two prospective jurors were not included in this census, Zacheus Payne and Charles Douglas. All the rest with the exception of Jonathan Havens are listed with no slaves in their households in 1790.

the venire from Sag Harbor in the over $1,000 group. The other four from Sag Harbor, all of whom did make it on the jury (John F. Havens, Silas Havens, Charles Douglas, Stephen Satterly), were all in the under $1,000 group. This probably goes some way toward explaining why, even though the jury was a predominantly Sag Harbor jury, it did not issue a verdict that was a ringing endorsement for Post. The jury was willing to give Post something for the fox, namely, an amount that approximated its bounty price or a token amount for the slight, 75¢. But as men of modest means they were probably unlikely to identify with English-style foxhunting or to grant significant damages for an affront done to the dignity of a wealthy man in pursuit of his sport. If the jury members chosen had been different, the result might have been different. Post may have garnered a higher award from wealthier men who could understand and relate to the insult he was done. Post by his own declaration was suing for the insult or the malice, as the 75¢ for the fox itself was hardly worth his trouble, especially when one sees that the costs involved in the jury trial amounted to $5. Indeed, the aggregate "feas" paid to the six jurors for their service totaled 75¢.[62]

All twelve of the jurors – with the exception of Charles Douglas – seemed to be upwardly mobile in having more property in 1818 than they did in 1801 or 1802.[63] By 1818, for example, Theophilus Cook had $6,600 and Thomas Beebe had really pulled ahead with $9,400. Zacheus Payne who was at the bottom of the group in 1803 had a very respectable $2,400 by 1818. Everyone who is listed (and there are three who are not – Silas Havens, Isaac Jessup, and Stephen Satterly) with the exception of Douglas had over $1,000, with the average total for these eight coming in around $4,200. The one juror we know was not moving up economically was, Charles Douglas, a "pump and blockmaker."[64] This was "a precision woodcarver" who crafted the block and tackle used to raise heavy cargo or sails, as well as the pumps used to keep water from building up below board on sailing

[62] See Judgment Roll, p. 10, Appendix B. The *Twenty-Five Dollar Act* set out the charge of each juror's fee at 12.5¢, to make a total charged here of 75¢ for six jurors. See s. 21, *Twenty-Five Dollar Act.*

[63] Although note that three are not on the 1818 list (Silas Havens, Issac Jessup, and Stephen Satterly). Silas Havens and Stephen Satterly are not on the list for 1806 either. Jessup had probably died by the time the assessment was made – his will was made on April 16, 1817 and probated on June 30, 1818 (*Abstract of Wills Recorded at Riverhead, Suffolk County N.Y., 1787–1842*, compiled by Elizabeth R. Van Buren, Liber D., p. 44. Suffolk County Historical Society, Riverhead, NY).

[64] Zaykowski, *Sag Harbor*, 348, 351.

ships.[65] Douglas was a neighbor of Captain John N. Fordham's in Sag Harbor in 1809.[66] He was chosen to be a town fence viewer from 1809 to 1812.[67] In 1818 he was taxed on $350 worth of real property.[68] He ended up on the final jury of six.

Cook, the most affluent of everyone at the time of the case, owned cattle – his earmarks from 1787 are included in town records c. 1787.[69] He was left a place called Yellow Spring in a will in 1775, purchased a homestead for his son, Silas Cook, and bought a place called Calf Neck for £1,237 in 1811.[70] Cattle were an important marker (and maker) of wealth, especially for Bridgehampton farmers, part of what would help them to be gentlemen rather than subsistence farmers.[71] Cook was elected to be an overseer of highways in 1806, a fence viewer in 1810, and one of the town trustees in 1812 and 1815.[72] James Sayre, who was among the jurors chosen and the only one with a combined property value of over $1,000 in 1803, was also from Bridgehampton and owned cattle.[73] He was repeatedly chosen to be a fence viewer by the town and twice held the position of overseer of the highway.[74] Abraham Topping, who was not among the chosen six but was another person in the jury pool with over $1,000 in property in 1803, was also very active in town government. He took turns as a fence viewer, overseer of the highway, town trustee, and overseer of the poor.[75] Indeed, in his work as Commissioner of Highways, he adjusted the line running past the Beebe and John N. Fordham properties in Sag Harbor in 1818.[76]

[65] See " James Brewer: Pump and Blockmaker," *Boston, 1775: History, Analysis and Unabashed Gossip about the Start of the American Revolution in Massachusetts* (July 14, 2007), available at http://boston1775.blogspot.com/2007/07/james-brewer-pump-and-blockmaker.html.

[66] *Town Records*, vol. 3: 355. [67] *Town Records*, vol. 4: 2, 4, 5, 8.

[68] See Tax Assessment Roll, 1818. [69] *Town Records*, vol. 3: 318.

[70] *Town Records*, vol. 6: 271, 223–24, 243.

[71] See Ann Sandford, *Grandfather Lived Here: The Transformation of Bridgehampton, New York, 1870–1970* (Sagaponack, NY: Poxabogue Publishing, 2006), 160–63 (on the cattle drives to Montauk and the earmarks).

[72] *Town Records*, vol. 3: 375; vol. 4: 4, 7, 24.

[73] *Town Records*, vol. 3: 324 (abstract of a 1788 earmark bought from Jeremiah Blower).

[74] *Town Records*, vol. 3: 351, 356, 358, 361, 371 (fence viewer in 1797, 1799, 1800, 1802, 1805), 341, 381 (overseer of the highway in the 6th district in 1794 and 5th to 6th in 1807).

[75] *Town Records*, vol. 3: 371; vol. 4: p. 2 (fence viewer in 1805 and 1810); vol. 3: 375 (overseer of the highway in the 5th district in 1806); vol. 4: 4, 30 (Commissioner of Highways in 1809 and 1817); vol. 3: 384; vol. 4: 5, 11, 23 (town trustee in 1808, 1811, 1813, 1815); vol. 4: 3, 32 (overseer of the poor in 1810, 1818).

[76] *Town Records*, vol. 4: 42–43.

As a group, the freeholders chosen to be in the venire were respectable property owners, generally upwardly mobile, and active in town governance. This last is especially noteworthy as economic power increases, although it is present across the property-owning levels recorded here. It is also noteworthy that unlike Post, Fordham, and many of the Piersons most of these individuals tended not to be slave-owners – at least not in 1790.[77]

All of the jury-related proceedings – summoning the panel of twelve, choosing the six jurors, swearing them in, hearing the evidence from the parties and witnesses – took place on the same day, December 30, 1802, "at the house of Hugh Gelston Jr" where Fordham made his court.[78] There are a number of things to notice here. First, lay justice was quick. Less than a month elapsed between the incident (December 10, 1802) and the determination of the case (December 30, 1802). Second, it happened at a relatively low cost – $5, approximately $118 in 2017 dollars.[79] Third, there seemed to be a certain amount of acceptable deviation from the strict requirements of the *Twenty-Five Dollar Act*, as evidenced by Fordham's handling of the tallying of the costs in the case and by the uncontested presence on the jury of James Sayre, a relative of Post's. Fourth, the Justice of the Peace proceedings were not conducted in a courthouse. Indeed, the "Court" of a Justice of the Peace in nineteenth-century New York was an informal place.

The painting in Figure 3.1 is from a later period – 1850 – but it gives a sense of the informality of the proceedings in a magistrate's court that would probably also have been present fifty years earlier. We see the Justice of the Peace, riding boots off, feet up, dog at his side, listening attentively along with a group of others – who might well be jurors – to the arguments of the parties. That could be a lawyer "friend" of one of the parties pointing to a helpful passage in a book, while a man in a top hat sits dispassionately awaiting his turn to speak. The location seems to be an inn or tavern, where many justices held their courts.

Hugh Gelston Jr. was the son of a Court of Common Pleas judge, Hugh Gelston, whose house was on the main street in Southampton village.[80] A genealogy of the Gelston family includes the following note in its entry on Hugh Gelston: the "village stock and whipping post stood on the

[77] With the exception of Jonathan Havens. See above.

[78] See Judgment Roll, pp. 3, 6, 8, 9, Appendix B.

[79] See Purchasing Power Calculator at www.measuringworth.com/uscompare/ using the Consumer Price Index from 1802–2017.

[80] At one point in the Judgment Roll the house is referred to by Fordham as Hugh Gelston's, without the addition of the "Jr." See Judgment Roll, p. 3, Appendix B.

FIGURE 3.2 Replica of a Pillory at the Southampton Historical Society, located on the Northeast corner of South Main Street and Job's Lane, Southampton, NY. Photograph by the author (2009).

North East corner of Main St., & Job's Lane. Judge Gelston's home was on the south corner. Persons punished for minor offences were said to be brought up to Gelston's fence."[81] Punished persons waited against the fence for their punishment to be meted out across the street. See Figure 3.2.[82]

Judge Gelston's house on the south corner of Main Street and Job's Lane is included on a historical map prepared by the late nineteenth-century local historian, William S. Pelletreau (see Figure 3.3). We can see on this map that the southwest corner of Main Street and Job's Lane lists Hugh Gelston and Hugh Gelston Jr. amongst its owners. Hugh Gelston Jr. is listed in this chain of title in 1775. His father, the judge, died late that year and left him the house.[83] Hugh Gelston Jr. is listed as having

[81] "Notes on the Southampton Gelston Family," Long Island Collection, the East Hampton Library, East Hampton, NY (13 pp.).

[82] Adams notes that the stocks and whipping post were abolished in 1811. See *Memorials of Old Bridgehampton*, 108.

[83] See William Smith Pelletreau, vol. 8 (1771–1776), *Abstracts of Wills on file in the Surrogates Office, City of New York* (New York Historical Society, 1900), 329 (available at www.archive.org/details/abstractswills006kellgoog). The information on the location

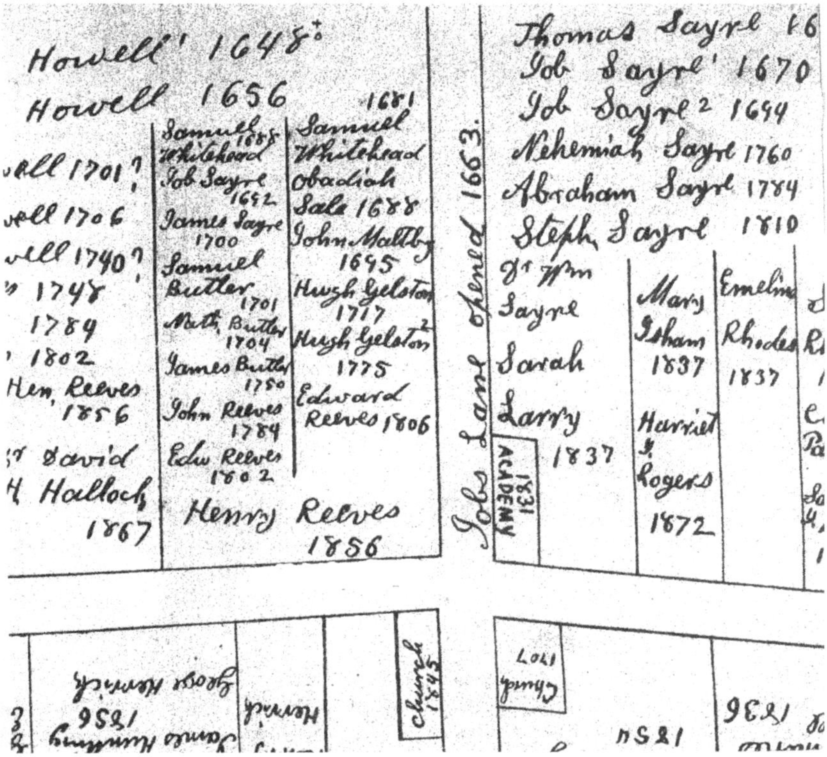

FIGURE 3.3 Panel from "Plan of Main Street of Southampton, L.I. showing owners of lots from laying out in 1648 till the present time" by William S. Pelletreau (1878). Southampton Historical Museum, Southampton, NY.

real property, "house and land," worth $1,150 in 1801 and $1,200 in 1802.[84] These figures would likely have included the value of the house his father left him. This in all likelihood was "the house of Hugh Gelston Jr." where the jury trial took place. It might have also been a tavern at that time, as Hugh Gelston Jr. was listed among those who took out licenses to retail liquor throughout Southampton town.[85]

of Judge Gelston's house, including the detail relating to prisoners waiting at his fence, in the handwritten genealogy in the Long Island Collection at the East Hampton Library is taken from this entry. See pp. 330–31.

84 Tax Assessment Rolls, 1801 and 1803.

85 See Sleight, *Sag Harbor in Earlier Days*, 17.

Hugh Gelston's household listed one slave in 1790 and one wonders if he or she was there on the day of the trial.[86] Gelston seemed to increase the number of slaves he owned. He registered the birth of a slave child named Charles who was born in 1801 and would have been a toddler at the time of the trial.[87] Gelston manumitted a slave named Judith, perhaps this child's mother, on May 19, 1803.[88] He also manumitted two slaves named Simeon and Caroline Prince many years later on November 8, 1814, not long before he died.[89]

As noted above, John N. Fordham also kept a tavern in Sag Harbor.[90] This appears to have been another violation of the statute as the *Twenty-Five Dollar Act* clearly stated that "no justice of the peace being an inn or tavernkeeper [...] shall try any cause by virtue of this act."[91] This provision appeared in the earlier *Ten Pound Act*, which in 1795 expressly gave magistrates the power to try violations under *An act to lay a duty of excise on strong liquors, and for the better regulating of inns and taverns.*[92]

In his study on New York Justices of the Peace in the colonial era, historian Sung Yup Kim explains that when the jurisdiction of the lay magistrates was expanded in the colonial period from £2 to £5 under the *Five Pound Act*, elite lawyers raised concerns about the fact that magistrates were trying cases in "private houses, dram shops, and obscure corners," where they mingled with the people and proceedings could easily degenerate into "disorderly conventions" lacking the appropriate "solemnity" and "awe."[93] The prohibition in later versions of the statute would prevent magistrates from benefiting economically by conducting legal proceedings in their own taverns (profiting from the feeding and drinking that would occur by attendants) and the *Ten Pound Act* would prevent them from presiding over cases involving the economic interests of competitors (would this person be fined or have their license revoked). Yet there was nonetheless a clear prohibition here even if the justice was not holding the proceedings at his own house.[94]

[86] See *First Census of the United States Taken in the Year 1790*, 167.
[87] See *Town Records*, vol. 3: 374. [88] See ibid., 365. [89] See *Town Records*, vol. 4: 21.
[90] Hedges, "Early Sag Harbor" in *Tracing the Past*, 202.
[91] S. 20, *Twenty-Five Dollar Act.*
[92] See s. 21, *Ten Pound* Act and p. 18 for the amendment.
[93] Sung Yup Kim, "Justices of the Peace, Lawyers, and the People: Local Courts and the Contested Professionalization of Law in Late Colonial New York" (Ph.D. diss., Stony Brook University, 2016), 403.
[94] See ibid., 119–20 (explaining that the change from a prohibition on a tavern-keeping Justice holding proceedings "at his own house" to an outright prohibition on tavern

We should be aware that the elite lawyers who raised concerns about the location for courts of Justices of the Peace, the same ones who criticized lay magistrates for being unlearned and illiterate, had their own reasons for painting the proceedings in taverns as unruly and inappropriate venues. While the humble backgrounds of most magistrates and scenes of local-lawmaking probably did genuinely offend elite sensibilities, the lawyers were also motivated in their opposition to the expansion of the jurisdiction of lay magistrates by the desire to prevent cases from being siphoned away from the New York courts in which they regularly practiced (the Supreme Court of Judicature, the inferior County Courts, the Mayor's Court in New York City and Albany, the Court of Chancery, and the Court of Vice Admiralty). Opponents stressed the educative impact of that shift, given the way that those courts served as an important training ground for young men studying to be lawyers. As one of the most vocal opponents of the statute, William Smith Sr., put it, the act would "discourage the study of the law, and all improvement in science."[95] However, it was not all about education and legal science. The professionalization that elite lawyers wanted so badly and that was so threatened by statutes like the *Five Pound Act* had practical and economic motivations intimately tied to professional self-interest.

As Kim explains in his study, the small claims system was one that worked very well for many people in New York and it was extremely popular with small farmers, tenants, artisans, and laborers, even if there were legitimate problems with issues like political appointments and complaints against justices for various infractions. Its popularity explains why the legislature kept renewing the *Five Pound Act* and expanding its jurisdiction. The higher courts, where lawyers were required in order to navigate the increased formality and complex procedure, were generally better for creditors and wealthy landowners who could afford to hire those lawyers. The lay courts favored debtors and less wealthy litigants who usually appeared without a lawyer. Hence, the rhetoric about the unseemliness of taverns must be taken with a grain of salt.

Other legal historians like William Novak have pointed out that licensed inn and tavern-keepers "were treated as virtual public

keepers trying any cases under the act happened between the 1758 and 1772 versions of the *Five Pound Act*).

[95] Ibid., 405.

officials."[96] "Inns and taverns were," Novak emphasizes, "*public* houses with special duties and high standards of decorum and orderliness."[97] So, yes, Hugh Gelston Jr. had a license to sell liquor, which he might have been doing out of his father's house, perhaps even operating it as a tavern. However, that tavern function would not be inconsistent with its *public* function as a local court house. Indeed, we have seen that "the house of Hugh Gelston Jr" had an established history of operating as a court under his father's tenure as a judge of the Court of Common Pleas under the civil side of the inferior County Court. Given that people who were to be punished at the village stock and whipping post waited against the fence of Gleston's house for their turn to be punished across the street, it would be fair to connect the house also to the criminal side of the inferior County Court's General Sessions of the Peace. It was, in other words, a *public* house that was also a house of the law, the local law of the County Court.

According to the Pelletreau map (Figure 3.3), Hugh Gelston Jr. sold his property on the southwest corner of Main Street and Job's Lane to Edward Reeves in 1806. Edward Reeves bought the property immediately to the south in 1802 and both lots went to Henry Reeves in 1856. There is currently a house one lot south of the corner on 21 South Main Street, known locally as "the Reeve House." This house was described in a building-structure inventory form as "the Reeves House/McCarthey House" and built sometime prior to 1858.[98] The form also records that the house was moved between 1904 and 1915 south of the corner.[99] Albert Reeves owned the house at the time of the move, which atlas maps indicate happened sometime between 1902 and 1916.[100]

96 William J. Novak, *The People's Welfare: Law and Regulation in Nineteenth-Century America* (Chapel Hill: University of North Carolina Press, 1996), 92.

97 Ibid., 173 (emphasis in the original).

98 "Reeves House/McCarthey House," Building-Structure Inventory Form, June 29, 1979 (MA 63 green/yellow). Located by Mary Cummings, Manager/Archives Southampton Historical Museum at the Southampton Historical Society.

99 One spot on the form says that the building was moved from the northwest corner of Job's Lane and South Main Street when the Tower Gallery Building was built c. 1925. This appears to be a typo, as the Tower Gallery Building is currently on the southwest corner of these streets. Elsewhere on the form it is noted that the house was moved *south* from the corner of Job's Lane and South Main Street. Two other Building-Structure Inventory Forms (JL 1A green and JL 4 green) from the same 1977 Historic District Study confirm that the Albert Reeves house was on the southwest corner. The first of these is the form for the Tower Gallery Building. Located by Mary Cummings with copies sent to the author November 2, 2009.

100 "The 1902 map shows a building (2 ½ story, 2 story and 1 story) on the SW corner of Jobs La and So. Main St. (land of Albert Reeves), the building then appears (1916 atlas)

FIGURE 3.4 The Reeve House at 21 South Main Street, Southampton, NY. Photograph by the author (2009).

Two photographs located by Mary Cummings of the Southampton Historical Society allow us to establish the time of the move as sometime in 1915. The first very old and faded (undated) photograph shows a house that looks a lot like the current Reeve house on the south part of the corner lot – it has the three dormer windows, a middle chimney, and five windows across the front, as the current house does. The main difference from the current house is what looks to be a quite elaborate front porch. That same house can be seen in the second photograph at the corner. This photograph is dated January 21, 1915.[101] In other words, the house must have been moved south from the corner after that date (January 21, 1915) but in time to appear on the 1916 atlas map, so sometime in 1915. What about the porch? The building inventory form records "Italianate detail added, 1870; porch removed." It does not say when the porch was

to have been moved south but remains on the same property of Albert Reeves. So this very well could be the 'Reeve House.' It actually resembles (stories) the current building at 21 So. Main St. However, on the atlas there are other buildings shown on the property." E-mail to the author from title searcher, Tammy Sweda, Fidelity National Title Insurance Co., Riverhead, NY (October 9, 2009).

101 Both photographs located and copies provided to the author by Mary Cummings on October 24, 2009.

removed. It seems to have been sometime after 1915, as the porch is still visible in the January 21, 1915 photograph.

The rather unusual shape of the entire building on the 1916 and 1902 atlases (when the property belonged to Albert Reeves) is reproduced in an 1873 atlas map naming the owner as Henry Reeves.[102] Henry Reeves ran a boarding house in the building that could accommodate fifty persons, according to a brochure published by the Long Island Railway in 1877.[103] It seems very possible that this was the house Hugh Gelston Jr. inherited from his father, sold to Edward Reeves, descended to Henry and then was moved south by Albert in 1915. It would certainly have been large enough to have operated as a courthouse/tavern (i.e. a "public house") and to have accommodated all of the persons involved in Post's case (at least seventeen people – two parties, six jurors, one magistrate, one constable, and seven witnesses).

Hugh Gelston Jr. did not live all his life and die in the house that his father left him on the corner of Job's Lane and South Main Street. He was among the many refugees who fled to Connecticut during the Revolutionary War when the British occupied Long Island, and he served as a Quarter Master during the War.[104] He married his second wife, Mary, daughter of Hachaliah and Mary (Culver) Foster, in 1773, before the War began. Their first child, the future Reverend Maltby Gelston, was born in 1791 in Sherman, Connecticut, and Hugh Gelston Jr. eventually died there in 1815.[105] However, when Mary died in April 1803, she was buried in the North End Cemetery in Southampton.[106] Hugh is described as having been a farmer at Southampton and he appears to have been there

[102] *Atlas of Suffolk County Long Island, vol. 1 Ocean Shore* (Brooklyn, NY: E. Belcher Hyde, 1902); *Atlas of the Ocean Shore of Suffolk County, L.I. (Easterly Section) Eastport to Montauk Point* (Brooklyn; Manhattan: E. Belcher Hyde, 1916). Copies of both maps provided by Tammy Sweda, Fidelity National Title Insurance Co. 1873 Atlas Map, copy provided by Mary Cummings, Southampton Historical Society.

[103] Noted in the "Reeves House/McCarthey House," Building-Structure Inventory Form.

[104] See *New York in the Revolution as Colony and State, vol. 1, A Compilation of Documents and Records from the Office of the State Comptroller* (Albany, NY: J.B. Lyon, 1904), 47. There was another Hugh Gelston who served in the Revolutionary War. He was a resident of Sag Harbor (died 1828) and should not be confused with the son of Hugh Gelston, the Court of Common Pleas judge in Southampton.

[105] See "Notes on the Southampton Gelston Family."

[106] "*Old Southampton-End Burying Ground; Old North-End Burying Ground; Burying Ground at North Seas; Part of Southampton where the First Settler's Landed in 1640*" (D.A.R. Southampton Colony Chapter, Southampton, NY, 1940), located at the Southampton Historical Society. I was unable to find this gravestone in the North End Cemetery.

both before and after the time of the case, namely, in December 1802. He was a witness to the will Nathan Post made in 1798 and then "personally appeared" before the Surrogate's Court in 1804 when the will was probated to swear that he saw Nathan Post sign it.[107] He appears in the town records registering the birth of a slave's child, Charles, in 1801 and occupying positions in town government in 1805.[108] He must have returned to Connecticut sometime after 1805, following a pattern of migration not uncommon among the refugees, many of whom did this, living in their later years with a child who stayed or returned to Connecticut. In fact, the sale of Hugh's father's house to Edward Reeves in 1806 might well have coincided with this final departure from home for Hugh Gelston Jr. He sold other land he inherited from his father to Edward Reeves that same year and the amount of real property he was taxed on decreased by a third from just a few years before.[109]

We now have a much clearer picture of what happened before the Justice of Peace in Post's case. We know that Lodowick Post chose a trial by jury and we have learned something of how the jury trial was conducted and the role played by the Constable. We have important economic and social information about the jurors, the Justice of the Peace, and the man in whose house the trial was held, Hugh Gelston Jr. We see a lot of slaveholding, not just by the families of Post and Pierson but also Justice of the Peace Fordham and Gelston. This may come as something of a surprise given the fact that the trial took place after the Revolution and in the North rather than the South.

In his book, *Freedom Bound*, Christopher Tomlins warns against the popular conception that freedom begins with the American Revolution. Slavery, the quintessential form of non-freedom, was extremely important in the post-Revolutionary period, North as well as South. For example, in 1788, New York "prepared itself for the coming of the new republic by adopting a new revised comprehensive slave law that guaranteed slavery's maintenance and perpetuation" and 10,000 blacks remained enslaved

107 Liber B, p. 272, Surrogate's Court, County Center, Riverhead, NY.

108 *Town Records*, vol. 3: 374, 371 (fence viewer and assessor in 1805).

109 See *Town Records*, vol. 6: 269. The editorial note on this page of the town records says that Gelston died in Sharon, Connecticut, in 1815. This likely is a mistake for Sherman. Gelston was much more likely to have gone to Sherman as it is in Fairfield County close to Long Island Sound. Sharon, on the other hand, is far inland in Litchfield County. The 1806 tax assessment roll has the real property at $1,000, decreased by $500, when it was $1,500 in 1803. See Tax Assessment Rolls, 1803 and 1806.

there in 1820.[110] In the country as a whole, 89% of blacks were enslaved in 1800, the same percentage that were enslaved in 1860.[111] Tomlins argues that "[t]hose who celebrate the American Revolution and its aftermath as the beginning of slavery's end do history no favors."[112]

We would certainly expect to encounter slaveholding in the South, given the region's plantation system. We might also expect to encounter slaves performing domestic labor in wealthy households in New York City, or industrial work on its dockyards and in its warehouses given the city's manifold connections to the Southern cotton trade, especially after the War of 1812.[113] But slavery in the New York countryside in 1802? This is the surprise that genealogists looking at small towns in the Northern United States have stumbled upon time and again – a surprise in that American history, popular and academic, persistently links freedom with the Revolution and associates movement north with increased freedom. As one genealogist strikingly puts it, "[f]or me, the idea of slavery in New England was like imagining Scarlett O'Hara aboard the *Mayflower*."[114] The association of the North with freedom is misleading – even in a Canadian context, where, as one historian writes, it must be recognized that:

> slavery was practised in a solid third of what is now Canada – in Upper Canada (Ontario), New France (Québec), New Brunswick, Prince Edward Island, and Nova Scotia; that it numbered thousands of slaves (with the greatest number in New France), held "legally" under various colonial regimes and traded globally; that it lasted for more than two hundred years; and that it ended only because it was not vital to the boreal economy.[115]

110 Tomlins, *Freedom Bound*, 505.

111 Ibid., 506.

112 Ibid., 504. See also 65 ("If one were to identify a transformational moment [it would not be the Revolution] it would necessarily be the massive and decisive turn to African slavery that began in the later seventeenth century and continued for nearly two centuries").

113 See Ira Berlin and Leslie M. Harris, "Introduction" to *New York Slavery* (New York: The New Press, 2005), 3–27, 22 (describing how New York City became the primary port for the shipment of raw cotton to European textile mills, its businessmen who helped planter's obtain "negro cloth" used to make slave clothes, obtain whips and slave tools, and its financiers who bankrolled the cotton economy by lending money to buy slaves and selling insurance to protect those investments).

114 Grant Hayter-Menzies, "Slavery and Freedom in a Colonial Connecticut Town," 13:3 *American Ancestors: New England, New York, and Beyond* (2012): 26–28, 26.

115 George Elliott Clarke, "Foreword" to Afua Cooper, *The Hanging of Angélique: The Untold Story of Canadian Slavery and the Burning of Old Montreal* (Toronto: Harper Collins, 2006), xvi. It is interesting to compare Angélique's arson with the alleged fire-burning slave conspiracies described in Jill Lepore, *New York Burning:*

Emphasis on the "boreal economy" here is important: it helps us understand that the issue was economic rather than moral. The point extends to the northeastern United States, where similar economic factors kept slavery from becoming as widespread and important as it was in the South. The traditional employments of small-scale farming and fishing in New England did not produce enough extra income to support widespread slave-owning. Families relied heavily on the labor of their own children.[116] There was no plantation system – Northerners were not growing staple crops like cotton or sugar cane given the climate.

Slavery was extensive in rural New York, however, in places like the Hudson Valley and Long Island. These were areas that opposed the manumission statute passed in 1799. Slaves were part of the economy, for both farming and domestic labor. Of the 582 households listed in the 1790 census in Southampton Town, for example, 56 listed slaves as members (almost 10%) and 28 of these consisted of 2 or more slaves per household (almost 5%).[117] Many were owned by members of the Pierson clan.[118] There were five slaves in the household of Jesse Pierson's grandfather, David Pierson Sr. in 1790.[119] They were presumably engaged in the agricultural work of the Pierson family.[120] Lodowick's Post's father

Liberty, Slavery and Conspiracy in Eighteenth-Century Manhattan (New York: Alfred A. Knopf, 2005).

116 See Daniel Vickers, *Farmers and Fishermen: Two Centuries of Work in Essex County, Massachusetts, 1630–1850* (Chapel Hill: Published for the Institute of Early American History and Culture, by the University of North Carolina Press, 1994).

117 Numbers based on *First Census of the United States Taken in the Year 1790*, 166–68. The total number of slaves in Southampton Town, according to this census, was 140. The population in 1800 of the smaller area of Bridgehampton (including Sagaponack but excluding Sag Harbor) was likely 1,257 people, including 52 free African Americans and 42 slaves. Sandford, "Rural Connections," 6.

118 The family name is variously spelled (e.g. Peirson, Parson, Parsons, Person, Persons, Pearson). On the different spellings, see Mather, *The Refugees of 1776*, 504. In the 1790 census, Matthew Pearson owned four slaves; another Mathew Pearson and Nathan Pearson two slaves each, Timothy Pearson, Samuel Pearson, Lemeual Pearson, and Zebulon Pearsons one slave each. See *First Census of the United States Taken in the Year 1790*, 167. The Piersons in next door Easthampton also owned slaves. See *First Census of the United States Taken in the Year 1790*, 162. There were also many Piersons in both Southampton Town and Easthampton who did not own slaves.

119 See *First Census of the United States Taken in the Year 1790*, 167. Jesse's father, Captain David Pierson, was the son of a David Peirson Senior. See Mather, *The Refugees of 1776*, 505. The 1790 Census list contains a David Pearson Senior (with the five slaves) and a David Pearson Junior with none.

120 For a sense of what slave housing in the countryside looked like, see John Michael Vlack, "Slave Housing in New York's Countryside" in *Slavery in New York* (New York: New Press, 2005), 72–73 (describing the "outer kitchens" or cabins in which slaves were

too, owned one slave, the smaller-scale style of slave-owning, which signaled that this work was not farm work but domestic labor.[121] H. P. Hedges later wrote disapprovingly of Nathan Post that in addition to having fancy wainscoting in his house, there was a slave whipping post in the kitchen, "a solitary and unused monument of the barbarity of a servitude and an age forever banished."[122] Hedges contrasted Post's wealth, generated from Sag Harbor-based trade with the West Indies, a compromised trade that including legal slave trading until 1808, with the Calvinist demeanor of the Sagaponack farming Piersons. Hedges was writing in 1895, long after the Civil War, and he expressed the Northern sentiment on slavery one would expect to see. His strictures, however, were not very fair, given that the Piersons, Calvinist though they may have been, were also slave-owners. (In his defense we may allow this is something Hedges would not necessarily have known.)

The 1799 manumission statute affected the status of children born to existing New York slaves. Those already enslaved at the time of the act's passage were not freed, and their children would remain in bondage well into their adulthood: until the age of twenty-eight for men and twenty-five for women. It was possible to negotiate the terms of an earlier emancipation, but this was fraught with risk: masters might renege; they might keep all sums paid if the total amount was not tendered on time, or if rules about decorum and respectful behavior owed by the slave to the former master often included in the contracts were breached. New Yorkers would also resell their slaves in the South in order to avoid the law, and there was a lot of kidnapping of freed slaves. In 1817, the New York legislature set a date for the end of slavery in the state, namely, July 4, 1827, which would coincide with the date of freedom for those enslaved in 1799. But now anyone born before the eve of July 4, 1827, could be "apprenticed" until the age of 21, meaning people might still be effectively enslaved as late at 1848.[123] This is not a legacy of freedom and emancipation. It is

housed and for a photo of one that looks like a tool shed). See Berlin and Harris, "Introduction," 4 (emphasizing that slavery in the New York countryside "often meant isolation in white households and labor on white-owned farms" and while there were free black communities in rural New York, they had little access to resources, land, and power and continued to live in households separate from their immediate family members).

121 See *First Census of the United States Taken in the Year 1790*, 167.

122 Hedges, "Pierson vs. Post," *Sag-Harbor Express* (1895).

123 See Patrick Rael, "The Long Death of Slavery" in *Slavery in New York* (New York: The New Press, 2005), 111–46, 133. The first census to list no slaves was in 1840. See 144.

a careful negotiation of the interest Northern slave owners had in their slaves, pushing slaves to buy their freedom (rather than flee) and maximizing the labor extracted in their best years, as well as control over behavior. Slavery in New York was very slowly being extinguished. But it evolved into new forms of restraint rather than definitively dying out as an institution. Future U.S. President Martin Van Buren built his political career on assuring Southerners of New York's reliability on the slavery issue, leading the movement to disenfranchise black men at the 1821 state constitutional convention by instituting a property requirement that few if any could meet.[124]

By unpacking *Pierson* at the local level we have gained instructive and eye-opening access to Northern post-Revolutionary slaveholding, a practice in which the families of both litigants, Pierson and Post, were engaged, as well as many of the other people involved in the case. Examination of the case at the local level has also allowed us to demonstrate that justice in a magistrate's court was dispensed in a private "public house" that was operating as a court and perhaps also a tavern, and that it is best described as a process oriented toward dispute resolution, concerned not with fine points of law but with quick settlement of a local dispute according to community standards of justice and with the goal of restoration of the community's *peace*, as Laura Edwards would phrase it.[125]

The local legal process that we have encountered was fast, relatively cheap, and informal. All of these features stand in sharp contrast to the case at the appellate level, which was slow, expensive, and extremely formal, and focused on a highly abstract question of law: Who acquired first possession of animals *ferae naturae*? This leads us to ask, what was the role of those most interested in this legal question – the lawyers – both at the first-level instance and on appeal? It is to this question that we now turn, the lawyers and the role they played in the case.

[124] Berlin and Harris, "Introduction" to *Slavery in New York*, 22.

[125] See Laura F. Edwards, *The People and Their Peace: Legal Culture and the Transformation of Inequality in the Post-Revolutionary South* (Chapel Hill: University of North Carolina Press, 2009).

4

Lawyerization

As Queequeg and I are now fairly embarked in this business of whaling; and as this business of whaling has somehow come to be regarded among landsmen as a rather unpoetical and disreputable pursuit; therefore, I am all anxiety to convince ye, ye landsmen, of the injustice hereby done to us hunters of whales. In the first place, it may be deemed almost superfluous to establish the fact, that among people at large, the business of whaling is not accounted on a level with what are called the liberal professions.

Herman Melville, *Moby-Dick, or the Whale* (1851), from "The Advocate"[1]

I made the claim in Chapter 1 that *Pierson* v. *Post* was a thoroughly legal affair from start to finish. Post turned to the law in order to redress the wrong he felt himself to have received by taking his case to a jury trial in Fordham's lay magistrate's court. Pierson responded to his $5.75 loss in that court by appealing to the New York Supreme Court. The writ of *certiorari* was the mechanism lawyers like Pierson's lawyer, Nathan Sanford, learned could be used to demand the supervision and correction of local or lay justice at the state court level. "Local justices had to be on their guard with [...] lawyers, for they could be reprimanded for high-handed behavior [...] and a writ of *certiorari* could remove proceedings from a county decision to a higher court."[2] Indeed, Sanford seemed to be among the group of lawyers firmly leading the way in opening up this market for legal services, which exploded in the years after *Pierson*.

[1] Quote from p. 118.

[2] A. G. Roeber, *Faithful Magistrates and Republican Lawyers: Creators of Virginian Legal Culture, 1680–1810* (Chapel Hill: University of North Carolina Press, 1981), 18.

As Laura Edwards has emphasized, the early nineteenth century was generally a time when local or customary law in America was being replaced by state-level actors, seeking to professionalize the law, its lawyers, and its judges.[3] Among the tools of professionalization were the turn to writing and publishing reports of judicial decisions at the state-court level, and the attempt to elevate the level of judges, by encouraging them to adopt a more scholarly and scientific demeanor and become less outwardly political in their orientation. Certainty, science, and principle became touchstones for what the law should aspire to become, signaling the way that a professionalized legal system would replace local or lay justice.[4]

In the case of a writ of *certiorari*, the Justice of the Peace would produce an account of what he had done in the case, and if all the "i"s were not dotted and "t"s were not crossed the verdict would be set aside. It was less an appeal on the substance of the plaintiff's case than a means to have the Justice of the Peace's handling of the procedure subjected to minute examination. This happened in England also where it was noted that: "[The Justice of the Peace] finds himself surrounded with numbers of pettifogging attorneys and solicitors, who watch his steps, and if there happens the least flaw in the method of drawing up and managing the proceedings, he finds himself obliged to attend a *certiorari* in the King's Bench."[5] As we saw in the previous chapter, Sanford challenged a variety of procedural points he alleged were violated by Justice of the Peace Fordham.

As it happened, the *Twenty-Five Dollar* contained a provision that expressly stated that reversals were not to be made for minor issues. This did not mean that procedural issues were considered minor per se. Certainly, however, some of those that Sanford raised were trifling

[3] See Edwards, *The People and Their Peace.*

[4] See ibid., where Edwards describes the Whiggish language of teleology used to describe such "modernization" of a legal system. Organic metaphors such as "grow" and "evolve" are often used to describe this process, making it sound not just inevitable but an uncontroversial improvement. Such an understanding ignores the way in which the purveyors of the improvements, state-level lawyers and judges, benefited by placing themselves at the center of the new professionalized system.
See also Roeber, *Faithful Magistrates*, who described the way that eighteenth-century Virginia contained a similar conflict between gentry/planter justices and lawyers, where the lawyers wanted more formal procedure, precedent, and proper form, and professionalized judges drawn from the ranks of the lawyers embracing the idea that law was a precise scientific enterprise.

[5] Quoted in Roeber ibid., 18.

(for example, that the venire did not state the purpose for which the twelve freeholders were summoned; that the summons did not require service by a particular constable).[6] S. 19 of the *Twenty-Five Dollar Act* stated that "the supreme court shall proceed and give judgment according as the very right of the case shall appear, without regarding any imperfection, omission or defect in the proceedings, before the court below, in mere matters of form."[7] Hence, so long as deviation could be characterized as a "mere matter of form," the Supreme Court was not supposed to intervene and reverse. The legislature was making it clear that what that court should be attending to was "the very right of the case." Hence, the New York Supreme Court's preference for the third exception and its question about Post's claim being sufficient in law.

Yet the appeal process shifted the balance of power in cases coming out of the lay magistrates' courts. As we will see, *certiorari* reversals were granted more often than they were refused. They also often left an original plaintiff like Post in a terrible position in relationship to costs, with cost awards routinely exceeding money damages at issue by many times after long delay. Lawyers of course were a, if not the, primary source of delay and expense. Hence a key question in a case-in-context study of *Pierson* is how and when lawyers became involved in the case.

Pierson and Post both appeared "in their proper person" in John N. Fordham's court on December 30, 1802.[8] To appear by "proper person" meant *not* to appear by way of attorney. When I first wrote about this, I said that appearance by way of attorney in a magistrate's court was not permitted at this time, and if it happened, even by consent of the parties, it constituted reversible error.[9] Dan Ernst correctly pointed out that the 1801 version of the *Twenty-Five Dollar Act* under which *Pierson* was tried was silent on the question.[10] An earlier version of the statute, the *Ten Pound Act* (passed in 1787 and added to in 1795) explicitly precluded lawyers from prosecuting, defending, pleading, or giving counsel in any suit or action tried under the statute unless they swore before the magistrate that they had

[6] We saw also in the previous chapter that Sanford did not but might have raised objections to at least three other irregularities or violations of the *Twenty-Five Dollar Act* – Fordham overcharging on costs allowed for by the statute, Post being related to one of the jury members, and if Fordham was an inn or tavern keeper, he was not supposed to try the case.

[7] S. 19, *Twenty-Five Dollar Act*.

[8] Judgment Roll, p. 4, Appendix B.

[9] See Fernandez, "The Lost Record," 165. In making this claim, I relied on *Smith* v. *Goodrich*, 5 Johns. 353 (N.Y. Sup. Ct, 1810) and the identification of that case in Brown, *The Justice's Directory*, 11. See 165 n. 72.

[10] Ernst, "*Pierson* v. *Post*: The New Learning," 34 n. 6.

received no fee or reward for doing so.[11] The purpose was to prevent "sundry persons [who] make a practice of pleading in courts held by a justice, and because of the emoluments therefrom arising, are induced to promote suits."[12] The failure to carry over this provision from the earlier version of the statute to the new one in 1801 suggests it was not in force at the time of the *Pierson* trial in late 1802. In which case, lawyers were permitted in the *Pierson* trial. However, if used, we know that they did not accompany their clients to court.

When the *Five Pound Act* was first passed in 1754 and the Justice of the Peace jurisdiction was raised from £2 to £5, leading colony lawyer, William Smith Sr., who sat on the legislative council of the colony of New York and chaired the council's committee for considering the bill, made sure lawyers were not excluded from these augmented lay magistrates' courts by adding to the draft of the bill that a litigant "or his attorney" could appear before the magistrate with his expanded jurisdiction.[13] However, Sung Yup Kim, who narrates this legal history, has found that lawyers seldom appeared and, when they did, they may have done so under a "power of attorney" given to a family member or friend of one of the litigants rather than as a licensed lawyer being paid as a professional.[14]

It is unclear how often lawyers or these more informal "attorneys" were appearing with litigants in our period. What is clear is that the issue of the presence of lawyers in magistrate lay courts became a very politically charged issue, involving, as it had under the *Five Pound Act*, a push and pull between popular sentiment (reflected in the legislature's desire to limit the lawyers' sphere of influence) and elite lawyers (wanting to push forward the project of legal professionalization). Clearly unable to kick the lay magistrates back down, the quest became, as William Smith Sr. had perceived in the earliest days of the *Five Pound Act*, to make sure lawyers were not barred from participation in the Justice of the Peace courts and then, as we will see, in the nineteenth century, to make a new and robust

[11] See s. 23, *Ten Pound Act* ("no person [...] shall be permitted by any justice to prosecute, defend, plead or counsel, in any suit or action to be tried in virtue of this act, unless such person so offering or appearing to prosecute, defend, plead, or give counsel [...] shall previously swear, before such justice, that he has not received or taken any fee or reward for the same, either directly or indirectly").

[12] S. 23, *Ten Pound Act.*

[13] See Kim, "Justices of the Peace, Lawyers, and the People," 400.

[14] See Sung Yup Kim, "'In a Summary Way, with Expedition and at a Small Expence': Justices of the Peace and Small Debt Litigation in Late Colonial New York," 57 *American Journal of Legal History* (2017): 83–117, 105 n. 84.

business of appealing from those decisions to the Supreme Court of Judicature on writs of *certiorari*.

There always was, as we have seen, a healthy dose of self-interest involved on the part of the lawyers who opposed the lay magistrate courts in New York. However, there was probably also a genuine belief on their part that a stable legal and political order was only possible if the trend toward legal professionalization continued. Lawyers were expressly excluded under the *Ten Pound Act* in 1787 and 1795 (at least for a fee), as we have seen, and given the silence in the 1801 *Twenty-Five Dollar Act* on the issue, they were presumably allowed to appear and to be paid for doing so. There was a restatement of the exclusion on lawyering (paid or unpaid) in the 1808 *Twenty-Five Dollar Act* and a further repeal on the ban in 1810.[15] These back-and-forth changes in the legislation over this twenty-or-so-year time span show that the issue of an overly legalized or lawyerized lay magistrate court was a contentious issue in the early American period.

Written pleadings were not required in a magistrate's court.[16] But they were not prohibited, which means they might be used. And, indeed, we know that they were used in *Pierson*. Livingston wrote that "*[b]y the pleadings* it is admitted, that the fox is a 'wild and noxious beast.'"[17] Calling the fox a "wild and noxious beast" is a quote from somewhere, specifically, from the pleadings. Fordham also referred to the fox in the exact same way and one assumes that he too was basing this upon the pleadings.[18] Pleadings would suggest the involvement of a lawyer, at least in Post's case. Charles Donahue thinks that the Judgment Roll "quite dramatically" confirms that Post's complaint was professionally made. Why? "Because even in 1802 only a lawyer could have produced the

[15] See s. 25, *New Ten Pound Act. An Act for the more Speedy Recovery of Debts, to the Value of Twenty-Five Dollars, passed April 11, 1808* (Albany, NY: Websters and Skinner, 1808) [hereafter *Twenty-Five Dollar Act (1808)*] ("it shall not be lawful for any justice in any cause to be tried at any court held before him, to admit or permit, any person to appear and advocate in the said court, in any cause to be tried before such justice, for any party in any manner whatever" except in the case of illness or absence from the county). See Ernst, "*Pierson* v. *Post*: The New Learning," 34 n. 6 (pointing out the repeal and thanking Fred Turner for spotting it). See *An Act for the payment of certain officers of government and for other purposes*, 193 *New York Laws* (April 5, 1810), 97, 100 ("Be it further enacted, That the twenty-fifth section of the act, entitled 'an act for the more speedy recovery of debts to the value of twenty-five dollars,' passed April 11, 1808, be and the same is hereby repealed").

[16] Esek Cowen, *A Treatise on the Civil Jurisdiction of a Justice of the Peace, in the State of New York* (Albany, NY: W. M. Gould 1821), 320.

[17] *Pierson*, 180. [18] See Judgment Roll, p. 4, Appendix B.

following piece of English prose: 'did upon a certain wild and uninhabited[,] possessed and waste land, called the beach, find and start one of those noxious beasts called a fox.'"[19] The reporter George Caines stated that he took the words from the declaration.[20] This would seem to confirm that there were pleadings and these words came from Post, as the declaration is the first part of the plaintiff's pleadings.[21] Donahue writes that Post's complaint "has all the hallmarks of a document carefully drafted by a lawyer who was firmly on Post's side."[22] Post's lawyer on appeal was Cadwallader David Colden.[23] We will see that Colden was Suffolk County's prosecutor for a number of years and it would make sense for him to be operating as Post's lawyer, pressing his case at its earliest stage. It is difficult for us now to know and I have not been able to confirm the point either way.

Pierson's lawyer on appeal, Nathan Sanford, was, like Colden, "a fancy New York City lawyer."[24] He had ties to the area even stronger than Colden's. Sanford, in fact, was related to his client, Jesse Pierson. The Piersons and the Sanfords (often spelled "Sandford") were connected through Nathan's father, whose paternal grandmother was a Pierson, as was his sister-in-law.[25] Nathan's father, Thomas Sandford, died in 1787 when Nathan was just ten years old.[26] Thomas was a Justice of the Peace and a man of standing and importance in the community, whose wealth probably came from whaling and cattle.[27] Thomas was elderly when he married Nathan's mother, Phebe (Baker) Howell. After he died, Phebe married David Hedges in 1791.[28] And David Hedges played an important role in paving Nathan's trajectory in state politics.

[19] See Donahue, "Papyrology," 181. [20] *Pierson*, 175.

[21] *Black's Law Dictionary*, 6th ed. (St. Paul, MN: West Publishing, 1990), s.v. "declaration."

[22] Donahue, "Papyrology," 181.

[23] See Judgment Roll, p. 14, Appendix B (naming Colden).

[24] Donahue, "Papyrology," 182.

[25] The father of Nathan's father, Thomas Sandford, married Sarah Pierson in 1709. She was the daughter of Colonel Henry Pierson. Also, Thomas's older brother, Zachariah, married Mary Pierson, sister of Sarah. Email to the author from Ann Sandford, September 1, 2009. Sandford writes in her biography of Nathan Sanford it was later said that as "[a] man on the go" Sanford "dropped the first 'd' in his surname in order to save time." See Ann Sandford, *Reluctant Reformer: Nathan Sanford in the Era of the Early Republic* (Albany, NY: State University of New York Press, 2018), 18.

[26] See Grover Merle Sanford, *The Sandford/Sanford Families of Long Island: Their Ancestors and Descendants* (Baltimore, MD: Gateway Press, 1975), 19.

[27] Phone conversation with Ann Sandford, August 25, 2009.

[28] Sandford, "Rural Wealth and American Property Law," 6–7.

David Hedges, Nathan Sanford's stepfather, was the head of a large extended family in Sagaponack, where the Piersons were also established, on land north of the beach where the fox is thought to have been chased and caught. Hedges used his land for dairy farming and cheese production.[29] He was also a slave-owner, one of many among the Long Island residents connected to *Pierson*, as we saw in the previous chapter. He had four slaves in 1790, whose labor was used to ditch Saag Swamp in order to build a new mill in 1793.[30] Hedges registered a number of "negro slave children" born in 1801, 1803, and 1805 (Jehu, Violet, and Kingston).[31] Hedges was an upstanding member of the community, a deacon of the Presbyterian Church in Bridgehampton and a prominent local politician, serving as Southampton Town Supervisor and as the representative for Suffolk County in the State Assembly.[32] He had already been a powerful politician when Phebe married him in 1791. He represented Suffolk County in the State legislature from 1786 to 1789 and participated in the vote in which New York decided to adopt the United States Constitution in 1788.[33] Phebe died in 1796.[34] Nathan was said to have been "carefully reared by his mother's relatives" and attended the prestigious Clinton Academy in East Hampton before entering Yale College in 1793.[35]

Clinton Academy was chartered in 1786 and named after then New York Governor George Clinton (the powerful uncle to Dewitt Clinton), who secured its charter (the first in the state) and donated its bell (still hanging in its belfry).[36] The school had three streams, the Classical Department, the English Academical Department, and the Common School.[37] Nathan Sanford was enrolled there by his mother

[29] Ibid. [30] See Sandford, *Reluctant Reformer*, 8. [31] See *Town Records*, vol. 3: 374.

[32] Sandford, "Rural Wealth and American Property Law," 7.

[33] Sandford, *Reluctant Reformer*, 8.

[34] Merle Sanford, *The Sandford/Sanford Families*, 19.

[35] Ibid., 27. Berger wrote citing to a conversation with Ann Sandford that Nathan Sanford "was the child of uneducated parents, but with the encouragement of the Piersons was able to attend the prestigious Hayground Academy." "It's not about the Fox," 1134. Hayground Academy seems to be a mistake for Clinton Academy. I have not been able to substantiate the point about being encouraged by the Piersons. Sanford was related to the Piersons on his father's side, not his mother's side. And it seems a bit off to say that his parents were uneducated, especially given his United States Constitution-ratifying stepfather. Between the substantial property his father Thomas left him and a stepfather like Hedges, Nathan was certainly of a privileged background.

[36] See www.easthampton.com/history/clinton.html.

[37] Tuition depended on which stream a student belonged to, 30 shillings per quarter for the Classical ("a regular classical education" plus other subjects such as geography,

when he was twelve years old in 1789.[38] Hedges was one of its largest financial contributors.[39] We do not know which of the three streams Sanford was in. However, one local historian wrote that "[h]e must have had an unusual mind and some unusual teachers [at Clinton Academy] who recognized it, for he quickly developed a taste for the best in literature and for problems of the mind."[40] He came to be known as "a finished scholar, as familiar with the French language as with his own, and in later life he made himself master of both Spanish and Italian. The Latin poets were his delight, and he solaced his leisure with their richness and beauty."[41] Sanford entered Yale College in the fall of 1793 at the age of sixteen.[42] After his mother Phebe died in 1796, he moved to New York City to study law with a lawyer named Samuel Jones.[43] In 1798, he attended the Litchfield Law School.[44]

Upon being called to the bar in 1799, Sanford was admitted as an attorney in the New York Supreme Court and the Court of Common Pleas of New York City, otherwise known as the Mayor's Court.[45] He was made a counselor of the latter court in early 1801 and a solicitor of the Court of Chancery in 1802.[46] Despite his attendance at Litchfield, a Federalist stronghold, Sanford became firmly identified with the Republican side of New York and national politics. James Kent wrote that Sanford "suddenly abandoned the federal [party] & joined the

navigation, and mathematics), 20 shillings a quarter for the English Academical ("a Miscellaneous Education" of reading, writing, arithmetic, English grammar, rhetoric, composition, "sentimental and epistolary," and French), and for the Common School it was 9 shillings, six pence per quarter for those who only read and 12 shillings per quarter for anyone else. See *Rules and Regulations for the Government of Clinton Academy in East-Hampton* (Sag Harbor, NY: David Frothingham, 1794), copy provided to the author by Rosanne Barons, Registrar, East Hampton Historical Society, East Hampton, NY.

[38] Sandford, *Reluctant Reformer*, 11. [39] Ibid., 12. [40] Clowes, *Wayfarings*, 120.

[41] Ibid., 121.

[42] Sandford, *Reluctant Reformer*, 12. It is possible his mother's death cut his studies at Yale short, as one source says Sanford did not graduate from Yale College. Halsey, *Sketches from Local History*, 184.

[43] Halsey, *Sketches from Local History*, 184. [44] Sandford, *Reluctant Reformer*, 17.

[45] Sanford's diplomas are in a set of his papers at the New York State Library in Albany. See "Certificate of admittance as Attorney at Law, January 25, 1799" and "Certificate of admittance as Attorney at Law, February 26, 1799," Nathan Sanford Papers SC14054, Folder 1. The first was his admittance to the New York Supreme Court and the second was to "the Court of Common Pleas called the Mayor's Court."

[46] "Certificate of admittance as a Counsellor at Law, February 4, 1801" and "Certificate of admittance as a Solicitor of the Court of Chancery, March 15, 1802," Nathan Sanford Papers SC14054, Folder 1, New York State Library, Albany, NY.

democratic Party, & became an admirer of Jefferson & corresponded with him."[47] Sanford's early attendance at a school whose patron was George Clinton signaled that his association with Republicanism went back to his youth and was connected to his hometown.[48] Certainly his association with Jefferson led to some excellent political appointments early on in his career, including a position as a Commissioner of Bankruptcy in 1800.[49] The best of these came in 1803, for an appointment as United States District Attorney for Southern New York, a position he held for twelve years that was reputed to bring him a lot of money – reported by some at $10,000 annually in fees, by others at $30,000 and even as high as $100,000.[50]

1803 was the year France and Great Britain went to war, a conflict in which the United States adopted a neutral position as between the two great European powers, but its ships were being seized by both sides claiming aid was being provided to their enemy. In an attempt to maintain the American right to trade as a neutral, Jefferson passed the Embargo Act in 1807, which resulted in many prosecutions of American merchantmen who violated the prohibition on trade with either belligerent.[51] Kent wrote that Sanford made a fortune in this office "by his multiplied & Vexatious Prosecutions during the Embargo times [1807–1809]. His Charges were enormous & he had the Control of the Confidence

[47] Donald M. Roper, "The Elite of the New York Bar as Seen from the Bench: James Kent's Necrologies," 56 *New York Historical Society Quarterly* (1972): 199–237, 230.

[48] Ann Sandford writes that Sanford's republican "views were consistent with those in his family and held by other men in his hometown. Sanford's republicanism was principled and grounded in his youth." See Sandford, *Reluctant Reformer*, 15.

[49] "Appointment as a Commissioner of Bankruptcy, District of New York," no date, signed by James Madison, Jefferson's Secretary of State. Nathan Sanford Papers SC14054, Folder 1, New York State Library, Albany, NY. Halsey gives the date of this appointment as 1800, the year Jefferson was elected. See Halsey, *Sketches from Local History*, 184.

[50] Edward Conrad Smith, "Nathan Sanford," *Dictionary of American Biography* (providing the $10,000 figure); Evan Cornog, *Birth of Empire: Dewitt Clinton and the American Experience, 1769–1828* (New York: Oxford University Press, 1998), 199 n. 19 (providing the $30,000 figure); Allan Nevins ed., vol. 2, *The Diary of Philip Hone, 1823–1851* (New York: Doss, Mead, 1927), 525–26 (providing the $100,000 figure). See Sandford, *Reluctant Reformer*, 56–57 (reviewing these figures). The discrepancies have to do with the differences between base salary for the position, fees for different actions taken when prosecuting a case, and the custom of the federal attorney receiving a percentage of the payments made to the court for the cases he won. See Sandford, *Reluctant Reformer*, 26–27.

[51] See Gordon S. Wood, *Empire of Liberty: A History of the American Republic, 1789–1815* (New York: Oxford University Press, 2009), 622–46.

of M.B. Tallmadge the district Judge. I remember that John Wells expressed the utmost abhorrence of the oppressive administration of Justice under Sanford & Tallmadge."[52]

In late 1802 when the scuffle over the fox took place, then, Sanford was a busy and up-and-coming lawyer, not yet as wealthy and super-eminent as he would later come to be as a United States District Attorney and then later still, like his stepfather, as a member of the State Legislature, State Senate, and United States Senate, but marked for success. Sanford skillfully navigated the transition from ally of Dewitt Clinton, to Martin Van Buren's "Bucktails," to the Tammany faction of the New York Republican party. Sanford would eventually replace James Kent as the Chancellor of New York State, a point that helps further explain Kent's animosity toward him.[53] In early 1803, when he filed the appeal for Jesse Pierson, Sanford had not yet received the United States District Attorney position, which came in the fall of that year.[54] By 1805, the time of the appeal in *Pierson*, Sanford was already a very important lawyer-politician and wealthy.

Although Sanford maintained a busy practice in both Albany and New York City, he continued to own the family house in Bridgehampton, where he was born and which had been left to him by his father Thomas.[55] He was taxed locally on "house and land" worth $2,000 in 1801 and $2,800 in 1803.[56] Hence, he continued to maintain family and financial

[52] Roper, "The Elite of the New York Bar as Seen from the Bench," 230.

[53] Kent said of Sanford: "He was always in my view a hard, avaricious heartless Demagogue [...] He removed to Albany after having buried two wives & was hated for his Character and Conduct [...] He spent his last years in building a most extravagantly expensive but inconvenient House." "He was a member of the Convention in 1821 & succeeded me as Chancellor." Roper, "The Elite of the New York Bar as Seen from the Bench," 230.

[54] See Sandford, *Reluctant Reformer*, 25 (quoting from the appointment letter, dated November 18, 1803).

[55] Sanford's house was located at the corner or Woolsey Lane and Scuttle Hole Road. It was destroyed a long time ago. See Appendix in Halsey, *Sketches from Local History* (marked on the map as "Hon. Nathan Sanford"); Ernest S. Clowes, *Wayfarings: A Collection Chosen from Pieces Which Appeared Under That Title in the Bridgehampton News, 1941–1953* (Bridgehampton, NY, 1941), 120 (writing that the "Old Sanford House" burned to the ground about two weeks ago). Scuttle Hole is in a village known as Mecox, southwest of Sag Harbor and north of Sagaponack.

[56] There is no entry for personal property, as presumably, living elsewhere, Sanford was taxed on this elsewhere. Sanford is also listed in 1806 as being taxed (in conjunction with someone named Silas White) on "house and land" worth $2,800. The tax assessment roll for 1818 lists his value of Sanford's house and land at $6,200. Tax Assessment Rolls, 1801, 1803, 1806, 1818.

interests in the area. Indeed, as late as 1821, when Sanford participated in the adoption of the new state constitution, he identified his occupation or profession not as a law or politics but as "Agriculture."[57] Others did this, including the large Federalist landowner Stephen Van Rensselaer, likely a rhetorical move to reject the role of full-time politician that was not yet an accepted one or to avoid the unpopular designation of lawyer. It is significant, nonetheless, that we see Sanford aligned with the Pierson family's agricultural identification despite the absence of day-to-day farming from his life and his modest agricultural land and farm rental income. This was nonetheless the agriculture of Sagaponack, the land of his influential stepfather (see "Hedges's Lane" in Figures 1.2 and 5.4).[58]

Then-Vice President of the United States Daniel Tompkins, the judge who sided with Sanford's argument in *Pierson*, presided over the Convention to adopt a new state constitution and appointed Sanford as Chairman to the Committee on the Suffrage, which was looking at whether the right to vote should be expanded or restricted and how (that is, whether military service, or labor on the roads, could stand in for a property qualification).[59] This was obviously an important issue and it is noteworthy that this was the Convention that effectively disenfranchised black men in the state. Sanford himself owned no slaves, although he did employ two free African Americans in his house in New York City in 1810 and one free African American in 1820.[60]

It is unlikely but possible that Pierson consulted Sanford prior to the jury trial on December 30, 1802. Sanford's record book shows a gap between December 10 and December 22.[61] He may have been working in New York City and not taking on new Mayor's Court clients or he may have been away, either in Albany or Bridgehampton. It is possible that he was home in Bridgehampton. Pierson would not have known he was being sued for certain until he was orally notified on December 22, by which time Sanford, if he was in Bridgehampton, would have been well on his

[57] Sandford, *Reluctant Reformer*, 94.

[58] Sandford writes that Sanford would easily "self-identify as a farmer, given the values he grew up with and the higher social status that he understood was conveyed by land ownership." Ibid.

[59] See ibid., 87–107.

[60] See ibid., 19.

[61] See "Registry of Court Cases 1799–1812," Sanford Family Paper SC23075, New York State Library, Albany, NY [hereinafter Mayor's Court Registry], 72 (in *Gelston* v. *Cornwall*, "9 December 1802 Gave notice of being retained to Bogert [attorney for the plaintiff – Sanford was retained by the defendant the day before on December 8]"), 73, 74, 75 (Sanford was retained by the plaintiffs in *Smith* v. *Davidson, Smith* v. *Harris*, and *Smith* v. *Pheonix* on December 23, 1802).

way back to New York City – he would have had to leave on December 19th given the three-day travel time to be back in New York City on December 22.[62] There is a further gap, in the Mayor's Court record book, from December 29 to January 10. However, even if Sanford was in Bridgehampton during that period, he could not have arrived in time to be consulted in person before the trial, which began at 2:00 p.m. on December 30. Could the consultation have happened by mail? The timing is very tight. Even if Pierson had written as soon as he was served on December 22, the letter would not have arrived until December 25. A return letter could have reached Pierson at the earliest on December 28, only two days before trial. Although there may have some back and forth between the two men about the incident, it seems most likely that Sanford got formally involved once the jury trial had been concluded. What we know for certain is that either a meeting or an exchange of correspondence occurred sometime before January 29, 1803 when Sanford was granted the writ of *certiorari* by then-Chief Justice of the New York Supreme Court, Morgan Lewis.[63]

Had Sanford visited the area in December/January of that year, or been in contact with his friends and family there over the holidays, he might well have heard about the scuffle. Recall that the jury trial before the Justice of the Peace involved seven witnesses.[64] We do not know who these people were or what role they played. At least some of them might have been the "companions" mentioned in one account of who was hunting with Post.[65] However, such a high number of witnesses shows that many people got involved in the case and many more would have had knowledge of it.

The picture in Figure 4.1 is obviously from a later date. However, it gives a sense of the way in which the capture of a fox could become a notorious event in Southampton. It helps us understand why Post wanted a jury trial, a public vindication of his claim before a jury of his peers, even if it was more expensive than a trial by magistrate alone and he probably would have been given a larger amount by Fordham than 75¢.[66] If the showdown on December 10 had anything like this level of interest, one can easily see how it might have come to Sanford's attention.

[62] Travel and post between New York City and Eastern Long Island would take three days by stage coach. See Adams, *Memorials of Old Bridgehampton*, 164.

[63] See Judgment Roll, p. 2, Appendix B. [64] Ibid., p. 10.

[65] Hedges, "Pierson vs. Post," *Sag-Harbor Express* (1895).

[66] See discussion of *Sharpe* v. *Sabin* in Chapter 5.

FIGURE 4.1 Fox on South Main Street, Southampton Village (c. 1900). Courtesy Town of Southampton, Office of the Clerk, Historic Division. Permission to reproduce granted by the Morris Studio, Southampton, NY.

We saw in Chapter 1 that Nathan and Lodowick Post had more property than David Pierson and that there may have been some declining gentry animus or motivation on Jesse Pierson's part when he insulted Post by interfering with his hunt, along with the urge to protect Pierson agricultural interests. We have also seen how the basic view of the fox was probably informed by clashing customs or worldviews, agrarian farming versus urban mercantile-shipping, Connecticut versus New York. Pierson's defensiveness and perhaps even aggressiveness, while not particularly admirable, would make sense as a matter of geography and human psychology as a member of the family whose properties were contiguous with the beach where the fox was said to have been caught and Post and his friends were hunting. It was unambiguously better for the Piersons to discourage sporting-style foxhunting next to their lands, given the likelihood of damage to their fields and fences, and to kill any fox on sight as a predator on their barnyards rather than engage in a sporting chase in which the animal might well get away. We saw that encouraging such chases would actually lead to an increase in the fox population.

While the Posts might have been materially better off than David Pierson at the time of the case, the Piersons were much more populous than the Posts were, specifically in that area of Sagaponack (see image at

Figure 1.2).[67] Nathan Post had two brothers, both of whom lived in Southampton, the town where Hugh Gelston Jr.'s house was and the trial took place, quite a bit further west from Bridgehampton and Sagaponack (see map at Figure 1.3). This meant that Lodowick Post lacked the dense kinship network that the Piersons clearly possessed, a network that, fortunately for Jesse Pierson, included an extremely competent lawyer, Nathan Sanford. As local historian, and descendant, Ann Sandford, has written, "Sanford probably took the appeal case as a favor to his cousin."[68] That form of social or cultural capital turned out to be worth its weight in gold. Post's lawyer, Cadwallader David Colden, was certainly competent, but we have seen that he did not object to Sanford's use of Justinian's *Institutes* or produce the Pothier text – moves that might have resulted in a win in what looked to be a game run on the principle he-who-brings-forward-the-best-authority wins.

Colden was a more senior lawyer than Sanford, having been called to the bar in 1791. He received a classical education before studying law, including private tutoring at his family estate near Flushing, Long Island (where Sanford later built an extravagant house) and one year of study in London, England, where he attended an Inn of Court.[69] From 1798 to 1801, Colden was an Assistant District Attorney for the First District of the City of New York, which included Suffolk County. He was not in that position in 1802 or 1805, but he must have maintained ties, as he was made its District Attorney again from 1810 to 1811.[70] Colden was not personally connected to Sagaponack, where the squabble took place, in the same way as Nathan Sanford, who had grown up there and maintained connections in the wider area that included property ownership and business interests. And he was not tied to Sag Harbor, as Post and the Justice of the Piece Fordham were. But Colden had only very recently given up the role of prosecuting cases from Suffolk County and would do so again. Colden was politically connected but his connections were to New York City: he would become mayor of New York City in 1818. Like Sanford, later in life, he held important political positions such as acting as

[67] There are many Piersons in neighboring areas also. East Hampton and Southampton Town, to name just two that stand out in the 1790 census.

[68] Ann Sandford, "Rural Wealth and American Property Law," 21.

[69] Cadwallader David Colden's father was a scholar and his grandfather was lieutenant governor and often acting governor of the province before the Revolution. See Paul David Nelson, "Colden, Cadwallader David" *American National Biography Online.*

[70] See https://en.wikipedia.org/wiki/Cadwallader_D._Colden.

a Congressman and a member of the New York State Assembly and the State Senate.

It is important to know that the message of *Pierson* v. *Post* for local Long Island was the foolhardiness of going to the law. Local lawyer, judge, and historian, Henry P. Hedges, wrote a newspaper article about the case in 1895 in which he reported that the case cost each side one thousand pounds.[71] We now know that was an exaggeration, although it is true that the amount of costs awarded, $126.37, probably did not include the lawyers' fees, which might well have been considerable. Even $126.37 was no small amount in 1805. And indeed, there is evidence that the judgment award and other costs associated with the case brought financial hardship to Lodowick Post.

As we have seen, Lodowick's father was a magistrate and probably played a role in encouraging his son to sue. The decision to appeal from the magistrate's court to the New York Supreme Court was Jesse Pierson's. At that stage, Lodowick Post actually had no choice but to defend his jury award. He was at a disadvantage in doing so given what we will see was close supervision of Justice of the Peace proceedings by the state Superior Court and high rates of reversal on *certiorari*. Also, by the time of the appeal, Lodowick had lost his father, who died on October 3, 1803.[72] So if Nathan was behind sending Lodowick to the law in the first place, he was no longer there to provide both economic and moral support.

There is evidence that in the wake of his father's death, Lodowick came down in the world. For instance, in 1805, the year judgment was rendered against him, Lodowick was listed in the town records as serving in what we have seen was the unpopular and fairly low-paid role of Constable.[73] He was listed (now alone on the tax roll) in 1806, taxed on $1,900 of real property, a substantial decrease from the listing for himself and his father at $2,900 in 1801 or the $2,800 in 1803.[74] By 1818, Lodowick's real property

[71] Hedges, "Pierson vs. Post," *Sag-Harbor Express* (1895) ("It was said the costs amounted to a thousand pounds each side; at that day an enormous sum and justifying the facetious epigram of one of my name and kin, 'Law is costive'").

[72] See gravestone record in Adams, *Memorials of Old Bridgehampton*, 334.

[73] *Town Records*, vol. 3: 371.

[74] Tax Assessment Roll, 1806, 1801, 1803. Nathan Post's will in 1798 includes bequests to his wife Mehetabel (bed and bedding, a cow, a horse and riding chair) and daughter Bethia (a cow) and legacies to son Nathan (£500) and daughter Peggy (£100). However, he revoked the legacy to Nathan in 1804, as Nathan Jr. died. The residue of the estate went to Lodowick, real and personal minus debts and legacies. See *Abstract of Wills Recorded at Riverhead, Suffolk County N.Y., 1787–1842*, Liber B, p. 64 and a copy of the will (giving dollar amounts

was listed as worth $1,200.[75] In 1817 he traded the house his father had left him, a house noted for its extravagance (decorated walls, wainscoted rooms, and finishings in a "superior style"[76]), for what was probably a more modest house owned by none other than a member of the Pierson family![77] It was located right in the heart of Pierson lands (see Figure 1.2, Hedges's Lane east of Sagg Street). One source identified the house trade as part of the settlement of the debt caused by the lawsuit, a claim I have been unable to substantiate.[78] It is worth noting that a tax assessment role from 1805 listing Lodowick, now on his own, listed no personal property and $1,900 of real property, suggesting that this was the amount of his inheritance (the real property value of the fancy house, which stayed the same in 1806).[79] It would have been extremely difficult for Lodowick to come up with $126.37 in cash to give to the Piersons in 1805 for two reasons. First, his sister Peggy was owed a £100 legacy from their father's estate.[80] And, secondly, early nineteenth-century Bridgehampton was generally not a cash-flush world, as suggested by the large number of people listed on the tax assessment rolls with low or no amounts of personal property, including the Posts.[81] In fact much of the economy was barter-based.[82]

and details of bequests) located in Liber B, p. 272, Surrogate's Court, County Center, Riverhead, NY.

75 Tax Assessment Roll, 1818.

76 Hedges, "Pierson vs. Post," *Sag-Harbor Express* (1895).

77 The trade was with John Pierson for the homestead in Sagaponack that had belonged to John Pierson's grandfather, Abraham Pierson. See Adams, *Memorials of Old Bridgehampton*, 219, 222. See also John E. Heartt ed., *The Story of a Celebration: Bridgehampton, Long Island, 1660–1910* (Long Island, NY: Hampton Publishing Co., 1910), 119. The original Post house is still standing on the main road, Montauk Highway, and is known locally as the Sayre house. See Geoffrey K. Fleming, *Images of America: Bridgehampton* (Charleston, SC: Arcadia Publishing, 2003), 54 for a photograph of the house c. 1880 then known as "Sayrelands."

78 See A. James Casner and W. Barton Leach, *Cases and Text on Property*, 2nd ed. (Boston, MA: Little, Brown, 1969), 15 ("Each party to the litigation spent more than £1000 on the case which required the family of one litigant to sell his home to the family of the other to get out of debt"). Casner and Leach state that a photocopy of the deed had been deposited at the Harvard Law School Library. It can no longer be located. Email to the author from Mary Person, Rare Books Cataloger, Historical and Special Collections, Harvard Law School Library, June 9, 2011. Nor can the deed be located at the Suffolk County Archives. Email to the author from Sharon A. Pullen, C.A., Archivist, Office of the County Clerk, Historic Documents Office, Riverhead, NY, June 13, 2011.

79 See Halsey, *Sketches from Local History*, 139 ("An Old Assessment Roll for the Year 1805").

80 Will of Nathan Post, Liber B, p. 272, Surrogate's Court, County Center, Riverhead, NY.

81 See e.g. Halsey, *Sketches from Local History*, 138–40. Even when Lodowick's father was alive and the two were listed as "Nathan & Son" in the tax assessments rolls from 1801 and 1803, there was no personal property listed.

82 See Ann H. Sandford, "Rural Connections: Early Republic Bridgehampton and Its Wider World, 1790–1805," 15 *Long Island Historical Journal* (2002/2003): 1–22, 6.

Indeed, there would seem to be something fundamentally unfair about asking a plaintiff who brought a claim under the *Twenty-Five Dollar Act* to pay costs so lacking in proportion to the upper limit that he could ever have been awarded under the act. After all, the act capped a defendant's costs at $5.[83] In Post's case, the $126.37 in costs awarded against him was 168 times his original money damages of 75¢, and five times the maximum amount he could have been awarded. The point of the *Twenty-Five Dollar Act* (like its predecessor the *Ten Pound Act*) was to create a small claims court for "the advancement of speedy justice and the saving of costs and trouble."[84] It was the writ of *certiorari*, appealing cases from the local level, asking the New York Supreme Court to review what the lay judge and jury decided, that had turned what would originally have seemed a quick low-cost way to obtain redress into a lengthy and potentially risky endeavor for a plaintiff. In the Supreme Court reversal rates were high and often had less to do with the merits of the case than whether a crafty lawyer on appeal like Nathan Sanford could find some error in the way that the Justice of the Peace had directed the case.

Consider another *certiorari* case that was decided by the New York Supreme Court in 1805. John Thompson used the *Twenty-Five Dollar Act* to bring a claim for the return of a 56¢ debt for liquor against Gerald Hendenbergh Junior. Hendenbergh's lawyer objected to fact that "Junior" had been left off Hendenbergh's name in the warrant that had been issued for his arrest and the jury summons. This objection was overruled by the Justice of the Peace, who simply added "Junior" to Hendenbergh's name on both documents. The jury was then called and approved of by both parties. They returned a verdict of 48¢ for Thompson and Hendenbergh was ordered to pay $5 in costs. Hendenbergh appealed to the New York Supreme Court, which reversed the decision ten months later. Thompson was forced to pay $36.78 in costs. This was an unreported case, presumably because it did not decide any important general legal or scientific principle.[85] Yet, it is important for our purposes because it shows just how dysfunctional the small claims process had become. What seemed by all the evidence to be a legitimate debt (albeit one that a jury found had to be read slightly down) ended up costing the original plaintiff over sixty-five times what he was claiming and over seventy-five times what a jury thought he was entitled to. The Judgment Roll does not

[83] See s. 21, *Twenty-Five Dollar Act*. [84] Amendments to the *Ten Pound Act*, p. 20.

[85] See *Hendenbergh* v. *Thompson*, Law Judgment #1805 T-44, Division of Old Records, New York County Clerk's Office, New York City, NY.

specify which error was the ground of reversal. If it was the misstep over the name, given that the documents had been amended, it seems a rather draconian consequence, the very definition of escaping on a technicality.

The New York Supreme Court did not decide many cases on *certiorari* in 1805. I could only find seven in the nearly nine hundred final judgments filed in the New York City archives for that year, including *Hendenbergh* and *Pierson*.[86] Of these seven, only three were reported cases.[87] In none were the amounts claimed and costs awarded included in the reported case. In *Brown* v. *Smith*, the reported case tells us that the jury in the case gave the plaintiff "one mill," 1/1000 of a US dollar, or 1/10th of a cent. Nathan Sanford, the same lawyer who argued Pierson's appeal, argued successfully for the defendant (the plaintiff on appeal) in this case that a verdict could not attach to a sum less than a cent.[88] However, the reported case does not include the amount that was originally claimed, 50¢ for damage to some grass and trees, or the amount – $86! – that the original plaintiff had to pay in costs after reversal of his award.[89] This case involved the same kind of extreme disproportion that existed in *Pierson* and in *Hendenbergh*. Indeed, the costs were a lot higher than in *Hendenbergh*.

The other reported case, *Seaman* v. *Patten*, was similar to *Hendenbergh* and *Brown* v. *Smith*, costing the original plaintiff $72.86 in a case that, like *Pierson*, was decided by jury trial in December 1802, although it took about seven months less time to be reversed than *Pierson*.[90] Livingston wrote the decision for the court, upholding the reversal of a jury verdict given at the court of a Justice of the Peace in which an inspector of provisions was sued by the original plaintiff who claimed that the inspector's refusal to allow the branding of a barrel of beef condemned it as unmerchantable. The original plaintiff sued for $25 for the beef and the abuse of authority, which the jury agreed with. Livingston upheld the inspector's discretionary authority to refuse to inspect the beef for not being in a properly branded barrel as

86 These files are not indexed and are very difficult to examine. They are almost all handwritten, very dirty, and in some cases in pieces. They fall apart easily as they are not stored in climate-controlled conditions. Many are tied with a small piece of string so they are cumbersome to work with.

87 *Pierson* and two cases described below, *Brown* v. *Smith* and *Seaman* v. *Patten*.

88 *Brown* v. *Smith*, 3 Cai. R. 81 (N.Y. Sup. Ct., 1805).

89 *Brown* v. *Smith*, Law Judgment #1805 S-82, Division of Old Records, New York County Clerk's Office, New York City, NY.

90 *Seaman* v. *Patten*, 2 Cai. R. 312 (N.Y. Sup. Ct., 1805); *Seaman* v. *Patten*, Law Judgment #1805 P-40, Division of Old Records, New York County Clerk's Office, New York City, NY.

supported by the relevant statute. He found that the plaintiff could have gone away and had the barrel properly branded and then returned it for inspection, and that there was no bad faith or malice on the inspector's part in the case.[91]

Not all of the seven *certiorari* cases from magistrates' courts in 1805 were extremely slow. *Pierson* is a high water mark at over two-and -a-half years. *Seaman* v. *Patten* took two years. *Brown* v. *Smith* took a year-and-a-half (another one that did not involve Sanford also took a year-and-a-half).[92] *Hendenbergh* took ten months. One took only four months and cost $41.25.[93] But on average the cases were slow and expensive, with *Pierson* as the upper bench mark of $126.37 (the least amount awarded against the original plaintiff upon reversal was in *Hendenbergh* at $36.78). Also noteworthy is that reversal seems to have been much more common than not. Of the seven cases, only one was not reversed against the original plaintiff in favor of the original defendant.[94] In other words, there seems to have been a disciplinary mechanism at work against the plaintiff-friendly jury verdicts and relative informal Justice of the Peace proceedings, a sure sign of the professionalization of bar and bench in the period. Indeed, given the colonial struggles over the *Five Pound Act*, it is almost as if the lawyers, unable to repeal or prevent the statute from being reenacted and the magistrates' jurisdiction from being expanded in that period and into the early American period, sought indirectly to undermine the speed and accessibility that made the scheme attractive and popular in the first place.

By 1813 enough *certiorari* cases had gone to the New York Supreme Court for one lawyer to publish a fifty-or-so-page digest of the principles

[91] See *Seaman* v. *Patten*, 2. Cai. R., 314–17.

[92] *Blydenburgh* v. *Sefford*, Law Judgment #1805 L-25, Division of Old Records, New York County Clerk's Office, New York City, NY. It cost $72.81, almost as much as *Brown* v. *Smith*.

[93] *Smith* v. *Mott*, Law Judgment #1805 M-50, Division of Old Records, New York County Clerk's Office, New York City, NY.

[94] *Woodworth* v. *Petrie*, Law Judgment #1805 P-30, Division of Old Records, New York County Clerk's Office, New York City, NY. It took about nine months and no costs were awarded in the case. This suggests that unlike a successful defendant who could show that the original plaintiff ought not to have received a jury verdict in his favor, a successful original plaintiff did not get reimbursed by the losing party in that case. However, s. 19 of the *Twenty-Five Dollar Act (1801)* set out that if a case was removed into the Supreme Court on *certiorari* and it "be there confirmed, then the party procuring such certiorari shall pay to the adverse party all costs of defending such suit in the supreme court."

of *certiorari* reversals.[95] By 1814, reportedly, there were nearly two hundred *certiorari* cases a year, a huge increase over 1805.[96] Multiple editions of the *Justice's Directory* appeared.[97] By 1821, one observer noted that "a considerable share, and in several instances, a majority of the causes which have occupied the large calendar of that court [the New York Supreme Court] [...] are brought there by certiorari from a justice's court."[98] Lawyers like Nathan Sanford seem to have led the way in opening this appellate work up for business. Here is our legal professionalization.

Amalia Kessler has documented the rise of lawyer-driven, oral, and adversarial legal culture in America, as it took over and eventually killed the Chancery Court in New York.[99] She demonstrates how lawyers came to push out scholar-judges like James Kent and Joseph Story, arguing that lawyers "rather than equity judges, were the nation's true civic republican elite."[100] Kent specifically came to regret letting lawyers into the Chancery Court in 1817.[101] This is especially poignant given that Sanford actually replaced Kent as Chancellor in 1823, an office which Kent did so much to build nationally and internationally and which he did not want to leave when he was forced to retire at age sixty.[102] Once he was gone, Kessler narrates how subsequent legislatures moved almost immediately toward changes based on oral adversarial procedure that resulted in lawyer control of equity proceedings.[103] Increased democratization found lawyers and others arguing that republican ideals were seriously offended by the secretive

95 See Samuel R. Brown, *The Justice's directory, or Points on Certiorari, being a digest of the cases reported by Johnson and Caines by a gentleman of the Bar* (Balston Spa [NY]: John Howe, 1813).

96 See James D. Folts, *"Duely and Constantly Kept": History of the Supreme Court of Judicature, 1691–1847, and an Inventory of its Records (Albany, Utica, and Geneva Offices), 1797–1847* (Albany, New York: New York State Court of Appeals and the New York State Archives and Records Administration, 1991), 20, available at http://www.nycourts.gov/history/legal-history-new-york/documents/History_Supreme-Court-Duely-Constantly-Kept.pdf (page numbers cited to the PDF document numbers)

97 See e.g. *The Justice's directory improved, or, Points on certiorari: being a digest of the cases reported by Caines and Johnson by a gentleman of the bar*, 3rd ed. (Auburn, NY: Printed by James Beardslee, 1816).

98 Esek Cowen, "Preface" to *A Treatise on the Civil Jurisdiction of a Justice of the Peace, in the State of New York* (Albany, NY: W.M. Gould, 1821), v.

99 Amalia D. Kessler, *Inventing American Exceptionalism: The Origins of American Adversarial Legal Culture, 1800–1877* (New Haven, CT: Yale University Press, 2017).

100 Ibid., 48. 101 See ibid., 62, 86–89. 102 See ibid., 45–47, 97.

103 See ibid., 97–101.

FIGURE 4.2 Fox and Vulture Coat of Arms, *The Daily Graphic* (February 23, 1877).

quasi-inquisitorial and written testimony-taking procedures of a court of equity. According to Kessler, this led to a fetishization of open oral adversarial culture and, ultimately, American exceptionalism given how "adversarialism [. . .] became part and parcel of a grand narrative of American exceptionalism."[104]

Like the earlier period Sung Yup Kim examines, 1805–1815 included some points of resistance against lawyer-driven professionalization. In 1808, the legislature brought back the old exclusion on paid lawyering,

[104] Ibid., 6.

at least for two years.[105] The other important change was to cap costs at \$25, the most that could be at issue under the statute.[106] The idea behind the second change, as the outcome in cases like *Pierson* and *Hendenbergh* suggested, was that the costs awarded should not exceed the uppermost amount that could be in dispute. That legislative change in 1808 looks like an explicit acknowledgement that there should not be such gross disproportion between the amount claimed/at issue and costs awarded, that what had happened in Post's case was not right. He should not have been forced to pay \$126.37 to defend a 75¢ claim.

Consider the Figure 4.2 from a New York newspaper later in the nineteenth century, not long before Hedges wrote his account of *Pierson* crediting to it the lesson that "Law is costive."[107] Here the lawyer says to each of the litigants "You each take a shell, I'll take the oyster." The top of the coat of arms reads "Laws I make and destroy." That the lawyer is a profiteer with no regard for consequence, even death, is strongly suggested by the cash bills in the crown, which is made of skulls. The bottom banner reads "Everyone for themselves, nothing for others," expressing the presumed motto of the lawyers.[108] Hence, the lawyer is the fox, or the vulture, or, worse still, both.

[105] S. 25, *Twenty-Five Dollar Act (1808)*; Ernst, "*Pierson* v. *Post*: The New Learning," 34 n. 6.

[106] See s. 17, *Twenty-Five Dollar Act (1808)* ("in all cases where the judgment before any justice of the peace, in any city or country of this state, shall be removed by certiorari to the supreme court, the plaintiff in error shall recover a sum not exceeding twenty-five dollars for cost, to be taxed on the reversal of any judgment so removed").

[107] "Pierson vs. Post," *Sag-Harbor Express* (1895).

[108] This image appears in Marc Galanter, *Lowering the Bar: Lawyer Jokes and Legal Culture* (Madison: University of Wisconsin Press, 2005), 273. I have added the date of the newspaper and translated the French in the banner slightly differently.

5

The Legal Fictions Needed for a State of Nature Debate

I do not know where I can find a better place than just here, to make mention of one or two other things, which to me seem important, as in printed form establishing in all respects the reasonableness of the whole story of the White Whale, more especially the catastrophe. For this is one of those disheartening instances where truth requires full as much bolstering as error. So ignorant are most landsmen of some of the plainest and most palpable wonders of the world, that without some hints touching the plain facts, historical and otherwise, of the fishery, they might scout at Moby Dick as a monstrous fable, or still worse and more detestable, a hideous and intolerable allegory.

Herman Melville, *Moby-Dick, or the Whale* (1851)[1]

The lawyers and judges in *Pierson* v. *Post* would have been prepared by their backgrounds and training to see in the facts of *Pierson* v. *Post* a set piece for a classic debate on how one acquires wild animals in a state of nature. As we have seen, the texts in which this issue received prominent attention were key elements in their legal training, in the apprenticeship arrangements that prioritized classical learning. They were tied to important and lucrative areas of practice such as the law merchant. We have also seen that Nathan Sanford was a politically ambitious lawyer with a penchant for the classics, who was no doubt familiar with Justinian's *Institutes*, on which the winning argument for Pierson (for better or worse) was based. Yet for two reasons we examine in this chapter *Pierson* was not, on its face, a good case for a general debate about wild animals caught in a state of nature. Or at least there were two specific

[1] Quote from p. 223.

obstacles to treating the case in this way. To get around them required all parties involved to engage in some convenient fictionalization.

First, the fox was not a good stand-in for all wild animals. At common law, foxes were considered vermin and hence an anomalous rather than prototypical category of animal *ferae naturae*. Second, the land where the fox was caught was not really "wild and uninhabited, unpossessed and waste land" as the declaration claimed; or at least this was only partly true. Interesting, then, that as Daniel Tompkins wrote at the outset of his majority decision, "*[i]t is admitted*, that a fox is an animal *feræ naturæ*, and that property in such animals is acquired by occupancy only."[2] Without those two admissions the state of nature debate that lawyers and judges alike seemed determined to have could not have taken place.

First, as for the fox, Post's pleadings described it as a "noxious beast."[3] We noted earlier that this was a somewhat odd choice of phrase for him (or his lawyer) to use: he wanted the jury to view the fox not as an economically insignificant object worth a nominal or trivial amount like 75¢ (about the amount the animal was worth as a bounty on vermin), but as a much more valuable object of recreational pursuit. Vermin are, by definition, "[a]nimals of a noxious or objectionable kind."[4] Foxes were vermin at common law,[5] as *Bacon's Abridgment* stressed by repeatedly using the phrase "fox, badger, *or any Animal of the Vermin Kind*" in its entry on "trespass."[6] This description of the fox also created a problem for Post in making out his case as a property claim, since it was difficult (although not impossible) to have a property in vermin. "[F]oxes were an anomaly within the genre of *ferae naturae*," Andrea McDowell explained. "Far from being potential property, foxes and other vermin were legally classified as nuisances, the killing of which

[2] *Pierson*, 177 (emphasis added).

[3] According to Caines these words came from the declaration, the first part of the pleadings, and Livingston stated that "*[b]y the pleadings* it is admitted, that a fox is a 'wild and noxious beast.'" *Pierson*, 180 (emphasis added).

[4] This is the *Oxford English Dictionary*'s first definition of "vermin." It includes the following usage example from 1900: "The fox is regarded in the Highlands by farmers and game-preservers as one of the worst species of vermin." The second definition of vermin is "[a] kind of class of obnoxious animals." It also includes a fox usage example from 1725: "A fox just suspended on a pole, the shepherds being much infested by this vermin all hereabouts." See *Oxford English Dictionary*, s.v. "vermin" 1a and 2a.

[5] McDowell, "Legal Fictions in *Pierson* v. *Post*," 746.

[6] See e.g. vol. 5, *A New Abridgement of the Law. By Matthew Bacon, of the Middle Temple, Esq.: The fourth edition, corrected, with many additional notes and References of and to Modern Determinations* ... (London, 1778), 180 (emphasis added).

was a service to the public."[7] Pierson's lawyer might have tried insisting on this traditional common law view of foxes as vermin. Sanford could have argued that based on Post's own characterization of the fox as a "noxious beast," Pierson was perfectly at liberty to kill any fox wherever and howsoever found. There is an echo of this point in Livingston's designation of the fox as a pirate and enemy of all humankind.

If Post had wanted to claim a property right in the fox, then, he (or his lawyer) probably should not have described it as a "noxious beast." However, there are several indications that Post never meant his case to be a property case. Recall, he was seeking a higher amount of money than the property value of the fox as bounty, or even as a pelt, up to $25, which was what the statute allowed. What Post was seeking was an amount of money for Pierson's impertinence and his malicious interference with the hunt rather than for the animal itself.

There are at least two indications that Post originally brought his claim in tort rather than property. The first is that he used the writ of trespass-on-the-case rather than trespass.[8] The second is that we now know that Post emphasized malice in the original complaint.[9] The case is even stronger now to say, as McDowell did, that "[t]here are signs that Post originally sued in tort."[10]

Trespass-on-the-case was the writ that eventually grew into the tort of negligence.[11] It evolved in Chancery as the way to construct new writs for different injuries that bore "a certain analogy to trespass" that were evaluated on a case-by-case basis or "on the particular circumstances of the case."[12] This is sometimes described as "a writ suited to the plaintiff's 'case.'"[13] "[T]he injuries themselves which are the subjects of such

[7] McDowell, "Legal Fictions in *Pierson* v. *Post*," 748. [8] *Pierson*, 175.

[9] See Judgment Roll, p. 5, Appendix B.

[10] McDowell, "Legal Fictions in *Pierson* v. *Post*," 738. McDowell made the point about malicious interference before we knew that the complaint explicitly alleged malice. See e.g. 738 ("the harm Post suffered was malicious interference with the hunt"); 739 ("Post's counsel could have framed his claim as malicious interference"); 739 ("Post's immediate grievance was not the loss of the fox, but that Pierson maliciously interfered with his hunt").

[11] *Black's Law Dictionary*, s.v. "Trespass on the case" (the action is "the ancestor of the present day action for negligence where problems of legal and factual cause arise").

[12] John Bouvier, *A Law dictionary adapted to the Constitution and Laws of the United States of America, and of the several states of the American Union; with references to civil and other systems of foreign law*, vol. 2 (Philadelphia, PA: T and J. W. Johnson, 1839) (New York: Lawbook Exchange, 1993), 503–504, s.v. "writ of trespass on the case."

[13] Elizabeth Jean Dix, "The Origins of the Action of Trespass on the Case," 46 *Yale Law Journal* (1936–37): 1142–76, 1143 n. 8 (citing and quoting from Blackstone's definition,

writs [...] have the general name of *torts, wrongs or grievances*."[14] Trespass-on-the-case or "case" is the form of action "adapted to the recovery of damages for some injury resulting to a party from the wrongful act of another, unaccompanied by direct or immediate force, or which is the indirect or secondary consequence of defendant's act."[15] Although Pierson's primary motive might well have been to kill the fox (seeing the fox through a farmer's eyes as a threat to livestock, particularly chickens), the indirect or secondary consequences of his actions were to wrong Post, whose hunt was spoiled.

If Pierson did "maliciously kill" the fox and did "maliciously take and carry [it] away," as Post charged in his complaint,[16] that would change our sense of how direct the wrong was. Consider the following example from Roman law, provided by Charles Donahue. Donahue asked whether an action would lie against a person who prohibited another from using the public baths.

> Clearly the action will lie in my favor if a strong man bars the doors of the baths against me, but what if he simply takes the last place in the baths and uses it himself? Normally, he would be free to do this; the baths are, after all, public. But he is not free to do this [...] if his purpose is not to take a bath himself but to prevent me from taking one.[17]

Malice and perhaps even just knowledge that there was an intention to take and the thwarting of that intention is an *inuria*. This is not about property (an *in rem* right against the world); it is about a wrong (an *in personam* right held by the victim, personal or specific to the person who committed the wrong). Or, as Donahue put it, "the point of Post's suit against Pierson is not that Pierson took Post's fox. The point is that Pierson interfered with the hunt."[18]

However, Post's lawyer did not take the matter forward as a tort claim even though the case was originally brought as a tort. There were at least two serious problems with proceeding in this way. The first was that there is no such tort as malicious interference with the hunt. As Brian Simpson has pointed out, the common law has traditionally refused to protect "things of mere pleasure and

borrowed from William Lambard, "a writ of case gives the suitor 'ready relief, according to the exigency of his business, and adapted to the specialty, reason and equity of his very case'").

14 Bouvier, 504 (emphasis in the original).

15 *Black's Law Dictionary*, s.v. "trespass on the case."

16 Judgment Roll, p. 5, Appendix B.

17 Donahue, "*Animalia Ferae Naturae*," 49–50.

18 Ibid., 48.

delight."[19] That would apply to foxhunting, which under ordinary circumstances has no economic value. Acknowledging Post's claim in the terms in which he brought it would have been like asking the court to create a new tort.[20] McDowell noted that "[e]ven today, it would be difficult to state a cause of action at common law for malicious interference with the hunt."[21]

The second problem was that unlike trespass where the plaintiff does not need to prove harm, trespass-on-the-case, like negligence, requires an injury in order to obtain damages, the remedy the writ requests.[22] Although trespass-on-the-case invited a court to find that a legal wrong had been committed "on the particular circumstances of the case"[23] or "as suited to the plaintiff's 'case',"[24] the fact that Post suffered no injury would have created a problem for his claim. As McDowell put it, Post "hunted for pleasure and suffered no economic loss."[25] Post needed a property claim in the fox. Without a property claim in the fox, namely, *something he was made to lose* by virtue of the wrong Pierson committed against him, Post could not show he suffered any harm. Without the property argument, Post would not have been able to make out the elements of his tort case.[26]

Blackstone defined "personal actions" as those in which a debt, personal duty, or damages were claimed and those "whereby a man claims a satisfaction in damages from some injury done to his person or property. The former are to be founded on contracts, the latter upon torts or wrongs."[27] In other words, a tort requires injury to person or property. Post's person, seemingly, was not injured. Arguably, however, an injury had been done to Post's property. Animals *ferae naturae* were a species of "qualified" property. As Blackstone clearly stated, "in animals *ferae naturae* a man can have no absolute property."[28] Generally, damage to things personal "while in the possession of the owner, as hunting a man's

[19] A. W. Brian Simpson, "The Timeless Principles of the Common Law: *Keeble* v. *Hickeringill* (1707)" in A. W. B. Simpson ed., *Leading Cases in the Common Law* (Oxford, UK: Oxford University Press, 1995), 45–75, 64.

[20] McDowell, "Legal Fictions in *Pierson* v. *Post*," 773. [21] Ibid., 774.

[22] See John G. Fleming, *The Law of Torts*, 8th ed. (Sydney, Australia: The Law Book Company, 1992), 17 ("Trespass was actionable per se, that is, without proof of actual damage, whereas generally damage was the gist of case").

[23] Bouvier, 504. [24] Dix, "The Origins of the Action of Trespass on the Case," 1143.

[25] McDowell, "Legal Fictions in *Pierson* v. *Post*," 772.

[26] McDowell called this "shoehorning" the case "into a property mold," 735. See also 738, 774 ("Post's claim depended on his having some property interest in the fox").

[27] Blackstone, *Commentaries*, 3: 117. [28] Blackstone, *Commentaries*, 2: 390.

deer, shooting his dogs, poisoning his cattle, or in any wise taking from the value of any of his chattels [...] these are injuries too obvious to need explanation," Blackstone wrote.[29] Such actions were either with force (*trespass vi et armis*) or not (a special action on the case).[30] In both of these suits "the plaintiff shall recover damages, in proportion to the injury which he proves that his *property* has sustained."[31] In other words, Post needed property in the fox.

These problems with Post's case explain why on appeal Post's lawyer agreed to reframe the case as a property-law case and argue it on the basis of who succeeded in occupation or first possession of the animal, agreeing in particular to omit the point about malicious interference that was in the original complaint. It was, as McDowell put it, "a defective torts case."[32] Trespass to Post's "'property' in the fox was the only legally cognizable harm he [Post] had."[33] Post needed to make out the property claim in order to get anywhere, including holding onto his $5.75 award at the appeal level, where Pierson was "the now plaintiff."[34] Colden was doing the best he could with some bad facts and law that went against him.

It is helpful to contrast *Pierson* v. *Post* with an unreported fox case from Connecticut which McDowell located, *Sharpe* v. *Sabin* (1796).[35] Here the plaintiff pleaded trespass, rather than trespass-on-the-case, and explicitly invoked the costs of keeping dogs and hounds and claimed, using property language, that the interloper hunter "convert[ed]" the fox pelt, worth twelve shillings to his own use. Conversion is clear property language. There was no jury in *Sharpe* v. *Sabin*. The parties appeared before an Assistant and the plaintiff was awarded 7 shillings.[36] Unlike *Pierson*, this was a true hunting case; the defendant was (unlike Pierson) another hunter. Hence, the plaintiff claimed that intentionally interfering with the hunt after he started the fox and was in close pursuit of it "was & is against Law & the Customs & rules of Hunting." The plaintiff did not specifically allege malice; but he did say that the defendant took the fox "with an intent to wrong & injure the Pltf." The defendant claimed, as Pierson also did, that "the matters therein contained are

[29] Blackstone, *Commentaries*, 3: 152. [30] Ibid., 152–53.
[31] Ibid., 153 (emphasis added). [32] McDowell, "Legal Fictions in *Pierson* v. *Post*," 735.
[33] Ibid., 772. [34] *Pierson*, 175.
[35] Reproduced in McDowell, "Legal Fictions in *Pierson* v. *Post*," 777 and reproduced here in Appendix D.
[36] Presumably because it was not a jury trial, the costs were less than $5, namely, £1, 5 shillings and 20 pence. Ibid.

wholly insufficient in Law to support any action against the defendant." However, the appeal court did not reverse. Both the lower court and the Superior Court agreed that the fox should be seen (i.e. valued) as vermin, bounty, or pelt, and that the original hunter would be given nothing for his investment in the hunt (he did not claim, as Post did, for a tortious interference with it). The property issue was just that, the market value of the fox, no more and no less.

Colden had a response if Pierson's lawyer tried to argue that Post had conceded foxes were vermin and there could be no property in vermin. Foxes *could* be property as vermin. Imagine an industrious exterminator who kills many foxes (or another species of vermin like rats), puts them in a bag planning to deliver them later to the relevant authority in order to collect the bounty, and the bag is stolen. According to Blackstone, there could be no larceny here at common law. Apparently, only animals that "serve for food" could form the basis for larceny. Other animals that are not eaten, which we can assume would include vermin, "the law holds to have no intrinsic value, as dogs of all sorts, and other creatures kept for whim and pleasure."[37] However, "a man may have a base property therein, and maintain a civil action for the loss of them [inedible animals], yet they are not of such estimation, as that the crime of stealing them amounts to larceny."[38] Hence, one could have "a base property" in vermin, or a bag of vermin, and have a civil cause of action to demand their return or to be indemnified for their value.[39] So a very direct and effective specific (if not entirely conclusive) argument for Nathan Sanford's client, Pierson, would have been to insist that there simply could not be property in the fox, as vermin, and without a property claim, Post's tortious claim failed. If Post had brought an action in conversion for the animal itself – once dead, there could be a base property in it. That left undecided of course whether a property could arise while the animal was still alive and being chased, and that was precisely what was at issue in *Pierson*.

To sum up, Post was not suing Pierson for the fox itself – in trespass for a conversion as in *Sharpe* v. *Sabin*. Post was suing in trespass-on-the-case for malicious interference with his hunt. The state Supreme Court would likely have said no to the later claim. However, they could have done so in

37 Blackstone, *Commentaries*, 4: 236. 38 Ibid.

39 I was wrong then to write that the court could have quickly and easily found for Pierson on the basis that one could not have property in vermin. See Fernandez, "*Pierson* v. *Post*: A Great Debate," 303.

a way that would have left undiscussed and undecided the old thorny issue of how possession/occupation is acquired in a wild animal. In other words, it was an unnecessary question to ask and answer in this case. Yes, Post needed property in the (dead) fox in order to be awarded damages for tortious interference. But damages for the dead fox was not what he was after. Deciding that Pierson, not Post, had property in the fox, was a very indirect way for the New York Supreme Court to deal with Post's claim when they could simply have said that there were no damages available for the tort of malicious interference with a hunt. That does not make the argument they did produce illegitimate or unfounded. It is clearly the *ratio deciendi* in the case, as the court controls the way it frames the question to ask and answer. But the argument, as put forward by the lawyers and accepted by the judges, does seem to be gratuitous.

What about the second concession, that property in animals *ferae naturae* was acquired by occupancy only? The problem here is that property in wild animals was often complicated by the issue of who owned the land on which the animal was caught. One view was that animals *ferae naturae* were free for the taking wherever they were. Absent statutory laws restricting hunting, anyone could take these animals, even when they were on another person's land. English game laws famously fettered this ability to access animals like deer and as such were seen by many as illegitimate. Two of E. P. Thompson's hunters convicted under England's *Black Act* "could scarcely be persuaded that the crime for which they suffered merited death. They said the deer were wild beasts, and that the poor, as well as the rich, might lawfully use them."[40] This was an attitude shared even by "persons of estate and quality," Thompson explained, who were involved in opposition to the exclusive attitude taken in the policing of deer parks and royal forests. They were "the old-established resident gentry [...] who perhaps shared some of the same attitudes to forest rights and to deer of their humbler tenants."[41]

Other authorities placed more weight on the principle of *ratione soli*, a principle of ownership "[o]n account of the soil; with reference to the soil."[42] In his *History of English Law*, John Reeves stated that animals *ferae naturae* were not the property of anyone. However, they had an incomplete property that accrued *ratione soli* and gave the owner title to

[40] See e.g. *Whigs and Hunters*, 162. [41] Ibid., 140.

[42] *Black's Law Dictionary*, 6th ed. (St. Paul, MN: West Publishing, 1990), s.v. "Ratione soli."

an action for injury done to them.[43] Blackstone stated that "if a man starts game on another's private grounds and kills it there, the property belongs to him in whose ground it was killed, because it was also started there, the property arising *ratione soli*."[44] However, if the animal was chased onto someone else's land and killed there, then the property vested in the hunter who started and chased it, although he would be guilty of a trespass against the first landowner.[45] Joseph Chitty wrote in his treatise on the game laws that a person could acquire property in the animals on the land of another but nonetheless be guilty of a trespass.[46]

The *Pierson* lawyers and judges were aware of these complications relating to animals *ferae naturae* and a free-taking approach versus limits imposed by *ratione soli*. Sanford cited to a passage in Blackstone very close to a passage relating to *ratione soli* in a section of the *Commentaries* called "Of Title to Things Personal by Occupancy."[47] According to Blackstone, animals *ferae naturae* could be taken by all mankind, and this was a natural right unless restrained by the laws of the country.[48] Tompkins referred to the principle of *ratione soli* twice in his decision. First, in the following passage, he explained why English case law was unhelpful in deciding *Pierson* v. *Post*:

> Most of the cases which have occurred in England, relating to property in wild animals, have either been discussed and decided upon the principles of their positive statute regulations, or have arisen between the huntsman, and the owner of the land upon which beasts *ferae naturae* have been apprehended; the former claiming them by title of occupancy, and the latter *ratione soli*.[49]

[43] John Reeves, *History of the English Law: From the Time of the Saxons, to the End of the Reign of Philip and Mary* (London: Reed and Hunter, 1814–1829), 370.

[44] Blackstone, *Commentaries*, 2: 419. [45] See ibid.

[46] See Joseph Chitty, *A Treatise on the Game Laws and on Fisheries: With an Appendix Containing All the Statutes and Cases on the Subject*, vol. 1 (London: W. Clarke, 1812), 6.

[47] *Pierson*, 176 (citing to Blackstone, *Commentaries*, 2: 403).

[48] See Blackstone, *Commentaries*, 2: 403 ("With regard likewise to animals *ferae naturae*, all mankind had by the original grant of the creator a right to pursue and take any fowl or insect of the air, any fish or inhabitant of the waters, and any beast or reptile of the field: and this natural right still continues in every individual, unless where it is restrained by the civil laws of the country. And when a man has once so seized them, they become while living his qualified property, or, if dead, are absolutely his own: so that to steal them, or otherwise invade this property, is, according to the respective values, sometimes a criminal offence, sometimes only a civil injury. The restrictions which are laid upon this right, by the laws of England, relate principally to royal fish, as whale and sturgeon, and such terrestrial, aerial, or aquatic animals as go under the denomination of game; the taking of which is made the exclusive right of the prince, and such of his subjects to whom he has granted the same royal privilege").

[49] *Pierson*, 178.

The second reference to *ratione soli* was to the duck hunting case, *Keeble* v. *Hickeringill*, in which the defendant shot guns to scare away ducks on the plaintiff's land. The plaintiff's duck-keeping was economic and not recreational (he invested in the construction of an elaborate duck trap). The ducks were on the plaintiff's own land (although they had not yet been reduced to possession) and the defendant shot the guns from his land which meant there was no trespass.[50] Tompkins pointed out that in *Keeble* v. *Hickeringill* the plaintiff's "possession of the ducks, *ratione soli*" made it "clearly distinguishable from the present."[51]

Post stated in his declaration that the fox was found, started, chased, and killed "upon a certain wild and uninhabited[,] unpossessed [,] and waste land called the Beach."[52] Everyone in *Pierson* agreed that the land where the fox was caught was not privately owned and so the principle of *ratione soli* did not apply. However, the situation was actually much more complicated than this, as the beach, while public land in some sense, was not unowned. It was owned by either the town or the state, although it seems likely that in 1802, the proprietors of the town saw the beach as undivided common land in which they had shared rights.[53] "Proprietor" was the term used to refer to "any descendent of the first settlers, who had originally purchased the town's lands."[54] Proprietors' shares in common undivided lands were important in order to do things like graze cattle and newcomers would commonly buy shares when entering the community, which were often traded and were also heritable. Hence, the beach was "unpossessed" only in the sense that it was not *individually* possessed. Possession need not carry with it the idea of individual possession, although it often does. Here even if the land was not individually possessed, it was certainly possessed.

Beaches were included in the Dongan Patent, the document that gave Southampton to trustees of the town in the seventeenth century.[55] If the fox was foraging for seafood washed up on the beach at the time he was found

50 On the problems related to figuring out what precisely *Keeble* v. *Hickeringill* stands for given no less than four versions of the reported case, see Simpson, "The Timeless Principles of the Common Law: *Keeble* v. *Hickeringill* (1707)," 64–65. Two of the reports emphasized malice.

51 *Pierson*, 179.

52 See Judgment Roll, p. 4, Appendix B.

53 See David Goddard, *Colonizing Southampton: The Transformation of Long Island Community, 1870–1900* (Albany, NY: State University of New York Press, 2011), 36 (noting that "the town's beaches [...] were long claimed to be proprietor land").

54 Ibid., 33.

55 A handwritten copy of the 1686 Dongan Patent is in Series 12943, Letters Patent, at Book 6, pp. 35–45. Copy of the document provided by the New York State Archives, Albany, NY. See p. 39 for a description of the granted land that specifically includes beaches.

and started, this was probably at low tide. If so, at least some of the chase, capture, and kill might have happened on the foreshore of the beach, "that portion of land which, lying between the low and high-water mark on a tide-washed shore, becomes alternately land and water."[56] This would pose a problem for saying that the beach was possessed by the town, as the town's jurisdiction ended at the high-water mark.[57] The foreshore would have been Crown land and Crown land became state land after 1776.[58] However, the town had long acted as if all beach land including the foreshore and underwater lands belonged to the town. The town issued fishing licenses, regulated the taking of fish, clams and oysters, leased the underwater land for oyster planting, sold seaweed from the beaches, and controlled the erection of wharves and docks.[59] The town's power to do all of these things was confirmed by legislative compromise in 1818, and again in 1831.[60] Post's complaint was inaccurate, then, in characterizing the beach as "unpossessed." It was not *individually* possessed. However, in 1802 it was *de jure* possessed by the state and *de facto* possessed by the town. I do not think that one could say that the beach was *de jure* owned by the town until 1889, when a court confirmed the town's title over the state's title based on long custom and usage.[61]

Was the beach "waste land"? That term was certainly used to designate the beach in colonial times. Other New England charters used the word in

[56] Frederick R. Coudert, "Riperian Rights: A Perversion of Stare Decisis," 9 *Columbia Law Review* (1909): 217–37, 217.

[57] "All the colonial charters on Long Island extended the boundaries of towns only to the outer limits of the mouths of all such waters and no farther," with all boundaries ending at the high water mark unless specifically designated otherwise. W. Keith Kavenagh, *Vanishing Tidelands: Land Use and the Law in Suffolk County, N.Y. 1650–1979* (New York Sea Grant Institute, 1980), 21.

[58] "Prior to the American Revolution, by English common and decisional law, all land and land under water not specifically granted by Crown Charter belonged to the Crown. After 1777, at least in New York, all land of any kind not included in a colonial grant became the property of the new state." Ibid., 108.

[59] See *Trustees of the Freeholders and Commonalty of the Town of Southampton* v. *Mecox Bay Oyster Company*, 116 N.Y. 1; 22 N.E. 387, 390 (N.Y. C.A., 1889).

[60] Ibid., 391.

[61] See ibid. Hedges represented the Mecox Oyster Bay Company (who were granted rights under a state statute passed by a group of trustees made up of a majority of proprietors) and (presumably a later different group of) town trustees were represented by none other than the great James C. Carter. The court held that the proprietors might have had equitable title but the town had legal title and the proprietors could not pass that to the oyster company.

reference to descriptions of fishing rights. In the 1662 Connecticut Charter, when settlers were given rights to "fishing on the coast, any of the seas, arms of the sea or salt water rivers where they have been accustomed to fish," they were also given the right "to build and set up on the *waste Land* belonging to the said Colony of Connecticut such wharves, stages and Work–Houses as shall be necessary for the salting, drying and keeping of their fish to be taken, or gotten upon that coast."[62] The Rhode Island Charter of 1663 contained a similar provision, also referring to what was clearly a beach right as a right to be exercised on waste land.[63]

Probably the most famous definition of waste was provided by John Locke in his section on property in the *Second Treatise*. Locke wrote that "land that is left wholly to nature, that hath no improvement of pasturage, tillage, or planting, is called, as indeed it is, waste; and we shall find the benefit of it amount to little more than nothing."[64] It is difficult to accept that the Southampton beach was waste in this sense. The beach was not land "left wholly to nature" that was *capable* of cultivation with the right amount and kind of agricultural labor. Beach land could never be transformed through that kind of labor; however ardent one's husbandry, one simply could not grow crops in sand. Moreover, it is extremely difficult to think of this as land that, when "left wholly to nature," would "amount to little more than nothing." This was a dubious claim in respect of regular uncultivated land that would have been used by indigenous people in a wide variety of ways: for the cultivation of crops, which they certainly undertook, but also as territory over which to travel, through which to pursue game and, of course, as a supportive environment for game animals to live and roam. However, the claim was also problematic in relationship to beach land in particular, given that such land was used to access important products of the sea like fish, whales, clams, oysters, seaweed, beach grass, and so on. The reason why this land would never have been considered "unpossessed" by the town was that it was so

[62] Connecticut 1662 Charter, reproduced in *The Federal and State Constitutions, Colonial Charters, and other Organic Laws of the States, Territories, and Colonies now or heretofore forming the United States of America*, vol. 1 (Washington, DC: Government Printing Office, 1909), 535 [emphasis added].

[63] See ibid., vol. 6: 3219. Also available as *Charters and legislative documents illustrative of Rhode-Island history: showing that the people of Rhode-Island, from the foundation of the state until their constitution of 1842, possessed and exercised the rights of self-government ...* (Providence, RI: Knowles and Vose, 1844), 15.

[64] John Locke, *Two Treatises of Government* (1689), Mark Goldie ed. (London: Everyman, 1993), 136.

valuable and important for the resources it contained and to which townspeople sought access.

All of this land had originally belonged to the Shinnecock and Montaukett Indians of Eastern Long Island. "Wasteland" and the portrayal of land as "wild" or "uninhabited" was an important way of justifying the seizure or purchase (often for nominal prices) of land from native peoples. As Stuart Banner put it, especially after the devastation of Aboriginal populations through contact with European diseases against which native inhabitants had no immunity, there seemed to be plenty of space.[65] Colonists had been writing for a long time about North America as "a desert Wildernesse replete onely with a kind of Savage People, and overgrowne trees," a place "where land lay idle and waste," and where "a great part of it lieth wild & inhabited of none but the beasts of the fielde, and the trees."[66] It is difficult not to think of this background when reading the *Pierson* case and its invocation of "wild and uninhabited, unpossessed and waste land."

In the case of the Shinnecock, their remaining land in the Shinnecock Hills was deeply coveted by proprietors and the town, who laying claim to title to the land entered into a lease arrangement with the Shinnecock for 999 years in 1703 reserving the ability to pasture livestock there and giving to the Shinnecock as the nominal quitrent one ear of corn a year.[67] Livestock trampling Indian crops and tussles over who was responsible for what fencing to keep animals and crops separate was a constant source of tension between the town and the tribe.[68] Relations were especially bad in the winter of 1805 when the town put more pressure on the Indians to gain control of these lands. Shinnecock leaders presented a list of complaints to the state legislature. In retaliation, Nathan Sanford, acting on behalf of the town trustees and proprietors delivered an opinion arguing that that any Indians who had intermarried

65 Banner, *How the Indians Lost their Land*, 29–30.

66 Ibid., 18, 21, 14.

67 Goddard, *Colonizing Southampton*, 181–82. See also 186–87 (explaining that the Shinnecock realized that the lease gave the whites outright possession and title and was strenuously opposed by some members of their communities but the sachems involved in the negotiations were bribed with £20 and heavily plied with rum; arguing that the thousand-year lease would have been seen by them as "essentially a deed in perpetuity" and the quitrent of the ear of corn "as a courtesy, a mere acknowledgement of the agreement, and not as a leasehold rent"; stating that "[t]he idea for a lease almost certainly originated with the town trustees"; and arguing that "the lease was the first step toward the eventual adoption of a reservation policy, toward confining an Indian community to a specific territory where it could be managed and generally disregarded").

68 See ibid., 188–95.

with "Negroes, Mulattoes (and) Whites" (which included leaders associated with the petition) ought to be debarred from drawings relating to lands under the lease.[69] This attempt to exclude certain individuals on the basis of mixed ancestry, as not Indians "properly so-called," was probably an indirect attempt to throw into doubt their ability to speak on behalf of the tribe and perhaps even to be considered members of it.[70] The incident Sanford involved himself in was an intensely racialized politics, described by David Goddard as part of Southampton's first colonization. A much later version played out specifically against African Americans has been explored by Andrew Kahrl in relationship to the issue of access to beach property along the Connecticut shoreline by minorities and the urban poor in the twentieth century.[71]

In 1805 struggles on Eastern Long Island that involved beach property did not involve conflicts between town trustees and proprietors in the manner of later tensions in the 1880s such as the Mecox Bay affair. In that dispute, proprietors took the position that their control of lands allowed them to sell off underwater lands (oyster beds) to outside interests, arrangements which froze out the towns.[72] Town trustees and proprietors

[69] Ibid, 202–203. Goddard explains that the Shinnecock probably presented the petition of grievances to the state legislature because the Montaukett had done this with some success in their struggles with Easthampton town trustees in 1800 over land that was further east in Montauk. See ibid., 203.

[70] Ibid., 202. See also ibid., 47–48 (explaining that a pattern of Shinnecock and African American intermarriage began to appear in the early years of the eighteenth century with members of both groups serving as indentured servants, both were heavily represented in the whale fishery shipping out of Sag Harbor, and then in the 1840s a branch of the underground railroad ran from the South and free slaves intermarried with displaced Montaukett in two free back communities, one in Easthampton and another in Sag Harbor), 48–49 ("The common historical experience of both groups, coupled with their low social status in the white community and their comparatively small size, would have encouraged or even necessitated it [intermarriage]. Other less tangible factors in traditional culture and religion where syncretism and polytheism played a central role in belief may also have contributed to a sense of commonality").

[71] See Andrew W. Kahrl, *Free the Beaches: The Story of Ned Coll and the Battle for America's Most Exclusive Shoreline* (New Haven, CT: Yale University Press, 2018).

[72] In the 1882 Mecox Bay affair, the proprietors' sale of underwater land to the oyster company created a scandal that woke the town from a slumber and spurred election of town trustees who were not proprietors in an attempt to protect town interests. Goddard explains how this incident operated as a catalyst for a new political consciousness, pitting Republican proprietors and those descended from them (like Hedges) against those who were living in the town and were not connected to the old established families and aligned themselves with the Democratic Party. See Goddard, *Colonizing Southampton*, 45–46. Hedges, the judge and local historian who wrote about *Pierson* in 1895, was central to organizing the Republican Party at the county level in 1856. He helped found Southampton's first bank, the Sag Harbor Savings Bank, and was elected its first president

also clashed in the 1850s and early 1860s over the seaweed taken from the shores of the bays on both sides of the Shinnecock Hills.[73] However, in 1805, there were no town trustees who were not also proprietors, so fighting over the products of the waters did not take place. And prior to what Goddard calls the second colonization of Southampton by the wealthy summer set, which happened from 1870–1900, there were no conflicts between summer residents and permanent residents over beachfront cottages or mansions.

While Locke's definition of waste has been influential, it was not the only one that was current. One nineteenth-century version of Locke's definition noted that "waste" was "sometimes used improperly to denote any land subject to rights in common or similar rights, although under cultivation."[74] This might not be a question of which was the correct definition, but as another source suggests, simply two non-competing definitions of waste, Locke's and "lands which are not in any man's occupation but lie common."[75] The colonial charters, documents that predated Locke's treatise in 1689, were likely using the term in this latter sense.

Southampton did seem to treat the beach as common land in this way. Consider whaling from the shore. This was practiced on eastern Long Island from whaling stations like the one on the beach below Peter's Pond (see Figure 1.2). These stations "were established along the coast some miles apart, where all of the equipment for killing whales was kept, such as boats, harpoons, lances, ropes, etc. [...] [and] a furnace for rendering the blubber."[76] When a stranded whale was spotted it would be brought in and divided between the inhabitants of the town.[77] In 1644, town records document a policy of appointing eleven men in each ward and by lot two of these would take on the work of cutting up any cast-up whale, "who for their paynes shall have a double share."[78] Originally each male inhabitant over sixteen years was allocated "an equall proportion" so long as he could be

in 1869. See Goddard, *Colonizing Southampton*, 44. For detailed description of the Mecox Bay Affair, see Goddard, *Colonizing Southampton*, 111–42.

73 Ibid., 221.

74 See e.g. Stewart Rapalje and Robert L. Lawrence, *A Dictionary of American and English Law*, vol. 2 (Jersey City, NJ: Frederick D. Linn, 1888), s.v. "waste," 1349.

75 Francis Nolan and Robert Rodney Kane, *The statutes relating to the law of landlord and tenant and land purchase in Ireland, from 1860 to 1896: containing the land law acts 1860 to 1896 ... and land purchase acts: with notes and cases, and an appendix of some of the prior statutes*, 5th ed. by Richard J. Kelly (Dublin: E. Ponsonby, 1898), 264.

76 Halsey, *Sketches from Local History*, 107.

77 Ibid.

78 Adams, *Memorials of Old Bridgehampton*, 257.

appointed in his ward to share in the work.[79] A division on the basis of land was introduced in 1647.[80] This certainly seems like a kind of common right regulated by the town.

Whales were an important economic resource. People always used the beach for access to lands under the water, specifically for things like oysters and seaweed. Proprietors and the town were at loggerheads over this very issue in 1818 when the proprietors were defeated by the state legislature in their attempt to lay claim to the products of the town waters.[81] Proprietors were given the management of undivided common land (including marshes and mill streams) and town trustees were given control over the town waters (including bays and ponds) and their products (e.g. seaweed), which left them able to raise money via permits and licenses for fishing and building wharves, and fines from breaches. For many generations, proprietors and town trustees were one and the same people, creating little opportunity for differences to arise. Moreover, most town inhabitants could easily acquire access to the commons. Shares, or fractions of a share, in common or undivided land were routinely sold for small amounts to town newcomers and subsequent generations acquired theirs by purchase or inheritance.[82] The amount of undivided land decreased over time, while the number of proprietors increased and the rights became increasingly subdivided, creating extremely small interests.[83] Even if tension might have existed in 1802 in relationship to the beach between proprietors and non-proprietors in the town, however, it would never have occurred to anyone thinking about the beach that foxes were an economic resource of any importance.

Bethany Berger's article about *Pierson* claimed that the conflict between Pierson and Post was "not about the fox" but rather involved parties, one of whom had proprietor rights (Pierson) in the undivided common land where the fox was caught, Peter's Pond, and one who did not (Post). There are a number of problems with this thesis. First,

[79] Ibid., 257–58. [80] Ibid., 259–60.

[81] S. 2 of this statute gave "undivided lands, meadows and mill streams" to the proprietors. However, s. 4 stated that "waters, fisheries, sea-weed and productions of the waters shall be managed by trustees of the freeholders and commonalty of the town of Southampton, for the benefit of said town." See *An Act relative to the common and undivided lands and marshes in Southampton, in the county of Suffolk*, Chap. 155 (passed April 15, 1818) in vol. 4 *Laws of the State of New-York, passed at the thirty-ninth, fortieth and forty-first sessions of the Legislature commencing January 1816, and ending April 1818* (Albany, NY: Printed for Websters and Skinners by the printer to the state, 1818), 140–41.

[82] Adams, *Memorials of Old Bridgehampton*, 58. [83] Ibid., 59.

FIGURE 5.1 Peter's Pond Lane at the corner of Daniel's Lane, Sagaponack, NY. Photograph by the author (2009).

Hedges wrote that the incident happened "near" Peter's Pond not at it.[84] Southampton has thirty miles of seacoast.[85] Hedges was probably using Peter's Pond to indicate where along the beach the confrontation took place.

Peter's Pond is no longer a proper pond; it is now marsh land and is not visible from the road or the beach due to the height of the sand dunes. However, the bed of the pond can still be seen in the same shape it had in 1800.[86] It is also still labeled "Peters Pond" on Google Earth. One local resident believes that the pond disappeared in the 1980s, as a result of various northeasters and other storms.[87] Another local historian

[84] See "Pierson vs. Post," *Sag-Harbor Express* (1895).

[85] J.H. French, *Gazetteer of the State of New York* (Syracuse, NY: R. Pearsall Smith, 1860), 638.

[86] Compare the pond marked "Peter's Pond" in the southeast corner of Figure 1.2 "Halsey Map (c. 1800)" with the Google Maps search available using "Peter's Pond Lane, Sagaponack, New York."

[87] As relayed to Ann Sandford and reported to me by Sandford in an email, September 16, 2009. Fairfield Pond Lane currently separates the land between the two old ponds, one of which filled in and one of which did not. This can be clearly seen on Google Maps/Google Earth.

FIGURE 5.2 Beach entrance at Peter's Pond Lane, Sagaponack, NY. Photograph by the author (2009).

FIGURE 5.3 Beach at Peter's Pond Lane, Atlantic Ocean side looking west, Sagaponack, NY. Photograph by the author (2009).

described it to me as "a swamp that occasionally floods."[88] It is currently on the property of a massive twenty-nine bedroom thirty-nine bathroom house/compound built for a reported $110 million dollars by businessman and investor Ira Rennert.[89] It is worth noting that Sagaponack generally is the most expensive zip code in the United States, with a median home sale price of $8.5 million dollars.[90] The Rennert house is reported to be one of the largest and most expensive houses in the country, valued at $248 million in 2015.[91] It is named after Fairfield Pond.

Berger argued that "Peter's Pond lay in the undivided lands" and it was "on some of the last common land in the community," but was unable to provide much evidence to support that.[92] The parcel north of the ocean and to the west of Peter's Pond Lane (the lot on which Peter's Pond would have been located) can be traced back to a Pierson who sold the land in 1865.[93] Indeed, it may have been private Pierson ownership of the land on which the pond was situated that created an association between it and the case in the stories Hedges heard. As Adams noted, Hedges did not move to Bridgehampton until 1854 (he had been a lawyer in Sag Harbor the ten previous years) even if he had been a child in Wainscott, the area just east of Sagaponack in the 1820s.[94] But this seems an unsatisfying explanation. We have seen that the Piersons owned a lot of land in

[88] Julie Greene of the Bridgehampton Historical Society.

[89] See Portia Crowe, "11 Crazy Facts about Junk Bond Billionaire Ira Rennert's $248 Million Hamptons Mansion," *Business Insider* [March 9, 2015] available at www.businessinsider.com/ira-rennerts-hamptons-mansion-2015-3.

[90] See https://en.wikipedia.org/wiki/The_Hamptons (citing Raisa Bruner, "The 25 Most Expensive ZIP Codes in America," *Business Insider* [March 7, 2016]).

[91] See Crowe, "11 Crazy Facts."

[92] See "It's Not About the Fox," 1120, 1121.

[93] The present 65-acre lot came from a family named Roesel. A 20-acre plot named the "Beech Close," bounded "[Ea]sterly by a highway called Peter's Lane," was sold to Paul Roesel by Samuel and Hannah Hedges in 1900. It was bounded "[so]utherly by the banks of the Sea and Westerly by lands of Rufus Sayre Mary Herwick and heirs of John [?] Herwick" (Liber 490, p. 262). No deed onto Samuel Hedges. However, there is an instrument releasing Hannah Hedges as an executor of Nyphens Wright. There is a deed to Nyphens Wright from Isaac M. Pierson in 1865, conveying "[a]ll the divided half of all the real estate of the said Isaac M. Pierson situated in the Town of Southampton County" (Liber 490, p. 257). There is an 1882 deed into Rufus Sayre (Liber 261, p. 293) confirming that Nyphens Wright and formerly Isaac Pierson owned the property east of Rufus Sayre. This means that Isaac Pierson would have had Rufus Sayre to the west, Peter's Pond Lane to the east, and the sea to the south. Title search performed by Laura Rissone.

[94] See Adams, *Memorials of Old Bridgehampton*, 166–67.

Sagaponack (see Figure 1.2). The Peter's Pond lot would not have stood out in this respect.

According to one source, Peter's Pond was also known as "Little Pond."[95] However, there was another "Little Pond," smaller than Peter's Pond, closer to the water and further east, closer to the town bounds with East Hampton which might have become confused with Peter's Pond in the stories Hedges heard (see "Little Pond" east of Fairfield and Peter's Pond in Figure 5.4).[96] This small pond was not included in some maps (e.g. Halsey's map in Figure 1.2). Hedges himself said the following: "Traditions sometimes grow like gossip. Both badly need sifting."[97] He knew of the other Little Pond, writing in one of his many celebration speeches, "I think the little pond near the extent of the Eastern Town bound is a little pond in the lot of Bethuel and James Edwards, near the ocean where the cows pastured and drank in my early days, about 100 rods west of the line between the towns."[98]

This body of water was probably being called "Sagaponack little pond" in the original laying out of Sagaponack in 1653.[99] It is still visible on Google Earth and, unlike Peter's Pond, has not been completely filled in by marsh. If Hedges was correct in his account of the case that Jesse was walking home from his schoolteacher's job in Amagansett, he would have taken Montauk Highway west and then gone south toward the ocean on Town Line Road (see Figure 5.4).[100] He would need to turn west in order to reach his house at the bottom of Sagg Street (see Figure 1.2). Walking along Hedges's Lane or Daniel's Lane would mean missing both ponds (see Figure 5.4). We can probably assume then that he opted for the more scenic route along the beach. In which case, he would have passed the other, truly little, "Little Pond."

[95] See ibid., 17 ("The present sheets of water in the neighborhood are Mecox Bay, Sagg Pond, Fairfield Pond and Little, or Peter's Pond").

[96] Figure 5:4 Plot of Encroachments is reproduced from Heartt ed., *Story of a Celebration*, between pp. 74 and 75.

[97] Hedges, "Memories of a Long Life" in *Tracing the Past*, 269.

[98] "Address of Hon. Henry P. Hedges," reproduced in Heartt ed., *Story of a Celebration*, 38–77, 73.

[99] See *Town Records*, vol. 1: 98–100.

[100] See http://easthamptonstar.com/Education/20151118/Old-Amagansett-Schoolhouse-Becomes-Museum-First-Donation (explaining that the Amagansett schoolhouse was built in 1802 and was originally located on Montauk Highway).

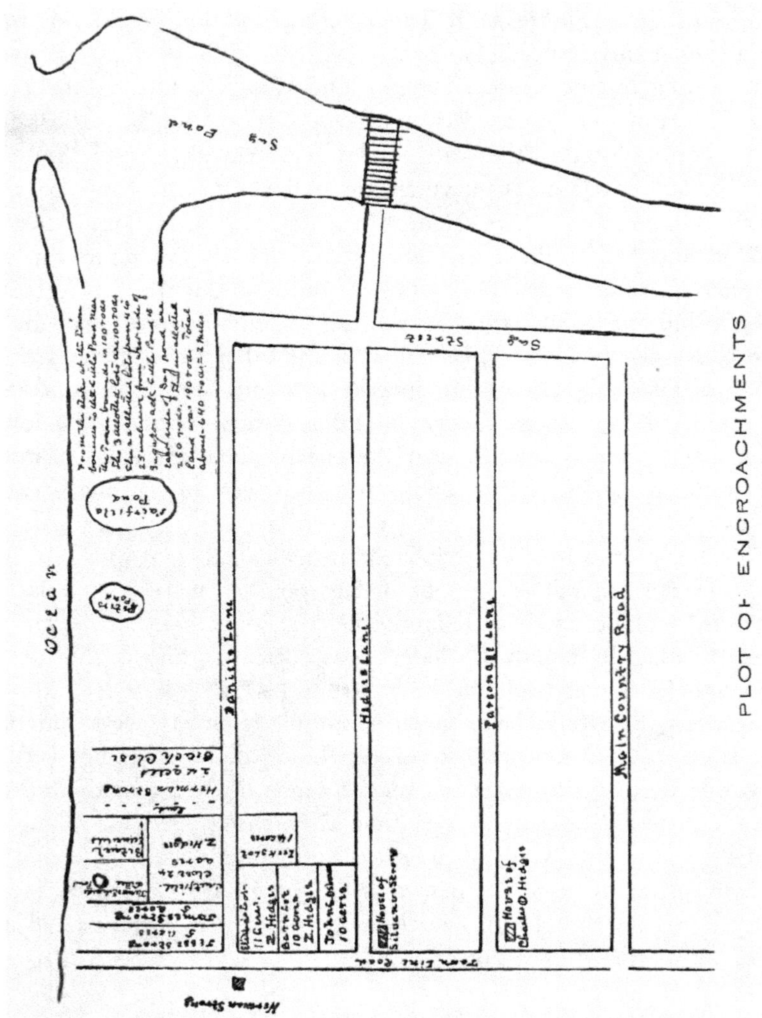

FIGURE 5.4 Plot of Encroachments. Reproduced from John E. Heartt ed., *The Story of a Celebration: Bridgehampton, Long Island 1660-1910* (Bridgehampton, NY: Hampton Printing and Publishing Co., 1910).

Hedges identified the place where the fox was clubbed as "an old shoal well." A "shoal" is a sandbank in a strip of water that is visible at low tide. A "shoal well" might be a kind of salt well used to procure brine for making salt.[101] Peter's Pond is not that close to the ocean and its shoals and sandbars. Local topography may have been quite different over two hundred years ago, but the basin of the pond is currently quite far back from the beach, behind some very high dunes and beach grass. The other pond, the truly little "Little Pond," may have been closer to the water and therefore more likely to have been the one with the shoal well.[102] A fox might well have been down by the water at any point along the beach, foraging for dead fish, clams, snails, or crabs.[103]

In any event, whatever happened at the point of the beach south of Peter's Pond, or near the other "Little Pond" further east, the second problem with Berger's thesis is that all of the action occurred on the beach itself – the start, the chase, and the kill. The original report always said that – Post "did, 'upon certain wild and uninhabited, unpossessed and waste land, called the beach, find and start one of those noxious beasts, called a fox,' and whilst *there*," i.e. on the beach, "hunting, chasing, and pursuing the same," Pierson "well knowing the fox was so hunted and pursued, did [. . .] kill and carry it off."[104] Peter's Pond was only ever brought up because Hedges spoke about it, probably, as we have seen, in an attempt to pinpoint where along this approximately 2 miles of beach the kill was supposed to have taken place (see Figure 5.4). The Judgment Roll confirms what was in the report, namely, that Pierson killed the fox on the beach: Pierson "upon the said wild and uninhabited[,] unpossessed[,] and waste land called the beach [. . .] [did] maliciously kill the said Fox."[105]

If the beach was waste in the sense of being common land, perhaps we can simply transplant Berger's interpretation of what the conflict was about to the beach. After all, before the legislative compromise in 1818, town proprietors saw beach land as undivided common land. But we cannot do this. The third problem with Berger's thesis is that I believe

101 The *Oxford English Dictionary* defines a salt well as "a salt spring, well, or pit [. . .] from which brine is obtained for salt-making." One might speculate a shoal well is a pit either formed by natural tidal forces or dug on a beach to collect brine. See *Oxford English Dictionary*, s.v. "salt well." Thanks to Christopher Tomlins for piecing this together.

102 I have not investigated this point in person. The pond does not appear to be closer to the ocean in Figure 5.4. However, this is clearly a very rough map.

103 See *Red Ben*, 169 ("Red Ben found crabs, fish, snails and clams washed up on the beach. He had never seen so much food. Some he ate, and some he carried to the dunes and buried for future use. He did not know that a new supply was washed in by every tide [. . .] Here indeed was the place in which to live and hunt – no traps, no hounds, no hunger").

104 *Pierson*, 175 (emphasis added).

105 Judgment Roll, p. 5, Appendix B.

she was wrong to claim that Post was a newcomer to the community who would have lacked proprietors' rights. Nathan Post was descended from one of the original inhabitants of the town, Richard Post.[106] Berger acknowledged that a genealogy by George Rogers Howell has Nathan descended from Richard.[107] But, she wrote, another does not,[108] citing another source that failed to list Nathan and Lodowick descended from Richard Post.[109] It is true that the entry in Berger's source mentions the original Richard Post, but the entry relates primarily to a different Richard Post, who settled in Hempstead (in Nassau County), married in 1732, and was having children in the 1740s, not the 1640s. This later Richard Post is probably a descendent of the original Richard Post, the Richard included in Howell.[110] But we cannot infer anything from its failure to mention Nathan and Lodowick among the descendants of this later Richard Post, who is from a different part of Long Island. The rejection of the very standard and reliable Howell (and of Mather, who relies on Howell) for another more obscure and narrowly focused genealogy is, in my view, a mistake.[111] There is no reason to doubt that Nathan Post was descended from the original town inhabitant Richard Post, who had proprietor rights, as town records clearly indicate.[112] Lists of the leading Southampton families, who were proprietors, routinely include both the Piersons and the Posts.[113]

[106] See Mather, *The Refugees of 1776*, 511 (giving the genealogy of Richard Post, whose great-great grandson was Captain Nathan Post). See also 512 (listing Nathan with his two brothers, Joseph and Jeremiah).

[107] See "It's Not About the Fox," 1125, 1125 n. 207. See George Rogers Howell, *The Early History of Southampton, Long Island, New York, with Genealogies*, 2nd ed. (Albany, NY: Weed, Parson and Company, 1887), 353–55. Nathan is listed on p. 354 as having been born on May 14, 1748 and Lodowick in listed on p. 355 child of Nathan and Mehetabel. Howell is the source relied on in Mather above. Both are available through https://archive.org/

[108] "It's Not About the Fox," 1125.

[109] Ibid., 1125 n. 208 (citing *Long Island Genealogies: Families of Albertson, Andrews, Bedell, Birdsall ... Willets, Williams, Willis, Wright, and other families. Being kindred descendants of Thomas Powell, of Bethpage, L.I., 1688*, Mary Powell Bunker comp. (J. Munsell's Sons, 1895), 263–65).

[110] See Howell, *The Early History of Southampton*, 353.

[111] That is not to criticize the genealogy by Mary Powell Bunker, which was tracing the descendants of someone named Thomas Powell of Bethpage, Long Island. Bethpage is in Nassau County, where Hempstead is also located. This is not Suffolk County.

[112] See e.g. *Town Records*, vol. 1: 98–101 (including Richard Post in the 1653/54 Sagaponack division), 144 (giving Richard Post a day for his oxen at pasture), 41 (giving Richard Post an additional two acres to his four acres next to the ancestor of the Pierson clan and his contemporary, Henry Pierson).

[113] See e.g. Adams, *Memorials of Old Bridgehampton*, 55; Goddard, *Colonizing Southampton*, 35.

Relying on Berger's work, Allan Hutchinson concludes that *Pierson v. Post* was about a "particularly heated [conflict] over the town's common lands" and its connection to "common land, which was used by the Pierson family and others to pasture their livestock."[114] Beach property was not being used to pasture livestock even if land like James Edwards's close to the ocean was used to support the pasturing of cows. Nor would it be accurate to say that "the dispute was really about control of the village common."[115] Even if the beach was common land in the sense of being a source of shared resources that proprietors saw as their own (albeit aspects were controlled by the town), the beach was not a "village common." Most importantly, both Pierson and Post were proprietors, so this could not be a case where one party thought he should have untrammeled access to anything that appeared on the beach because he was a proprietor and the other should not because he was not a proprietor. Berger was right that the fight between Pierson and Post "was not about the fox." Nor, however, was it about proprietors versus non-proprietors. It was about the underlying culture clash between the young sons of two established and leading families, and their different ways of being wealthy in this community. Farmers like the Piersons would have opposed the more mercantile wealth of the Posts and, specifically, Lodowick Post's aping of aristocratic English-style foxhunting given a farmer's interest in protecting fields, fences, and chickens, especially if it was understood that more organized foxhunting would ultimately mean more foxes in the neighborhood.

What, then, can we conclude about the land itself? There is a sense in which the beach on which the fox was caught was indeed "unpossessed." It was not individually possessed. Proprietors like Pierson *and* Post would have thought of it as undivided common land or land possessed by the town. There is also a sense in which it was indeed "waste" or common land. However, it was not waste in Locke's sense. Words like "wild" and "uninhabited" conjure up an image of a state of nature, unregulated, unowned, unoccupied, a place where there is no law and for which law is yet to be made. Waste land in the Lockean sense is "land that is left wholly to nature" and that is not useful because it is unimproved.[116] That

[114] Allan C. Hutchinson, *Is Eating People Wrong?: Great Legal Cases and How They Shaped the World* (New York: Cambridge University Press, 2011), 70, 74.

[115] Joseph William Singer, Bethany R. Berger, Nestor M. Davidson, Eduardo Peñalver eds., *Property Law: Rules, Policies, and Practices*, 6th ed. (New York: Wolters Kluwer Law and Business, 2014), 135 n. 6.

[116] Locke, *Two Treatises of Government*, 136.

was just not an accurate image or description of the beach in this case. It was waste only in the sense of being public or common land. It was thought of by both the town and the proprietors as valuable, though probably not for the foxes it supported.

James Kent did not write any of the *Pierson* decision. However, he did visit Long Island on one of his Circuit Court trips about ten years earlier in 1795, and he wrote about his stay in the town of Riverhead.[117] Kent did not travel down the South Fork toward the Hamptons and Montauk, writing that "one of the pleasantest rides with a carriage *must be* from S[outh] Hempstead [in Nassau County] to Montock [sic] Point along the S[outh] side of the Long Island."[118] He described his familiarity with the island as a "slight acquaintance" and seems to have based most of what he recorded on what he was told by others. He wrote, for instance, that "above one half of Long Island *is said* to be waste and unfit for cultivation," its "natural sterility [...] *is said* to be occasioned by being burnt frequently by the Indians for the sake of hunting deer," and that "Agriculture on the Science of manuring and improving land is here studied and practiced as a Science more and more successfully than in any other Part of the State. *So I am informed* by judicious observers."[119]

"River Head," Kent explains, "stands at the Head of the fork into which the East end of Long Island branches [...] Shelter Island lies in between the two Forks." See Figure 1.3. "I am told that S[outh] and E[ast] Hampton are beautiful towns, well settled and the land [found?] therein in a very high pre-eminent State of Cultivation. There is fine land at Montock [sic] Point." As for the beach, Kent wrote about the strip extending from Rockaway Beach to Southampton that "for 200 Miles the S[outh] side is defended from the Ocean by a Sandy Beach of about 80 Rods wide and encloses within it a long Bay of 2 or 3 Miles wide into which small craft enter at the Inlets and which abounds with oysters, clams and fish and yields on the N[orth] side a long extent of Saltmeadow." Generally, he

[117] See "Memories of my Journey to Riverhead, September 6–10, 1795 to attend the Circuit Court," Reel 1, Volume 2, *The Papers of James Kent*, Library of Congress, Manuscript Division, Washington, DC.

[118] Ibid. [emphasis added].

[119] See ibid. [emphasis added]. See William Cronin, *Changes in the Land: Indians, Colonists, and the Ecology of New England* (New York: Hill and Wang, 1983), 50–51 (on native people's burning of the land and the agricultural advantages of doing so, increasing the rate at which forest nutrients were recycled into the soil and thinning the forest canopy allowing light to reach the forest floor).

recorded that "the S[outh] side derived their greatest benefit from the range of Salt Meadow."[120] Kent recorded that there were some fine farms in the area, noting that "the grandest single farm in this State" was owned by Mr. Gardiner on Gardiner's Island, also lying between the North and South forks in Peconic Bay, certainly very high praise. Also "Gentlemen have fine farms on the Necks and facing the long Bay and Beach." However, he described the area around Riverhead as "a barren heap of Sand as one half of the Island appears to be." Travel for the most part "is very tedious and very heavy on account of Sand."

Kent's comments capture a contemporary understanding of Long Island as wild, beautiful, some parts cultivated, some parts not. It was advanced in the study of agriculture as a science and bore witness to some great successes on that score, even if the land generally suffered from "natural sterility" and was difficult to work with in other respects. Sand specifically posed obstacles for travel and agriculture. Yet the waters of the beaches made up of that sand abounded with valuable sea life such as oysters, clams, and fish. The salt marsh hay or beach grass from the salt meadows Kent noted was so important was used as bedding and fodder for farm animals and to create garden mulch and to top haystacks in farming.[121] "Judicious observers," the source for most if not all of Kent's information about the place, in other words, saw and described the beach specifically as both wild (its sands posing challenges to cultivation and agriculture) and valuable (for its sea life and beach grass) even if it was also waste, a word which Kent used specifically when he wrote "one half of Long Island is said to be waste and unfit for cultivation."

Livingston, interestingly, described the beach in his dissent simply as "waste and uninhabited ground," leaving out both the "wild" and "unpossessed."[122] This description was more technically accurate, if the sense of "waste" meant was common land, that is, land that was valuable (i.e. for access to sea life and resources) and not Lockean waste land (that had the potential of being cultivated for crops but was not and, as a result, "the benefit of it amount[ed] to little more than nothing"). And it would

[120] Salt meadow is a meadow subject to flooding by salt water.

[121] The grass is a species of cordgrass native to the Atlantic coast of the Americas, which grows from Newfoundland south along the Eastern coast of the United States to the Caribbean and Northeast Mexico. See https://en.wikipedia.org/wiki/Spartina_patens, which also describes the uses to which it was put and its current ecological importance even if it is considered an invasive species on the West coast of the United States.

[122] See *Pierson*, 180.

seem to be relatively unproblematic to call the beach "uninhabited," for although many people used it, no one – at least no human animals – actually lived on it. Summer residents did not start coming to Southampton to build vacation houses on the beach until the 1860s.[123] The phrase "wild and uninhabited, unpossessed and waste land," used no less than three times in the Judgment Roll,[124] created a kind of half-truth, a legal fiction, about the land.

Like the agreement to allow the fox to stand for animals *ferae naturae* when the fox was in truth, and rather more problematically, vermin in which it would be difficult (though not impossible) to claim a property right (at least when it was dead), the legal fiction that the land was "unpossessed" and "waste land" was essential for the case to take on the form of a state of nature debate. The lawyers and judges seemed very interested in arguing over how one acquires possession in a wild animal caught on waste land belonging to no one. The very wildness of it – as if the question was itself "unpossessed" and unoccupied in an early American context – made it attractive to these early American lawyers and judges. It was a point open for consideration, as a matter of first principle, in keeping with the classical texts and authorities with which the lawyers and judges were familiar. The question whether it was even possible to have property in a fox caught on state land under *de facto* control of the town would have been of considerably less general interest, especially as a precedent. And there were certainly no old Roman and civil law authorities dealing with the latter kind of question. There was, in other words, no opportunity lurking in the narrower (and arguably more accurate) set of issues to have a great debate. And a great debate with a bevy of classical and other impressive sources these classically trained and elite lawyers and judges seemed determined to have. There was "a knotty point" that would turn on pure principle with an animal that was not economically important.[125]

The fox was not a valuable animal farmed for its fur, or hunted for food or like the whale valued for bone to make hoopskirts and corsets and blubber and sperm to make lighting oil and machine lubricant.[126] Bereft of valuable use, the verminous fox was not economically important in the way that animals such as seals, or whales, or fish have been. The legal fictions that the lawyers built into the case and their treatment of it as

[123] See Goddard, *Colonizing Southampton* (describing the process of colonization that took place by the summer set).

[124] See Judgment Roll, pp. 4–5, Appendix B.

[125] *Pierson*, 180.

[126] See Deal, *The Law of the Whale Hunt*.

a question of pure principle have enabled legal scholars down to the present day to treat the issue of first possession of a wild animal unencumbered by all the social and economic context that complicates instincts about what the rule should be and puts into play competing values familiar to us, such as preservation of a limited resource, versus job creation, versus cruelty to animals, all embodied in fished-out cod stocks, whale species hunted to extinction, or baby seals clubbed to death on ice floes. These are difficult questions. *Pierson*, greatly facilitated by the supposed innocuousness of the humor in Livingston's dissent, has allowed scores of legal scholars and students to discuss the issue of first possession of a wild animal in hunting contexts and beyond without acknowledging those contentious debates. It has allowed us to depoliticize the environmental implications of the capture rule. The next part of the book explains precisely how this academic transformation of *Pierson* in the nineteenth and twentieth centuries took place, starting with its report at the appeal level, its uptake by James Kent, and its making and remaking in law school casebooks and in the hands of influential theorists of American property law. The suggestion here is that these scholarly legal theorists flew off with the fox much in the manner of the eagle in Cecil Aldin's picture of the dead or dying fox reproduced on the cover of this book.

PART III

THE INTELLECTUAL HISTORY OF *PIERSON*

6

The Reporter

If you should write a fable for little fishes, you would make them speak like great whales.
[Oliver] Goldsmith to [Samuel] Johnson

Herman Melville, *Moby-Dick, or the Whale*, "Extracts" (1851)[1]

About the "whaling voyage" – I am half way in the work [...] It will be a strange sort of a book, tho', I fear; blubber is blubber you know; tho' you may get oil out of it, the poetry runs as hard as sap from a frozen maple tree; – & to cook the thing up, one must needs throw in a little fancy.
Herman Melville to Richard Henry Dana Jr., May 1, 1850[2]

It has been the fate of law reporters to enjoy little acknowledgement in the general conception we have of where our law comes from. We treat a written report as if it came from the mouth or pen of the judge when, in actual fact, at least in the British tradition, reports, in the minority of cases in which they are available, were created by a court reporter scribbling down what he thought the judge was saying in a busy and often extremely noisy courtroom, without transcripts or even the benefit of shorthand until the seventeenth century.[3] The court reporter did not hold an official position. As a consequence, there was not likely to be

[1] Quote from p. xxx.
[2] *The Letters of Herman Melville*, Merell R. Davis and William H. Gilman eds. (New Haven, CT: Yale University Press, 1960), 108, quoted by Ferguson, *Law and Letters in American Culture*, 270.
[3] See Harry M. Scharf, "The Court Reporter," 10 *The Journal of Legal History* (1989): 191–227.

any judicial oversight or approval of what was recorded, or even any working relationship with the clerks of the court. We treat the words of a case by Lord Coke or Lord Mansfield as if they were their own words; but they were in fact the words of the reporter, subject to a wide variety of factors that could and probably would almost inevitably corrupt what was recorded.

In New York at the time of *Pierson* v. *Post,* "court reporter" was an official position. John Langbein has described this as "the American solution" to law reporting, adopted in 1804 in both New York and Massachusetts. "The state legislatures provided for the designation of official reporters, who were paid stipends that effectively subsidized the reports."[4] George Caines was the first person to hold this position in New York. He prepared three volumes of cases, which he published from 1804 to 1806.[5] He included *Pierson* in the third and last volume of these reports.

At least two matters should be emphasized in relation to the *Pierson* report. First, we must acknowledge that it appeared very early in the history of reporting in New York. James Kent famously said when he came to the bench in 1798 that there were no reports and the opinions were all delivered orally from the bench.[6] One unofficial volume of cases was published in print in 1801, *Coleman's Cases*. It contained cases going back to 1794.[7] Second, only a small percentage of cases were reported. Caines made reports for 222 cases in 1805. Yet there are approximately 900 Judgment Rolls from cases heard by the New York Supreme Court in 1805 in the New York City Archives.[8] Approximately 2,375 money judgments were filed by the New York Supreme Court in Albany in

[4] Langbein, "Chancellor Kent and the History of Legal Literature," 574.

[5] See George Caines, vol. 1, *New-York term reports of cases argued and determined in the Supreme Court of that state* (New York: I. Riley, 1804). Volume 1 contained cases from 1803 and 1804. Volume 2 contained cases from 1804 and 1805, published in 1805. And the last, volume 3, which contained *Pierson*, were all 1805 cases published in 1806.

[6] See Kent, *Memoirs*, 117.

[7] John H. Moore, "One Hundred Fifty Years of Official Law Reporting and the Courts in New York," 6 *Syracuse Law Review* (1954–55): 273–306, 274. William Coleman, *Cases of Practice, Adjudged in the Supreme Court of the State of New-York together with the Rules and Orders of the Court* (Albany, NY, 1801). Langbein noted that Coleman's work was rare and may not have been well-marketed or well-received. See Langbein, "Chancellor Kent and the History of Legal Literature," 573.

[8] I also did a count from the Docket Books and found close to the same number, 924 entries for 1805. See Supreme Court of Judicature (New York), Docket of Judgments, J0131-82, vols. 3 and 4, New York State Archives, Albany, NY.

1805.[9] That would make for a total of 3,275 cases, about a 15 percent reporting rate. Purely oral decisions certainly persisted.[10]

Early reporters and their advocates like Kent, firmly on the professionalization side of the push and pull between local or lay justice and professionalized justice, would be keen to create the impression that what they provided approached complete or near-complete coverage. Caines's successor as New York's official reporter, William Johnson, went back to print publish reports for 1803, before the start of Caines's tenure in 1804.[11] In doing so, Johnson wrote that the profession was thereby provided with "an unbroken series of adjudications of our higher courts, from the year 1799, inclusive to the present time."[12] This seems like an exaggeration if what it is taken to mean is that there was now a full record of all of the adjudications during that period of time. Reporting was highly selective, as in the British tradition. It never aspired to provide complete coverage. Even a collection of early United States Supreme Court reports contained at best guess only a third of the decided cases.[13]

Reporters and those in favor of legal professionalization were keen to create the impression that an unbroken chain of precedents existed from which to craft an indigenous common law. The truth is that individuals like Kent and Johnson were busily in the process of creating the conditions that could support this kind of law, both as a practice and as a concept. The reports were the equivalent of the raw material out of which, with the right kind of determination, it could and would be made. Laura Edwards

[9] Docket of Judgments, J0141, Roll No. 1 (Microfilm), New York State Archives, Albany, NY.

[10] In 1847, the legislature in New York required written opinions in cases where the opinion was not delivered in open court, which seems to imply that exclusively oral opinions continued. See William D. Popkin, *Evolution of the Judicial Opinion: Institutional and Individual Styles* (New York: New York University Press, 2007), 94. For a reproduction of the text of this legislative provision, see Moore, "One Hundred Fifty Years of Official Law Reporting," 290–91.

[11] Historians of the book consider it very important when speaking about publication to distinguish between print and manuscript. See Harold Love, *The Culture and Commerce of Texts: Scribal Publication in Seventeenth-Century England* (Amherst: University of Massachusetts Press, 1998). This is especially true for legal materials like reports of cases that often circulated in small communities of lawyers and judges in manuscript form. However, this becomes less important once there is reliable print publishing in the nineteenth century, even though the circulation of manuscript sources certainly continued.

[12] William Johnson, Preface to vol. 1, *Reports of Cases Adjudged in the Court of Judicature of the State of New York from January Term 1799 to January Term 1803, both inclusive together with cases determined in the Court for the Correction of Errors during that period* (New York: I. Riley, 1808).

[13] See Popkin, *Evolution of the Judicial Opinion*, 79.

has written eloquently of how elites in North and South Carolina who championed state-level law set out to dismantle the local legalism she terms "the Peace," the on-the-ground adjudication of disputes that included the voices of those – women and even slaves – who lacked formal equality in the state-law system but who had a participatory (if far from equal) role to play in the way that local law operated. This process of displacement resulted, Edwards argues, in a transformation of legal inequality in the post-Revolutionary South.[14]

Edwards documents that in South Carolina a court reporter was appointed in 1811 but that the results were spotty until the 1820s. In North Carolina, judges designated as court reporters began issuing decisions from the state's higher courts in the 1790s, but as in South Carolina reports of decisions appeared only occasionally and at irregular intervals. The appearance of regularity, however, was important enough to license a retrospective numbering of the reports.[15] A key rhetorical trope in the early American period was to try to build greatness by speaking as if it already existed; the appearance of professionalized law proceeded in advance of its actuality. As Edwards emphasizes, the men who were staffing the growth of this kind of law left a voluminous historical record, one that is generally a record of their own triumph.[16] Collections of reports and statutes created "the impression of orderly progress over time."[17] However, "[t]he results conjured up order out of a past that was anything but orderly."[18] Certainly a neat and orderly legal science was intended and desired by elite legal professionals in 1804. That does not mean that it was by any means already in place. Edwards quotes the great intellectual historian Perry Miller, who stated: "We take the success of the courts in defending their integrity so much for granted that we forget how in the early nineteenth century their champions believed they barely survived the gale."[19]

[14] Edwards, *The People and Their Peace.* [15] Ibid., 37–38. [16] See ibid., 28.

[17] Ibid., 39.

[18] Ibid., 40. See also Roman Hoyos, "A Province of Jurisprudence? Invention of a Law of Constitutional Conventions" in Angela Fernandez and Markus D. Dubber eds., *Law Books in Action: Essays on the Anglo-American Treatise* (Oxford; Portland, OR: Hart Publishing, 2012), 108–26 (on the use of a treatise on the law of constitutional conventions later in the nineteenth century to conjure up reassuring order out of a disconcerting disorder).

[19] Edwards, *The People and Their Peace*, 28 (quoting Perry Miller, *The Life of the Mind in America, from the Revolution to the Civil War* (New York: Harcourt, Brace and World, 1965), 236).

Where Caines did make a report, he seems to have had access to both the judges and the clerks of the New York Supreme Court. In the preface to the first volume, he thanked the judges who "have unreservedly given their written opinions."[20] He also thanked "the clerk of the court" for "an unlimited recurrence to the papers and pleadings his office contains."[21] It seems as if lawyers who were involved in the cases also helped, perhaps by offering their own notes. Caines thanked "the whole bar" who had "frankly and generously afforded their cases and every other communication, that was wished or desired."[22] Interestingly, he did not, like other reporters such as Ephraim Kirby in Connecticut, assure the reader that the judges had reviewed his work prior to print publication.[23] Kirby was not an official reporter and probably felt it important to signal to his readers that nonetheless the collection was reliable as it had a judicial *imprimatur*. It seems unlikely that Kent at least reviewed the work, as his copy of Caines's reports contains many of the kind of corrections he probably would have made on an advance copy had he been given an opportunity to review it.[24]

Kent did not work closely with Caines. Indeed, he stated that he thought Caines was a bad reporter. It is true we will see that there were accuracy issues with Caines's reporting. However, other factors help explain Kent's animosity toward Caines, specifically political disagreement, unsurprising to find in factious New York and generally amid the political upheaval that resulted from the shift in power away from the Federalists in national politics. Caines was an ardent enthusiast of Thomas Jefferson and Jeffersonian Republicanism, sure to attract Kent's ire, staunch Federalist as he was. Kent was not yet Chief Justice when Caines was appointed. It is extremely unlikely he would have supported

20 Caines, Preface to *New York term reports*, iv.

21 Ibid. The New York Supreme Court had two clerks at this time, one in Albany, Francis Bloodgood, and the other in New York City, James Fairlie. See *Duely and Constantly Kept*, Appendix E, "Supreme Court Clerks (1797–1847)," 158. At least in 1794, the New York City clerk was considered "the clerk" (presumably James Fairlie), while the Albany clerk was considered his deputy. See William Wyche, *Treatise on the Practice of the Supreme Court of Judicature of the State of New York in Civil Actions* (New York: Printed by T. and J. Swords, 1794), 4–5. This might explain why Caines used the singular here.

22 Caines, *New-York term reports*, Preface to *New York term reports*, iv.

23 See Ephraim Kirby, "Preface" to *Reports of Cases Adjudged in the Superior Court of the State of Connecticut: From the Year 1785, to May 1788, with Some Determinations in the Supreme Court of Errors* (Litchfield, CT: Collier and Adam, 1789).

24 See Caines, *New-York term reports*, Kent Law Library, New York State Library, Manuscripts and Special Collections, Albany, NY (hereafter Kent's copy, 1st ed. *New York Term Reports*).

the choice of a Republican for the newly created position. Caines's unofficial predecessor, William Coleman, was a Federalist. Indeed, he was recruited by Alexander Hamilton to be the editor of the *New York Evening Post*, a newspaper funded by Federalists in New York and organized by Hamilton in order to continue to espouse Federalist politics and policies after Jefferson was elected President in 1800.[25]

First, let us examine the evidence for the claim Kent made that Caines was a bad reporter. Kent wrote the following rather scathing note at the end of the November Term in the first volume of the reports Caines prepared:

> I have perused this number and corrected some mistakes. I think the Reporter does not take Notes very correctly and that the work is full of mistakes. The decisions of the Court when in writing, as most of them are, appear correct and this source of accuracy stamps the whole value on the Book for without that aid, I should have no reliance on the Reporter. His own annotations in the margins might have been spared. However, as the first essay, the work deserves great indulgence.[26]

I can find three places in the hundred or so pages of reports from this term where Kent writes things like "[t]his is not correct,"[27] "[t]his is very obscurely reported,"[28] and a qualification stating "the remark of the Reporter to the contrary notwithstanding."[29] In conjunction with this last, Kent wrote, "See note at the end of this volume," by which he meant the passage above quoted. In cases where there was no decision of the court in writing, Kent criticizes Caines's note taking.

Unlike other early American law reporters, such as the first official reporter in Massachusetts Ephraim Williams, Caines knew shorthand and so was probably doing a better job than most at the difficult task of taking notes where there was no written decision.[30] Scholars have agreed that some allowance must be made for mistakes made in this hectic oral context or where a written opinion was available if a judge's handwriting was difficult to read.[31] There are a lot of mistakes, it is true, although true

[25] Caines noted that Coleman left law reporting in order to be the editor for the *New York Evening Post*. Caines, "Preface," *Lex Mercatoria*, vii. See Nevins, *The Evening Post*, 14–34.

[26] Kent's copy, 1st ed. *New York Term Reports*, 107.

[27] Ibid., *Dow* v. *Smith*, 1 Cai. Rep. 32 (N.Y. Sup. Ct., 1803), 36.

[28] Ibid., *Jackson* v. *Reynolds*, 1 Cai. Rep. 20 (N.Y. Sup. Ct., 1803), 21.

[29] Ibid., *Riddles* v. *Mitchell*, 1 Cai. Rep. 11 (N.Y. Sup. Ct., 1803), 11.

[30] See Caines, Preface to 2nd ed., where Caines refers to his ability to write shorthand. See Surrency, *A History of American Law Publishing*, 42, noting Ephraim Williams did not know shorthand.

[31] We ought to be careful about being too scrupulous on the question of mistakes, especially when "the reporter had to transcribe orally delivered opinions whenever a written

mistakes on substance seem to be relatively few. Kent is probably exaggerating when he says that the work is "full of mistakes."[32] Greater coordination and cooperation between Kent and Caines would have prevented Caines from making the mistakes Kent would have caught, but the second edition reflects few of the corrections Kent made.[33] In other words, Caines did not seem to be working with Kent's corrections.[34] Indeed, the tone of Kent's comments makes it unlikely that Caines was ever meant to see the note and the other corrections and

opinion was unavailable and that manuscripts received from judges in their own hand were not always easy to read." Popkin, *Evolution of the Judicial Opinion*, 80.

32 There are two other mistakes like this after Kent wrote the note. See Kent's copy, 1st ed. *New York Term Reports, Spencer* v. *Webb*, 1 Cai. Rep. 118 (N.Y. Sup. Ct., 1803), 120 ("This case is very badly reported") and *Martin* v. *Bradley*, 1 Cai. Rep. 124 (N.Y. Sup. Ct., 1803), 124 (writing a correction to a footnote that "The Reporter here is inaccurate"). Kent repeats the issue with *Spencer* v. *Webb* in his annotations in the second edition, also located in Kent Law Library, New York State Library, Manuscripts and Special Collections, Albany, New York (hereafter Kent's copy, 2nd ed. *New York Term Reports*). See Kent's copy, 2nd ed. *New York Term Reports, Spencer* v. *Webb*, 1 Cai. Rep. 117 (N.Y. Sup. Ct., 1803), 120 (it becomes "This case badly reported").

33 See Kent's Copy, 1st ed. *New York Term Reports, Riddles* v. *Mitchell*, 1 Cai. Rep. 11 (N.Y. Sup. Ct., 1803), 11, where Kent changed the spelling of the first party's name to *Rideller* – not changed in 2nd ed. *New York Term Reports, Riddles* v. *Mitchell*, 1 Cai. Rep. 11 (N.Y. Sup. Ct., 1803), 11; Kent's Copy, 1st ed. *New York Term Reports, Seaman* v. *Drake*, 1 Cai. Rep. 9 (N.Y. Sup. Ct., 1803), 9, where Kent crosses out the third ground on which the application was made and on p. 10 has crossed out "in law" – Kent's Copy, 2nd ed. *New York Term Reports, Seaman* v. *Drake*, 1 Cai. Rep. 8 (N.Y. Sup. Ct., 1803), 8, retains the third ground and p. 9 retains "in law," which Kent has again crossed out and written to replace it "ex gratia"; Kent's Copy, 1st ed. *New York Term Reports, People* v. *Youngs*, 1 Cai. Rep. 37 (N.Y. Sup. Ct., 1803), 42, *Smith & Stanley* v. *Wright and Wright*, 1 Cai. Rep. 43 (N.Y. Sup. Ct., 1803), 44, *Miller* v. *Drake*, 1 Cai. Rep. 45 (N.Y. Sup. Ct., 1803), 45, *Elijah Bentley*, 1 Cai. Rep. 47 (N.Y. Sup. Ct., 1803), 47, *Muir & Boyd* v. *United Insurance Company of the City of New York*, 1 Cai. Rep. 49 (N.Y. Sup. Ct., 1803), 53, were all cases where Kent fixed a "per curiam" judgment to a specific judge, which did not result in a change in the second edition; *Potter* v. *Briggs*, 1 Cai. Rep. 57 (N.Y. Sup. Ct., 1803), 57; *Vandyck* v. *Van Beuren and Vosburg*, 1 Cai. Rep. 84 (N.Y. Sup. Ct., 1803), 86, where Kent has written "by Kent" rather than "per curiam," which also remained the same in the second edition.

34 There are a few instances where changes were made. One was a case in which Caines had inadvertently reversed the plaintiff and the defendant. See Kent's Copy, 1st ed., *Post* v. *Wright & Buchan*, 1 Cai. Rep. 111 (N.Y. Sup. Ct., 1803), 111–12; 2nd ed., *Post* v. *Wright & Buchan*, 1 Cai. Rep. 111 (N.Y. Sup. Ct., 1803), 111–12. This might well have been pointed out by any number of people involved in the case. Another was correction of the word "direction" for "discretion." See Kent's Copy, 1st ed., *Bogert and Lewis* v. *Hildreth, Sheriff of Montgomery*, 1 Cai. Rep. 1 (N.Y. Sup. Ct., 1803), 4; 2nd ed., *Bogert and Lewis* v. *Hildreth, Sheriff of Montgomery*, 1 Cai. Rep. 1 (N.Y. Sup. Ct., 1803), 4. This was the kind of mistake akin to a typo that anyone reading the original could well pick up. Another example like this was Kent writing "physician" for "doctor," in one case, see Kent's Copy, 1st ed., *Hart* v. *Hosack*, 1 Cai. Rep. 25 (N.Y. Sup. Ct.,

comments on his "first essay" or try. Perhaps Kent was angry, not having been invited to contribute, or it may have been he would not have wanted to help.

Mistakes or no mistakes, it is extremely unlikely that Kent, an ardent Federalist, either liked or sought out Caines, an enthusiastic Republican. Perhaps Kent was unwilling to work with him. Or it might have been Caines who rejected Kent. We do not know, but Caines exhibited an independence of spirit that Kent would not have appreciated. Caines dedicated his 1802 book on *lex mercatoria* or the law merchant to Thomas Jefferson.[35] He also argued in the New York Supreme Court before Kent against Kent's hero, Alexander Hamilton, in the important case of *People* v. *Croswell* in which Federalist newspaperman Harry Croswell was tried for a libel he was accused of having made against Jefferson. Hamilton famously argued in a speech that reportedly went on for six hours before the New York Supreme Court that truth should be a defense in such a charge.[36] This case counted as a defeat for Hamilton in the sense that the New York Supreme Court did not agree with his argument in early 1804, despite Kent speaking in its favor. However, the following year, in 1805, the New York legislature adopted the truth-as-defense position.[37] It was an important case to Kent, who wrote about it many years later in his *Commentaries*.[38] It seems likely that Kent did not appreciate Caines's appearance and efforts on the opposing side of a case that was, like the earlier trials

1803), 26. That change did appear in the second edition. See 2nd ed., *Hart* v. *Hosack*, 1 Cai. Rep. 25 (N.Y. Sup. Ct., 1803), 25.

35 George Caines, *An enquiry into the law merchant of the United States, or, Lex mercatoria americana, on several heads of commercial importance: dedicated by permission to Thomas Jefferson, President of the United States: in two volumes* (New York: Isaac Collins and Son, 1802).

36 See " The Speeches at Full Length of Mr. Van Ness, Mr. Caines, the Attorney-General, Mr. Harrison, and General Hamilton, in the Great Cause of the People against Harry Croswell, on an indictment for a libel on Thomas Jefferson, President of the United States" (New York: G. and R. Waite, 1804) in vol. 41, *Albany Institute Pamphlets*, New York State Library, Albany, NY. Caines did not include the case in those for 1804. It was later reported by Johnson in 3 Johns. Cai. 337 (N.Y. Sup. Ct., 1804).

37 See https://en.wikipedia.org/wiki/People_v._Croswell. Truth as a defense had been allowed under the original *Sedition Act* passed by John Adams in 1798 in order to prosecute Republicans criticizing the government prior to Jefferson repealing it. These trials took place in Federal Courts. For a list of the most significant prosecutions, see https://en.wikipedia.org/wiki/Alien_and_Sedition_Acts.

38 See *Kent's Commentaries*, 2: 16–22 (where Kent explains that the New York law adopted truth as a defense with the important proviso that the words or speech even if truthful must also not be made with malice to hurt or humiliate a public official).

under the *Alien and Sedition Acts*, a hot political issue in the early American period.[39]

The legislation empowering the court to appoint a reporter was passed on April 7, 1804.[40] The timing of the appointment (May Term 1804) suggests it was a lame-duck decision made by then Chief Justice Morgan Lewis, who won the state governorship on April 24. Kent was appointed as Chief Justice on July 2, too late to be able to oppose Caines's appointment. Kent and Lewis may not have been on good terms at the time, as Kent's memoirs record his refusal of Lewis's offer of support for the New York Supreme Court Chief Justice position in exchange for Kent's support of Lewis's bid for state governor, an election in which Lewis ran as a Republican.[41] Given these circumstances, it seems unlikely that Kent had much if any say in who obtained the first reporter position.

Kent was generally not shy about expressing negative views of other people, especially those he judged harshly for having abandoned the Federalist cause.[42] Historians have noted he "had a tendency toward sharp, personal attacks on others that could accurately and charitably be called mean-spirited."[43] Kent's comments about Caines on the flyleaf to the second edition of Caines's reports amply demonstrate that tendency. Kent wrote that Caines took up "the business of reporting" because he failed as a lawyer. He also wrote that after Caines ceased being a reporter "he had never been prosperous nor greatly respected either for Sound Judgment or pure Morals." He appeared to suggest that Caines had little property of his own that did not belong to his wife, an odd charge given the rampant hypergamy of legal and political elites at the time, as well as the way that fortunes were so often made and lost on land and other kinds of

39 See Kathryn Preyer, "*United States* v. *Callender*: Judge and Jury in a Republican Society" in Mary Sarah Bilder, Maeva Marcus, and R. Kent Newmyer eds., *Blackstone in America: Selected Essays of Kathryn Preyer* (New York: Cambridge University Press, 2009), 92–112.

40 See Moore, "One Hundred Fifty Years of Official Law Reporting," 273, quoting the text of the provision.

41 See Kent, *Memoirs*, 120–21.

42 For example, Sanford came under fire for changing from Federalist to Jeffersonian Republican as discussed in Chapter 4. See Roper, "The Elite of the New York Bar as Seen from the Bench: James Kent's Necrologies," 230.

43 See e.g. Shields, "Chancellor Kent's Abridgment of Emerignon's Maritime Insurance," 1145 n.169. Shields notes that the tendency Kent had toward sharp personal attack and comments he made to Alexander Hamilton helped precipitate Hamilton's fatal duel with Aaron Burr in 1804, when those comments were relayed to Burr by a third party.

speculation.[44] This second edition appeared in 1813, many years after Caines's dismissal. Such a republication was consistent with the idea at the time that reporters held a property in their reports of cases.[45] These might still be Caines's cases, Kent seemed to be saying, but he really was a worthless fellow.

Much more admirable in Kent's opinion was his old friend and loyal Federalist William Johnson. The reporter position was an appointment made by the Court and held "at pleasure."[46] Kent did not have to wait too long to replace the undesirable Caines with a person more to his liking. Kent's memoirs record that he (Kent) was indispensable in getting Johnson his appointment in 1806.[47] John Langbein has documented the close working relationship between Kent and Johnson. The two produced an impressive number of reports, many of them reports from the Court of Equity once the position for a reporter for that court was created and Kent was made Chancellor in 1814.[48] Their collaboration was a deep one, with Kent going so far as to dedicate his famous *Commentaries of American Law* to Johnson.[49] Langbein wrote that "[t]he two men were so closely identified that when Kent retired in 1823 in some political disfavor, Johnson fell with him."[50]

Kent's issues with Caines certainly would have included political affiliation as well as the level of care Kent thought were put into the preparation of the reports. However, there was also a question of attitude. Caines wrote the following in the Preface to the offending second edition,

44 See e.g. Gore Vidal, *Inventing a Nation: Washington, Adams, Jefferson* (New Haven, CT: Yale University Press, 2003), 35 (speaking of John Adams, "[e]ach Adams had seemed instinctively to be obeying an old law of new societies, by marrying above his social station: farmer John to a Boylston, while Abigail's mother was a storied Quincy"). See John Fabian Witt, *Patriots and Cosmopolitans: Hidden Histories of American Law* (Boston, MA: Harvard University Press, 2007), 15–82, 30–31, 75–78 (on sitting United States Supreme Court judge James Wilson's disastrous land speculations).

45 The reporter's copyright was extinguished in the 1834 decision involving the first official United States Supreme Court reporter, Henry Wheaton. See Surrency, *A History of American Law Publishing*, 46.

46 See N.Y. Laws 1804, c. 68.

47 See Kent, *Memoirs*, 125 (noting also that it was largely through Kent's influence that Johnson's appointment was made).

48 Langbein, "Chancellor Kent and the History of Legal Literature," 579.

49 Ibid., 580–81.

50 Ibid., 582–83. A similar close relationship developed at the United States Supreme Court between Joseph Story, who (rather than John Marshall) took the lead in securing an official reporter, and the very close working relationship he developed with the first person to fill that role, Henry Wheaton. See Popkin, *Evolution of the Judicial Opinion*, 77–78.

noting that he had taken some license preparing the first edition: "Encouraged by legislative patronage, and a permission to exercise his own discretion, the author, in the second volume, began a little to dress the cases in his own language, and to discard from the opinions of the judges the statements of facts, by which they were, when delivered, in general preceded."[51] This behavior, "exercise[ing] his own discretion" and "dress[ing] the cases in his own language," exhibited an independence of spirit that Kent was certain to dislike. Johnson's docile behavior in the Chancery reporter's position would have been more to Kent's taste. In contrast to Caines, Johnson wrote that "[t]hese judgments are given exactly as they were delivered in writing."[52] As Langbein put it, "Johnson was learned and genteel, diligent but unambitious, a Federalist by disposition and hence politically congenial, yet recessive in the extreme – in short, an ideal minion. Kent had found his Boswell, happily named Johnson."[53]

Consider the following contrast between Caines and Johnson. Caines's *Lex Mercatoria Americana*, a book setting out the law that applied to American ships engaged in foreign trade, coastal trade, and the fishing trade, does not shy away from direct, substantive and critical engagement with its issues. Caines states his disagreement with an admiralty rule that allowed an exemption to be made for goods of an enemy nation found aboard the ship of a friendly nation, for example, and does so in strong terms. Calling this practice of "neutral bottoms making neutral goods," recently agreed upon in a treaty with France, a "monstrous incongruity," he wrote the following: "it is hoped that the veil of peace will forever hide from our sight the baneful results of such a convention; a compact which unnerves the arm of the warrior, and flattens the edge of his sword."[54] He then wrote: "But I forget that my office is to relate what is, not that which ought to be."[55] Compare this with William Johnson's contribution to an area of law closely related to the law merchant and so important to New York during this period: a careful translation from the French of Azuni's famous book on maritime law, virtually guaranteed – by the fact that it was a translation – to include nothing in the way of

[51] Caines, "Preface to the Second Edition," *New-York Term Reports of Cases*.
[52] Johnson, "Preface" to *Reports of Cases Adjudged in the Court of Chancery of New York*, vii.
[53] Langbein, "Chancellor Kent and the History of Legal Literature," 582. Kent would have known Johnson's personality prior to the appointment, as the two were good friends.
[54] Caines, *Lex Mercatoria*, 121. [55] Ibid.

substantive comment or strong language of the sort Caines was wont to produce.[56]

The struggles between Kent and Caines and the contrast between Caines and Johnson highlight an important point about the power of invisible personnel in a case-centered law-making process.[57] The clerk is completely invisible. The reporter is present to some extent – we read his version of the facts and his marginal notes, and older collections include the reporter's name in the citation: 3 Cai. R. 175 (1805) stands for the third volume of *Caines's Reports* containing cases closed during the year 1805, at page 175.[58] Despite their relative invisibility, reporters have long played an important role in common-law jurisdictions. Lord Campbell famously said of his days as a law reporter in England, "I had a drawer marked 'Bad law,' into which I threw all the cases which seemed to me to be improperly ruled."[59] Frederick Pollock exercised an enormous influence over the development of British common law in the nineteenth century from his position as chief editor of the semi-official English *Law Reports*, "largely responsible for determining which judgments were and which were not reported."[60] Early American reporters were considered far more important than the judges.[61] It was the reporter "who selected the cases, stated the facts, summarized the views of counsel, summarized

[56] See *The Maritime Law of Europe by M.D.A. Azuni ... Translated from the French* [by William Johnson], 2 vols. (New York: I. Riley, 1806). The work was originally published in Italian and translated into French, from which Johnson translated it into English for Americans. Its importance lay, as the translator put it, in knowing "the principles by which neutral commerce is to be regulated in time of war," given the high level of conflict and war between the great trading nations, especially Britain and France after the Revolutionary War. See "Translator's Preface," xiii.

[57] Paul Halliday has written eloquently about the invisibility of clerical practice in eighteenth-century England and the important role King's Bench clerks played in literally making the precedents by turning them into things and then making it possible through their clerical practices to find those things again, a process integral to them being operationalized as precedents. See Paul D. Halliday, "Authority in the Archive," 1:1 *Critical Analysis of Law* (2014): 110–142.

[58] See Surrency, *A History of American Law Publishing*, 45 (identifying the trend reducing the importance of the reporter with the shift to citing reports by the name of the state rather than the name of the reporter).

[59] James Oldham, *The Mansfield Manuscripts and the Growth of English Law in the Eighteenth Century*, vol. 1 (Chapel Hill: University of North Carolina Press, 1992), 184.

[60] Neil Duxbury, *Frederick Pollock and the English Juristic Tradition* (Oxford: Oxford University Press, 2004), 6. Duxbury writes at p. 11, that Pollock consulted with judges and counsel about what the *Law Reports* should include and as to their wording. However, "[d]eterminations of what should and should not be reported were [...] ultimately his alone." Duxbury notes at p. 286 that Pollock held this position for forty years.

[61] Surrency, *A History of American Law Publishing*, 44–45.

the views of those judges who gave oral opinions, and supplied annotations of his own."[62]

Judges who cared about their own intellectual legacy and about founding a professionalized legal science on a common-law case method realized that the relationship with a reporter mattered tremendously to what they were trying to build. The close working relationships important judges had with their reporters, and their tender aspects, are striking. Justice Joseph Story shared food and lodging with Henry Wheaton, the first United States Supreme Court reporter.[63] In dedicating his *Commentaries* to Johnson, Kent wrote "[i]n compiling these volumes [...] I have frequently been led to revisit the same ground, and to follow out the same paths, over which I have so often passed with you as a companion to cheer and delight me."[64] He continued: "You have reported every decision which I gave in term time, and thought worth reporting, during the five and twenty years that I was a Judge at Law and in Equity, *with the exception of the short interval occupied by Mr. Caines' Reports*."[65] One might easily read in here "with the exception of the [fortunately] short interval occupied by [the unfortunate] Mr. Caines." When Caines tried to return to his position as reporter after Kent and Johnson were forced out, Kent said that Caines's claims to the position "as an old original & persecuted Reporter [...] mortified & extremely disgusted" him.[66]

Less widely discussed is how lawyers become invisible in the reports. This happened under Kent and Johnson, in a way that was not true of Caines's reports. Caines saw the lawyers' arguments as indispensable to the report. He included them and wrote about how important he thought they were in the preface to the first edition of the *Reports*: "To omit altogether what the advocate has urged, and specify his points alone, has more than once been suggested; but believing the reasonings of the barrister to form the link which connects the case with the decision, it was thought impossible, without in some degree preserving the language of the pleader, to do justice to either."[67] When Johnson took over publication of

[62] Langbein, "Chancellor Kent and the History of Legal Literature," 578.
[63] Popkin, *Evolution of the Judicial Opinion*, 77.
[64] See "To William Johnson, Esq." in Kent, *Commentaries*, vol. 4 (1830) np. Kent moved this dedication from the fourth volume to the opening pages of the first volume in the second edition in 1832.
[65] Ibid [emphasis added].
[66] Roper, "The Elite of the New York Bar as Seen from the Bench: James Kent's Necrologies," 213 n. 23.
[67] Caines, Preface to *New York term reports*, v.

the New York Supreme Court reports from Caines, Johnson wrote to Kent that "Mr. C. [Caines] offered me his notes on Arguments, but I declined the acceptance of them, thinking it best to omit the Arguments of Counsel, and give only the facts & opinions of the Court."[68] Johnson may not have been keen on including lawyers' arguments because, unlike Caines, he did not know shorthand, without which it would be extremely difficult to reproduce those arguments anything close to verbatim.[69] Preparing summaries of the lawyers' arguments was generally considered to be the most arduous of the reporter's tasks.[70]

Johnson did reproduce some of the lawyers' arguments in his New York Supreme Court reports. However, he ceased the practice for Kent's Chancery Court decisions. Johnson explained that his decision was not based on the inconvenience it would have caused him to attend every oral argument. It was rather "a deliberate judgment confirmed by the opinion of persons entitled to very great respect, and which, if necessary, might be supported by the highest legal authority."[71] His defense was that "mutilation" was inevitable in any abridgement and that he had an obligation to keep the reports from getting too "voluminous."[72] Such elaborate attention to the point suggests awareness that members of the bar would not be pleased to see their arguments discarded. Johnson wanted to avoid any negative inference to be drawn about his own dedication to the role.

It seems likely that Kent's was one of those opinions "entitled to very great respect" and that he would have been against the inclusion of lawyers' arguments. Why? Well, this seemingly innocuous editorial choice, was of great consequence to a jurist with an ego like Kent's. Omitting the lawyers' arguments generally operated to aggrandize the judge, who now appeared to be the source of everything in the opinion,

[68] William Johnson to James Kent, December 23, 1805, Reel 2, vol. 3, *The Papers of James Kent*, Library of Congress, Manuscript Division, Washington, DC. Reproduced in Kent, *Memoirs*, 125–26.

[69] Johnson wrote in the preface to the twenty-volumes of New York Supreme Court cases the following: "Unused to the practice of short-hand writing, I have been obliged to rely on a quick pen and on memory." William Johnson, Preface to *Reports of Cases Argued and Determined in the Supreme Court of Judicature and in the Court for the Trial of Impeachments and the Correction of Errors in the State of New York*, vol. 1 (New York: I. Riley, 1807), vii. Caines refers to his ability to write short-hand in the Preface to the 2nd ed. *New York Term Reports*.

[70] Surrency, *A History of American Law Publishing*, 43.

[71] William Johnson, Preface to *Reports of Cases Adjudged in the Court of Chancery of New York* (Albany, NY: E.W. Backus, 1816–23; New York: Van Winkle and Wiley), vii.

[72] Ibid.

(the authorities, the ideas) even when much of what the opinion was built on in fact came from the lawyers. Excluding the lawyers' arguments was not necessarily (or at least not exclusively) a bid to augment judicial authority. There were important practical considerations, as Johnson indicated. The practice of including lawyers' arguments greatly increased the length of the reports and consequently their expense. Reporters walked a fine line between increasing costs (if they included too much of the lawyers' arguments) and offending their professional consumers (if they included too little).[73] Reporters had to be careful not to antagonize the prominent lawyers whose help they needed to sell the volumes.[74] All this suggests that lawyers cared deeply about garnering due credit and were not content to live in the shadows like the law clerk or Kent's "ideal minion," Johnson.

The 1804 New York statute that created the reporter position said that the reporter would report cases as the judges may direct or "as may be deemed important to be reported."[75] We do not know how Caines and Kent navigated the question which cases were to be selected; but the bad relationship between the two men and Caines's feistiness suggests it is unlikely Caines would simply do whatever Kent demanded. Caines's own references to "dress[ing] the cases in his own language," "exercise[ing] his own discretion," suggest he saw the role otherwise. When the position for a Chancery Court reporter was created in 1814, the same year that Kent was named Chancellor, it left no doubt as to who was in charge – the legislation stated that the reporter would "from time to time [...] report and publish such decisions of the court of chancery, as the chancellor of this state [i.e. Kent] shall deem of sufficient importance to be reported and published."[76] The Chancery Court was actually held at James Kent's house, in his study, and there seems to be little doubt that he was fully and completely in charge.[77] However, at the New York Supreme Court in 1805, Caines's view was by no means insignificant.[78] This means that in *Pierson*, though invisible to us, George Caines was an important person.

[73] See Popkin, *Evolution of the Judicial Opinion*, 99. [74] Ibid., 79.

[75] Moore, "One Hundred Fifty Years of Official Law Reporting," 273.

[76] See ibid., 278.

[77] See Kent, *Memoirs*, 120. See also Kessler, *Inventing American Exceptionalism*, 36–48, 55–61 (on Kent's role systematizing the law of equity in New York State), 45 (emphasizing how Kent and Joseph Story were attracted to the law of equity given "the increasingly democratic (and thus, to them, distasteful) thrust of American political life"), 47 (and "a response to the perceived dangers of democratic rule").

[78] See Langbein, "Chancellor Kent and the History of Legal Literature," 577 ("it was the reporter and not the judges who had the final say about which cases would be reported").

When Kent and Livingston were arguing over what Ricard, Beawes, and Emerignon said in a law merchant case involving a maritime law dispute, Caines inserted a marginal note filling out who Emerignon relied on for his understanding of "the Rhodian law," the earliest code or collection of Maritime laws: "Faber, Vinnius, Duarenus, Kuricke, Loceenius, Devicq, Roccus & Marquardus."[79] This note was obviously connected to knowledge Caines had from working on his book on the law merchant. Much of this book was a fairly prosaic recounting of Federal Congressional law on ships and shipping.[80] It also included extensive and detailed discussion of maritime law cases, mostly from England but also from various states in the Union, where available.[81] However, it too had its more learned or exotic moments, unsurprising given the inevitably international dimensions of maritime law. Thus, Caines cited Vattel on the obligation to honor a promise to pay in the case of a ransom of ship and cargo, so strong was "the power of contracting."[82] In addition to Vattel, the work contains references to Valin and Vinnius.[83]

Caines clearly would have felt comfortable in the world of the authorities invoked in *Pierson* – Justinian, Pufendorf, Barbeyrac, and Bynkershoek. Is it possible that Caines may have elaborated on what actually happened in the case? Did he "dress" the cases "a little [...] in his own language" or "write a fable for little fishes" and "make them speak like great whales," as Oliver Goldsmith wrote to Samuel Johnson in one of the epigraphs Melville chose to append to the beginning of *Moby-Dick*?

[79] See *Walden* v. *Le Roy*, 2 Caines Reports 262 (N.Y. Sup. Ct., 1805), 272. The French lawyer Antonius Faber (1557–1624); Arnoldus Vinnius (1588–1657), a Dutch lawyer who was a professor at Leyden; Francisco Duarenus (1509–1559); Reinhold Kuricke (1610–1667), a German expert on maritime law; Johannes Locceenius (1598–1677), a Swedish historian of maritime law; Francesco Rocco (1605–1676), an Italian expert in maritime law; Johannes Marquardus (1610–1668), another expert on maritime law.

[80] See e.g. Caines, *Lex Mercatoria*, 12, explaining the Congressional law requiring that each American ship contain "a chest of medicines" and another provision setting out the minimum amount of water, salt meat, and ship bread for each passenger on a transatlantic crossing. Caines writes, "[i]t is in provisions like these that we recognize in our country, the parental tenderness of an affectionate mother." See also pp. 13–15 on the (largely futile) attempts to legislate fines for ships engaged in the slave trade and the provision on p. 45 setting out a fine between $200 and $2,000 for bribing or offering to bribe a customs officer. Other sections treat items such as the customs and duties on goods for exportation, going into detail on the particular type of good, e.g. sugar, pickled fish etc., rules relating to the making of manifests for passengers and goods and penalties for breach, the proper labeling of goods and the like.

[81] See e.g. ibid., 69–79. The chapter "Of Commercial Neutrality" relies heavily on Charles Robinson's British *Admiralty Reports*. See ibid., 108–30.

[82] Ibid., 106. [83] See ibid., 362, 231.

Certainly there existed a tradition in English law reporting to worry less about the exact words of the lawyers or judges and to capture instead the gist or sense of what was being said, "the broad underlying sense of arguments and decisions," as one commentator on the law reporter's role put it.[84] This could result in making a judge sound much more eloquent than he in fact was. A certain nineteenth-century English Vice Chancellor "appears to have had no voice to speak of and very little wit; he frequently becomes inaudible, and yet the pundits of the Inns of Court and elsewhere, having read him as rendered by shorthand writers, held him to be a great master of lucid, elegant and forceful language."[85] But judges of the New York Supreme Court wrote their decisions (at least those that were reported), so it seems unlikely that Caines could have significantly altered either Tompkins's majority decision or Livingston's dissent. He might have created a tidier debating structure for the lawyers' arguments than occurred in reality.[86] As he put it, "it has been necessary to condense; to shorten but not to deviate from the path, counsel have been pleased to elect."[87] In reporting the lawyers' argument, the concern is to capture the essence of that argument, not to provide a faithful reproduction. We must be careful not to imagine the reporter operating faithfully as a stenographer would in a courtroom today, creating a transcript of the proceedings. What was produced was nothing like a verbatim transcript; it was a much more creative account, with facts, lawyers' argument, and the judge's opinion woven together from different sources, oral argument, and written papers in the possession of the clerk, the judges, and the lawyers themselves.

The high-minded *Monthly Anthology, and Boston Review* editors criticized Livingston, not Caines, for the humor *Pierson* demonstrated. It did not seem to occur to them that Caines rather than Livingston might have been to blame. And, indeed, they seemed to think that Caines was in

[84] Scharf, "The Court Reporter," 192. [85] Ibid., 224.

[86] I wrote in "The Lost Record" that oral argument might have been in Riverhead at an adjourned session of the New York Supreme Court on September 19, 1805. However, I now think that is unlikely. Judgment was given on September 10, 1805 and it would be odd for the argument to come later than the decision in the case. The hearing probably took place on Wednesday, August 7, 1805. See Supreme Court of Judicature (New York), General and Special Term Minute Books, J0130-82, New York State Archives, Albany, New York, highlighted in the "Archival Note" at the end of the Introduction, where I explain two new archival findings since finding and writing about the Judgment Roll in "The Lost Record." I have been unable to find out what occurred in Riverhead on September 19.

[87] Caines, Preface to *New York term reports*, iv.

general a little *too* faithful to what transpired in the cases he reported, suggesting that he did not interfere enough with the words of counsel in the reports of his cases. It was, they wrote, "the duty of a reporter to exhibit the counsel in a decent garb, however slovenly they may themselves consent to appear. A filthy, or a tattered dress is neither decorous nor dignified before the most respectable tribunal in the state."[88] This sounds like a criticism of Caines for failing to make the lawyers appear to be *better* than they were when they actually appeared.

The *Monthly Anthology, and Boston Review* editors appear to be suggesting that it was the job of the court's invisible personnel or support staff to help both judges and lawyers appear before the public, in the law report, in the best state possible. Why? Early nineteenth-century law reports were both more literary and political than they are today. Collections of reports were, for instance, regularly reviewed by publications like *The Monthly Anthology, and Boston Review*. And literary collections included case reports, and not just burlesque examples like Livingston's dissent in *Pierson*.[89] William Coleman, New York's first unofficial law reporter, went on to be the editor of an important daily newspaper, *The New-York Post*, which would have carried, among many other things, reports of trials thought to be of public interest.[90] As the politics between Kent, Caines, and Johnson demonstrate, law reporting was intimately connected to, not hermetically sealed from, the rough and tumble of politics. Indeed, struggles over the reports and who would be the reporter were yet another theatre for those politics. That is the point that appears to be missing in the evaluations of what kind of reporter Caines was, specifically that Kent would have disliked him and been critical of him probably no matter what, given their differing politics and the circumstances of Caines's appointment.

As Joanne Freeman puts it, the early national period was characterized by a "politics of friendships and enmities [that] was fluid, unpredictable, and difficult to manage. Under the two umbrellas of principle known as Federalism and Republicanism lay a mass of shifting loyalties, [in which] no one figure [was] ever entirely predictable in his actions or allegiances."[91] This uncertainty created "a politics of anxious

[88] "The Boston Review" (July 1, 1806), 368.

[89] See Surrency, *A History of American Law Publishing*, 40 (referring to Francis Hopkinson's inclusion of case reports in a literary collection in 1792).

[90] See Nevins, *The Evening Post*, 14–34.

[91] Joanne B. Freeman, *Affairs of Honor: National Politics in the New Republic* (New Haven, CT: Yale University Press, 2002), 214.

extremes"[92] that was, at times, "like a war without uniforms [in which] it was difficult to distinguish friends from foes and often impossible to predict the strange combinations of circumstances that could alter a man's political loyalties or lead to an alliance between former enemies."[93] Richard Hofstadter famously called the highly personal nature of post-Revolutionary politics "the paranoid style."[94] In such a highly personal and confrontational political culture, any opposition was immediately associated with anarchy, subversion, and disloyalty, all of which – whether real or imagined – elicited extreme responses.

In this touchy and fluid period, Kent came down regularly and firmly on the Federalist side of political issues, as his allegiance to Alexander Hamilton during Hamilton's lifetime, and eulogizing after his death, testifies, along with the acerbic comments in the *Necrologies* on those who – in his eyes – opportunistically turned their backs on Federalism. Interestingly, Livingston was one of the few Republicans whom Kent spared. Donald Roper argues that Livingston became "politically dormant" once he went to the bench in 1802 and that Kent was in Livingston's debt for the role Livingston played in helping secure Kent's professorship at Columbia and for Kent's receipt of an LL.D in 1797.[95] Kent's role as Chief Justice and as Chancellor insulated him from a certain kind of party politics. However, Federalism remained strong among the merchants of New York City, so there was a point in continuing to fight. And Kent continued to yield indirect influence until the 1820s through positions on the Council of Revision and the Council of Appointments, essentially until New York adopted a new state constitution in 1821, which failed to repeal the mandatory retirement for judicial officials and therefore resulted in his own unwelcome retirement alongside the repeal of those arguably undemocratic institutions.[96] The *Commentaries* sprang from that forced retirement. They were a way to push for a more

[92] Ibid., 10. [93] Ibid., 223.

[94] See Richard Hofstadter, *The Paranoid Style in American Politics, and Other Essays* (New York: Knopf, 1966).

[95] See Roper, "The Elite of the New York Bar as Seen from the Bench: James Kent's Necrologies," 205. Livingston had been once very vigorously anti-Federalist, which Kent expressed upset over in 1792 when Livingston constitutionally justified George Clinton's election as Governor in a questionable election.

[96] The Council of Appointments and the Council of Revision – which included judges, along with the Governor – controlled appointments to all offices and reviewed state legislation. See Alvin Kass, *Politics in New York State, 1800–1830* (New York: Syracuse University Press, 1965), 13–15 (on the Council of Appointments); 45–47 (on the Council of Revision).

conservative approach to the law by promoting common-law doctrines that would lean toward the protection of property and older forms of wealth from what Kent and fellow old-guard members of the "Junto" (what they were called by their enemies) condemned as "Jacobin" (what they called their enemies) legislative intrusions.[97]

It would be a mistake to fail to place the struggles over New York's first official (and allegedly unsuccessful) reporter Caines against this broader political background and context. So too, we must recognize the way in which law reports themselves played a role in political life. Important intellectuals debated issues surrounding law reports. Daniel Webster reviewed one of Johnson's collection of cases and offered a number of important criticisms of it.[98] One was to chastise the judges of the New York Supreme Court for disagreeing too much among themselves. Webster wrote: "We know of nothing more unhappy for the publick, or more discouraging to those engaged in professional pursuits, than the disagreement of the judges."[99] He noted that the Court of King's Bench in England for eleven successive years had not produced a dissent and "perhaps for thirty years, in that court, there was hardly as much difference of opinion on the Bench, as happened in the New-York court" in this one term.[100] Law reporting was a political issue for Webster, connected to the topic of constraint or control of the judiciary, who were left with less discretion and room for personal and private decision if cases were reported.[101] Disagreement and dissent among the judges would muddy

[97] See e.g. Charles Warren, *Jacobin and Junto; or, Early American Politics as Viewed in the Diary of Dr. Nathaniel Ames, 1758–1822* (Cambridge, MA: Harvard University Press, 1931), 3 ("Never in American annals has there been a period when men 'took their politics so hard' as in the twenty-five years between the framing of the Constitution and the end of the War of 1812. Households, families, communities, trades, and professions were split on political lines, in hot and abusive enmity, according as they held Federalist or Antifederalist views. Men patronized the taverns, shops, stage lines, banks, and other enterprises which were conducted by their party associates; they even regarded the political complexion of their doctors"). On New York specifically, see Kass, *Politics in New York State*, 136–37. See also David Hackett Fischer, *The Revolution of American Conservatism: The Federalist Party in the Era of Jeffersonian Democracy* (New York: Harper and Row, 1965), 182–87.

[98] "The Boston Review: Article 17 *Reports of cases argued, and determined, in the Supreme Court of Judicature of the State of New York* ..." by William Johnson in *The Monthly Anthology and Boston Review Containing Sketches and Reports of Philosophy, Religion* [...] (April 1, 1807): 206–208.

[99] Ibid., 208. [100] Ibid.

[101] See Alfred S. Konefsky, "Law and Culture in Antebellum Boston," 40 *Stanford Law Review* (1987–88): 1119–59, 1132–33. It is included in Alfred S. Konefsky and Andrew J. King eds., *The Papers of Daniel Webster: Legal Papers, vol. 1, The New Hampshire*

the waters of what Webster called "the legitimate use of precedents," the promotion of reliable rule and restrain arbitrary authority or private opinion.[102] "Precedents," according to Webster, "not only *assist* the judge; they, in a good measure, *control* him."[103] Publicity (in governance generally and in the courts in particular) was a crucial nineteenth-century political concern.[104]

Caines might well have added "a little fancy" to what was, looked at one way, just blubber (as in talk). "[B]lubber is blubber you know; tho' you may get oil out of it," as Melville wrote to Henry Dana Jr. However, that blubber, or perhaps the oil that could be got out of it, was just what the common law was, a primarily oral tradition in which cases were more like remembrances, often imperfect, and reports were only evidence of what that law was, not texts that lawyers learned to parse very specifically into binding *ratio decidendi* and non-binding *obiter dictum*.[105]

Many scholars and legal historians have noted that the idea of precedents as binding in a strict way is a relatively recent phenomenon. For centuries the common law operated in a much looser, customary, and primarily oral way.[106] Our more rigid and positivistic, even legislative, understanding of the common law probably dates only from the nineteenth century, or at least it "hardened," as it is sometimes put, over the course of the nineteenth century.[107] If we examine the differences between

Practice (Hanover, NH: Published for Dartmouth College by the University Press of New England, 1982), 172–74.

102 "The Boston Review" (April 1, 1807), 208. 103 Ibid.

104 See Kessler, *Inventing American Exceptionalism*, 94, 109–11 (discussing the general publicity concern in the context of New York's Chancery Court). Kessler discusses publicity primarily in terms of taking evidence through open court witness examination that could be subject to cross-examination by the opposing party as opposed to the private interrogatories of equity examiners and masters and the way that this secrecy was thought by many to be a problem with equity procedure. She does not deal with Chancery reporting practices specifically. To the extent that there were reports, a practice that was taken on intensely in the Kent-Johnson collaboration, one wonders how that fact bears on contemporary views expressed about Chancery being secretive and unfair, especially in the decades after Kent's tenure when objections were no longer synonymous with criticism of him as an individual and more about the institution and how it was perceived.

105 Popkin helpfully characterizes the shift to a precedent-based system in a more strict sense as a movement to treat case law legislatively as if it were a statute. See *Evolution of the Judicial Opinion*.

106 See Simpson, "The Common Law and Legal Theory."

107 See Jim Evans, "Change in the Doctrine of Precedent during the Nineteenth Century" in Laurence Goldstein ed., *Precedent in Law* (Oxford: Clarendon Press, 1987), 35–72, 35 n. 1.

Caines's early reports and what happened during Johnson's tenure, we can see that New York seems to exemplify this "hardening" process. Where Caines had nothing to say about what was strictly speaking binding in a decision in 1805, by the time he republished the cases in 1813 he spoke of "leaving to the student the labour of separating the gold from the dross."[108] In 1815, eleven volumes into his twenty-volume coverage of the New York Supreme Court and the Court of Errors, Johnson published a Digest, in which he omitted the usual marginal notes and carefully extracted "from the opinions of the judges, the principles of law."[109] He also separated from these the *obiter dicta*, defined as the "observations of the judges, not embraced in the points decided by the court."[110] In other words, Johnson had turned to the hardened, clearly separated and delineated perspective that was clearly not part of Caines's legal culture ten years earlier in 1805. Only when a significant number of cases are reported can one have the view that legal science will involve "separating the gold from the dross" in this way. Reporting as a widespread practice was a necessary precondition for this particular theory of the common law.[111]

Caines's "fancy" might well have been needed "to cook things up" in the sense of creating the report as precisely we now see it.[112] However, the kind of creativity at the reporter's disposal, while great by today's standards, was probably not of the kind in which it would have been permissible to make up arguments from whole cloth. Put another way, Caines was working *with* the judges and lawyers involved in the cases he reported, not making them up from scratch. They might not have minded a little elaboration or "corruption," especially if in doing so Caines crystallized the arguments and streamlined the analysis; in the report they would look a little more learned, or sophisticated, or wittier than they had been in real life. However, it is likely that they would have condemned wholesale reportorial fabrication. Johnson might well have been more fastidious than Caines. Johnson wrote for instance that

[108] Caines, Preface to the Second Edition.

[109] William Johnson, Preface to *Digest of the Cases Decided and Reported in the Supreme Court of Judicature and the Court for the Correction of Errors in the State of New York* (1815).

[110] Ibid.

[111] See Neil Duxbury, *The Nature and Authority of Precedent* (Cambridge UK; New York: Cambridge University Press, 2008), 35 n. 18 and the sources citing there, noting that in the United States, the modern doctrine of *stare decisis* starts to take shape in the early decades of the nineteenth century.

[112] Johnson, Preface to *Digest*.

"imperfect or inaccurate reports of judicial determinations, are justly to be reprobated as the bane of legal science."[113] However, we cannot conclude that Caines was apt (and allowed) to take great and free license. Indeed, he said in the preface to the second edition of the reports that he refrained from correcting errors from the first edition because he did not consider himself to be free to deviate from "what had been publicly delivered."[114]

There are two excellent reasons to conclude that Caines did not deviate greatly from what the lawyers and judges said in *Pierson*. First, he certainly did not make the whole thing up, despite the feeling of fable or fairy tale the case report sometimes stirs up. There was a case, as the discovery of the Judgment Roll confirmed. Moreover, the feature of the report most directly responsible for its fictional feel, the assumptions that allowed the lawyers to have their great state of nature debate set out in Chapter 5, with the fox standing for all animals *ferae naturae* – namely, the legal fiction surrounding the status of the land on which the fox was caught – was already in the Judgment Roll. In other words, the state-of-nature set up came from the original pleadings and papers (including the account as recorded by the Justice of the Peace): Post "did upon a certain wild and uninhabited[,] unpossessed and waste land, called the beach, find and start one of those noxious beasts called a fox." As we saw in Chapter 4, we do not know if those words came from Post himself, from Colden or from another lawyer he might have originally hired (but who did not appear with him at the jury trial). They might have come from Post's father (himself a magistrate), or even from the magistrate of record, John N. Fordham, if he assisted in helping to prepare the case. We do know that those words did not come from Caines. They were there from the earliest days of the action. Hence, as non-literal as the process of creating a law report was in the period, the pleadings and papers did create some essential parameters.

Secondly, there is Kent. As we have seen, he was not shy about expressing his negative views of people generally and of Caines in particular. Minute books of the New York Supreme Court confirm that

113 William Johnson, Preface to *Reports of Cases Adjudged by the Supreme Court of Judicature of the State of New York from January Term 1799, to January Term 1803, both inclusive; together with the cases determined in the Court for the Correction of Errors during that Period* (New York: I. Riley, 1808).

114 Caines, Preface to the Second Edition. It is unclear if this meant "publicly delivered" in court or simply what had been "publicly delivered" in the first edition. I am inclined to think the latter. In either case, it is an example of Webster's concern that law reports were intimately linked to questions of accountability and limits on arbitrary power.

Kent was present for the argument in *Pierson*.[115] One imagines that if Caines had been taking extensively free license, Kent would have objected on those grounds and not confined himself to the complaint that Caines made too many (really very minor) mistakes, or to comments on his moral character. It is true that standards were different than today. The reporter was extremely important. His name was on the reports. He held a copyright in them. The appointment was a lucrative office, like other offices, themselves often thought of as property, distributed under one political regime, taken away as spoils of war, and reallocated when the regime changed as a reward for party loyalty. The law reporter operated with the cooperation of the bench, but he was very independent. Still, it is difficult to believe that Kent would *not* have objected to Caines making up written reports for the judges, especially when they were unorthodox as in Livingston's case. As we have noted, *The Monthly Anthology, and Boston Review* article that was critical of Livingston's dissent in *Pierson* did not blame Caines. On the contrary, they absolve him of responsibility: "The reporter tells us in his preface, that in most cases he received the written opinions of the court; of course he is not responsible for the defects of their manner or matter."[116]

In fact, rather than condemn Caines for including or preparing a report that was too much a flight of fancy, both Kent and Johnson took it up in avid and serious ways. Johnson relied on it in his *Digest* under the section relating to "animals *ferae naturae*."[117] And, as we saw in the Introduction, Kent discussed it in earnest and at length in his *Commentaries*. Kent was actually the first person to put *Pierson* into scholarly circulation in a really influential way as we will explore in the next chapter. What occurred, in other words, was the kind of transformation so important to the acceptance of a case as a "leading" case. As Brian Simpson, a pioneer of legal archaeology, wrote, "common law rules enjoy whatever status they possess not because of the circumstances of their origin, but because of their continued reception."[118] It is this "continued reception" that makes the case what it is, the one that the profession knows. Indeed, one may even say that the cases are remade in the way that they are taken up. Their uptake just becomes

[115] Supreme Court of Judicature (New York), General and Special Term Minute Books, J0130-82, New York State Archives, Albany, NY. This is one of the two new sources highlighted in the "Archival Note" at the end of the Introduction that I had not yet found when I wrote "The Lost Record" and "*Pierson* v. *Post*: A Great Debate."

[116] "The Boston Review" (July 1, 1806), 368. [117] See Johnson, *Digest*, 35.

[118] Simpson, "The Common Law and Legal Theory," 86.

their new meaning.[119] That is why it is so important for historical investigation to extend beyond the case in its original context to its broader scholarly and intellectual trajectory and to focus specifically on the role played by those staffing that process of uptake, the treatise writers and later law teachers and casebook compilers – other invisible but important actors in a case-based, law-making process – who signal to the lawyers and would-be lawyers which cases are important and why.[120] For a prominent law school case like *Pierson*, we need to ask how the staffers framed that importance. This is not just a matter of what the case is taken to "stand for" by lawyers who might argue using the case in a court of law but what, following an older and less positivistic understanding of the common law, the case is supposed to show or illustrate. In this older tradition, the cases are examples of the law rather than the law itself. They are "best evidence" of a law greater than the sum of its cases.[121] The trans-historical and trans-jurisdictional tilt of the case method of teaching continues to ascribe to this older less positivistic understanding of what a case is, what is does. Hence, the dizzying approach casebooks take in reproducing cases good at exemplifying a point or a lesson despite having come from a relatively low level of court, an obscure jurisdiction, or a time long ago that is no longer very relevant. The skill of "thinking like a lawyer," whatever else it involves, is supposed to come from immersion in those examples and a development of what Karl Llewellyn famously called

[119] See Gerald J. Postema, "Classical Common Law Jurisprudence (Part I)," 2 *Oxford University Commonwealth Law Journal* (2002): 155–80, explaining that the view of law that is "taken up" (rather than "laid down") emerges from the disagreement between seventeenth-century British jurists, Coke and Davies (who ascribed to a static view of the common law as what existed since time immemorial) versus Seldon and Hale (who argued for a historical understanding of the common law incorporating variations on an evolving consensus as it grows and changes).

[120] See Angela Fernandez, "Legal History as the History of Legal Texts" in Christopher Tomlins and Markus Dubber eds., *Oxford Handbook of Legal History* (forthcoming Oxford University Press).

[121] See Gerald J. Postema, "Classical Common Law Jurisprudence (Part II)," 3 *Oxford University Commonwealth Law Journal* (2003): 1–28, 14. See also John H. Baker, *Introduction to English Legal History*, 4th ed. (Oxford: Oxford University Press, 2007), 196 ("There was probably never a time when the common law was not in some sense 'case law,' the result of solutions found in real cases"), 198 (however, it was thought of as "common learning" and "[n]o single precedent would be taken as common learning: it was evidence of practice and professional opinion but no more"), 198 ("[judicial] opinions were not sources of law, but simply evidence as to what the law was commonly held to be"); Duxbury, *The Nature and Authority of Precedent*, 32–33 ("a precedent could make an impression on lawyers because it was evidence of common learning, but no single precedent would be accepted as authority in preference to such learning [...] precedents must not be mistaken for law").

"situation sense."[122] A case will always have an importance for its original litigants in terms of how it affected their rights. However, without the uptake the case will be nothing in a common-law system even if that uptake it limited to its narrow use as a precedent in a subsequent case.

Perhaps, even though Livingston wrote his dissent, he never intended that it be published. I say this because one of the biographical notices written about Livingston after his death suggested he was "rather too averse to the parade of display and publication," noting that "many of his most elaborate opinions, the result of laborious and profound investigation, were communicated only to the counsel interested."[123] That notice appeared in *The North American Review* in a review of a collection of reports from the United States Supreme Court Circuit Court on which Livingston sat, written to promote the prompt public reporting of cases to strengthen the common law (a move crucial to helping to stave off state legislative codification, the reviewer argued), and, therefore, bemoaning the reservation of decisions in cases for private contemplation. Such a practice, if engaged in by Livingston, raises the distinct possibility that Livingston provided a copy of his decision in *Pierson* to the lawyers and that it made its way to Caines through one of them, most likely Colden. Livingston accepted Colden's characterization of the case as a case of hot pursuit, rejected the majority's view that it was a case of mere pursuit, and adopted the point from Barbeyrac that Colden recommended. Doubtless, Colden would have felt vindicated that someone on the bench had understood his argument and been happy to see his arguments make some impact.

If Caines received Livingston's decision from Colden (or Sanford or Livingston himself), he might then have very legitimately decided to exercise his prerogative as the true author of the report to include the

[122] Karl Llewellyn, *The Common Law Tradition* (Boston, MA: Little, Brown, 1960).

[123] Review of Elijah Paine Jr., vol. 1 *Reports of Cases Argued and Determined in the Circuit Court of the United States, for the Second Circuit, Comprising the Districts of New-York, Connecticut, and Vermont*, 27 *The North American Review* (July 1828), 167–91, 188–91 (on Livingston), 191. This review quotes repeatedly from Kent's *Commentaries*. I come to it through yet another one of Donald Roper's footnotes, where he noted that Kent did not say much about Livingston in his notes or "necrologies" of his contemporaries but gave reference to a sketch published here. The sketch is buried quite deeply in the review and not what one would expect to find in a review of a set of reports. See Roper, "The Elite of the New York Bar as Seen from the Bench: James Kent's Necrologies," 202 n. 4. One wonders of course if the article (and sketch) was written by Kent, standing in lieu of the usual evaluations Kent made of his contemporaries in his "Necrologies," as Roper termed them.

dissent along with the majority opinion. The boldness of his character makes this a believable move. Nor was there anything unjustified about it for Kent or anyone else to criticize. It was Caines's decision, even if Livingston never had any intent or thought that the text would be made public when he so wittingly penned it. It would be analogous to privately circulated musings among friends or colleagues that end up in the public sphere. If Livingston never expected his decision to appear publicly, this would help explain why he felt free to take the license in it that he did. It came from his pen; but it was only publicly preserved for posterity due to Caines – and that was Caines's decision.

If Caines published Livingston's work when Livingston had not meant for it to appear in public print, there is some irony in the situation, since Livingston's dissent in *Pierson* has been singled out as the only one of his decisions that appears in modern casebooks.[124] There is a distinct possibility, then, that its solemn foolery gives us a window on a Court of Dover world inhabited by legal professionals that was not so unique. Perhaps such expensive (to the parties) moot court-like performances and quasi-private determinations were more common than we would think, among members of a small elite bar, who knew each other well and belonged to many of the same social, legal, and political clubs. One has the feeling that Johnson would have used his discretion to suppress anything even slightly embarrassing had anyone offered the slightest hint that it would be important to do so. Caines, on the other hand, strikes one as a person who was open to, and may indeed have reveled in, showing the law as it was, perhaps even knowing that the reporter position would not be his for long with Kent in charge, given the political patronage system and the way that "faction" divided up the world and created friend and foe.[125]

Published legal reports sadly do not report costs. Old English reports such as the Yearbooks recorded the lawyers' oral arguments, which could be used for future study, specifically the *how* or procedure that was all-important in the King's Courts in Westminster Hall.[126] Pleadings became written (in order to constrain what the case would be about) and a trial was used to determine

[124] Dunne, "Brockholst Livingston," 399 (noting that *Pierson* "appears to be his [Livingston's] only opinion to be carried in modern casebooks").

[125] See generally, Patricia U. Bonomi, *A Factious People: Politics and Society in Colonial New York* (New York: Columbia University Press, 1971); Freeman, *Affairs of Honor*.

[126] Substance was "secreted through the interstices of procedure," as Maine famously put it. Quoted in Postema, "Class Common Law Jurisprudence (Part I)," 162. See Baker, *Introduction to English Legal History*, 53–57 (on the writ system and the forms of action), 179 (on the Yearbooks).

both the relevant law and its application to these facts (as opposed to oral pleadings, a disputation on a hypothetical set of issues and then determination in the local neighborhood of the facts by a jury who had information about the dispute that they relied on when the judge later traveled there on circuit).[127] In other words, the way the common law worked changed tremendously over the centuries and those changes, specifically technological change such as the print publishing of law reports that now included reasons, altered how *uptake* of a case actually worked, how it could or would be taken up and to what ends.[128] In the United States, the shift to written reasons for judgment was a move that both augmented the authority of judges like Kent who saw the enterprise in grand terms and limited it, as the judge was required now to explain himself, saying why he did what he did and how it was consistent with past decisions. Written reasons for judgment made a positivistic precedent-based system possible. And by making the case a central unit of analysis, it also allowed for the emergence in the 1870s of a case-based method of legal education, the case method, divided along the lines of clearly delineated substance-based areas of the law (e.g. public law v. private law, and private law divided into discrete subjects such as contracts, property, and later tort). This is what Thomas Grey called "Langdell's secret triumph," as those basic categories channel attention and silently structure thinking and experience even if the narrow formalism or classical orthodoxy associated with Langdell failed.[129] As Robert Gordon has emphasized, even for lawyers who dismiss the importance of theory, these categories "soak gradually into the marrow of lawyers' bones."[130]

[127] See Postema, "Classical Common Law Jurisprudence (Part I)," 162, relying on John H. Baker, *The Common Law Tradition: Lawyers, Books, and the Law* (London: Hambledon Press, 2000).

[128] Postema credits coinage of the term "uptake" (as opposed to being "made," "posited" or "laid down" by will or nature) to an unpublished manuscript of James Murphy on "Law's Positivity in Thomas Aquinas." See "Classical Common Law Jurisprudence (Part I)," 166 n. 52. See also Duxbury, *The Nature and Authority of Precedent*, 52, emphasizing the shift toward an increasing expectation of reason-giving absent from the older system where judges were more like mediators navigating what legal issue was to be settled by the oral pleadings. "As the focal point of the trial moved from the pleadings to the decision, lawyers, their clients and even law reporters increasingly expected judges to provide reasons for what they decided."

[129] See Thomas C. Grey, "Langdell's Orthodoxy," 45 *University of Pittsburgh Law Review* (1983–1984): 1–53, 49–50.

[130] Robert W. Gordon, "The Case For (And Against) Harvard [Review of *Logic and Experience: The Origin of Modern American Legal Education* by William P. LaPiana]," 93 *Michigan Law Review* (1994–1995): 1231–60, 1244 (quoting Grey's comment on "Langdell's secret triumph" at p. 50).

Yet information about costs was and still is difficult to obtain. We would often be shocked, I think, to learn how much it cost to vindicate this right or defend against that action. The $126.37 amount Post was left to pay did not accompany the published report and so those who later appreciated the literary and legal finery on display were spared from thinking about who had to pay for it. Yet much profit in terms of intellectual fodder or food for thought lay for those standing downstream of the celebrated case and it was taken up in a variety of interesting ways that must be included in a proper history of the case.

7

Mandarization

Many are the men, small and great, old and new, landsmen and seamen, who have at large or in little, written of the whale. Run over a few: – The Authors of the Bible; Aristotle; Pliny; Aldrovandi; Sir Thomas Browne; Gesner; Ray; Linnaeus; Rondeletius; Willoughby; Green; Artedi; Sibbald; Brisson; Marten; Lacépède; Bonnaterre; Desmarest; Baron Cuvier; Frederick Cuvier; John Hunter; Owen; Scoresby; Beale; Bennett; J. Ross Browne; the Author of Miriam Coffin; Olmsted; and the Rev. Henry T. Cheever.

Herman Melville, *Moby-Dick, or the Whale* (1851)[1]

Pierson might well have languished in relative obscurity in the third volume of George Caines's Reports had it not been brought to the attention of a larger audience by James Kent in his *Commentaries on American Law*.[2] At most, Livingston's dissent would have resulted in *Pierson* acquiring the status of an oddity or a curiosity, purely a product of what Joseph Story called Livingston's "vivacities."[3] But that did not happen. Instead, the serious treatment *Pierson* received in 1827 from Kent's *Commentaries* launched it on the road to serious fame and fortune as a scholarly precedent. Kent ignored the dissent, probably because it was funny (in both senses, humorous and peculiar), which would detract from the serious holding in the rest of the case and interfere with its operation as a working precedent in cases like *Buster* v. *Newkirk* and in his *Commentaries*. Kent might also

[1] Quote from p. 146. [2] Kent, *Commentaries*, 2: 281–83.
[3] Quoted in Dunne, "Brockholst Livingston," 391.

have known or suspected that Livingston had not intended his dissent to be for public consumption.

We do not know how Kent felt about Livingston's dissent, but I do not think Kent would have liked it. Its solemn foolery risked making a mockery of the serious law-building he was engaged in. However, as we saw in the previous chapter, he would have had little or no control on whether or how Caines reported the decision.

Kent was abstemious, at least by his own report.[4] As Donald Roper put it, Kent was a "gentleman of moderation [...] most temperate in his living habits."[5] Kent was virtually the only lawyer or judge not involved in *Pierson*, who was not a Freemason.[6] He was clubbical to some extent, but he seemed to belong to different clubs, dictated probably for the most

[4] See Kent, *Memoirs*, 165 (where Kent states in a letter to his brother "I never have been drunk, and, by the blessing of God, I never will get drunk, but I have a constitutional privilege to get drunk, and that privilege I will not sign away").

[5] Roper, "The Elite of the New York Bar as Seen from the Bench: James Kent's Necrologies," 203.

[6] Indeed, some of the lawyers and judges in *Pierson* belonged to the same lodge, Holland Lodge. The judge who granted the writ of *certiorari* and was Chief Justice at the time the appeal was filed, Morgan Lewis, was a member of Holland and he went on to be the Grand Master of the Grand Lodge of New York. See "Morgan Lewis" in William R. Denslow, vol. 3, *10,000 Famous Freemasons*, 84.

Pierson's lawyer, Nathan Sanford, was "raised," as the Masons put it, to the third level of membership in Holland and made a full member in 1800, and he was elected Master of this Lodge in 1803, the same year he filed the appeal in *Pierson*. See *Bicentennial Commemorative Volume of Holland Lodge No. 8 of the Ancient and Honorable Fraternity of Free and Accepted Masons* (New York: Published by the Lodge, 1988), 135 (giving the year for Sanford as 5800. i.e. 1800), 109 (giving the year of Sanford's election as Master as 5803, i.e. 1803). One must subtract 4,000 from these years, which are given in "Anno Lucis," "a Masonic thing." Email to the author from Thomas M. Savini, Director of the Chancellor Robert R. Livingston Masonic Library of Grand Lodge, New York City, September 29, 2010.

Daniel Tompkins, who wrote the majority opinion, was not a member of Holland. However, he was the Grand Secretary of the Grand Lodge of New York at the time of the case. See "Daniel D. Tompkins" in Denslow, vol. 4, *10,000 Famous Freemasons*, 246 (Tompkins held this position from June 25, 1801 until June 13, 1805).

Post's lawyer, Cadwallader David Colden, although not a member of Holland, served as Senior Warden of the Grand Lodge of New York. Colden later renounced his Masonic ties. See De Alva Stanwood Alexander, vol. 1, *A Political History of the State of New York*, (Port Washington NY: I. J. Friedman, 1969) 370. Denslow does not give the five-year period. However, Colden was serving as Senior Warden in 1810 when Holland Lodge was given a new warrant after its previous one was stolen. See *Bicentennial Commemorative Volume of Holland Lodge*, 22. Denslow wrote that Colden's bid to denounce Freemasonry for political gain failed to win him election as governor of New York in 1834. See vol. 14, *10,000 Famous Freemasons*, 235.

part by political affiliation and later geographical location.[7] For example, Kent belonged, along with fellow Federalists William Johnson and the first unofficial reporter in New York, William Coleman, to "the Friendly Club."[8] This club was "an earnest, intense, rigidly ethical and highly self-conscious group" of Federalists who met in New York City in the 1790s, to discuss politics, novels, history, and books of travel.[9] Unlike most Courts of Dover their meetings were "sober gatherings, serious and almost grim, dedicated to 'improvement.'"[10] Kent moved to Albany in 1798. There was much less clubbical activity there than in New York City.[11]

Kent was certainly not insensitive to the leanings of literature, as his membership in the Friendly Club attests. His library included Virgil, Horace, Byron's Poems, and a ten-volume set of Shakespeare, as well as copies of *Tristram Shandy* and *Robinson Crusoe*.[12] The list of books he

The Chancellor Robert R. Livingston Masonic Library of the Grand Lodge in New York City is named after a prominent member of Brockholst Livingston's family. Robert Livingston studied law with the father of Brockholst Livingston, William Livingston. James M. Banner Jr., "Livingston, Robert R," *American National Biography Online*.

The Chancellor Robert R. Livingston Masonic Library of Grand Lodge, New York City holds two biographical essays on Kent but the connection seems to be based on Kent's being a notable person not one based on actual membership. Thomas Savini explains that the biographical clipping files on prominent Masons "have grown to include files on men who were thought to be Masons but really weren't; men of illustrious historical standing; and in some cases, people who had some tangential relationship to Freemasonry or individual Freemasons. It's possible that James Kent is included for this final reason [...] [There is] no mention of any involvement in Freemasonry on Kent's part" in either of the files. Email to the author from Thomas M. Savini, Director of the Chancellor Robert R. Livingston Masonic Library of Grand Lodge, New York City, September 30, 2010.

7 Freemasonry did not necessarily mean rowdiness. Membership was very common operating almost like church membership, especially in New York City, where the anti-Masonic movement of the 1830s had the most trouble gaining ground. See Paul Goodman, *Towards a Christian Republic: Antimasonry and the Great Transition in New England, 1826–1836* (New York: Oxford University Press, 1988).

8 See Langbein, "Chancellor Kent and the History of Legal Literature," 582 (on Kent and Johnson). William Coleman also belonged to the Friendly Club. See Nevins, *The Evening Post*, 15.

9 See James E. Cronin, "Elihu Hubbard Smith and the New York Friendly Club, 1795–1798," 64:3 *Publications of the Modern Language Association* (1949): 471–79, 472.

10 Ibid., 476.

11 See Roy Victor Peel, *The Political Clubs of New York City* (New York: Putnam, 1935).

12 See *Kent Family Papers*, vol. 8: 39, 23. Ferguson notes that Kent felt ashamed as a young lawyer riding circuit with Edward Livingston in 1786 when Livingston pulled out a pocket Horace and read some passages to him, assuming he understood. Kent wrote "I said nothing, but was stung with shame and mortification. I purchased immediately Horace and Virgil ... and formed my resolution [...] to recover the lost languages." Ferguson,

helped compile for the Mercantile Library Association of the City of New York contain many books that the Friendly Club would have been interested in, particularly books on travel, history, and politics.[13] Ferguson notes that Kent followed his hero, Alexander Hamilton, in careful study of French literature, and Kent also added copious notes to those books and copies of most of Shakespeare's plays.[14] This was all pretty serious stuff.

I have the impression that Kent generally would not have had much time or patience for Court-of-Dover playfulness by virtue of temperament. Also, importantly, he had less interest in using clubbical activity to build the kind of alliances that would advance his political career, which took a decidedly non-populous turn. As Donald Roper put it, quoting David Hackett Fischer, "Kent was one of those 'Federalists of the Old School' who withdrew into political hibernation after Jefferson's calamitous victory of 1800 rather than engage in the turbulent struggle for popular support."[15] He also was not interested in the kind of economic investments that drove so many of his contemporaries, like Cadwallader David Colden, whom he described as having "a restless love of political office and a sanguine Zeal for Stock Speculations," all of which would have involved a great deal of information sharing and trading in clubs and other social meeting

Law and Letters in American Culture, 27. In his 1794 Columbia College lectures, Kent "urged every American lawyer to master the Greek and Latin classics as well as moral philosophy, history, logic, and mathematics, and his emphasis was on the ability that flowed from general knowledge." Ferguson, *Law and Letters in American Culture*, 28. See also Kessler, *Inventing American Exceptionalism*, 42–43.

[13] There are no works of literature included in the Mercantile Library list that Kent helped compile. See *Outline of a Course of English Reading: Based on that Prepared for the Mercantile Library Association of the City of New York*, Henry A. Oakley ed. (New York: G.P. Putnam, 1853). This was despite the fact that the work was offered as "a truly valuable guide to the student of English literature," according to its editor, Henry A. Oakley. See "Preface," iii–iv, iv. Oakley preserved Kent's notes on different titles, which are interesting to peruse, especially famous works like the *Federalist* or Montesquieu's *Spirit of the Laws*. There are many biographical works and the books on travel include a range of aspersions cast at those he called barbarian or savage races or peoples. Kessler notes that Kent wrote that English literature was "accorded to evenings [...] in company with my wife" whereas law was for the "business part of the day." See Kessler, *Inventing American Exceptionalism*, 44–45.

[14] See Ferguson, *Law and Letters in American Culture*, 66, 67–68.

[15] Roper, "The Elite of the New York Bar as Seen from the Bench: James Kent's Necrologies," 208 (quoting Fischer, *The Revolution of American Conservatism*).

places.[16] Colden went on to be mayor of New York City; Daniel Tompkins, like Morgan Lewis, eventually became the Governor of the State. These were lawyer-politicians who threw themselves into the hurly-burly of political and economic life. Kent, on the other hand, was "a cautious investor [...] censorious of greedy lawyers [such as Colden or Sanford] who became overly concerned with amassing wealth."[17] Although he relished his seat on the Council of Revision, a state body empowered to review all state legislation and veto statutes considered objectionable, Kent's style of politics was, as Roper put it, elite.[18] It allowed him to play "a leading part in shaping policy while being at the same time above the rancor and intrigue so prevalent in New York politics."[19]

Kent's private note on Livingston described him as "an amiable polished Man, of a good deal of Talent & learning but rather speculative & ingenious than solid."[20] Whatever, he thought of the frolic in 1805, as we saw in the Introduction to this book, Kent's own use of *Pierson* in the *Commentaries* edits out its literary or playful dimensions and presents the decision as a purely serious precedent. Kent's serious presentation makes perfect sense given his aims and aspirations for the *Commentaries* and judge-made law generally in New York State. The objective was to build non-legislative law that could be copied in other states and strengthen centralized power in the new nation by making judge-made law common for all states.[21] Codes were thought by many conservatives to be dangerous because they were the product

[16] Roper, "The Elite of the New York Bar as Seen from the Bench: James Kent's Necrologies," 218.

[17] Ibid., 204.

[18] Ibid., 210, 209 (referring to Kent's "form of elitism"). Kent's biography emphasizes his conservatism. See John Theodore Horton, *James Kent: A Study in Conservatism, 1763–1847* (New York; London: D. Appleton-Century Co., 1939). For other biographical essays on Kent, see Carl F. Stychin, "The Commentaries of Chancellor James Kent and the Development of an American Common Law," 37 *American Journal of Legal History* (1993): 440–63; David W. Raack, "'To Preserve the Best Fruits': The Legal Thought of Chancellor James Kent," 33 *American Journal of Legal History* (1989): 320–66; G. Edward White, "The Chancellor's Ghost," 74 *Chicago-Kent Law Review* (1998): 229–62.

[19] Roper, "The Elite of the New York Bar as Seen from the Bench: James Kent's Necrologies," 209.

[20] Ibid., 206.

[21] Most other states lacked an equity court, and so Kent's decisions as Chancellor would have a limited reach. However, the *Commentaries* allowed Kent an influential vehicle through which to state the law of New York, which, in subsequent editions, dropped qualifiers such as "in this state." Kent's son, William Kent, was the editor of many

of legislatures, an interesting idea given that codes are almost always lawyerly projects assigned and drafted by conservative legal elites.[22] But whatever the basis or lack of it for Kent's fears, didactic explanations of judge-made common law in a set of books like the *Commentaries* was a serious project; there was no room for silliness or solemn foolery.

In the first part of this chapter, we explore how Kent's serious treatment of *Pierson* paved the way for its serious academic uptake in the nineteenth century by legal mandarins such as Oliver Wendell Holmes Jr. and Frederick Pollock, who gave it an actual "taking" interpretation. We will see in the second part of the chapter that Livingston's dissent was invariably omitted in early law school casebooks in the twentieth century. When the dissent finally began to appear, it was for very specific serious reasons. Only in the 1970s was the humor of the dissent openly appreciated. Then in the 1980s, *Pierson* took yet another serious turn in the hands of the New Mandarins, legal academics interested in using the case to demonstrate a point related to law and economics. Its history is a microhistory of trends, preoccupations, and styles in professionalized academic legal commentary in the nineteenth century and the twentieth-century American law school.

THE OLD NINETEENTH-CENTURY LEGAL MANDARINS: KENT, HOLMES, POLLOCK

The later nineteenth-century story begins with none other than Oliver Wendell Holmes Jr. Holmes, who edited the twelfth edition of Kent's *Commentaries* (1873).[23] Holmes had been quite obsessive about this project in his "proving years," exhibiting what his biographer Mark DeWolfe Howe called a "frightening intensity" about the work.[24] In a letter to the novelist Henry James his mother remarks that when Holmes dined with the family he refused to be parted from the manuscript, and that this was true even in his own house:

subsequent editions of the *Commentaries* and scholars have not explored to what extent he brought this more national perspective to bear on the work.

22 See Gordon, "Book Review [of *The American Codification Movement: A Study of Antebellum Legal Reform* by C. M. Cook]."

23 James Kent, 4 vols, *Commentaries on American Law*, Oliver Wendell Holmes Jr. ed., 12th ed. (Boston, MA: Little, Brown, 1873).

24 Mark DeWolfe Howe, *Justice Oliver Wendell Holmes II: The Proving Years, 1870–1882* (Cambridge, MA: Belknap Press of Harvard University Press, 1963), 22.

His whole life, soul and body, is utterly absorbed in his *last* work upon his Kent. He carries about his manuscript in his green bag and never loses sight of it for a moment. He started to go to Will's [William James's] room to wash his hands, but came back for his bag, and when we went to dinner, Will said, "Don't you want to take your bag with you?" He said, "Yes, I always do so at home."[25]

Holmes probably took such care of the book because he saw the project as important to his determination to be recognized for greatness, a status that he believed had to be achieved before the age of forty.[26]

Four years after publishing his twelfth edition of Kent's *Commentaries*, Holmes published an article on possession in the *American Law Review*.[27] Much of what appeared in the article was repeated in his famous Lecture VI on "Possession" in *The Common Law* in 1881, another project he saw as intimately connected to the greatness he felt he needed to establish before he turned forty.[28] In the *Common Law* lecture, Holmes wrote that "[t]he Roman law and the common law agree that, in general, fresh pursuit of wild animals does not give the pursuer the rights of possession. Until *escape has been made impossible* by some other means, another may step in and kill or catch and carry off the game if he can."[29] Gone was Barbeyrac's idea that an actual taking was not required, a point preserved by the majority in *Pierson* and by Kent in his discussion of *Pierson* in the *Commentaries*.[30] Recall how carefully each of these texts had framed *Pierson* as a situation of mere pursuit, in which what was key was the power or control of the pursuer. This power or control required for

[25] Quoted in Howe, ibid., 22 (from a letter included in Ralph Barton Perry, *The Thought and Character of William James, as revealed in unpublished correspondence and notes, together with published writings*, vol. 1 (Boston, MA: Little, Brown, 1935), 519). Howe refers to William James's mother as "Mrs. Henry James." Mary Robertson Walsh was the mother of William James (the philosopher) and Henry James (the novelist). Their father was also Henry James and so she was also "Mrs. Henry James."

[26] Howe, *Justice Oliver Wendell Holmes*, 49 ("[t]hose minds which are fittest to survive must prove their strength. Holmes was resolved that for him the proving must occur before he was forty years of age"). See Robert W. Gordon, "Holmes's *Common Law* as Legal and Social Science" in *Taming the Past: Essays on Law in History and History in Law* (Cambridge UK; New York: Cambridge University Press, 2017), 50–74, 54–55 (on *The Common Law* and the lecture on possession).

[27] See Oliver Wendell Holmes Jr., "Possession," 12 *American Law Review* (1877–78): 688–720.

[28] Holmes, *The Common Law*, 206–46; Howe, *Justice Oliver Wendell Holmes*, 135 (Holmes wrote, "I remember that I hurried to get it [*The Common Law*] out before March 8, because then I should be 40 and it was said that if a man was to do anything he must do it before 40").

[29] Holmes, *The Common Law*, 217 (emphasis added).

[30] Kent, *Commentaries*, 2: 282–83.

occupancy might be established by an actual taking but an actual taking was not required.[31] In Holmes, however, we now find the idea of *impossible escape*. Because Kent had said that "[t]he civil law contained the same principle as that which the Supreme Court adopted" and he went on to discuss the Roman law and Justinian, Holmes quite understandably linked the idea in Justinian to the common law as it was adopted in those cases. He cited to the *Commentaries, Pierson*, and *Buster* v. *Newkirk* after stating that "it has been held that an action does not lie against a person for killing and taking a fox which had been pursued by another, and was then actually in the view of the person who had originally found, started, and chased it."[32] Yet it is not clear that the majority did adopt Justinian – recall those sections from Justinian related to wounding and not mere pursuit, even if that idea was pressed upon them by Pierson's lawyer, Nathan Sanford. Livingston had suggested that Justinian was the view he was rejecting as well. Kent at least was careful in talking about *Pierson* as a situation of mere pursuit (not hot pursuit or impossible escape). Somehow Holmes, standing downstream from all this nuance, came to see it all thrown into the general soup of impossible escape, actual taking, or what would come to be known as the capture rule.

Holmes was impressed by the relativity involved in the line-drawing exercise when it came to the question of establishing possession in wild animals. Hence he wrote in his own inimitable style: "the difference between the power over the object which is sufficient for possession, and that which is not, is clearly one of degree only, and the line may be drawn at different places at different times."[33] It seems likely that this language of *power* came from Kent (who probably took it from Pothier's use of the word *puissance*). Holmes then went on to discuss the 1844 deer hunting statute in New York that changed the rule of capture from *Pierson* to a hot pursuit rule, a point that had been added to the sixth edition of Kent's *Commentaries* and continued down to the twelfth.[34]

[31] See Introduction. [32] Kent, *Commentaries*, 2: 282–83.

[33] Holmes, *The Common Law*, 217.

[34] See Holmes, ibid. See also James Kent, vol. 2, *Commentaries on American Law*, 6th ed. (New York: W Kent, 1848), 348–49 n. e. ("The legislature of New York have enlarged the right of acquisition of game by pursuit, in the case of deer in the countie[s] of Suffolk and Queen's, by declaring, that any person who starts and pursues such game, shall be deemed in possession of the same, *so long as he continues in fresh pursuit* thereof. Laws of N.Y. April 1, 1844, ch. 109. *N.Y.R.S.* 3d edit. Vol. 1. 883") [emphasis in the original]. See also vol. 2 in 7th ed. (New York: W. Kent, 1851), 410 n. d; 8th ed. (New York: W. Kent, 1854), 417 n. e; 9th ed. (Boston, MA: Little, Brown, 1858), 484 n. a; 10th ed. (Boston, MA: Little, Brown, 1860), 446 n. c; 11th ed., George F. Comstock ed. (Boston, MA:

The influence of Kent on Holmes's lecture fairly bristles from the page. Holmes took an idea that was in Kent (and was certainly bumping around in the lawyers' arguments and Livingston's dissent in *Pierson*), shook off its complexities and nuance, and presented it in a way that was quite at odds with what Kent had originally said, although an understandable misstatement. Things, in other words, did not stay the same in these scholarly writings and rewritings. Instead, one influential version replaced or at least competed with the others, creating a palimpsest in which it becomes increasingly difficult to say what was scraped off and what was now written on the manuscript page. Holmes's interpretation of *Pierson*, and of Kent on *Pierson*, in *The Common Law* must have been influential. As we will see, it certainly seemed to influence Holmes's friend Frederick Pollock. However, before we leave Holmes, we must examine the way in which Holmes seemed bothered by where his interpretation of *Pierson* took him.

The first concern relates to the arbitrariness of the line-drawing exercise, i.e. figuring out "the difference between the power over the object which is sufficient for possession, and that which is not."[35] Holmes used a Herman Melville-like review of the variety of customs in the whaling industry in order to make his point. In Greenland, Holmes explained, the first person to strike the whale needed to hold it "fast" in order to maintain priority to it.[36] Whereas in the Galapagos, the first striker took half the value of the whale even if he lost the line.[37] And in the Massachusetts case of *Swift* v. *Gifford*, the first person to strike and leave their iron in the whale took all of it.[38] All of these different ways

Little, Brown, 1866–67), 429 n. d; 12th ed., Oliver Wendell Holmes Jr. ed. (Boston, MA: Little, Brown, 1873), 350 n. d.

35 Holmes, *The Common Law*, 217. 36 Ibid., 212. 37 Ibid.

38 Ibid. See *Swift v. Gifford*, 2 Lowell 110, 23 F Cas 558 (Mass D.C., 1872). This case was decided not long before Holmes wrote his 1877 essay, and he draws on it quite extensively in what he wrote in the essay and later in the lecture, which makes sense as it was a Massachusetts case. See Deal, "Judicial Invention of Property Norms," 90–92, explaining how what Holmes said about *Swift* v. *Gifford* around the norms of cutting-in caused subsequent confusion around rules relating to dead whales found drifting by a second taker (where cutting-in was a custom influencing priority i.e. if the cutting-in had been completed by the time the first striker appeared on the scene) and the pursuit of a live whale by competitors (in which cutting-in was not used to establish priority). The confusion was passed down through Holmes and made its way into Robert Ellickson's work on whaling rules, where it continued to be said that iron-in was combined with cutting-in in cases of competitors who both chased a living whale. Although Deal notes, 91, that it is the judge in *Swift* v. *Gifford* who "must bear most of the blame for the subsequent confusion."

of formulating the rule, as Holmes put it, "tends [...] to shake an *a priori* theory of the matter."[39] He noted the range on the issue from Justinian, who said that even wounding the animal was insufficient, to *Swift* v. *Gifford*, where it was enough to put in a harpoon.[40] Apparently, there was a different rule for foxes and many different ones for whales, but not for fish, which were a separate case again.[41]

As Bruce Ziff has explained in his work on a set of late nineteenth-century sealing cases, seals, even when killed, can still "escape," as sealers would leave the slaughtered animals in piles on the ice and floating ice, or bad weather would often cause the original ship to be unable to return to collect them. The capture rule, being the first to *kill* the animal, was an inadequate way to deal with the issue of who owned such seals when another ship came to "save" the dead seals that would otherwise go to waste.[42] Holmes did not discuss these cases.[43] However, had he known about them, they could only have exacerbated his sense that the decision about what kind of exercise of power was sufficient for possession in wild animals was "clearly one of degree only, and the line may be drawn at different places at different times."[44] We could, and probably should, add, *and for different animals*, a point that it has been difficult for legal scholars to acknowledge as rules and text books tend to treat all non-human animals as interchangeable regardless of their size and other unique features.

There was a larger nagging concern for Holmes, which was that although the Roman law (Justinian) and the common law (*Pierson* v. *Post* and *Buster* v. *Newkirk*) had established a high threshold with respect to the degree of power in relationship to the object to be possessed, there was a tension between this and "the general tendency of our law [which] is to favor appropriation."[45] Here Holmes went on to discuss

[39] Holmes, *The Common Law*, 213. This point and all three of the whale-rule positions were set out in the earlier piece. See Holmes, "Possession," 719.

[40] Holmes, *The Common Law*, 217–18.

[41] On this last point relating to what constitutes the capture of fish, see ibid., 217 (where Holmes discusses *Young* v. *Hichens*, 6 QB 606 [1844]).

[42] Ziff, "The Law of Capture, Newfoundland-Style."

[43] The first four of the five cases Ziff discusses were reported from 1859 to 1872 and so were theoretically eligible for inclusion by the time of the publication of *The Common Law* in 1881 (and even in the article on possession in 1877). Evidently, the Newfoundland Law Reports were not on Holmes's radar screen, probably unsurprisingly. We only ever know what it is in our world to know.

[44] Holmes, *The Common Law*, 217.

[45] Ibid., 237 ("We have adopted the Roman law as to animals *ferae naturae*, but the general tendency of our law is to favour appropriation").

a case in which a man found logs that were afloat and tied them up. The logs then broke free and were found by another who tied them up for himself. The court held that "the first finder retained the rights which sprung from his having taken possession, and that he could maintain trover against the second finder, who refused to give them up."[46] In other words, *the law wanted to assign possession in response to relatively light touching*. Why? Well, precisely in order to avoid the kind of "quarrels and litigation" Tompkins talked about in the majority judgment in *Pierson*.[47]

Blackstone discussed this problem at the beginning of his volume on property, referring to the "innumerable tumults" that would result from property that "unavoidably remain[ed] in common" and belonged to the first occupant like animals *ferae naturae*.[48] "[D]isturbances and quarrels would frequently arise among individuals, contending about the acquisition of this species of property by first occupancy."[49] Arguably then, it was better to implement a rule that accorded possession in response to *relatively light touching*, which would leave less of this potentially troublesome kind of property lying around. As Holmes put it, our law "abhors the absence of proprietary or possessory rights as a kind of vacuum."[50] If the law favored easy appropriation, then this was better, *as long as the signal was clear enough*. The kill and capture that *Pierson* implied was superior to hot pursuit as a way of establishing possession in the fox was actually more than was required. The fox could escape just like the logs in the case Holmes discussed: that would not justify depriving the original possessor of their property right. On the policy point that was put forward by the majority in *Pierson*, the decision arguably went the wrong way.

Is it not the whole point of property law to allow people a legal right to protect precisely that which they are unable to hold tightly in their hands? This is true most obviously in the case of land. However, it also applies to objects that move, movables in the civil law. Property rights in a movable allow a person to put that object down and walk away but still exclude others; to sell it, lease it, be recognized as its owner. The degree of possession required for first possession is greater than that required in order to maintain possession, in the case of both movables and immovable land. However, it does not follow from this that the degree of possession required for first possession should be the greatest possible degree, namely, the capture rule. As the judgment in *Popov* v. *Hayashi*, put it,

[46] Ibid. [47] *Pierson*, 179. [48] Blackstone, *Commentaries*, 2: 4, 14. [49] Ibid., 15.
[50] Holmes, *The Common Law*, 237.

"absolute dominion and control is not required to establish possession" because "such a rule would be unworkable and unreasonable." Why? "The 'nature and situation' of the property at issue does not immediately lend itself to unequivocal dominion and control. It is impossible to wrap one's arms around a whale, a fleeing fox or a sunken ship."[51] So long as the signal was clear enough, pursuit with the imminent prospect of taking, should have been enough to exclude Pierson.

There is an irony in Holmes refraining from following this instinct about the mismatch *Pierson* presented, since if he had looked into it more closely, he might have learned of Barbeyrac's preference for the law of the Salians, as discussed by Pothier.[52] The law of the Salians was old German customary law. Holmes was always on the lookout for "Frankish" or "Teutonic" rather than Roman antecedents that explained the history of English law.[53] "Teutonic" meant traceable to the law of the Salian Franks.[54] The Salian connection might well have motivated Holmes to follow his instinct that there was a problem with *Pierson* further than he did. However, his strong identification with Kent's *Commentaries*, living with them in the intense way that he did, might have made it difficult for him to disagree with them and with Kent, who (we now know) in full knowledge of the alternatives (Trebatius, Barbeyrac, and Pothier) nonetheless rejected mere pursuit and, if we are to include *Buster* v. *Newkirk*, even pursuit with wounding.

Holmes's interest in possession, and the treatment of *Pierson* in Kent's *Commentaries* that Holmes helped popularize by editing the twelfth edition of the *Commentaries* and discussing these issues at length in his famous lectures on *The Common Law*, trickled out into the rest of the common-law world. Holmes's famous correspondence with Frederick Pollock was an important point of contact into England.

Holmes and Pollock talked about Holmes's *American Law Review* article on possession in their letters in 1878.[55] Then, ten years later, and

[51] *Popov* v. *Hayahsi*, para. 5. [52] Pothier, *Traités du droit de domaine de propriété*, 18.

[53] See Howe, *Justice Oliver Wendell Holmes*, 153.

[54] See ibid., 211–12. Holmes thought that Kent and Story were wrong about the Roman origins of possession. See ibid., 221. Specifically, he argued that the English law of bailment was like the law of the Salian Franks; it was not Roman law. See Holmes, "Possession," 697–98.

[55] See Mark DeWolfe Howe ed., *Holmes-Pollock Letters: The Correspondence of Mr Justice Holmes and Sir Frederick Pollock, 1874–1932*, vol. 1 (Cambridge, MA: Harvard University Press, 1941), 8–14.

seven years after Holmes published *The Common Law*, Pollock co-authored his own book on possession.[56] In it, Pollock discussed the capture of wild animals, asking: "At what point in the process of capture is the taker's control complete enough to make him a possessor? This is in its nature as much a question of fact as anything can be, yet it is one upon which the law cannot escape having an opinion."[57] Here was recognition of Holmes's point that the line-drawing exercise was an arbitrary one. Yet here also we encounter strong deference, as there was in Holmes, to Kent. Pollock used Kent's *Commentaries* to support a claim that "[t]he general principle [is] that *pursuit short of capture will not do*."[58] We have seen that Kent was careful to say in the *Commentaries* that *Pierson* was only a rule on mere pursuit and *Buster* v. *Newkirk* was also to be thought about that way. However, when the text traveled, it tended to be interpreted as insisting on a capture rule, that is a Justinian rule on actual taking. This is certainly what Pollock endorsed. And we saw above that Holmes did the same when he wrote that "*[u]ntil escape has been made impossible* [. . .] another may step in and kill or catch and carry off the game if he can."[59]

Precisely the same thing happened when the Supreme Court of Canada received *Pierson* in the late nineteenth century. *Pierson* came into Canada in a case called the *Frederick Gerring Jr.* v. *Canada* in 1897.[60] In this case, the Supreme Court of Canada decided an out-of-bounds fishing case involving an American vessel found to be engaged in the act of fishing, having drifted into the treaty-prohibited three-mile limit, despite the fact that the fish were netted outside the limit where fishing by the foreign vessel was permitted. One of the three concurring judges, King J., refers to both Pollock's book and Kent's *Commentaries* in discussing the point that the vessel may have had enough control of the fish to have had a qualified property in them; however, he thought that the fish could still get away and had not yet been reduced to possession, and so the treaty-prohibited fishing happened within the three-mile limit thereby violating the treaty and justifying seizure of the *Gerring* by

[56] Frederick Pollock, *An Essay on Possession in the Common Law* (Oxford: Clarendon Press, 1888). This book was co-authored with Robert Samuel Wright but Pollock wrote the part where the quotes below appear.

[57] Ibid., 37. [58] Ibid., 37–38; 38 n. 1 (emphasis added).

[59] Holmes, *The Common Law*, 217 (emphasis added).

[60] *Frederick Gerring Jr.* v. *Canada*, 27 S.C.R. 271 (Sup. Ct. Canada, 1897).

Canadian authorities.[61] "The remedy for cases of hardship," King J. wrote, "lies in the pardoning power of the Crown."[62]

Sedgewick J. concurred, although he preferred not to opine on the general question of how one establishes possession in a wild animal or to determine at what precise time the fish became the property of the catchers.[63] Instead he focused on the (very convincing) practical point, King J. also made, that there was hours of work left to be done once the purse seine, the type of net being used, was set around the fish, an action that would only take between ten and twelve minutes.[64] Because the men continued to bale the fish from the purse seine, what they were doing when they drifted into the three-mile limit was fishing. Sedgewick J. wrote the following:

> The act of fishing is a pursuit consisting, not of a single but of many acts according to the nature of the fishing. It is not the isolated act alone either of surrounding the fish by the net, or by taking them out of the water and obtaining manual custody of them. It is a continuous process beginning from the time when the preliminary preparations are being made for the taking of the fish and extending down to the moment when they are finally reduced to actual and certain possession.[65]

The fish are never all taken, many escape, the net is still in the water and it might break away: "The 'fishing' is not over [...] until *as a fact they are secured*."[66]

The third concurring judge, Girouard J. relied on Kent for his direction to both *Pierson* and *Buster* v. *Newkirk*, reproducing sections of each case, including much of Tompkins's majority opinion in *Pierson*.[67] The standard – whether the fish could still escape – was Justinian's actual capture standard. And it had come to be commonplace, it seems, in

61 See ibid., 298.

62 Ibid. The Crown refused to grant the pardon and the case remained a thorn in the side of the Department of Fisheries and Oceans for over a decade and created serious problems in British/Canadian-American relations for at least another decade, the very definition of a diplomatic nightmare that would not go away.

63 See ibid., 284.

64 King J. also emphasized the time point, namely, that handling and emptying the net would take two hours, whereas "[t]he setting and drawing of the seine is the work of a short time." Ibid., 294.

65 Ibid., 280–81. King J. also used the language of "continuous." See ibid., 298 ("the act of fishing cannot be said to be entirely at an end in a useful sense until the fish are reduced into actual possession. The whole is a continuous act").

66 Ibid., 282 (emphasis in the original). 67 Ibid., 305–308.

authorities, like this one, that canvassed Kent, Pollock, *Pierson*, and *Buster* v. *Newkirk*.

Indeed, Girouard J.'s opinion in the *Gerring* was more *Pierson* than *Pierson* v. *Post*, outdoing the famous New York case in exploration of exotic sources. McGill-trained, cosmopolitan and academically-oriented Girouard J. cites and quotes at length from the British fishing case *Young* v. *Hitchens*, refers to the English treatise *Angell on Tide Water*, reproduces Chapters 12 and 13 of Justinian's *Institutes*, as well as Gaius in Justinian's *Digest* and the view of Trebatius contained in it, and discusses the British case *Blades* v. *Higgs*. He also refers to a bevy of civil law writers: Domat, Savigny, Pufendorf, Heinneccius, Barbeyrac, and Pothier.

Sedgewick J., combining the forthright/practical with the quasi-literary in a style somewhat like Livingston's solemn foolery in *Pierson*, wrote parts of his concurrence in a flowery way, referring, for example, to his own fly fishing, the work of English intellectual and imperial apologist James A. Froude and his book *The English in the West Indies* (1888) giving a description of fishing by boys in the West Indies, the biblical multitude of fishes, and the city of Troy, which was under siege but did not fall for ten years.[68] This bundling of references to classicism, Christianity, and romanticized colonial racism was presented by Sedgewick J. through a lens that was decidedly gendered masculine and "Aryan." He wrote that to give fishing a strict interpretation would be "to emasculate language, to filch from that word – a word, which, with recognized variations, appears to be common to all the Aryan races – all but a fraction of its meaning."[69] It is a feature of solemn foolery that it often does not date very well, as we saw in several examples in Chapter 2.

Responding to the point that the Captain and crew of the ship had inadvertently slipped into the three-mile limit and were unaware of their whereabouts when baling the fish, Sedgewick J. wrote that *they* were not being punished under the statute and the treaty: "In the eye of the statute *the vessel itself* is the offender. The statute gives to it a moral consciousness – a personality – a capacity to act within or without the law, and imposes upon it the liability of forfeiture in the event of transgression."[70] Here we encounter anthropomorphism of the ship rather than

[68] See ibid., 282–83. *The English in the West Indies* was a travelogue written in response to fears colonial administrators had that British colonies in the West Indies would go the way of Haiti and to give advice on how the colonies should be governed. See Thomas Walter Thompson, *James Anthony Froude on Nation and Empire: A Study in Victorian Racialism* (New York: Garland, 1987).

[69] *Gerring*, 285. [70] Ibid., 284–85 (emphasis added).

anthropomorphism of the fox, the ship as a legal person. This rationale would not have been very satisfying to the owner of the ship, a man from Massachusetts, who found a tremendous amount of political backing in the United States for the grievance he felt he had been done by seizure of the vessel, which was subsequently handled carelessly by the Canadian authorities, turning his plight into a popular *cause célèbre*. Adopted by many a prominent politician the case became a significant international incident, taking a number of diplomatic turns in the foreign relations between Canada/Great Britain and the United States that went on until the 1920s.

Sedgewick J. also brought out an important political and environmental dimension of the case less out-of-step with present-day ideas, namely, strong condemnation of the "nefarious" and "barbarous" practice of overfishing, which we now know turned out to be extremely prophetic in terms of what happened to fish stocks in Eastern Canada in the late twentieth century: "We Canadians are in a sense the world's trustees," Sedgewick J. wrote, "[t]he North American fisheries have been committed to our guardianship, not for ourselves alone, but for posterity, not for Canada alone, but for humanity."[71] He singled out the purse seine net as an incredibly destructive instrument "inimical" to preservation of the fisheries, contributing to their "annihilation, their absolute destruction for all time" and emphasizing the importance of the treaty to both countries to protect "the goose that lays the golden egg."[72] The fisheries needed protection, according to Sedgewick J., so as to "conserve them for the benefit of future generations."[73]

Sedgewick J. was no doubt motivated by nascent nationalism and a desire to augment the authority of his relatively young institution still rather humiliatingly subject to reversals by the Privy Council in London. The lack of sympathy toward Mr. Morris and the mistake his Captain made letting the boat slip into the three-mile limit is a loud silence in all three of the concurrences. The "masculinity" of the still young nation would be protected by the Canadian court taking a tough stance toward its larger more powerful neighbor, backing up the Canadian and British authorities' attempt to protect a shared natural resource in order to preserve future extraction, and refusing, at least in this case, to step down. The striking combination of imperial/colonial prose that we would no longer appreciate in Sedgewick J.'s opinion with a strong and

[71] Ibid., 286. [72] Ibid. [73] Ibid.

sweepingly prescient ecological call that would echo in present-day sentiments would make the *Gerring* case a good Canadian law school classroom case, a Canadian *Pierson*, dealing with fish rather than foxes, especially if it includes Girouard J.'s scholarly exoticism, outdoing *Pierson* itself on that score.[74]

Did anyone by the late nineteenth century disagree with how Kent had come to be understood, or with Holmes or Pollock, on actual taking? In fact an American treatise on *The Law of Animals* published in 1900, at the dawn of the twentieth century, registered disagreement with the rule of actual capture. According to its author, John Ingham, *Pierson* and *Buster* v *Newkirk* held that "[m]ere pursuit of a wild animal is not sufficient to confer property."[75] Ingham also included a quotation from Gaius noting that Trebatius had said that any wounding of the animal made it the pursuer's, as indeed did mere pursuit, so long as the animal was not abandoned. This was hot pursuit. He also included a quotation from Justinian's *Digest* paraphrasing Gaius that "[t]he opinion of most has been that it is not ours unless we have captured it, because much may happen to prevent our capturing it; which is the better opinion."[76] Ingham wrote that "Chancellor Kent appears to consider that this principle of the civil law is the one adopted" in both *Pierson* and *Buster* v. *Newkirk*, namely the principle of actual capture received from the Roman law (Justinian) adopted into later civil law.[77] "But," Ingham pointed out, "in *Pierson* v. *Post* it is said ... " and then quotes from the majority opinion where Tompkins concedes that Barbeyrac was correct to say

[74] Given that Girouard J.'s opinion reproduces what is essential to the majority in *Pierson*, the only down-side to using the *Gerring* exclusively as a Canadian *Pierson* would be not letting students see Livingston's dissent and the original context for solemn foolery. The dissent could be included, perhaps also with the British fishing case *Young* v. *Hitchens*, as the interpretation of that case, was at least the only stated basis for the dissent in the *Gerring* written by Gwynne J. and joined in by the Chief Justice Sir Henry Strong.

[75] John H. Ingham, *The Law of Animals: A Treatise on Property in Animals, Wild and Domestic, and the Rights and Responsibilities Arising Therefrom* (Philadelphia, PA: T and J.W. Johnson, 1900), 5.

[76] Ibid. Ingham does not cite directly to the *Digest* but rather to a compilation of Roman law. Indeed, the way Ingham quotes from this passage, it sounds like Trebatius might have made the point, or at least Gaius said Trebatius did. Perhaps the Roman law compilation Ingham was using did not make it clear who said what. In the *Digest*, Justinian includes passages from Gaius, who provides the view of Trebatius. Trebatius, however, thought that any wounding established the right. He was far from thinking that an actual taking was required.

[77] Ibid.

"that actual bodily seizure is not indispensable to acquire right to or possession of a wild beast; but that on the contrary, the mortal wounding of such beasts by one not abandoning his pursuit may with the utmost propriety be deemed possession of him."[78] *Pierson* did not of course involve wounding, and, although *Buster* v. *Newkirk* did, the wounding was not mortal, and Newkirk arguably abandoned pursuit even with the dog left in place. As we have seen, Kent's original meaning was simply that mere pursuit was not sufficient *and not necessarily* that an actual taking was required.

Pierson appeared in other sources in the early twentieth century characterized in the same way, namely, presupposing that an actual taking was not required. The aptly named Harry Chase published a handbook for game wardens in 1910 that cited *Pierson* in support of a rule of mere pursuit. Chase also quoted from the same part of Tompkins's majority decision citing Barbeyrac on the point that an actual taking was not required, that a mortal wounding or using a trap from which the animal could not escape would be enough.[79]

The point about wounding and trapping and the absence of a need for actual taking was important to Ingham and Chase, both writers interested in the animal-related aspects of *Pierson*, because these facts would appear in actual disputes, hence were crucial information for game wardens intervening in on-the-ground altercations. Some situations might indeed involve the pure or mere pursuit of the *Pierson* majority, which meant that the original reading of Kent's *Commentaries* would be apt. But more commonly the facts would involve wounding or other indications that the original hunter was closing in after significant labor, which most (non-lawyer) observers would grant ought to be rewarded in some way (a share in the kill, meat rather than the skin, say, in *Buster* v. *Newkirk*). The second hunter might also have put in much labor (staying up and out into the cold night, on New Year's Eve no less in *Buster* v. *Newkirk*) even if that labor should be subject to a discount (Buster's use of Newkirk's dog). It would be valuable for game wardens to know whether the wounding required by law had to be mortal, or that a trap had to be one from which the animal could not escape.

[78] Ibid., 6.

[79] See Harry Chase, *Powers, Duties, and Work of Game Wardens: A handbook of practical information for officers and others interested in the enforcement of fish and game laws* (Rutland, VT: Tuttle, 1910), 85–87.

Chase was content simply to report these principles, referring to *Pierson* and *Buster* v. *Newkirk* (and for fish *Young* v. *Hitchens*). Ingham, in contrast, seems to have been keen to provide readers with arguments in favor of hot pursuit, casting doubt on Kent who "appears to" be saying that absolute taking or capture is the civil law rule adopted in *Pierson* and *Buster* v. *Newkirk*. Ingham followed the point that Barbeyrac, as interpreted by Tompkins, did not require an absolute taking, pointing to a Canadian case from Québec that held that pursuit could be sufficient if there was wounding and persistent chase.

In the Québec case, *Charlebois* v. *Raymond*, the judge rejected Roman law and Justinian's requirement that the wild animal (a bear) must be taken, choosing instead what he called the French law in which following the animal gave the pursuer possession of it against an interloper who killed and took it.[80] Perhaps unsurprisingly, given that the case was decided in a civil law and predominantly French-speaking jurisdiction by a French-speaking judge, Pothier's property treatise was cited by the winning party.[81] Unlike *Buster* v. *Newkirk*, where the use of the dog had not established continuous pursuit, the original hunter's dogs in the Québec case, having been set upon the bear since the previous morning, was taken to be in continuous uninterrupted pursuit, as the scent of the bear had not been lost. The dogs wounded the bear, and were wounded by it. Some died. It does not appear that the wounding of the bear was mortal. The intervening hunter who killed the bear had only been hunting it one or two hours and was doing so with the help of the original hunter's remaining dogs. The judge was unwilling to grant the intervenor first occupancy of the animal.

Now the *Gerring* would appear to have overruled the Québec case, at least as it might be relied upon in a Canadian common-law province, for it was from a higher-level court, the Supreme Court of Canada, and in it Girouard J. discussed *Charlebois* explicitly, rejected it, and gathered together a concentration of authorities, as we have seen, more intense than *Pierson* itself, all in order to establish the point that seizure of the animal is indispensable given the possibility of escape.[82] But the point to

[80] See *Charlebois* v. *Richmond*, 12 *The Lower Canada Jurist-Collection des décisions du bas-Canada* (Montréal: John Lovell, 1868), 55–56.

[81] Private law (property, contract and tort – known as extracontractual obligations) was left to be regulated by the province using civil law in the 1866 *Civil Code of Lower Canada*.

[82] The Supreme Court of Canada has the power to review decisions from Québec, including private law decisions; but they are supposed to apply Québec civil law to the private law cases that come before them. Arguably then, the *Frederick Gerring* overruling *Charlebois*

notice is that in the wider common-law world, Kent as interpreted by Holmes and Pollock, and Holmes and Pollock in their own right, had created an intellectual or academic trajectory that became difficult to counter. In most cases, discussion started in Kent's *Commentaries* and moved to *Pierson* v. *Post* as sure as night follows day, with some stops in Holmes and Pollock along the way. Consider, for instance, an excellent short survey article written by Earl C. Arnold in the *American Law Review* in 1921 on cases involving wild animals. In it, Arnold used Kent's *Commentaries* to establish the point that control was the key to property in a wild animal, and once control was lost and the animal escaped, property in it was lost.[83] Arnold used *Pierson* to establish that "[i]t is essential that the animal be brought within the power and control of the pursuer. Mere pursuit does not give any rights."[84] He acknowledged that physical taking was not necessary in every case if nets, traps, or other devices were used so that "the animal in all probability will not escape."[85] He used Pollock on possession to discuss the fish that were not yet reduced to capture in *Young* v. *Hitchens*.[86] Arnold then went on to assert that according to *Pierson* "even pursuit accompanied with wounding is equally ineffectual for that purpose (to vest property in the pursuer), unless the animal be actually taken" and the note refers the reader to Kent's *Commentaries*.[87] Arnold then discussed *Buster* v. *Newkirk*.[88] After this, he used Holmes to support the idea that "the common law was in agreement with the Roman law" in "holding that fresh pursuit of an animal did not give the pursuer the right of possession."[89] In other words, here was an actual taking interpretation

would apply to the common-law provinces but not to private-law cases coming from Québec. See John E. C. Brierley and Roderick A. Macdonald, *Quebec Civil Law: An Introduction to Quebec Private Law* (Toronto: Emond Montgomery Publications, 1993), 57–58 (explaining the contentious history of appeals to the Supreme Court of Canada which strove for a uniformity in which the civil law solution would often be sacrificed and noting that appeals from Québec on the civil law are heard by panels of five in which a majority of judges are drawn from Québec; three of the nine appointments have – since 1949 when appeals ceased to the Privy Council – been drawn from the bench and bar of Québec). The convention of applying Québec civil law to private-law cases coming out of Québec in the nineteenth century is another matter.

[83] Earl C. Arnold, "The Law of Possession Governing the Acquisition of Animals *Ferae Naturae*," 55 *American Law Review* (1921): 393–404, 395.

[84] Ibid. [85] Ibid. [86] Ibid., 396, 396 n. 11. [87] Ibid., 396, 396 n. 12. [88] Ibid.

[89] Ibid., 396, 396 n. 14. For another example of reliance on *Pierson* through Kent's *Commentaries* and Holmes, see Taylor Hannis, *The Science of Jurisprudence: A treatise in which the growth of the law is unfolded by historical method and its elements classified and defined by the analytical* (New York: Macmillan, 1908), 544.

of *Pierson*, founded on Kent's *Commentaries* and on Holmes's interpretation of the case.

Yet Arnold then proceeded to discuss a relatively new case that had been decided in Wisconsin in 1915 called *Liesner et al.* v. *Wanie*.[90] In this case, the plaintiff had "mortally wounded" a wolf and was in continued pursuit of it. "When its capture by the plaintiff was inevitable," Arnold explained, "defendant pointed his gun so it reached within three foot of the animal, and shot, killing it."[91] The court held for the plaintiff, writing that "[t]he instant a wild animal is brought under the control of a person so that actual possession is practically inevitable, a vested property interest in it accrues which cannot be divested by another's intervening and killing it."[92] Here was a new standard: *practical inevitability*. And it seemed to be inconsistent with how *Pierson* had come to be understood; it was much more in keeping with Livingston's dissent and the hot pursuit rule. One ought not to intervene (intrude saucily) and take another's kill in the moment before they are about to make it. That wrong might well give rise to a legal right.[93]

The court in *Liesner et al.* v. *Wanie* referred explicitly to John Ingham's treatise to say that control was sufficient and an actual taking was not required, distinguishing between what the civil law held versus the common law.[94] Here was the idea that, as Ingham saw it, that Kent had stated that the civil law required an absolute taking but that was not what the common law required. This was a rather odd position to take as both *Pierson* and *Buster* v. *Newkirk* were common law cases and Kent had gone out of his way to emphasize that these cases were both situations of mere pursuit. Holmes's interpretation of Kent had forged a connection between the common law and civil law positions. It was a connection that Pollock had also accepted (influenced as he would have been by *Young* v. *Hitchens*, which was a British case) and that Arnold also believed. However, the court in *Liesner et al.* v. *Wanie* followed a different track. It saw a situation of practical inevitability. The plaintiffs had the wolf "so in their power that escape was highly improbable, if not impossible" that a property right vested in them, "which cannot be divested by another's intervening and killing it."[95] Relying on Ingham, the court said "[s]uch is the law of the chase by common law principles, differing from the more

[90] *Liesner et al.* v. *Wanie*, 145 *Northwestern Reporter* 374–76 (Supreme Court of Wisconsin, 1914).

[91] Arnold, "The Law of Possession," 396. [92] Ibid., 397. [93] Ibid.

[94] *Liesner et al.* v. *Wanie*, 376. [95] Ibid.

ancient civil law which postponed the point of vested interest to that of actual taking."[96] In other words, contrary to Holmes, there was a difference between the common law and civil law; the common law was the "the law of the chase" not the capture rule.

Hence, there were two trajectories or lines of thinking about *Pierson*. In one, according to Holmes and Pollock, escape had to be made impossible and the animal actually taken (à la Justinian) – the capture rule. In the other, articulated by Ingham, an actual taking was not required, so something like practical inevitability was a viable common law position – what the wolf case *Liesner et al.* v. *Wanie* called "the law of the chase."[97] Kent can be read as supporting both positions in so far as he originally gave *Pierson* a mere pursuit interpretation, as Tompkins had in *Pierson* by agreeing with Barbeyrac that an actual taking was not required. However, Kent also seemed (to Holmes, to Pollock, to Ingham, and to Arnold) to be arguing that the Roman law (i.e. Justinian), which required actual taking, was the rule adopted in the civil law and in *Pierson* and *Buster* v. *Newkirk*. Here were two rival interpretations, one of which left open the possibility of a hot pursuit rule. A hot pursuit rule was available where there was mortal wounding as in *Liesner et al.* v. *Wanie* and in situations that involved inescapable traps (unlike most fish nets where many fish will still escape, and "fishing" is a long process with many steps). This was not necessarily inconsistent. Indeed, one might say that in general, an absolute taking was required unless there was mortal wounding (as in *Liesner et al.* v. *Wanie*) or traps and nets from which it was unlikely that the animal would escape (unlike *Young* v. *Hitchens*).

The point to notice is that the above understanding of the rule in *Pierson* was not worked out clearly in *Pierson* itself. Nor was it made clear in Kent's *Commentaries*, which conflated the common law position on mere pursuit with the Roman law point on wounding and actually taking. Holmes simply made the leap to actually taking, wounding or no wounding, and read Kent in that way, as did Pollock and later commentators like Arnold and Ingham, as well as the court in *Liesner et al.* v. *Wanie*. The idea that hot pursuit was a viable rule, but applied only where there was mortal wounding or inescapable traps or nets, was not an obvious outcome of *Pierson*. Generating it required a lot of intensive interpretation. And, at least according to some (e.g. Pothier and Trebatius) the wounding in a valid hot pursuit did not need to be mortal nor would a net or trap be absolutely inescapable (according to Arnold). In *Pierson* Livingston had spoken up for a hot pursuit

[96] Ibid. [97] Ibid.

rule in a situation that was not mortal wounding and did not involve inescapable nets and traps, but it is difficult to know how seriously to take his dissent. Yes, as Barbeyrac put it, the animal might be within reach of taking; but an animal within reach of a taking that did not involve wounding or trapping was an animal that could still escape, no?

THE NEW (QUIET) TWENTIETH-CENTURY LEGAL MANDARINS: CASEBOOK EDITORS

Pierson gained a prominent place in an American casebook for the first time in 1915 in the Harvard Law School collection on the law of property compiled by Edward Warren.[98] Warren did not include Livingston's dissent. Neither did the University of Chicago Law School teacher Harry

[98] Edward H. Warren ed., *Select Cases and Other Authorities on the Law of Property* (Cambridge, MA: The editor, 1915), 1–3.

Pierson was included in earlier casebooks but not in a first-page first-place way to introduce the idea of possession. See e.g. William Sullivan Pattee, *Illustrative Cases in Personality*, vol. 1, (Philadelphia, PA: T. and J.W. Johnson, 1893), 19–22 (where *Pierson* appears early on in a section on animals *ferae naturae*, following light, air, and water); John Davison Lawson, *Select Cases in the Law of Personal Property: with analysis and references to other cases* (Columbia, MO: E.W. Stephens, 1896), 164–67 (where *Pierson* appears deeper in although it is in a section on "Modes of Obtaining Title to Personal Property" "By Original Acquisition (A) Occupancy"). Neither of these casebook reproductions included the dissent or the lawyers' arguments.

John Chipman Gray did not include *Pierson* in his six-volume *Select Cases and Other Authorities on the Law of Property* (Cambridge, MA: C.W. Sever, 1888–1892). It had no wild animal or first possession section; it did contain sections on air, earth, and water under "Natural Rights" in vol. 2. See pp. 32–179.

A helpful reference used in this chapter to track property law casebooks has been Douglas W. Lind, *Bibliography of American Law School Casebooks, 1879–2004* (Buffalo, NY: William S. Hein, 2006), 624–61. I have not, however, searched for *Pierson* in all the casebooks listed there. In other words, it is a selected collection of property law casebooks I have chosen to discuss here. Of the personal property casebooks listed in Lind, *Pierson* does not appear in Everett Fraser, 2 vols., *Cases and Readings on Property; Introduction to Real and Personal Property* (Chicago, IL: Foundation Press, 1933–1936); Richard H. Chused, *A Modern Approach to Property: Cases, Notes, and Materials* (St. Paul, MN: West Publishing, 1978); or Olin L. Browder Jr., Roger A. Cunningham, and Joseph R. Julin eds., *Basic Property Law* (St. Paul, MN: West Publishing, 1966).

I have made an effort to use the most up-to-date edition of the casebook where available, but I have not followed to see if *Pierson* eventually appears in later editions of Fraser, Chused, or Browder et al. above.

Teachers' Manuals are not readily available (although Lind reports that they are consistently produced from the 1950s on – he discretely refers to them as "supplementary materials" – see "Introduction," x) and I have not consulted these except in the case of the 5th edition of Casner and Leach (2004), the last edition of this casebook to carry the

A. Bigelow when he first reproduced *Pierson* in his casebook on personal property two years later.[99] Bigelow's book was part of the American Casebook Series published by the West Publishing Company.[100] In the first edition *Pierson* did not appear on the first page, as it had in Warren's collection, but in the second (1931) edition of Bigelow's book it assumed the first-case position.[101]

Bigelow seems to have complicated his thinking about *Pierson* between 1931 and 1942, when the third edition of his casebook appeared.[102] Bigelow was the Dean of the University of Chicago law school from 1929 to his retirement in 1935. He was an avid big game hunter, who traveled to Africa for several expeditions. Probably with fewer duties at the law school after 1935 – he continued to teach long after his retirement – he had more time to delve into the intricacies of a topic like possession as it was connected to an activity, hunting, that was important to him.[103] In the third edition, Bigelow moved *Pierson* further into the book, as if to decrease its importance, and he added a long and extremely interesting footnote.[104]

First, Bigelow's footnote paraphrased Livingston's dissent, omitting all of its solemn foolery. It was given the following utterly serious paraphrasing:

> Livingston J. dissented upon the ground that there was no precise test or unanimity of judicial opinion as to when a wild animal should be regarded as sufficiently reduced to possession to become private property; that the destruction of foxes should be encouraged and to allow a person to intervene and obtain title by possession when another had the labor of arousing and pursuing the animal and was still closely on his trail would be against public policy.[105]

Second, Bigelow included a long quotation from the wolf case, *Liesner et al. v. Wanie*, which included the new standard of "practical inevitability" and

names of the original editors, kindly provided to me by one of its co-editors Lea S. VanderVelde.

99 See Harry A. Bigelow ed., *Personal Property* (St. Paul, MN: West Publishing, 1917), 141–43.

100 See ibid., v–ix.

101 Harry A. Bigelow ed., *Personal Property* 2nd ed. (St. Paul, MN: West Publishing, 131), 4–6.

102 Harry A. Bigelow ed., *Cases and Materials on the Law of Personal Property*, 3rd ed. (St. Paul, MN: West Publishing, 1942), 13–15.

103 The biographical information in this paragraph is based on the "Biographical Note" to the Finding Aid for the Harry A. Bigelow papers, Special Collections Research Centre, University of Chicago Library. I have not searched in the papers for discussion of views on *Pierson* or possession more generally.

104 Bigelow ed., *Personal Property*, 3rd ed., 15 n. 2.

105 Ibid.

was grounded by the Wisconsin court in John Ingham's treatise.[106] The Wisconsin court wrote, and Bigelow quoted from it, that practical inevitability, giving rise to a vested property right that cannot be divested by another intervening and killing the animal, "is the law of the chase by common-law principles, differing from the more ancient civil law which postponed the point of the vested interest to that of actual taking."[107]

Third, the footnote also referred to Arnold's *American Law Review* article. Probably Bigelow had read Arnold's 1921 article, which directed him to *Liesner et al.* v. *Wanie* (1915), which, in turn, led him to Ingham's treatise (1900). He had discovered in reading these sources that, despite Kent (or at least Kent as interpreted by Holmes and Pollock), there was an alternate understanding of *Pierson*, a parallel track as it were, that rejected the capture rule and was grounded in Livingston's dissent and the hot pursuit rule (or what *Liesner et al.* v. *Wanie* called "vigorous pursuit").[108] This view, "the law of the chase by common-law principles," deserved to be presented to property students and scholars trying to understand possession.[109]

Bigelow's first footnote in the section on possession headed by *Pierson* referred to Holmes's work on *The Common Law*, Pollock's book, and two law review articles on possession.[110] The first of these articles is a long two-part excursion into the various definitions of property, title, ownership, title, and legal possession published by Joseph W. Bingham in 1915.[111] Bingham offers intelligent observations about property as "commercially wealth, however slight," and possession as "to have or to hold in some sense or other."[112] However, he also engages in a lot of hand-wringing over "the endless controversies" that persist over the understanding of legal possession despite "the accumulated learning of the books," without making a lot of progress on the point.[113]

The second article cited by Bigelow was written in 1932 and strikes a more realist tone, appropriate to its time. Its author, Burke Shartel, begins by stating that possession is "the vaguest of all vague terms."[114] But instead of "add[ing] one more to the already imposing array of suggested

[106] Ibid. [107] Ibid., 4–5 n. 2 (cont.). [108] *Leisner et al.* v. *Wanie*, 376.

[109] Bigelow ed., *Personal Property*, 3rd ed., 4–5 n. 2 (cont.). [110] Ibid., 13 n. 1.

[111] Joseph W. Bingham, "The Nature and Importance of Legal Possession," 13 *Michigan Law Review* (1914–15): 535–65, 623–45.

[112] Ibid., 538, 553. [113] Ibid., 535–36.

[114] Burke Shartel, "Meanings of Possession," 16 *Minnesota Law Review* (1931–32): 611–37, 611.

definitions of possession," Shartel states that he wishes "to make the point that there are many meanings of the word 'possession.'"[115] The reason why the notion is still vague, according to Shartel, is that legal theorists have been attempting "the impossible."[116] Rather than trying to bring "as many cases as possible together, on the basis of some feature of similarity among them [...] all under one conceptual head," it is more profitable to "emphasize instead differences between cases," which are "for legal purposes, far more significant than the likenesses which constitute the basis of unification under one concept."[117] Gone is the faith that more discussion will necessarily bring more precision, more understanding, more clarity on a unified concept. There is not one meaning; there are many meanings.

Holmes, we recall, was uncomfortable about where the capture rule in *Pierson* took him. He was skeptical about embracing an *a priori* view of what degree of power or control was required in order for there to be possession of a wild animal. This is a strong and obvious point if an animal is large like a whale, if it is difficult to get ones arms around it (as *Popov* v. *Hyashi* put it), and if there are different customs and subsequently different rules. Depending on the animal and its relationship to human use, killing (or even processing or "sculping") might not be enough. In the case of Ziff's seals, killing them was not enough to create possession if they were deemed abandoned on the ice and would otherwise go to waste. In *Liesner et al.* v. *Wanie* a common law court said that whatever the civil law on possession of a wild animal (and the disagreement among its authorities) might be, the common law could be and was different: the practical inevitability of killing the animal was sufficient to vest the possessory right. Bigelow was reading all these texts – Holmes, Ingham, Arnold, *Liesner et al.* v. *Wanie*, Shartel – and by 1942 seems to have had his faith in the rightness of the capture rule in *Pierson* comprehensively shaken, Kent et al. notwithstanding. This change of heart, indicated by the discovery and citation of the parallel track established by these other authorities in the third edition of his casebook, was probably connected to Bigelow's own hobby, big-game hunting, which encouraged receptivity of a hot pursuit rule and of the Lockean point about expended labor – even when it was labor expended in recreational pursuit.

Casebook editors who came after Bigelow were less shy about putting their views forward. We will see that they did not hesitate to use notes and questions after the reproduced or excerpted case in order to express doubts or issue gentle prompts to further thinking along more complicated lines

[115] Ibid., 612. [116] Ibid., 611. [117] Ibid., 612.

that they thought edifying, or simply provided shortcuts to the view they believed was correct. This is not a format or style that Bigelow adopts, so one is left to decode footnotes in order to ascertain the editor's thinking. Easy access to electronic resources makes this a relatively straightforward exercise today – HeinOnline provides PDFs of the law review articles, case law databases such as LexisNexis make the report in *Liesner et al.* v. *Wanie* available, and the *Making of Modern Law* database provides access to the texts of treatises such as Ingham's *The Law of Animals* and Chase's handbook for game wardens. The research can all be done without even getting out of one's pajamas. It would have taken considerably more effort in 1942 to chase down paper copies of all these sources, and even more effort to read and digest them. Frankly, one must wonder whether any student ever bothered to do this. I am not even certain that other property teachers would have done so.[118] More than anything intended to guide the reader, that is, the footnote might better be interpreted as a guide to Bigelow's own thinking.[119] Treated as such, it suggests a counternarrative of (and counterweight to) the way that Kent–Holmes–Pollock operated to establish the correctness of the capture rule and the civil law's congruence with the common law. The footnote records Bigelow's realization that this was not the only line of thinking on *Pierson*.

Bigelow's footnote also provides our first glimmer of the inclusion of Livingston's dissent in a law school casebook. It is significant that as Bigelow was wrestling seriously with his own thinking on possession, he does not (and would not) consider it appropriate to include the dissent itself, using instead a serious paraphrasing of its points. The dissent in other words started creeping in through the back door but was not yet allowed to make its own full-on rowdy appearance.

[118] Although starting in 1999, the historically minded Dick Helmholtz and the co-editors of his casebook present and discuss *Liesner et al.* v. *Wanie* after first-case first-page appearance of *Pierson* and then *Buster* v. *Newkirk*. See Barlow Burke, Ann M. Burkhart, and R. H. Helmholtz eds., *Fundamentals of Property Law* (Charlottesville, VA: Lexis Law Publishing, 1999), 7 n. 2 (where students are asked to question whether *Buster* v. *Newkirk* accurately states the rule in *Pierson*, tells them about the practical inevitability standard in *Liesner* where the pursuit is "vigorous," and asks about its rationale). This note is maintained (albeit in shorter form) in the most recent edition of the casebook. See Barlow Burke, Ann M. Burkhart, Thomas P. Gallanis, and R. H. Helmholtz eds., *Fundamentals of Property Law*, 4th ed. (Matthew Bender and Co., a member of LexisNexis, 2015), 6 n. 1.

[119] See Angela Fernandez, "An Object Lesson in Speculation: Multiple Views of the Cathedral in *Leaf* v. *International Galleries*," 58 *University of Toronto Law Journal* (2008): 481–519 (on how idiosyncratic and incomprehensible casebook notes and questions can be).

The first property casebook to include the actual text of Livingston's dissent was the successor to Warren's Harvard Collection, edited by James Casner and Barton Leach, and published by Little, Brown in 1951.[120] The editors added a note to the dissent that revealed what was behind their thinking. Gone was Bigelow's discrete footnote and small print that required close reading and serious scholarly study and decoding. Calling sources like Justinian "outmoded," the dissent was included for its insistence on the need to develop an Anglo-American common law separate from the civil law and Roman law.[121] The editors wrote that "Justice Livingston, as evidenced by his dissent, was willing to make the separation complete in the early nineteenth century."[122] This point was made more explicitly in the second edition where the editors wrote that it was of interest, "but little else," what English authorities indicated about the relationship between pursuit and possession of wild animals, and "of no interest at all" what Justinian said. Why? As they put it in the second edition in 1969, "[w]e should have been developing an *American* law suited to our needs and based upon our own situation – geographic, political, social."[123]

As we have seen, the dissent certainly made the point about independence ("Whatever Justinian may have thought of the matter [...] [Have we not] a right to establish a rule for ourselves[?]").[124] We have also seen that it is true that Livingston expressed frustration with civil law sources and their contrary indications in *Pierson* and other cases.[125] However, he also relied heavily on foreign law in his later decisions on the United States Supreme Court, where he carved out a specialization in commercial and maritime law, areas that relied heavily on such sources.[126] One could not conclude, then, that Livingston was willing to make the separation between American law and foreign law "complete" in 1805.[127] The editors appear to be using Livingston to make a provincially inflected

[120] See A. James Casner and W. Barton Leach eds., *Cases and Text on Property*, 1st standard ed. (Boston, MA: Little, Brown, 1951), 13–14.

[121] See ibid., 15. [122] Ibid.

[123] Casner and Leach eds., 2nd ed., *Cases and Text on Property* (1969), 15 (emphasis in the original).

[124] *Pierson*, 181.

[125] See ibid., 181 ("[w]riters on general law, who have favored us with their speculations on these points, differ on them all"). See also *Penny and Scribner* v. *The NY Insurance Co; Lawrence* v. *Sebor; Leavenworth* v. *Delafield* and the discussion of these cases in Chapter 2.

[126] See Cushman, "Henry Brockholst Livingston," *Dictionary of American Biography*.

[127] See Casner and Leach eds., 1st standard ed. (1951), 15.

and, I suppose it seemed to them at the outset of the Cold War, patriotic or nationalistic point, pushing it to the fore in the way that they edited the decision and presented it. They also edited out some of the more eccentric parts of the dissent.[128] Students were expressly warned not to "permit [Livingston's] facetiousness of expression which must have caused some tongue clucking at that time to obscure the trend of his thought."[129] The editing was clearly intended to prevent the more puzzling aspects of the text from luring students away from the point about the irrelevance of so-called foreign law and the importance of an indigenous and truly *American* (their emphasis) perspective. We should remember that it was the way that the lawyers and Tompkins used the authorities – as if the best would necessarily win – not their use *per se* that bothered Livingston. It was unthinking use of foreign sources that Livingston was objecting to, not the use of foreign sources in which he himself was expert.

Casner and Leach's point about independence was not so different from the point that Bigelow probably wanted his students to see by including reference to *Leisner et al.* v. *Wanie*; namely, that there was an American common-law decision that differentiated American common law from the civil law, that there was no need to believe (slavishly) that the civil law answer to this question, the capture rule, was the best answer for this time and place (and for all animals). As *Leisner et al.* v. *Wanie* framed it, hot pursuit with an imminent taking, or practical inevitability, was also an available rule, advanced in this homegrown wolf case, in John Ingham's treatise, and in Livingston's dissent. Here were all the elements for an indigenous American counter-story. But Bigelow buried his revisionism in a footnote where it could not have enough weight to counterbalance the immense authority, influence, and established intellectual trajectory set out in the Kent–Holmes–Pollock triad. Could those theoretical/historical giants of the law have been wrong? Could the Roman law itself, at least according to Justinian, have been wrong? Casner and Leach wanted to establish the point that Americans were not required to follow the civil law (or Roman law) – they had to think for themselves. Bigelow's revisionism was more subtle: the titans of the law might have indeed got it wrong. Why not hunt them as he would his big-game animals? Subtlety meant his point was more easily missed. Why avoid the spotlight? Likely he felt outgunned: a short no-nonsense decision by the Wisconsin Supreme Court versus an elaborate and learned New York Supreme Court decision (two if one counts

[128] Ibid., 14. [129] See ibid.

Buster v. *Newkirk*); John T. Ingham, an obscure treatise-writer from Philadelphia, versus Kent–Holmes–Pollock.

Casner and Leach noted Livingston's impatience with the parties and the "pomposity" of Tompkins's majority opinion.[130] They did not contemplate the possibility that Livingston might have been reacting to the pomposity of the lawyers and the ridiculous amount of energy and money spent on this 75¢ fox. Like earlier casebooks – Warren's, Bigelow's – Casner and Leach excluded the lawyers' arguments. They did not even use ellipses to indicate something had been removed.[131] Oddly, Casner and Leach still asked students to consider "how far Tompkins, J., was justified in stating that *Pierson* v. *Post* 'was argued with much ability by the counsel on both sides.'" How could students answer without seeing the arguments? The question appears designed to lead students to conclude that the case had *not* been argued with much ability.[132] Rather than include the lawyers' arguments in the second edition, the editors' leading question was removed.[133] The tendency to exclude the lawyers' arguments continues and has in fact increased.[134] Without them, it is impossible to see that Post's lawyer objected to the characterization of the case as one of mere pursuit, and to understand what he wanted the court to adopt from Barbeyrac – not the point about wounding that Tompkins discussed but the idea of vesting possession in one within the "Reach of taking" that was invoked by Livingston.

The only casebook reproduction I have seen that included the lawyers' arguments is the collection produced by Harvard Law School's Charles

130 See ibid., 15 (Livingston "plainly showed [...] that he was impatient with the petty squabble between country squires [...] and disapproved the pomposity of Tompkins J. in dealing with it").

131 See ibid., 11. 132 Ibid., 15.

133 See Casner and Leach eds., 2nd ed. (1969), 15, 11. No lawyers' arguments or ellipses appeared in the third edition either. See A. James Casner and W. Barton Leach eds., *Cases and Text on Property*, 3rd ed. (Boston, MA: Little, Brown, 1984), 10–11. This remains true in the later Aspen publications of this casebook in the 2000s. See A. James Casner, W. Barton Leach, Susan Fletcher French, Gerald Korngold, and Lea VanderVelde eds., *Cases and Text on Property*, 4th ed. (New York: Aspen Law and Business, 2000), 23–29; 5th ed. (New York: Aspen, 2004), 34–40; French and Korngold eds., *Cases and Text on Property*, 6th ed. (2015), 72.

134 Joseph William Singer's casebook used to indicate with ellipses where the lawyers' argument had been removed. See e.g. Joseph William Singer ed., *Property Law: Rules, Policies and Practices*, 5th ed. (New York: Aspen Law and Business, 2010), 152. However, the ellipses have disappeared in the 6th edition. See Joseph William Singer, Bethany R. Berger, Nestor M. Davidson, and Eduardo Peñalver eds., *Property Law: Rules, Policies and Practices*, 6th ed. (New York: Aspen Law and Business, 2014), 131.

Donahue, which put *Pierson* in its first pages in three editions from 1974 to 1993.[135] This casebook also provided translations of the Latin passages in *Pierson*, which are so apt to confuse (students) and obfuscate (issues), and included notes and questions providing context on the various authorities cited in the decision such as Blackstone and Justinian. In other words, it rejected the ahistoricism and patriotism of Casner and Leach and instead put emphasis on making sense of the authorities employed, along with emphasizing the role of the lawyers. Like Bigelow, Donahue cast doubt on the capture rule, asking in articles he wrote on the subject why we have an anti-Lockean decision in an age where Locke and labor theories of property were so important. He also argued that the passage from Justinian's *Institutes*, while tending to, did not conclusively establish Pierson's claim.[136] Donahue wrote in 2009, "I remain of the view that we should focus on the lawyers."[137]

Inclusion of the dissent in American property law casebooks became standard in the 1970s. Some casebooks allowed the jocular tone of the dissent to influence the kind of notes and materials appended to the case rather than attempting to contain and control it as Casner and Leach had. In 1977, Charles Haar and Lance Liebman included the dissent (unedited) and added to the notes and questions section excerpts from a 1974 case in which a show parrot named Chester "flew the coop."[138] Another note provided a quotation from the historian Perry Miller proposing that in the early American republic, knowledge of civil law operated as "a badge of cultivation," a way to "dazzle clients and juries" and to allow elite lawyers to "express their contempt for those who did not follow the law 'as a liberal and scientific study.'"[139] A third included a story in which a man discovered that he and his adversary in a dispute were described by his adversary's lawyer as "[t]wo fat geese" and that the adversary's

[135] Charles Donahue Jr., Thomas E. Kauper and Peter W. Martin eds., *Cases and Materials on Property: An Introduction to the Concept and Institution* (St. Paul, MN: West Publishing, 1974), 1–2; 2nd ed. (1983), 1–2; 3rd ed. (1993), 2–3.

[136] See Donahue, *Animalia Ferae Naturae*," 61; Donahue, "Noodt, Titius, and the Natural Law School," 610–11.

[137] Donahue, "Papyrology," 182.

[138] See Charles M. Haar and Lance Liebman eds., *Property and Law* (Boston, MA: Little, Brown: 1977), 25–27; 28 n. 4 (the court held that the rule of *ferae naturae* did not prevail, as Chester was a domesticated animal and the person who had used food to lure him away from the ASPCA educational exhibitions for children had not acquired a property in him by capture).

[139] See ibid., 28–29 n. 5.

lawyer recommended to the lawyer the man was about to retain: "You pluck one. I'll pluck the other."[140] A supplement in 1982 provided students with a large portion of the "Fast Fish, Loose Fish" chapter of Melville's *Moby-Dick*.[141] Haar and Liebman's second edition included a witty *repartee* or imaginary dialogue about jackasses and the ownership of their offspring.[142] Here were editors who were not afraid of the mock aspects of the case, its literary dimensions, and its wider historical context.

Casebooks that appeared in the 1980s and 1990s tended to put *Johnson* v *M'Intosh* before *Pierson*, in order to begin at the real beginning, with white settlers and their relationship to lands previously owned by Native peoples. Jesse Dukeminier and James Krier first published their law-and-economics oriented collection in 1981.[143] Beginning with its second edition in 1988, it put *Pierson* second to *Johnson* v *M'Intosh*.[144] Joseph Singer's casebook, first published in 1993, pushed *Pierson* back a little further, after two Native Indian land cases (including *Johnson* v *M'Intosh*), and followed it with cases relating to oil and gas, making explicit the connection between wild animals and other fugitive resources.[145] Dukeminier and Krier asked: "What are the benefits of 'certainty' in a property system? Might there be disadvantages in advancing the objective of certainty?"[146] Singer asked: "What rule of Law – Tompkins' or Livingston's – creates the most certainty about ownership rights? Is the rule that creates the most certainty also the most just?"[147]

A new free *Open Source Property* electronic casebook launched in 2015–2016 not only gives *Pierson* first-page position, it uses a foxhunting scene as the banner picture on the casebook's homepage.[148] In addition to

[140] Ibid., 29 n. 6.

[141] See Haar and Liebman eds., Supplement to the 1st ed. (1982), 7–9.

[142] See Haar and Liebman eds., 2nd ed. *Property and Law* (Boston, MA Little Brown, 1985), 40–41.

[143] See Jesse Dukeminier and James E. Krier eds., *Property* (Boston, MA: Little, Brown, 1981), 34–38.

[144] See Jesse Dukeminier and James E. Krier eds., *Property*, 2nd ed. (Boston, MA: Little, Brown, 1988), 15–19.

[145] See Joseph William Singer ed., *Property Law: Rules, Policies, and Practices* (Boston, MA: Little, Brown, 1993), 56–72.

[146] Dukeminier and Krier eds., 1st ed., *Property* (1981), 40 n. 2.

[147] See Singer ed., 1st ed., *Property Law* (1993), 61 n. 4.

[148] See https://opensourceproperty.org/ edited by Stephen Clowney, James Grimmelmann, Michael Grynberg, Jeremy Sheff and Rebecca Tushnet (2015–16). The editors are all scholars of intellectual property, a fact that helps explain their launch of a casebook in

questions about certainty (or "administrability") (à la Dukeminier and Krier) *versus* fairness and justice or morality (à la Singer), the editor of this section, James Grimmelmann, follows the case with questions relating to "ecology," asking if the rule is consistent with the "responsible stewardship of resources" and the consequences for "an exhaustible resource [. . .] for the benefit of future generations." Conquest appears later in its own section with *Johnson* v. *M'Intosh* and is connected to Singer and his writing on the ongoing injustice of conquest, and there is also a later reading on the ownership of oil and gas and questions about wastefulness versus the tragedy of the commons.[149] It is good that the ecological question is raised in connection to *Pierson* but it is a bit unclear what context the students would have for appreciating it in connection to the capture rule at this early point in the text. The ecological question is followed by a series of questions relating to "incentives" folded together under the banner of "efficiency":

> Does the rule encourage or discourage the conversion of idle resources to productive use? Does it encourage excessive, duplicative, or wasteful efforts to exploit resources? Does it encourage or discourage disputes or violence among rival occupants? Does it encourage would-be claimants to expend resources on protecting themselves *against other* would-be claimants, instead of on more productive pursuits? When weighing these incentives in the aggregate, is the rule *efficient*? That is, does it extract the greatest possible value from available resources at the lowest possible cost?[150]

In this very expansive idea of incentives, value is not necessarily the ruthlessly extractive "certainty" of the capture rule for wild animals or other fugitive resources. Yet it is a rather cabined notion of value even while it encompasses ideas as various as reducing wastefulness, avoiding violence, and minimizing unnecessarily exerted effort. When asking about morality, the editor expresses skepticism about whether we have a standard for measuring moral or immoral behavior.[151] Yet one might just as equally wonder about our ability to compute "greatest possible

this format. It will be interesting to see if other areas of the law will follow and if they do what this will do to the older for-profit business model for casebooks, specifically will it render the older format obsolete. And will there be different ideological versions of free electronic casebooks to choose among, as there were among the earlier print-published casebooks.

149 See *Open Source Property*, Part 1, 48–53, 61–62 (*Johnson* v. *M'Intosh*), 200–208 (oil and gas as a fugitive resource akin to wild animals).

150 Ibid., 11.

151 Ibid, 10 ("Morality: Does the rule reward moral behavior and punish – or at least refrain from rewarding – immoral behavior? (This assumes of course that we have a standard for moral and immoral behavior)").

value" at "lowest possible cost," which assumes a metric of measuring disparate values and costs.

As more and more students are exposed to *Pierson* over time, a trend that the *Open Source Property* casebook demonstrates shows no signs of abating, what material the casebook editor includes or omits, what questions are asked after the text, just like the questions asked in the classroom itself, will shape what the case comes to mean collectively for the profession. What you see depends literally on what you can see, and certainly on what is emphasized to you as a student. From the perspective of the authoritative casebook editor or treatise writer, you make sure to keep in sight what you think should be seen. For *Pierson*, that seems to have largely meant, at least in its early law school casebook days and until the 1970s, suppressing or carefully managing the dissent to keep its oddities from becoming too distracting and making no space at all for the lawyers' arguments.

The point is to recognize that although the case itself might seem unchanging, it has not actually been the same text over time. Its meaning has been greatly influenced by the ways in which it has been reproduced, edited, and presented by casebook editors. Some of this reflects scholarly preoccupations and approaches, such as the extent to which the editor is interested in legal history (for example, Donahue and Helmholtz); some looks like it could be roughly captured by differences of time, with the rough ten-year law-lag one so often sees (for example, Casner and Leach in the patriotic and conservative 1950s and 1960s versus Harr and Liebman in the irreverent 1970s); some represents ideological differences between those to the right and the left of the political spectrum in the 1980s and 1990s (Dukeminier and Krier's law-and-economics approach versus Singer's more liberal approach); some reflects the rise of an Aboriginal rights consciousness that makes the concerns associated with *Johnson* v *M'Intosh* relevant, starting in the 1970s and groups such as the American Indian Movement and continuing today. Currently we see a connection to the Animal Rights Movement.[152] All these changes in law school casebooks show that the law school curriculum is not disconnected and insulated from the wider intellectual, social, political, and cultural world in which law schools exist. One might think the tracking of external trends is obvious, but the hard-bound and expensive casebooks (they have, at least until *Open Source Property*, been hard-bound and expensive) have a way of conveying an impression that they capture

[152] See e.g. French and Korngold eds., *Cases and Text on Property*, 6th ed. (2015), 80 n. 4.

something like an essential and natural world of what the law is, not just one authoritative version that is out there competing intensely with other versions that claim to be equally authoritative with different emphases and interests.

THE NEW (LOUD) TWENTIETH-CENTURY LEGAL MANDARINS: PROPERTY THEORISTS

Starting in the 1960s, *Pierson* v *Post* began to be featured (or at least mentioned) in the writing of prominent American legal scholars, who unlike the legal mandarins of the nineteenth century, would have encountered the case in their law school casebooks when they were students. Prominent in this scholarship were Charles A. Reich's famous article on New York City taxi medallions, "The New Property," published in the *Yale Law Journal*, and Frank I. Michelman's "Property, Utility, and Fairness," published in the *Harvard Law Review*. Both are among the top twenty most-cited law review articles of all time.[153] In 1977 *Pierson* also received a mention by Justice William Rehnquist in a United States Supreme Court case involving state fishing regulations prohibiting non-residents (otherwise federally licensed) from fishing in Virginia waters.[154] Attention in these prominent fora – the two most highly ranked law reviews and comment by

[153] Charles A. Reich, "The New Property," 73 *Yale Law Journal* (1963–64): 733–87, 778 n. 209; Frank I. Michelman, "Property, Utility, and Fairness: Comments on the Ethical Foundations of Just Compensation Law," 80 *Harvard Law Review* (1966–67), 1165–1258, 1244. Reich ranks seventh and Michelman twelfth. See Fred R. Shapiro and Michelle Pearse, "The Most-Cited Law Review Articles of All Time," 110 *Michigan Law Review* (2011–2012): 1483–1520, 1489.

[154] See *Douglas* v. *Seacoast Products Inc. et al.*, 431 U.S. 265, 97 S. Ct. 1740 (U.S. Sup. Ct., 1977). Virginia argued that because the state "owned" the fish in its waters, it could exclude federal licensees. The majority wrote that "[a] State does not stand in the same position as the owner of a private game preserve and it is pure fantasy to talk of 'owning' wild fish, birds, or animals. Neither the States nor the Federal Government, any more than a hopeful fisherman or hunter, had title to these creatures until they are reduced to possession by skillful capture" (citing to a case by Oliver Wendell Holmes Jr. *Missouri* v. *Holland* and the dissent in *Geer* v. *Connecticut*). "The 'ownership' language [...] must be understood as no more than a 19th-century legal fiction expressing 'the importance to its people that a State have power to preserve and regulate the exploitation of an important resource.'" Rehnquist in his dissent agreed that "States do not 'own' free-swimming creatures within their territorial limits in any conventional sense of that term" (citing to *Missouri* v. *Holland* and *Pierson* v. *Post*). However, he preferred to call the State's "substantial proprietary interest" in the fish and game within their boundaries "common ownership" (citing to *Geer* v. *Connecticut*) and thought more weight ought to be given to the State's rights.

a United States Supreme Court justice – seems to have encouraged resort to the case as a precedent after a long sleep, a nearly unbroken eighty-three years, at least among reported cases.[155] Secondary source citation, in law journals and the like, followed much the same pattern, declining after the 1890s with numbers beginning to increase only in the 1970s and 1980s, with enormous jumps in the 1990s and the first fifteen years of the 2000s.

It is difficult to say exactly why *Pierson* becomes so popular and widely referenced in this fifty-year period. Certainly it must be significant that virtually all judges and law professor were exposed to it in their property casebooks as law students. Most casebooks carried it, often very prominently as we have seen. It was memorable, it was funny. Charles Reich himself wrote in a later short review of a book on legal reasoning that featured *Pierson* that "[s]tudents are likely to remember these cases for almost anything except the type of reasoning at issue" and, specifically, in the case of *Pierson*, are "more likely to remember the learned and humorous dissent by Livingston, J., as a gem of legal wit."[156] For law professors writing law review articles, the dominant mode of scholarly legal conversation in the twentieth century, what they learned as students and remembered from their student days provided a ready source of reference. *Pierson* featured vivid facts and a memorable dissent. Its binary of hot pursuit versus capture was easy to grasp even if the textual references were subtle and debatable and one was apt to forget or confuse Pierson with Post and perhaps even fail to recall which way the court had ruled. Given the way that *Pierson* was used in law school casebooks, as an introduction to the fundamental question of how one has property in anything and how to establish possession via occupancy over unowned things, law professors saw it as eminently applicable to new property questions – property in parts of the human body, property in new technology discovered using those human body parts (e.g. gene cells and their stem lines), related questions of patents and the like in intellectual property, as well as unowned baseballs when they are hit into the stands.[157] It seems likely that *Pierson* will continue to be used in this way to deal with off-world ownership in space of objects like asteroids.

[155] With the exception of a Massachusetts Supreme Court case in 1926 about a hunted deer, *Dapson* v. *Daly*, 257 MA 195, 153 N.E. 454 (MA: Sup. Ct., 1926). See "Appendix A: Citation History," recording the gap.

[156] Charles A. Reich, "All the Right Moves [Review of *Tactics of Legal Reasoning* (Durham, NC: North Carolina Press, 1986) by Pierre Schlag and David Skover]," 85 *Michigan Law Review* (1986–87): 1201–1203, 1203. *Pierson* is reproduced and discussed in the book at pp. 55–62.

[157] See examples given in the Introduction.

One is struck when reviewing the enormous number of references to *Pierson* in law reviews of the twentieth century that many of the references are tangential. Even in situations in which the topic of the piece is not tied very directly to questions of possession, whether of new property or original entitlements, still *Pierson* makes an appearance. Such cursory references show just how deeply *Pierson* has become embedded in a common legal culture, common legal language, so much so that it need not be much related to the topic under discussion. It is as if reference to *Pierson* is now an obligatory hat tip that authors feel the need to make, rather like the nudge-and-wink of those telling an in-joke to an in-crowd (a bit like *hostis humani generis* explored in Chapter 2), the creation of rapport with audience or reader.[158] Nor have judges been immune to the temptation to use *Pierson* in this way, as some of the non-animal case citations in Appendix A demonstrate.

As interesting and revealing as the cursory references can be, I have chosen to discuss here instances in which the case plays a central role for property theorists who have written influential articles, or where the secondary use illustrates a noteworthy trend or phenomenon in legal scholarship. The relatively recent history of the case, following its canonization in casebooks, is important to understanding the range of ways in which *Pierson* has been used. These more substantial deployments have themselves been very influential and have undoubtedly contributed to the kind of cursory or tangential uptake that is so striking and prevalent in law reviews from the 1980s on; they will likely continue in judgments and law reviews as long as the case it is still taught in American law schools. It is as if each new legal scholar who touches the case feels compelled to contribute to its collective meaning as it morphs and changes over time, creating a version of Ronald Dworkin's "strange literary exercise": the chain novel.[159] As Stanley Fish pointed out in his criticism of Dworkin's use of the idea of the chain novel to explain the way that invention operated within constraints in legal interpretation, it is impossible to maintain "[t]he distinction between explaining a text and changing it."[160]

158 See e.g. K. Scott Hamilton, "Prolegomenon to Myth and Fiction in Legal Reasoning, Common Law Adjudication and Critical Legal Studies," 35 *Wayne Law Review* (1988–89): 1449–80, 1456–57.

159 Ronald Dworkin, "Law as Interpretation," 60 *Texas Law Review* (1981–82): 527–50, 542.

160 Stanley Fish, "Working on the Chain Gang: Interpretation in Law and Literature," 60 *Texas Law Review* (1981–82): 551–67, 562.

This is because "[t]o explain a work is to point out something about it that had not been attributed to it before and therefore to change it by challenging other explanations that were once changes in their turn Explaining and changing [. . .] are the same activities."[161] In *Pierson*, to explain Livingston's dissent as a literary text offers insight into its puzzling features, while at the same time changing how we think about the case and the dissent, as an example of legal solemn foolery. It is unlikely the case would ever have become as famous (and infamous) as it did without that witty dissent. Yet we will see that the deployment of *Pierson* by law and economics professors in the twentieth century has been, like the use of it by Kent, Holmes, and Pollock's use in the nineteenth century, utterly serious.

Hence, we are left to process a somewhat paradoxical situation. Fun and frolic (whatever we might feel about it) is the reason why *Pierson* assumed such a well-known and prominent place in the American legal canon; yet, its seriousness, the solemnity of its foolery, is often the sole focus of scholarly attention. This occlusion of what is undeniably present in the case – its humor – what was there from its beginnings in Livingston's hands and living on in law school classrooms for over a hundred years, creates a new kind of "surreal" feel.[162] The new (loud) mandarins, just as the old (quiet) ones, have created a dissonance in putting the foolery once more out of sight. They have made appreciation of the text as a primarily literary text extremely difficult, and in doing so have simultaneously greatly increased the likelihood of being misled by it. Let us examine then some of the twentieth-century treatment of *Pierson* in the hands of influential property law scholars.

University of Chicago law professor Richard Epstein made *Pierson* very central to an influential article he published in 1979.[163] For Epstein, the assumption and failure to demonstrate in the case that the fox was unowned illustrated what he called "the legal reluctance to examine first principles afresh."[164] He noted that what he called "the little question – what counts as taking first possession – received exhaustive attention" in the case, while "[t]he large question – why is first

[161] Ibid. While Dworkin sees legal interpretation as "an activity in need of constraints," Fish sees it as "a *structure* of constraints" in which there is no such thing as a free independent and uninterpreted text.

[162] McDowell, "Legal Fictions in *Pierson* v. *Post*," 765.

[163] See Richard A. Epstein, "Possession as the Root of Title," 13 *Georgia Law Review* (1978–79): 1221–1243, 1224–31.

[164] Ibid., 1224.

possession sufficient to support a claim for ownership – received no consideration at all."[165] He took the case as a challenge to try to articulate "how given bits of property are matched with given individuals."[166] And in such an investigation "taking possession of unowned things" as a way of acquiring ownership was the key focus.[167]

Carol Rose put *Pierson* front and center in her famous article "Possession as the Origin of Property," published in 1985 in the *University of Chicago Law Review*. Rose used the majority judgment to support her theory that property is about communication and that possession, specifically, requires a "clear act." Rose wrote that "[p]ossession as the basis of property ownership, then, seems to amount to something like yelling loudly enough to all who may be interested."[168] However, it is unclear what was not clear about starting and chasing a fox. Anyone who saw that, hunter or no hunter, would know what it meant – they might not respect it, as in Pierson's case, if they had reasons not to; but that is not a problem of comprehension or clarity. Starting and chasing a fox with "dogs and hounds" is a clear declaration by the pursuer that he has demonstrated what Rose took to be required, namely, "an unequivocal intention of appropriating the animal to his individual use."[169] When Tompkins spoke about a clear rule being best, he meant *a clear rule to decide who should get the fox*, the hunter or the interloper. There was no lack of clarity in the signal the hunter sent; the problem lay in the degree of control Post had obtained when compared against Pierson. Indeed, Post probably alleged Pierson took the fox with malice precisely because it was so clear what he, Post, was doing, hunting the fox.[170] Rose posed a series of questions meant to make a "slippery slope" point about the difficulty of pinpointing when exactly pursuit would be deemed sufficient. Rose wrote that "[t]he problem with assigning 'possession' prior to the kill is, of course, that we need a principle to tell us when to assign it. Shall we assign it when the hunt begins?"[171] No. "When the hunter assembles his dogs for the hunt?"[172] Clearly, no. "When the hunter buys his dogs?"[173] Clearly, clearly, no. Why not assign it when the hunter finds and starts the fox? Livingston included a similar kind of continuum when he implied that it could not be

[165] Ibid., 1225. [166] Ibid., 1221. [167] Ibid., 1222.

[168] Rose, "Possession as the Origin of Property," 81.

[169] Ibid., 76 (quoting *Pierson*, 178).

[170] The point about malice was a new element revealed in the Judgment Roll in the case. See Judgment Roll, pp. 4–5, Appendix B. However, we always knew that Post and his "dogs and hounds" were in Pierson's sight and Pierson swooped in "well knowing the fox was so hunted and pursued." *Pierson*, 175.

[171] Rose, "Possession as the Origin of Property," 76. [172] Ibid., 76–77. [173] Ibid., 77.

enough "to acquire dominion over a thing, before in common" that "we barely see it, or know where it is, or wish for it" – those things would clearly not be enough. However, to "make a declaration of our will respecting it"? – that would be enough, so long as we had a "reasonable prospect" of catching it, an ambit that could be circumscribed by uninterrupted and vigorous or hot pursuit and\or wounding.[174]

Henry Smith took Rose's argument about possession as communication and used it and *Pierson* to focus on a point about audience-specificity. "The certain-control rule is naturally addressed to a larger and more anonymous audience," Smith wrote, "whereas the hot-pursuit rule, with its greater detail, is more appropriate to a small group."[175] The small group is hunters who will know the custom that pursuit is putting in a claim to the animal. Smith used *Pierson* as an illustration of how possession "relates to how we define objects for purposes of ownership, which involves the widest set of anonymous interactions among the most heterogeneous audience that the law addresses."[176] In a later piece on custom, specifically on the way that "informationally demanding customs require an audience with a high degree of common knowledge," Smith refers to *Pierson* to support the point that strangers to a community in which people hunt for wild animals who may not "know when it is still subject to capture raises a more difficult informational question" than neighbors in an area who will know the community norm and will abide by it.[177] These points seem fine as far as they go; but again they presuppose that a non-hunter would not understand or have difficulty understanding what pursuit with "dogs and hounds" signaled. That conclusion seems to stretch beyond common sense.

Recall here Livingston's statement that he would decide the case according to the size of dog Post used.[178] Smith refers to this as an example of a "very particularized bright line rule" that would "impose a large processing burden on non-hunters," who would have little reason to know about the applicable edict from the twelve-century Holy Roman Emperor Frederick I.[179] The edict we might recall was that if there was a disagreement between an initial hunter and a "chance occupant," the

[174] *Pierson*, 181, 182.

[175] See Henry E. Smith, "The Language of Property: Form, Context, and Audience," 55 *Stanford Law Review* (2002–2003) 1105–1191, 1118.

[176] Ibid., 1119.

[177] Henry E. Smith, "Community and Custom in Property," 10 *Theoretical Inquiries in Law* (2009): 5–41, 5, 16 n. 44.

[178] *Pierson*, 182. [179] Smith, "The Language of Property," 1118–9.

animal would be given to the first hunter if he used "large dogs and hounds," but the "captor" succeeded if he used "beagles only."[180] Smith notes parenthetically that Livingston's reference was meant "quite possibly ironically."[181] I think it almost certainly was and Smith's use is an excellent example of the way that legal scholars in the process of the serious mandarization of the case have ignored, or, in this case, relegated to a parenthesis, the solemn foolery of Livingston's dissent.

There is a presumption in both Rose's and Smith's work that vagueness is bad (in Rose's case) and a limited audience is bad (in Smith's).[182] This seems to translate into a different but related presumption that that the greatest amount of clarity is best and that the most extensively understood communication is best. However, each of these positions fails to recognize that a signal that is clear enough (i.e. finding and starting a fox) is sufficient, and a heterogeneous audience no detriment to its reception, as long as heterogeneity is not a barrier to communication and comprehension. *Pierson* is just not a very good case to illustrate that more – more communication of intent, a more homogenous audience – is always better. At least in this context, more is just overkill. To use Rose's metaphor, the yell given was loud enough. More clarity and, indeed, perhaps even the maximum amount of clarity, can be very important in many legal situations – consider something like the ranking as between secured and unsecured creditors. But context-specificity should be brought to bear when evaluating the sufficiency of clarity. One should not automatically assume that more clarity and more certainty are always better than enough.

Sufficiency notwithstanding, the idea that clarity is the most important thing and that more clarity is always better even if it is overkill, as well as a failure to appreciate that a significantly lighter degree of attachment might well have been enough in this case, seems to inform the preference other property law teachers have for using *Pierson* to make a point about the superiority of rules over standards. Here, the clear capture rule, "he who seizes takes," is held to be superior to the allegedly "fuzzy" standard that the person in hot pursuit with a reasonable prospect of taking has possession, the standard Livingston articulated in his dissent in *Pierson*. James Krier has written about *Pierson* that "[t]he majority wanted a clear and certain rule, and here capture served best: it's easier to determine who first caught a fox than to determine, as the dissenting judge would have it,

[180] *Pierson*, 182. [181] Smith, "The Language of Property," 1118.

[182] See e.g. Rose, "Possession as the Origin of Property," 78 ("Society is worst off in a world of vague claims").

who first pursued it with a reasonable prospect of capture."[183] And, he continued, "[t]he rule of capture is just that – a firm fixed rule. The approach of the dissent is what we would today call a standard, as opposed to a rule (An example of a rule is a stop sign posted on a roadway; an example of a standard is a sign that says 'drive carefully when roads are wet')."[184]

Robert Ellickson also expressed a preference for the majority over the dissent in similar terms in a well-known article on the whaling industry in the late 1980s.[185] "[U]tilitarian whalers," according to Ellickson, "concerned with the transaction costs associated with their rules [...] would prefer [...] bright-line rules that would eliminate arguments to fuzzy rules that would prolong disputes."[186] Later he added, "[c]ompared to rules, however, standards are more likely to provoke disputes about proper application."[187] Speaking specifically about the dissent, Ellickson wrote:

> Somewhat more responsive to incentive issues would be a rule that a whale belonged to a ship whose crew had first obtained a "reasonable prospect" of capturing it and thereafter remained in fresh pursuit [citing to Livingston's dissent in *Pierson*] [...] A reasonable-prospect standard, however, is by far the most ambiguous of those yet mentioned, invites transaction costs, and, like the other rules so far discussed, was not employed by whalers.[188]

Robert Deal has argued that Ellickson was mistaken about this. A reasonable-prospect standard was alive and well in the custom of iron-holds-a-whale, which held that "a first striker in pursuit deserved some consideration" and included "assessments[s] of the first striker's prospects for capturing the whale."[189]

Given the level of disagreement between the authorities citied in *Pierson*, Krier wrote that "the *Pierson* case *should have been* resolved exactly as it was. (Whether it actually would have been resolved in the same manner is, of course, hardly clear)." Krier was speaking, as he put it, "[f]rom an instrumental point of view – where the end in mind is to have rules that promote constructive competition in the production of goods."[190] Whether the rule of capture does promote constructive competition is another question. Krier

183 Krier, "Facts, Information, and the Newly Discovered Record," 192. 184 Ibid., 193.
185 See Robert C. Ellickson, "A Hypothesis of Wealth-Maximizing Norms: Evidence from the Whaling Industry," 5 *Journal of Law, Economics, and Organization* (1989): 83–97.
186 Ibid., 87. 187 Ibid., 94. 188 Ibid., 88.
189 Deal, *The Law of the Whale Hunt*, 49, 52.
190 Krier, "Facts, Information, and the Newly Discovered Record," 192 n. 8 (emphasis in the original).

himself seemed to suggest that, in the environmental context, it creates waste. This is because, as he put it, the capture rule "has been shown in any number of instances to result in relatively rapid depletion rather than long-term conservation, because it induces people who seek to exploit common property resources to gear up, to get more, and to get it faster."[191] This has certainly been the case for groundwater, oil and gas, and the hunting to extinction of animal species such as the American passenger pigeon and the North American bison.[192]

Dale Goble and Eric Freyfogle write in their casebook on wildlife law that "*Pierson* v. *Post* is the law of the resource rush: the first possessor wins."[193] According to these scholars:

> There were gold rushes and timber rushes, rushes to grow cows and to claim newly opened lands [...] When technology created a market for a previously unvalued piece of nature – as was the case with bison skins and great auk feathers – or allowed marketing of it – as was the case with passenger pigeons – the rush was on [...] A pure rule of capture encourages such resource rushes by awarding the first taker the exclusive rights to the resource. When first in time is first in right, speed becomes everything. Because to wait might be to lose, it often makes economic sense to capture in excess of need.[194]

Goble wrote in 2005 that "[w]ildlife, as vagrant stuff subject to capture, requires the tolerance of everyone who might kill it or destroy its habitat – and much of the story of wildlife in America has been a recurring demonstration of the tragedy embedded in the saga of Pierson, Post, and the fox."[195] The California Gold Rush, timber rushes, cattle overgrazing, as well as new markets devastating animal species (e.g. great auk feather pens or a taste for passenger pigeons or buffalo skins, as well as beaver and sea otter pelts) created "Tragedy of the Commons" scenarios that might be better thought of "Tragedy of the Market," given the "often profligate waste" created by the capture rule. If the prize goes to he who seizes it and "first in time is first in right, speed is all."[196]

191 James E. Krier, "Capture and Counteraction: Self-Help by Environmental Zealots," 30 *University of Richmond Law Review* (1996): 1039–1054, 1052.

192 See Griggs, "Does Groundwater Management Work?"; Craft, "Of Reservoir Hogs and Pelt Fiction."

193 Dale D. Goble and Eric T. Freyfogle eds., *Cases and Materials on Wildlife Law* (New York: Foundation Press, 2002), 124.

194 Ibid., 124–25.

195 Dale D. Goble, "Three Cases/Four Tales: Commons, Capture, The Public Trust, and Property in Land," 35 *Environmental Law* (2005): 807–53, 813.

196 See ibid., 814–19 for extensive citations for each situation and animal, quotations from 819, 818.

Legislatures and courts (or both) have had to work around the capture rule in a number of situations in order to prevent antisocial consequences.[197] A string of cases exists in which *Pierson* has interfered with or complicated a state's ability to regulate or conserve its wild life, since according to the case the state cannot own animals that have not been reduced to possession.[198] If the capture rule ever made sense in order to stimulate economic development, it was for a world in which there was "a seemingly infinite supply of wild animals, minerals, water and other fugitive resources."[199] We know that world is not our world.

Even if the rule did not create problems for waste reduction and environmental protection, we need to recognize that the instrumental view is just one perspective, one that requires us to surrender an instinct about what would have been fair in *Pierson* when we really do not have to. Really, all the majority said was needed in order for there to be acquisition by first possession was a clear signal to take, and that signal (hunting with dogs and hounds), by Rose's own understanding of property as communication, was quite clear enough. It might be true that a clear capture rule deters law suits; it might not. Robert Deal found that the jumble of norms whalemen used to decide disputes between them over who owned a contested whale were remarkably successful at keeping disputes out of courts.[200] Even if there are more "transaction costs" involved in the use of

[197] See e.g. *Knighton et al* v. *Texaco Producing Inc.*, 762 F Supp 686 (US Dist Ct, W Dist of Louis, Shreveport Div, 1991); The City of San Marcos *v.* Texas Commission on Environmental Quality, 128 SW 3d 264 (Texas CA, 3rd Dist, Austin, 2004) (lamenting the legislature's failure to replace the capture rule with a reasonable use rule for groundwater).

[198] See e.g. *Douglas* v. *Seacoast Products Inc et al*, 431 US 265, 97 S Ct 1740 (US Sup Ct, 1977) (question "can a state own its wild animals" first posed by the US Supreme Court); *United States* .v *Long Cove Seafood Inc*, 582 F 2d 159 (US CA, 2d Cir, 1978) (New York clams could not be "stolen" by another state); *Idaho ex rel Evans* v. *Oregon*, 462 US 1017, 103 S Ct 2817 (US Sup Ct, 1983) (Idaho suing Oregon and Washington for equitable apportionment of fish in a shared river); *Clajon Prod Corp.* v. *Petera*, 854 F Supp 843 (US Dist Ct, Dist of Wyoming, 1994) (constitutional challenges to the state regulation scheme governing the allocation and distribution of hunting licenses for elk, deer and antelope by landowners); *State of Texas* v *Bartee*, 894 S W 2d 34 (CA Texas, San Antonio, 1994) (is theft of white-tailed deer possible). Like Wyoming and New York, Texas had a statute stating that its wild animals were the property of the state. Even if the state could use its police power to preserve and regulate wild animals, the law of capture created a problem. See Blumm and Ritchie, "The Pioneer Spirit and the Public Trusts" (tracing the survival of state-ownership of its wild animals despite a variety of challenges).

[199] John G. Sprankling, "Environmental Critique of Adverse Possession," 79 *Cornell Law Review* (1993–94): 816–84, 857.

[200] See Deal, *The Law of the Whale Hunt.*

a standard rather than a rule in an individual case, it might well be the right thing to do to adopt the standard when the rule is a bad rule. There are also many relevant differences between animals, their size (whales), how easily they escape (fish), and how humans hunt them (seals) that demand differentiated responses rather than the one-size-fits-all capture rule. One of the points that Deal makes repeatedly in his book is that courts and legal scholars have treated small animals like foxes, ducks, rabbits, mackerel, and bees as if they are the same as large and difficult to catch animals such as whales as interchangeable when they are not.[201] What is true of animals in also true of other varied fugitive resources that have different properties, employ different methods of extraction, and raise different policy considerations in terms of what extraction means for the environment and for different stakeholders, not least the animals and resources themselves and their sustainability.

The idea that clarity and certainty are the most important factors in the choice of the best rule even when they are more than what is required seems to have led to a fixation on rules versus standards that has received undue emphasis and has left scholars unable to challenge the holding in *Pierson* even when desirous of doing so, as in Krier's case.[202] That seems like an odd (and undesirable) place to be, admiring the case for having been decided correctly (i.e. efficiently), while at the same time recognizing that the rule is actually a bad rule (from the perspective of societal consequences).

The current successor to Casner and Leach's 1951 casebook is probably a good snapshot of where things currently stand. With the original compilers long gone, recent editions have ceased editing the dissent to contain and control it, and have replaced the conservative and patriotic notes and questions that had their origins in the 1950s with new ones. One of these notes reads: "What are the advantages of certainty in legal rules? Property rules range from "bright line" clear rules, like first in time gets it all, to "mushy" rules that require sharing resources like water "reasonably" or that mandate "equitable" division of property on dissolution of

[201] See e.g. ibid., 2 ("Courts, when thinking about wild animal cases, imagined ducks, rabbits, mackerel, or even bees. The stakes in a dispute over a single animal worth potentially thousands of dollars bore little resemblance to a contest concerning a small animal that individually was of little value"), 3 ("Whales, deer, and foxes were all – in the eyes of the law – pretty much the same"), 23 ("Whaling, in the eyes of the law, was much like hunting a rabbit").

[202] See Krier, "Facts, Information, and the Newly Discovered Record," 193; "Capture and Counteraction," 1052.

marriage.[203] The note then asks: "How would you characterize the rule that Post wanted the court to adopt?" The answer to the question is clearly that Post's rule is "mushy." Who is going to speak up in favor of that? Is "mushy" ever good? It seems doubtful.[204] Carol Rose has called these "mud rules," which again are difficult to see in a positive light.[205] And in this way, new (or relatively new) law students are being told that clear and certain rules are superior to vague "fuzzy," "mushy," or "muddy" standards.[206]

This is a frustrating bias in the law and economics literature. Well-known and influential legal scholars have repeatedly pointed out that rules are not always superior to standards. William Eskridge and Philip Frickey, for example, have pointed out that when the language of rules and standards was first used by Hart and Sacks and the Legal Process School, it indicated no pre-decided preference for rules over standards. Both were recognized as legitimate, and a preference for one over the other was supposed to be determined by the desired social outcome.[207] In a well-known article on rules and standards (referred to me by my colleague and leader in the Canadian law and economics movement Michael Trebilcock), Louis Kaplow pointed out that "the familiar suggestion that rules tend to be over- and underinclusive relative to standards [...] is misleading because typically it implicitly compares a complex standard and a relatively simple rule, whereas both rules and standards can in fact be quite simple or highly detailed in their operation."[208] "[T]here are

[203] French and Korngold eds., *Cases and Text on Property*, 6th ed. (2015), 77 n. 7.

[204] The Teacher's Manual to the 5th edition (which contained substantially the same text as the 6th edition does) said the following about this note: "Post's proposed rule would certainly be mushier than the one the court adopted, but not as mushy as the kind of rule you might get if you pursued some sort of sharing, or punish-undesirable-behavior resolution of the dispute." A. James Casner, W. Barton Leach, Susan Fletcher French, Gerald Korngold and Lea S. VanderVelde eds., *Teacher's Manual: Cases and Text on Property*, 5th ed. (New York: Aspen Publishers, 2005), 14 ("Page 40, Question 6").

[205] Carol M. Rose, "Crystals and Mud in Property Law," 40 *Stanford Law Review* (1987–88): 577–610.

[206] But see ibid., 609 (acknowledging that "there is a version of certainty and predictability in mud rules").

[207] See William N. Eskridge Jr. and Philip P. Frickey, "The Making of the Legal Process," 107 *Harvard Law Review* (1993–94): 2031–2055, 2044.

[208] Louis Kaplow, "Rules versus Standards: An Economic Analysis," 42 *Duke Law Journal* (1992–93): 557–629, 565. See also 589 (the suggestion that is made is that "rules limit the range of permissible considerations whereas standards do not. Observe, however, that a rule cannot be over- or underinclusive relative to a standard if one is comparing the standard to the rule equivalent to the standard. Implicitly, therefore, commentators must be comparing a complex standard to a simple rule"); 594 (calling it "a romantic

simple and complex rules as well as simple and complex standards [...] in some instances in which the complex standard is superior, it may be that complexity is better than simplicity [...] or, it may be that a standard is better than a rule, but a simple standard would be preferable to a complex one."[209] In *Pierson*, we arguably have a simple rule and a simple standard and it is not clear which one is superior, especially when one factors in the point that a standard effectively becomes a rule once it establishes a precedent.[210]

Such lucid arguments notwithstanding, American students and scholars of law and economics have tried to implement the crude rules versus standards way of looking at *Pierson*, and the assumption that rules are superior to standards, by turning this complex and multifaceted text into an algorithm.[211] Unfortunately their failure to understand what Livingston was doing in the dissent seems to have led these economists to repeat Livingston's assumption – or alternatively take seriously a point he did not mean should be taken seriously – that foxhunting means fewer foxes, a factor that wreaks havoc with their calculations.[212] If scholars from Holmes to Ellickson can be accused of having read too much Herman Melville, these scholars could have done with reading a bit more Anthony Trollope. Those novels make it clear how important healthy fox populations were to the hunt and what a terrible crime it was ("vulpecide") to poison or otherwise exterminate foxes from a neighborhood as mere vermin.[213] One of the characters in Trollope's *The American Senator* (1877) is described in the following way: "Of course, Goarly was a brute. Had he not threatened to shoot foxes?"[214] Another member of the community says about him, disapprovingly, "It wouldn't have been the first fox he's *murdered*."[215] A reductionist way of thinking about the case has even resulted in its use

perspective" to imagine that standards allow more room to maneuver); 596 ("there is no universal tendency for standards as they are actually applied to be more complex than rules that would plausibly be promulgated").

209 Ibid., 566–67. 210 See ibid., 577.

211 See Dhammika Dharmapala and Rohan Pitchford, "An Economic Analysis of 'Riding to Hounds': *Pierson* v. *Post* Revisited," 18 *The Journal of Law, Economics, & Organization* (2002): 39–66.

212 See ibid., 44. For a litany of criticisms of this approach, see McDowell, "Legal Fictions in *Pierson* v. *Post*," 768–69.

213 See Watson, "Introduction to Law for Second-year Students," 441 (relying on Trollope for the claim that foxhunting meant more foxes not less).

214 Anthony Trollope, *The American Senator* (New York: Oxford University Press, 1931, reprinted 2008), 22.

215 Ibid., 27 (emphasis added). The "vulpecide" reference is at p. 62.

in artificial intelligence modeling, certainly a sign that we have lost anything approximating a nuanced perspective.[216]

It is probably an inescapable human truth that some people like nuance and others do not; or, as the question is sometimes put to legal scholars, what do you prefer, the unrelenting desert heat of law and economics or the swampy terrain of law and society?[217] As Ellickson has written, "the law-and-economics scholars believe that the law-and-society group is deficient in both sophistication and rigor, and the law-and-society scholars believe that the law-and-economics theorists are not only out of touch with reality but also short on humanity."[218] My own view is that at least on *Pierson*, the law and economics perspective has failed to understand what the case was about, and that to see the case in its fullest and most interesting light requires approaching it socially, historically, and culturally, rather than as a parsed down, apparently pre-decided, instance of the superiority of rules over standards. On the one hand, as I have tried to demonstrate, there are many interesting things to say about the case from a social, historical, and cultural perspective. On the other, the case actually does a pretty poor job of communicating what law and economics scholars want it to say. In the same way that the authorities upon a closer inspection do not clearly support Pierson, the allegedly "fuzzy," "mushy" or "muddy" standard was actually quite clear enough.

Why has the case come to be seen as a parsed down lesson about rules versus standards? This is a complicated question and one would have to undertake a study of the American legal academy in the twentieth century and the rise of the law and economics movement in the 1980s in order to answer it properly. Some of the explanation is related to "path dependence," as the economists themselves would put it. People learn the case in a certain way and it makes it difficult for them to see it in any other way. As Alan Watson has written: "First-year law students are misled because their teachers were themselves misled in their own first year."[219] It is true

216 See Thomas F. Gordon and Douglas Walton, "Pierson vs. Post Revisited: A Reconstruction using the Carneades Argumentation Framework" in Paul E. Dunne and Trevor J.M. Bench-Capon eds., *Computational Models of Argument* (Amsterdam, The Netherlands: IOS Press, 2006), 208–19.

217 See Robert C Ellickson, *Order Without Law: How Neighbors Settle Disputes* (Cambridge, MA: Harvard University Press, 1991), 147 (attributing this language of desert and swamp to Arthur Leff).

218 Ibid., 7. See also Robert C. Ellickson, "The Entitlements of Unallied Hunters After a Sequential Capture," 63 *University of Toronto Law Journal* (2013): 126–37, 136–37 (comparing "scientific and humanist camps").

219 Watson, "Introduction to Law for Second-year Students," 443.

that law professors are free to choose whichever one of the casebooks they think provides the best overall perspective. But it is also true that they probably often choose, as a matter of default, the casebook with which they were taught and consequently know best. Teacher Manuals (a phenomenon that exists for American casebooks but not for Canadian ones, given the much smaller law school market in Canada) contribute tremendously to cementing an already rigid perspective about what is important in a case and what is not. A canonical case like *Pierson* can easily become a kind of sacred cow to those who are invested in seeing it in a particular way. That seems fundamentally problematic from the perspective of what we should be trying to do as scholars of the law, and certainly as scholars of legal history.

Indications of an appreciation that there is overkill in the certainty accorded the majority ruling in *Pierson* have appeared in a collection of law and economics essays on possession published in 2015.[220] Consistent with her earlier influential writing on *Pierson*, Carol Rose described the majority opinion as saying that "first possession required a clear and decisive signal that the hunter controlled the now-defunct animal"; however, Rose now calls it a "strong requirement of physical control" and goes on to discuss what would be required in terms of control of the beast itself (so it does not escape) as against others who might want it (Pierson on the one hand, Post on the other), noting that the requirement need not be a complete current control.[221] Though not exactly a response to the criticism about overkill, there is recognition here that there is something "strong" (and perhaps too strong) in the majority's rule.[222]

Another article in the collection on the psychological or behavioral dimensions of how people understand possession calls the requirement of the majority position in *Pierson* "too stringent" and notes that "[t]he minority view [Livingston's], which sufficed with a reasonable likelihood of physical capture, may better accord with people's perception of

[220] Yun-Chien Chang ed., *Law and Economics of Possession* (Cambridge, UK: Cambridge University Press, 2015): 103–127.

[221] See Carol M. Rose, "The Law is Nine-Tenths of Possession: An Adage Turned on its Head," in *Law and Economics of Possession*, ibid., 40–64, 51–52.

[222] Rose refers to the 2009 *Law and Social Inquiry* piece on *Pierson* and not the 2011 one where I first published the overkill criticism. See ibid., 51 n. 21. A version of this criticism was also made in the 1980s in Schlag and Skover, *Tactics of Legal Reasoning*, 56 (calling the occupancy standard in *Pierson* an "ideological overstatement" given that "there are standards other than occupancy that could well serve to define the point at which one acquires a property right in a wild animal"). Quoted by Reich, "All the Right Moves," 1203.

possession."[223] This author relies on comments Epstein included in his 1979 article to this effect in a discussion of whaling.[224] This is a far cry from the use made of Epstein in the 1990s, where, for instance, a scholar on the market as a property institution and trading financial assets relied on *Pierson* and on Epstein's essay to briefly note: "capture rule works satisfactorily and no point in changing rule in mid-stream."[225] There does seem to be some appetite, in other words, to reconsider the self-evident correctness of the majority rule in *Pierson* in order to attend to adverse social and environmental consequences in certain contexts that are now, sitting down-stream, difficult to deny. As Eric Freyfogle wrote in the mid-1980s, addressing specifically issues of water justice, "[c]apture rules in all settings are hard to justify today, particularly when applied to resources that are scarce and valuable."[226] Rose acknowledged in the mid-1990s that the rule of capture does not work very well for environmental resources "because the goods that we consider environmental usually belong to a kind of natural commons."[227] Indeed, "our usual property-defining act, the unregulated rule of capture, turns into a horror story for these great natural commons," destroying the resource which it is in the collective best interest to preserve.[228] "Through a series of small decisions, the larger environmental resource is wasted," Rose continued, "[a]ir gets polluted, fisheries get fished out, forests get felled, bird populations get depleted, and aquifers get pumped dry [...] people leave behind a *wasteland*, where the resources are exhausted to a point that they cannot renew themselves."[229] This is the wasteland of the capture rule in *Pierson*.

[223] Daphna Lewinsohn-Zamir, "What Behavioral Studies Can Teach Jurists about Possession and Vice Versa," in *Law and Economics of Possession*, 128–48, 134.

[224] See ibid., 134 n. 10.

[225] David E. Van Zandt, "The Market as a Property Institution: Rules for the Trading of Financial Assets," 32 *Boston College Law Review* (1990–91): 967–1025, 989–90 n. 90.

[226] Eric T. Freyfogle, "Water Justice," *University of Illinois Law Review* (1986): 481–519, 494.

[227] Carol M. Rose, "Given-ness and Gift: Property and the Quest for Environmental Ethics," 24 *Environmental Law* (1994): 1–31, 5.

[228] Ibid., 6 (Rose described the tragedy of the commons here as human acquisitiveness gone wild: "each human actor, fearing to be the last in the race to capture the vast wild things, vies with all the others to take while the taking is free").

[229] Ibid. (emphasis added).

Conclusion

To produce a mighty book, you must choose a mighty theme. No great and enduring volume can ever be written on the flea, though many there be who have tried it.

Herman Melville, *Moby-Dick, or the Whale* (1851)[1]

Is *Pierson* a flea, as Melville put it, or a whale? Is it an insignificant dispute over a 75¢ fox between two stubborn young men from wealthy backgrounds that legal professionals (lawyers and judges) blew up until it reached Rabelaisian (dis)proportions? Or is it a case on "a mighty theme," first possession in animals *ferae naturae*, highlighted by an important legal scholar, James Kent, taken up by later nineteenth-century legal mandarins such as Holmes and Pollock, placed on the first pages of property law casebooks, written about in scholarly articles by a generation of new twentieth-century American law professor-mandarins, for over a hundred years giving untold hundreds of thousands of law students their introduction to the law of property, and providing a classical problem for legal academics to chew on from a variety of perspectives (historical, economic etc.)?

This book has argued that *Pierson* can be seen as, and is indeed, both a whale and a flea. I have approached the case from both of these perspectives. Part I focused on Brockholst Livingston's dissent as an instance of solemn foolery in order to highlight the playful dimensions of professional law in-the-making and its echoes in law and literature. We saw that those "vivacities," to use Joseph Story's coinage, were, like the phrase

[1] Quote taken from p. 497.

"saucy intruder" itself, not innocuous.[2] They came at a price and they carried (and continue to carry) various kinds of ideological freight, including and perhaps especially the way that the production of law and legal culture in male fraternal space trades in male and female gender in complicated and problematic ways. The camaraderie, the ribaldry anchored in a joke or lighthearted fun has an object or a butt, and it is often an animal-gendered female being subjected to slaughter.[3] Solemn foolery itself is arguably the very definition of a lack of professionalism by modern standards. Yet it is there in the history of the legal profession demanding to be seen, acknowledged, and explained. It is actually often there just under our noses, but we usually just laugh (or frown disapprovingly), depending on the moment and the context, and turn our heads away. I think it would be better to problematize and try to understand what are the implications or consequences of legal solemn foolery. The first step, always so important, is identification, naming. That allows us to see the instances we encounter here and there; really see them, and not discount them as anomalies.

Part II's explanation of the social history of the case is a view of *Pierson* as a flea, a dispute that, due to the discovery of the Judgment Roll we can now know much more fully – where the jury trial took place, who the jury members were and their economic backgrounds, how the trial worked, the role lawyers played on appeal, the amounts of money at issue, and the legal issues and how they were transformed from tort to property. Yet the reason why there is an appetite for learning more about *Pierson*, the reason why it is such an interesting flea to legal historians and other legal scholars, is because of its intellectual trajectory, the role it has played in what we might think of as the common law of the law school curriculum and the extent and range of ways in which it has been chewed on and deployed by legal academics.[4] All this is what we have just explored in Part III.

The process of mandarization outlined in Part III began in the nineteenth century with Kent, Holmes, and Pollock. It continued in the twentieth century in a wide variety of casebook presentations. Casebooks are

[2] Dunne, "Brockholst Livingston," 391; *Pierson*, 181.

[3] Livingston referred to Renard as he (see e.g. *Pierson*, 180).

[4] Fernandez, "An Object Lesson in Speculation," 518 (discussing the process of creating "a common law in the law school curriculum").

our anthologies of the law, creating a canon intended to include that which is important and to exclude that which is not.[5] When a case appears in so many different casebooks and anthologies in first-place first-case position (or not far off), as *Pierson* has for so long and for such a wide range of editors with different scholarly aims and agendas, we must stop and learn more about it and not just use it to demonstrate one theory of property or another. The "mighty theme" of first possession or occupation (*occupatio*) has at least two important dimensions we have explored, both of which echo in Roman law and in American empire.

First, there is the issue of slavery. We might recall that Kent wrote that "the law of chattels, once so unimportant, has grown into a system, which, by its magnitude, overshadows [...] the learning of real estates."[6] One of the most significant reasons for the importance of chattel property in Kent's day was slavery: slaves were chattel property and an important form of property in both the North and the South. This was true even if treatise-writers like Kent treated slavery as if it were a feudal remnant on its way out.[7] The popularity of a work like Justinian's *Institutes* in the antebellum period was probably due in part to the way that the text dealt with slavery. As Alan Watson explains, in the *Institutes*, the slave is a conquered foe who, but for the vicissitudes of the battlefield, would have been an equal or a brother. This would have been a lot more attractive than the kind of slavery Americans actually found themselves living with, premised as it was on notions of profound and inherent racial inequality.[8] While Southern slaveholders pointed to Roman slavery as justification for American slavery, Northern abolitionists countered by pointing out that Roman slavery was not permanent. Unlike the African American slave, those slaves could buy their own freedom and even rise to high political office.[9] In addition to serving as a textbook for law students,

5 See Balkin and Levinson, "Legal Canons: An Introduction."

6 Kent, *Commentaries*, 2: 278.

7 See e.g. Tapping Reeve, *The Law of Baron and Femme; of Parent and Child; of Guardian and Ward; of Master and Servant; and of the Powers of the Courts of Chancery* (New Haven, CT: Oliver Steele, 1816), 339–41; Kent, *Commentaries*, 2: 201–209. Both treat slaves as persons analogous to servants rather than chattel property. See Christopher L. Tomlins, *Law, Labor, and Ideology in the Early American Republic* (Cambridge UK; New York: Cambridge University Press, 1993), 259–68.

8 See Alan Watson, *Slave Law in the Americas* (Athens: University of Georgia Press, 1989), 23–24 (explaining how, in contrast to slavery in the American South, Roman slaves were often highly educated and they might be of any racial or national type; so there was no sense that they "were of an inherently inferior racial stock").

9 See Carl J. Richard, *The Golden Age of the Classics in America: Greece, Rome, and the Antebellum United States* (Cambridge, MA; London, England: Harvard University Press,

Justinian's *Institutes* probably also helped colonizers and early Americans feel better about their own institutions of slavery.

We know that American slave owners often gave their slaves Roman names like Caesar, Nero, Pompey, and Cato. Were they imagining that they were participating in a more noble form of slavery, the pedigree of which helped justify what they were doing in their own eyes? Or was it some kind of cruel joke? It seems likely that the naming of slaves, like the naming of towns and cities referring to Ancient Greece and Rome, was at least in part due to what Carl Richard, has described as "[t]he urge to re-create classical civilization in the United States."[10] It extended to ships in the ports of coastal cities.[11] Americans gave their children names like Claudia, Cornelia, Hannibal, Homes, Horace, Lucius, Virgil, and Ulysses.[12] "Masters continued to give their slaves classical names," Richard noted, "though none named them Spartacus," the rebel slave leader.[13] African Americans in the North sometimes retained their classical given names (rather than changing them to Christian names) and sometimes gave their children similar names.[14] "Even Native Americans were sometimes swept up in the classical mania."[15] The classical allusions clearly echo ideologically in empire and naming is a powerful tool of empire.[16] "What's in a name?" asks one historian of colonial American slavery, "Mastery," she answers, noting that the first thing

2009), 181–93 (on Southern uses of ancient slavery to justify American slavery), 198 (quoting African-American abolitionist David Walker's 1829 *An Appeal to the Coloured Citizens of the World* that "every body who has read history knows that as soon as a slave among the Romans obtained his freedom, he could rise to the greatest eminence in the State, and there was no law instituted to hinder a slave from buying his freedom. Have not the Americans instituted laws to prohibit a man of colour from obtaining and holding any office whatever under the government of the United States of America? Now, Mr. Jefferson tells us that our condition is not so hard as the slaves were under the Romans!").

10 Ibid., 31 (noting that the most popular names of towns and cities were Athens, Sparta, Rome, Troy, Carthage, and Arcadia. Ohio topped the Northwest with thirty-five classically named towns).

11 Ibid., 32 (ship names included the *Hector*, the *Horace*, the *Venus*, the *Leonidas*, and the *Spartan*).

12 Ibid. 13 Ibid.

14 See Joseph Carvalho III, "Researching Black Families in Hampden County, Massachusetts: 1650–1865," 12:3 *American Ancestors: New England, New York, and Beyond* (2011): 37–39, 38.

15 Richard, *The Golden Age of the Classics in America*, 32 (one Penobscot tribe leader called himself Neptune and a Cherokee leader used the name Roman Nose).

16 It is interesting that the categories of things commonly given classical names include liminal categories of persons denied full legal personhood such as slaves or children.

Cotton Mather did when he received a slave from his congregation was to rename him.[17]

Notwithstanding that it took place in a Northern state after the American Revolution, there was slavery all over the *Pierson* case, in the high number of people involved who were slave owners: the Piersons, the Posts, the Justice of the Peace, the stepfather of Nathan Sanford, and Hugh Gelston Jr., at whose house the trial took place.

As Christopher Tomlins has put it, "Roman law, not common law, gave the activity of colonizing much of its juridical cosmography."[18] This was true both for land and for the important category of chattel property, slaves. Francisco de Vittoria cited Justinian on the point that whatever was captured in war became the property of the captor, including the people themselves.[19] In Roman law, "slavery originated in capture" in the sense that those captured during war, instead of being killed, were "spared" (*servari*) by being enslaved.[20] This form of capture could reduce a person to "the condition of a beast," making them chattel property instead of a person.[21] Hence, capture was important to Roman law conceptions of slavery. In his famous work, *Ancient Law* (1861), Henry Sumner Maine explicitly linked "[t]he Law of Warlike Capture" to "the Roman principle of Occupancy."[22] Later, Pollock, in his notes on Maine's text, wrote that Maine's statements "about the Roman doctrine of capture in war" were "misleading."[23] Pollock thought it not appropriate for Maine to look to the passages from Gaius in Justinian's *Digest* about wild animals in peacetime and say that they applied to human beings and their property or their very persons in wartime. "[T]he ideal law of nature," Pollock wrote, "would not justify treating captives of free condition as slaves."[24] Yet that seemed to be what some legal scholars wanted the Roman law on occupation to do.

As for land, Tomlins describes how Grotius added land to the list of things that were open to first takers in Justinian. In the *Digest*, Justinian records Gaius's discussion of "all animals taken on land, sea, or in the air,

[17] Wendy Warren, *New England Bound: Slavery and Colonization in Early America* (New York: Liveright, 2016), quoted in Maya Jasanoff, "The Great Trap for All Americans," *The New York Review of Books* (October 13, 2016).

[18] Tomlins, *Freedom Bound*, 188. [19] Ibid., 420. [20] Ibid., 421. [21] Ibid., 422.

[22] *Ancient Law: its connection with the early history of society and its relations to modern ideas by Sir Henry Sumner Maine; with introduction and notes by Sir Frederick Pollock*, 1st ed. (London: J. Murray, 1920), 260. Pollock first published his edition with notes in 1906.

[23] Ibid., 311, Note O, "Capture, Occupation, Possession." [24] Ibid.

that is wild beasts" that "may escape from our custody and return to their natural state of freedom."[25] Next came "gems, stones, and pearls lost on the seashore" that belonged to the first taker. And then "things taken in war" that were a legitimate (if forcible) transfer. There is but one reference to land as something that is open to appropriation by a first taker and that is "an island arising in the sea." This was said to be "a rare occurrence."[26] There was nothing in the *Digest*, Tomlins emphasizes, to justify taking newly discovered land, that is. what would become America. Yet Grotius added uncultivated land to the *Digest*'s class of things open to first takers.[27] Vitoria made the same move, relying on "the law of nations and the natural law, the property of the first occupant," citing to Chapter 12 of Justinian's *Institutes*, the same passage Sanford relied on in *Pierson*.[28] Tomlins explains how Maine later included "lands newly discovered or never before cultivated" in his list of "objects which the Roman lawyers called *res nullius* – things which have not or never had an owner [...] wild animals, fishes, wild fowl, [and] jewels disinterred for the first time."[29] In other words, justification for the colonial seizure of America was to be found in the Roman and civil law, specifically Justinian. This was despite the fact that, as property law and wildlife scholar Dale Goble puts it, there is a pretty obvious difference between property in a wild animal like a fox that is wont to escape and a continent, which will not.[30]

The ideological importance of Roman law for both capture-justified slavery and first-taker occupation of land and chattel property provides an important explanation for a phenomenon noted by many scholars of civil law in America, which is that Roman or civil law played a merely ornamental role for jurists like Joseph Story and James Kent.[31] Historians have made the same point about the founders using the classics as mere "window dressing."[32] Yet the exotic

[25] This was the passage in the *Digest* Kent added to the *Commentaries* in connection to *Pierson* and the capture rule. See Kent, *Commentaries*, 2: 283 n.b.

[26] Tomlins, *Freedom Bound*, 118. [27] Ibid., 119 n. 81, 145.

[28] Tomlins, ibid., 115 n. 67; *Pierson*, 176. [29] Tomlins, *Freedom Bound*, 119 n. 81.

[30] See Goble, "Three Cases/Four Tales," 807.

[31] See Watson, "Chancellor Kent's Use of Foreign Law" (on Kent); Hoeflich, *Roman and Civil Law and the Development of Anglo-American Jurisprudence in the Nineteenth Century* (on Story).

[32] See Richard, *The Golden Age of the Classical in America*, 209 (citing Bernard Bailyn, *The Ideological Origins of the American Revolution* (Boston, MA: Harvard University Press, 1967)).

authorities were not mere ornament. They were also doing serious (and seriously dirty) ideological work, albeit selectively and in a rather haphazard way.[33]

So, although the passages relied on in *Pierson* from Justinian's *Institutes* did not actually apply to the situation of capture and loss (Chapter 12) and wounding (Chapter 13) of a pursued animal, the work was important to early Americans in at least two senses: first, in terms of an attachment to slavery; and, second, in terms of the colonization of land by legal purchase and by seizure or occupation in wartime.[34] Great political events in the early nineteenth century such as the Louisiana Purchase in 1803 (and how the acquisition of a further 828,000 square miles facilitated westward and southern expansion) and doctrines on display in events like the War of 1812 that would eventually give rise to the idea of "manifest destiny," demonstrate the extent to which expansion was a priority. Rome was consciously adopted as a model of expansionist nationalism for early Americans.[35] "During this age of Manifest Destiny, Americans saw their expanding nation as a new empire that would exceed the past empires of Athens and Rome."[36] It is not routinely acknowledged that the imperialism of this young and new Rome often met with disappointment, such as the embarrassing ransoms resulting from weak naval power and the lost protection of the British in the Mediterranean during the Barbary Wars.[37] But like early modern states in the sixteenth and seventeenth centuries, there is no denying that in the nineteenth century the United States was building empire at home and abroad, colonizing Native peoples and competing against European powers for influence and territory, nations that appeared to them to be exhausted by mid-century.[38]

Historically, possession played a very important role for early modern states in their competing claims against each other. As two scholars interrogating how arguments of *res nullius* (things belonging to no one)

[33] See Lauren Benton and Benjamin Straumann,"Acquiring Empire by Law: From Roman Doctrine to Early Modern European Practice," 28 *Law and History Review* (2010): 1–38 (emphasizing the inexact way in which arguments about *terre nullius, res nullius*, occupation, and possession were made by imperial agents on the ground in the sixteenth and seventeenth centuries).

[34] See Banner, *How the Indians Lost their Land* (emphasizing the role of legal purchase and contract rather than force in the process of dispossession and colonization).

[35] See Richard, *The Golden Age of the Classical in America*, 112–14. [36] Ibid., 105.

[37] See Franklin Lambert, *The Barbary Wars: American Independence in the Atlantic World* (New York: Hill and Wang, 2005).

[38] See Richard, *The Golden Age of the Classical in America*, 118 (quoting from Henry David Thoreau's journal where in 1851 he described America as "the she wolf to-day, and the children of exhausted Europe [...] have founded a new Rome in the West").

from the *Digest* were inappropriately turned into questions of *terra nullius* (land belonging to no one) write:

> If there was a single identifiable Roman legal idea that was more prominent in empire than any other, it would seem to have been possession, rather than *res nullius*. In Roman law, possession, based on brute fact rather than entitlement, could potentially lead to ownership [. . .] and then the question concerned who of the two contenders had the *better* claim, rather than who had absolute title.[39]

These authors emphasize that *possession* was key for imperial agents on the ground, seeking to fend off claims by competing empires. Proving absolute title was much more difficult and possession could be established and protected more easily.[40] The question then, who has the *better* claim to possession, is exactly the way that *Pierson* v. *Post* was framed, with the majority choosing Justinian and Pierson, and Livingston – despite what Joseph Story described as Livingston's own aquiline Roman face – choosing Post.[41] In other words, the sixteenth- and seventeenth-century European preoccupation with possession and the Roman law of occupation appears in *Pierson* dressed up in an early nineteenth-century American toga.[42] This was part joke (at least for Livingston), part participation in "classical mania," in the way that so many other things at the time were (perhaps most strikingly the architecture of court houses, banks, houses, and taverns), and part utterly serious language, sources, and ideas justifying empire.

And in *Pierson* the connection to expansionist nation-building is even clearer in Livingston's argument about the inappropriateness of slavishly following Justinian, the stance taken by the lawyers and by Tompkins that likely set him off in the first place. In Livingston's objection, we can see a variant on a common trope found later among American transcendentalists (1830–1860) who issued warnings about the dangers of slavishly copying classical sources.[43] The idea is well summed up in John Adams's

39 Benton and Straumann, "Acquiring Empire by Law," 30.
40 Ibid., 17 ("rather than having to establish title tout court, they [competing states] simply could aim to show that they had a better claim than the competing power in question").
41 Dunne, "Brockholst Livingston," 391.
42 Jean-Louis Halpérin, *The French Civil Code*, Tony Weir trans. (London: University College London Press, 2006), 69 (writing that the points supposedly based on Roman law that made their way into the French Civil Code of 1806 were also "almost always 'modern ideas' developed in the seventeenth and eighteenth centuries, dressed up in a toga").
43 See Richard, *The Golden Age of the Classical in America*, 123–25 (providing examples from Walt Whitman, Nathaniel Hawthorne, Ralph Waldo Emerson).

advice to son John Quincy, to study the "great Masters of Antiquity [...] but never imitate them."[44] It is significant that this idea of rejecting imitation and slavishness became important to those trying to build a uniquely American literature starting in the 1830s, as Livingston's own call for independence and what would later become Emersonian self-reliance in law in the *Pierson* dissent, appeared in the literary guise that it did. Indeed, a true empire would require great literature.[45] There is something appropriate then about Livingston's dissent entering the canon (and perhaps even inaugurating it) of great *legal* literature, even if it was not his intent at the time he wrote it for that decision to become as public as it did.

The combination of slavery and European colonization is well represented in two points that come out in Ann Sandford's biography of Pierson's lawyer Nathan Sanford. The first is that the Pierson family played a prominent role in the deed that was drawn up between Southampton trustees and the Shinnecock Indians in 1703.[46] The second is that shortly after Sanford argued and won the *Pierson* case for Jesse Pierson, he defended a group of white wealthy Southampton town trustees and proprietors against a challenge brought against them by some members of the Shinnecock tribe who alleged abuse by proprietors in pasturing sheep, cattle, and horses on land that the Shinnecock leased from them.[47] The lease also dated to 1703. Sanford's argument? In addition to his usual procedural challenges, some of the petitioners of mixed ethnic ancestry, Native and African American, lacked a pure bloodline, which, Sanford argued, made them eligible to participate as leaseholders.[48] This bid to exclude Native Americans of mixed ancestry connects to issues of race (the unexpectedly high levels of slave owning among those involved in the case) and colonization (echoing in its use of the image of a wasteland there for the taking) reverberating in *Pierson*. Like the injury to the animal itself, those issues are difficult to see beneath Livingston's solemn foolery.

Pierson then is like *Moby Dick* in that it works simultaneously (and dizzyingly) on a number of different levels. *Moby Dick* is full of purported facts – the whaling rules Robert Deal writes about or Robert Ellickson drew upon, or the immense volume of nautical and sealife information it

[44] Quoted in ibid., 124.

[45] See ibid., 122 (quoting from a writer arguing that great literature did not require monarchy, who said about the future greatness of American letters: "We shall then have an empire").

[46] See Sandford, *Reluctant Reformer*, 156 n. 22. [47] See ibid., 23. [48] Ibid.

contains.[49] Yet it is also metaphysical – Ahab's maniacal pursuit of the white whale and what that means about humanity, or God, "the unseen and unaccountable old joker."[50] The chapter "Cetology," which approaches whales as a classification in zoology, is written in an encyclopedic style from which it abruptly departs with the following words:

> I now leave my cetological System standing thus unfinished, even as the great Cathedral of Cologne was left, with the crane still standing upon the top of the uncompleted tower. For small erections may be finished by their first architects; grand ones, true ones, ever leave the copestone to posterity. God keep me from ever completing anything. This whole book is but a draught – nay, but the draught of a draught.[51]

Moby Dick is a text that defies attempts to classify it as serious (literal) or not serious (non-literal or figurative). It is both – it is a work of fiction that trades in the factual in order to generate the fantastical and metaphorical to gesture toward the metaphysical. In it Melville transforms the stuff of whaling into a "grand" or "true" building/erection, the kind that is never really finished (and remains ever a draft). Melville wanted to write a great novel; he was not concerned about making sure that all of the factual information he conveyed was absolutely correct, reliable and not going to mislead.

In *Moby-Dick*'s famous Chapter 89, "Fast-Fish and Loose-Fish," the chapter that Ellickson and other legal scholars have relied on so heavily, Melville discusses the 1805 British whaling case, *Gale* v. *Wilkinson*, although he did not name it.[52] One of the lawyers in that case, the eminent Scottish-trained John Erskine, engaged in some solemn foolery that we would now consider very offensive.[53] He drew an analogy, as the *London Times* report put it, between the law on married women and rules in the Greenland whale fishery – "a woman out of her husband's protection was described to be exactly in the case of a loose fish."[54] A longer account of the case reproduced in a work about whaling explained that the argument was that if the woman became a "loose fish," then "any one [would have] had a right to seize" her.[55]

[49] See Deal, *The Law of the Whale Hunt*; Robert C. Ellickson, *Order without Law: How Neighbors Settle Disputes* (Cambridge, MA: Harvard University Press, 1991), 191–206.

[50] *Moby-Dick*, 247. [51] Ibid., 157.

[52] See Deal, "Fast-Fish, Loose-Fish," 218 n. 162 (identifying *Gale* v. *Wilkinson*, its reference in *Moby-Dick*, and citing to a report in the *London Times*, quoted from below), 210 n. 97 (identifying a longer report of *Gale* v. *Wilkinson* in Scoresby, quoted from below).

[53] See Deal, ibid., 219 (describing Erskine). [54] *The Times (London)*, December 24, 1805.

[55] The extension of the metaphor comes from "Account of a Trial Respecting the Right of the Ship *Experiment*, to a Whale Struck by one of the Crew of the *Neptune*" by

The husband "had originally harpooned the lady; he had her fast; but when he found she ran out too much line, he left her to plunge into the sea of folly and dissipation by herself, dragging the weight of her marriage vow along with her."[56] The husband thought he could recover her but "[n]o, – he had given her up, – he had left her to her fate, and as another had harpooned her, he had a right to retain her."[57] The bawdy analogy convinced Lord Ellenborough, who was Chief Justice of King's Bench from 1802–1818. He held that the whale belonged to the second-taker or interloper (the captain of the ship *Experiment*). The smaller whaling boat used by the initial pursuers of the whale (from the ship *Neptune*) was to be returned to them. However, Lord Ellenborough held that as for the harpoon and lines *the whale itself* had acquired "a kind of property in them."[58] Since the *Experiment* successfully fastened the Neptune's "loose fish," practically speaking, this meant that harpoon and lines could stay with them and the request by the plaintiff/*Neptune* to have them returned was denied. This striking formulation – *the whale as property holder* – helps explain the notoriety and fame of the case. It gives one pause as this would, indirectly, make the whale a legal person who can hold property. Lord Ellenborough in making the point was likely responding with his own humor, to "the witty Erskine," as Melville called him, matching wit for wit.[59] The case was not included in the *Law Reports*. The analogy between the loose woman and the loose whale and the statement of the whale as property-holder was probably all too much for its Reporter, Lord Campbell, who stated in his autobiography that as reporter he had suppressed "bad Ellenborough law."[60] Did *Gale* v. *Wilkinson* find its way into the drawer he marked "bad law" along with the other cases by Ellenborough that Campbell found to be suspect?[61]

William Scoresby Jr., vol. 2, *An Account of the Arctic Regions: With a History and Description of the Northern Whale-Fishery* (Edinburgh: Printed for Archibald Constable and Co., 1820), 518–21, 521.

[56] Ibid. [57] Ibid.

[58] Ibid. The *London Times* reported this as "the whale actually acquired *a sort of property* in the *harpoon*."

[59] *Moby-Dick*, 433.

[60] See Deal, "Fast-Fish, Loose-Fish," 229, quoting from James Oldham, "Law-Making at *Nisi Prius* in the Early 1800s," 25 *Journal of Legal History* (2004): 221–47, 223. Oldham explains that only ten percent of the trials conducted by Lord Ellenborough when he was Chief Justice of King's Bench were reported. Hence, one probably should not read too much into the exclusion of any particular one. However, *Gale* v. *Wilkinson* might not have been one Campbell was keen to record.

[61] Oldham, *Mansfield Manuscripts*, 184.

Melville reported the exchange between Erskine and Ellenborough slightly differently but kept surprisingly true to the facts in substance, describing the marital issue as a case "wherein a gentleman, after in vain trying to bridle his wife's viciousness, had at last abandoned her upon the seas of life; but in the course of years, repenting of that step, he instituted an action to recover possession of her."[62] According to Melville, Erskine argued successfully (presumably for his client, the lover) that

> though the gentleman had originally harpooned the lady, and had once had her fast, and only by reason of the great stress of her plunging viciousness, had at last abandoned her; yet abandon her he did, so that she became a loose-fish; and therefore when a subsequent gentleman re-harpooned her, the lady then became that subsequent gentleman's property, along with whatever harpoon might have been found sticking in her.[63]

The language is more sexually explicit, in keeping with the sexual ribaldry that runs throughout *Moby-Dick*.[64] Here we have the phallic imagery of the harpooning, the reharpooning, and "the harpoon [that] might have been found sticking in her."[65] Melville's account of the case is also more explicit about describing the woman as the property of one man and then another, made so by the initial harpooning and reharpooning, as the phallic metaphors put it. No one uses the word "adultery," but that was presumably the criminal charge against Erskine's client, the second-taker.[66] The judge's repartee, according to Melville, was to say that as for the harpoons and line "when the fish made off with them, it (the fish) acquired a property in those articles; and hence anybody who afterwards took the fish had a right to them."[67]

[62] *Moby-Dick*, 434. [63] Ibid.

[64] Such as the talk of erections above. See Robert Shulman, "The Serious Functions of Melville's Phallic Jokes," *American Literature: A Journal of Literary History, Criticism, and Bibliography* 33:2 (1961): 179–94, 186–87 (characterizing the passage quoted from above as Melville using a phallic joke to communicate what creating books means to him – a never-ending process of creation with all the qualities of sexual process, the basic source of animal life, and audaciously identifying his book "with the sexual principle itself" – a "grand" or "true" erection that will give pleasure to generations of readers).

[65] See ibid., 180–82 (on the loose-woman/loose-whale analogy). This last part about "the harpoon [that] might have been found sticking in her" suggests that the loose lady was found *in flagrante* with the second man by the first.

[66] Shulman, ibid., 181 ("The source makes perfectly clear that it is a case of adultery, but Melville makes the same point wittily and indirectly through [. . .] innuendo"). It would be the original creators of the story, the lawyer and judge, who do this though, or whoever wrote the first report of it who was responsible for the wit and indirect innuendo. Melville embellishes in the re telling there is no doubt; but not as much as one might think.

[67] *Moby-Dick*, 434.

A literary scholar, Robert Shulman, writing about the phallic imagery in *Moby-Dick* and specifically of the Erskine-Ellenborough exchange in "Fast-Fish, Loose-Fish," thinks that in telling the story Melville was having Ishmael react to the "obviously unjust" decision to give the second striker the whale and the equipment since "those who have labored to catch the whale not only lose it but also their own lines and harpoons."[68] In the retelling, Shulman thinks that Ellenborough figures as pimp, sanctioning the lady/whale's whoring/adultery by accepting Erskine's bawdy analogy. If that is correct, one can see why Lord Campbell wanted to keep it out of the *Law Reports*. Shulman reads the sexual jokes and phallic metaphors in *Moby-Dick* generally as having a hostile underbelly, even when they are good natured on the surface. The point then would be for the jokes to operate as a form of social satire, here to see Ellenborough as a hypocrite, since the judge's decision is "immoral and corrupt in terms of the very standards of respectability which a Lord Ellenborough piously upholds."[69]

Melville's use of *Gale* v. *Wilkinson* may or may not have been intended to make the moral point and to engage in the social satire Shulman describes. It certainly seems plausible. As a non-literary expert, it seems to me that the sexual jokes/imagery operate in a range of ways in *Moby-Dick* and as Shulman himself acknowledges they are often random and gratuitous, as if Melville is saying "I know it's a big book. Are you still awake?"

We certainly see the inclusion of an actual legal case, albeit one in which both lawyer and judge took to legal solemn foolery in relationship to the whale, analogized first to a married woman fallen into "dissipation" (Melville used a slightly different word, "viciousness") and then to a propertied (i.e. male) rights holder that can now own things like harpoons and lines. The flipping between male (property holder) and female (sex object) should probably be understood in relation to the bisexuality that ran through Melville's life and works.[70] Shulman explores how the

[68] Shulman, "The Serious Function of Melville's Phallic Jokes," 181. [69] Ibid.

[70] Melville has been described as "*the* American master of male bonding narratives" or the homosocial. See Robyn Wiegman, "Melville's Geography of Gender," 1:4 *American Literary History* (1989): 735–53, 735. *Moby-Dick* contains important scenes on the homoerotic such as the shared bed between Ishmael and Queequeg (lying "in our hearts' honeymoon [...] a cosy, loving pair" p. 58) and the scene in the chapter in which Ishmael revels in the sperm of a sperm whale ("Squeeze! squeeze! squeeze! all the morning long; I squeezed that sperm til I myself almost melted into it" and upon "unwittingly squeezing my co-laborers' hands in it [...] that at last I was continually squeezing their hands, and looking up into their eyes sentimentally; as much to say [...] Come; let us squeeze

male–female flipping worked in descriptions of the great white whale itself in the three-day chase with which the novel ends, the whale being described alternately as a male aggressor and a female object of breach.[71]

The famous chapter, "Fast-Fish, Loose-Fish," that began with a hail to "the waif" that "grand symbol and badge" (a flag that was often left in a dead whale to indicate the slayer's ownership), rises to ask the following "mighty" questions relating to the conquest of America (by way of a planted flag) and those who conquered it (the ancestors of his European-descended readers): "What was America in 1492 but a Loose-Fish, in which Columbus struck the Spanish standard by way of waifing it for his royal master and mistress? [. . .] What is the great globe itself but a Loose-Fish? And what are you, reader, but a Loose-Fish and a Fast-Fish, too?"[72] Melville is ultimately concerned in this chapter (as he is in most) to make a point about humanity, namely, that we are all loose fish (i.e. free) and fast fish (i.e. colonized or owned in some sense). So, the serfs, the slaves, the poor widows, the bankrupts, and even the archbishops and the dukes are fast-fish held so by their owners, their creditors, their fancy houses, annual incomes, and other property.[73] Possession is not just "half of the law"; it is often "the whole of the law," as *Gale* v. *Wilkinson* showed in relationship to the harpoon and lines of the *Neptune* and the whale itself.[74]

Tomlins argues that Melville was engaged in "foolery, though less [. . .] solemn foolery than a deeply subversive foolery, anti-foundational foolery."[75] How? Well, first, Melville said that the Fast-Fish, Loose-Fish rule was so "terse" it "might be engraven on a Queen Anne's farthing."[76] However, "the admirable brevity" of fast-fish, loose-fish as soon as it is uttered "necessitate[s] a vast volume of commentaries" to sort out just what is meant by "fast" and "loose."[77] And, as Tomlins puts it, Melville made the issue "hopelessly confused" by adding into the mix the older custom of iron-holds-the-whale as a way of technically holding fast.[78]

ourselves into each other; let us squeeze ourselves universally into the very milk and sperm of kindness" p. 456). Wiegman's article demonstrates how queer theorists and feminists have battled over how to think about sexuality in Melville's work. See Laurie Robertson-Lorant, *Melville: A Biography* (New York: Clarkson Potter, 1996), which argues that it is more accurate to think about Melville's life and writing in terms of bisexuality rather than homosexuality.

71 See Shulman, "The Serious Function of Melville's Phallic Jokes," 190–94.

72 *Moby-Dick*, 432, 435. 73 See ibid., 434–35. 74 Ibid., 434.

75 Tomlins, "Animals Accurs'd," 40. 76 *Moby-Dick*, 432. 77 Ibid., 433.

78 Tomlins, "Animals Accurs'd," 39.

This bit of the text is confusing as Melville blended together both the waif and the iron in iron-holds-the-whale, writing "a fish is technically fast when it bears a waif, *or any other recognized symbol of possession*; so long as the party waifing it plainly evince their ability at any time to take it alongside, as well as their intention so to do."[79] This was mashing together the very separate rules and customs relating to live and dead whales, where the iron-in would be used to identify a first striker in pursuit of a live whale (often very contested), whereas a waif/pole was usually used to mark a dead whale.[80] Yet, if these ways of marking possession sufficed, despite the fact that they did not entail maintaining a physical connection to the animal, then holding fast really was something less even than "a strand of cobweb," the striking metaphor Melville chose to capture the loosest but yet sufficient hold.[81]

Indeed, in what sense was iron-holds-the-whale or the waif/flag holding fast at all? As Melville knew, and he goes on to report, the whale with the harpoon and cut lines of the *Neptune*, was deemed by Lord Ellenborough to be a loose whale in *Gale* v. *Wilkinson*. There is then an undermining of the idea that there was a basic truth. Why? Because fast-fish, loose-fish could be made to be both *consistent* (an iron-in can "technically" hold a whale fast for a first striker) and *inconsistent* (*Gale* v. *Wilkinson* held that the whale was a loose fish successfully taken by the second striker) with iron-holds-the-whale. If these "two great principles," "the fundamentals of all human jurisprudence," were so unstable, then how could any of it make sense?[82] Morality aside, that nonsense was a profound indictment of the law on its own terms as purportedly rational and logical. Melville was married to the daughter of Massachusetts Supreme Court Chief Justice Lemuel Shaw and was no legal innocent.[83] Here we have an example of what

[79] *Moby-Dick*, 433 (emphasis added).

[80] See Deal, "Judicial Invention of Property Norms," 82, 89–92 (explaining that customs/rules/norms relating to dead whales were clearer than those governing situations of pursuit of a live whale by competitors using different marked irons). See also Deal, *The Law of the Whale Hunt*, 119 ("[w]hile whalemen harbored many different ideas about what constituted possession of a live whale [...] the custom concerning a harpooned whale was, by whaling standards, well settled at sea").

[81] *Moby-Dick*, 433 ("a mast, an oar, a nine-inch cable, a telegraph wire, or a strand of cobweb, it is all the same" – they may all be said to hold a whale fast).

[82] Ibid., 434.

[83] See Brook Thomas, "The Legal Fictions of Herman Melville and Lemuel Shaw," 11:1 *Critical Inquiry* (1984): 24–51.

Tomlins highlighted as a key literary technique of Melville's, namely, "one that states plain truths and then works assiduously to undermine them."[84]

According to Robert Deal, there was a truth in the nonsense or "jumble of competing rules" that Melville presented as "the two great principles."[85] Deal's conclusion, after having reviewed a wide range of competing testimony and ideas from whalemen in the litigated cases he examines and the lawyers, judges, and treatise writers involved or invoked in those cases, is that iron "sort of held the whale."[86] "An affixed iron in an injured whale might preserve some rights in the first striker." However, there was "such a welter of conflicting standards" that "[b]eyond a general statement that, in certain circumstances, an affixed iron in an injured whale might preserve some rights in the first striker, it is difficult to draw anything resembling a rule."[87] The evidence Deal gathered suggests that whalemen were resolving controversies as they arose on an ad hoc basis using a variety of norms, customs, and law, including iron-in giving rights to the first striker, fast-fish, loose-fish giving rights to the second taker. Neither of these were treated as, strictly speaking, grants of conclusive rights with trumping power; rather they created claims in a negotiating process when a dispute arose over a whale between competing takers, sometimes more than two. Important also were ideas about honesty and fairness based on efforts exerted, forgone opportunities, and appeals to honor that were neither law (fast-fish, loose-fish) nor custom (iron-holds-the-whale). In my favorite line from Deal's work, one Captain is recorded as having said "[i]t is customary *with me* to give up anything that belongs to another man."[88]

Pierson is similar to "Fast-Fish, Loose-Fish." The case has its serious dimensions, namely, the lawyers' arguments and the sophisticated deployment of Roman and civil law authorities on the question of how one acquires possession of a wild animal. Alongside them we encounter Livingston's dissent, begging to be understood as an example of solemn foolery and sporting wit. Yet it also put forward a serious contender to the capture rule – hot pursuit, seen and appreciated as a rival rule by scholars like John Ingham and, probably not coincidentally, the University of Chicago law professor, Dean, and big game hunter, Harry Bigelow. His dual perspective, as hunter and legal scholar, made him hesitant to

[84] Tomlins, "Animals Accurs'd," 37.
[85] Deal, "Judicial Invention of Property Norms," 75; *Moby-Dick*, 434.
[86] Deal, "Judicial Invention of Property Norms," 94. [87] Ibid., 92.
[88] Ibid., 93 (emphasis added). See also Deal, *The Law of the Whale Hunt*, 125, 129.

endorse the capture rule, when it was at odds with what many hunters would say, and indeed, with what had been taught to game wardens for over thirty years in Harry Chase's handbook, if game wardens were apt to consult such a book. Indeed, one must wonder if the hot pursuit rule, as it started to get going in cases like *Liesner et al.* v. *Wanie*, might have had a better (or at least a fighting) chance of becoming the common law on the chase and capture of wild animals if Livingston *had not* pontificated on it in the way that he did in *Pierson*, where the serious and legitimate rule became hopelessly mixed up in his literary frolic. It certainly seemed to create uncertainty for serious-minded legal mandarins, who were just not sure what to do with it and so, like Kent, ignored it.

As we saw in Chapter 6, George Caines decided that unlike *Gale* v. *Wilkinson* the dissent would not be stashed out of sight in a "bad" or "embarrassing" law drawer. And as we have examined in Chapter 7, Kent used the majority holding on mere pursuit as a serious working precedent along with *Buster* v. *Newkirk* in the *Commentaries* in a way that was very influential, at least among decided cases and legal academics. Caines having included Livingston's dissent, Kent and those who came after him had to decide whether the alternative to the capture rule should be discussed. Twentieth-century casebook editors were faced with the same question. They had to decide whether or not to include the dissent and, if included, whether they should edit it to remove its eccentricities or follow it with notes and questions to try to control and contain it, or revel in it.

As Chapter 7 explained, starting in the 1980s and early 1990s, casebook editors became increasingly comfortable including the dissent and fitting it into their overall approach, or ideology, treating it as if it were a case that was always there "in the beginning" (in a *Genesis* sense) and had to be accounted for (as if it were a great Biblical principle). Haar and Liebman went for joviality. The law does after all contain some, and there is certainly a rich intersection between law and literature well worth exploring, as we did in Part I of this book. The juxtaposition of the hot pursuit rule and the capture rule made for what was taken and presented as a clear contrast between two approaches (as in Singer, concerned to tie the contrast into a conversation about justice/fairness) and it fed into a dominant discourse about rules and standards that was fashionable amongst those enamored with the Coase Theorem and efficiency approaches to property (as in the case of Dukeminier and Krier). As a legal historian, Charles Donahue opted for using *Pierson* as an opportunity to teach students about some of the authorities important to early American lawyers (Blackstone and Justinian) and, by including the lawyers' arguments, to bring them into the story. Donahue was careful to translate the Latin, making it possible to assess clearly the arguments about mere pursuit versus hot pursuit and the inapplicability of Justinian to the facts of the case.

Then in the 2000s *Pierson* started to appear in artificial intelligence and computational theorems by legal scholars assuming a clear contrast between the two approaches and rule choices, a binary structure being essential to those studies, and determined to leave complication, nuance, and ultimately, law, behind.[89] The earliest example I have found of *Pierson* being used in this way is in reference to a project by Mark J.F. Fischer, who was a Law and Computer Fellow at Stanford in the early 1970s, who (unsuccessfully) used *Pierson* to "simulate the method of teaching thought to be characteristic of today's law professors" in a computer.[90] The functional or reductionist understanding has come to cast a long shadow, with the case parsed between analogical and dialectical ways of thinking in an essay devoted to narrative and the law.[91] Even an account of *Pierson* seeking to reconstruct its historical context through exploration and explanation of its Roman and civil law sources comes back to questions of what is the best rule in terms of rules and standards, efficiency and certainty.[92]

Absent Livingston's frolic, Kent might have been more inclined to speak up in favor of the hot pursuit rule, since his annotations suggest that (at least later) he knew about Pothier's support for Barbeyrac. Had Kent done so in the *Commentaries*, Holmes almost certainly would have been encouraged to expand upon his doubts about the firmest hold being the best. Late-nineteenth-century legal scholar/philosopher/historians like Holmes and Maine would have been inclined by their general views and mindsets to think of the firmest hold as what would have been required in order to hold property in *primitive societies* or in *ancient times*, a kind of might-makes-right inconsistent with the rule of law for civilized modern

[89] See e.g. Gordon and Walton, "Pierson vs. Post Revisited."

[90] See William E. Boyd, "Law in Computers and Computers in Law: A Lawyer's View of the State of the Art," 14 *Arizona Law Review* (1972): 267–311, 310 n. 268. Also reported on in "Stanford University Computer Study and Research Program," 12 *Jurimetrics Journal* (1971–72): 113.

[91] See Linda H. Edwards, "The Convergence of Analogical and Dialectic Imaginations in Legal Discourse," 20 *Legal Studies Forum* (1996): 7–50, 14–17 (confusing Tompkins for Livingston on custom, see pp. 15–16).

[92] See e.g. Josh Blackman, "Outfoxed *Pierson* v. *Post* and the Natural Law," 51 *American Journal of Legal History* (2011): 417–60, 453–60.

peoples. The progressive and enlightened European non-feudal mindset would honor an intention sustained and serious and capable of being made actual. Yes there was a difference between property that was already owned and first possession by occupation; however, thinkers like this would have been attracted to the idea that there should be consistency and reason in making the rules more, not less like each other, and this would have been important to them.

Robert Gordon has used the lens of positivism to understand "the Victorian legal and social science that defined the problems for which Holmes and his contemporaries thought it was important to offer solutions."[93] Yes, Holmes's discussion of possession contained pragmatic insights such as his point about the relativity of line drawing discussed in the previous chapter. However, the *Common Law* was, as Gordon elegantly put it, "a book at war with itself" given the way that it combined the pragmatism (for which Holmes is well known) with scientific positivism. The positivism is there, "well and truly entrenched," Gordon argues, despite Holmes's famous aphorism about the primacy of experience over logic.[94] Holmes had a deep belief in "the regularity and order" that he thought was already present in legal ideas and rules and saw as vital the role that the legal scholar plays in excavating those ideas and rules and subjecting them to re-examination, dragging them out into the light of day like a dragon from its cave.[95] In relationship to the capture of wild animals specifically, Holmes would have appreciated the Teutonic roots of the hot pursuit rule, which Pothier grounded in Barbeyrac and the law of the Salians – yet another factor that would have augured in its favor had it been put seriously on the table.

Gordon criticizes the *Common Law* for failing to follow through on the historicist program, dragging the archaic rules forward, counting the dragon's teeth and claws before deciding what to do with him. "[O]ne

[93] See Gordon, "Holmes's *Common Law* as Legal and Social Science," 52. See also 54 (explaining that positivism in this sense is "the belief that explanation must be scientific, and that to be scientific it must confine its investigation to observable phenomena – facts – and its method to induction, from regularities in the occurrence of past facts, of laws or statements of the probability of the occurrence of future events").

[94] Ibid., 56.

[95] Ibid. See also Robert W. Gordon, "Introduction" to *Taming the Past: Essays on Law in History and History in Law* (Cambridge UK; New York: Cambridge University Press, 2017), 1–13, 4 (providing "The Path of the Law" quotation from Holmes about taming the dragon, the process Holmes likened to the examination of old archaic common law rules, which had either to be killed or reformed, i.e. tamed and made into "a useful animal"). The book provides an image of St. George slaying the dragon on its cover.

of the puzzles of the *Common Law*, Gordon writes, "is that it fails to undertake any sustained development of what is announced as its major theme."[96] So rather than any genuine re-examination of the capture rule in the chapter on possession, we see instead what we would call nowadays path-dependency, following along, more or less, on the track Kent set, even in the face of doubts and counter-authority with which Holmes would have been sympathetic.

The next step in the historicist program, deciding what to do with the dragon, kill him or turn him into "a useful animal," namely, discard the archaic legal rule or reform and turn it to good use, is difficult to get to when its alternative, in this case, hot pursuit, was presented in the hodge-podge of serious and silly that is Livingston's dissent. In other words, Livingston probably damned the hot pursuit rule by treating it in *Pierson* in such a whimsical way. No wonder the nineteenth-century mandarins like Kent, Holmes, and Pollock ignored it. Once this path had been set their twentieth-century successors approached hot pursuit as a foil to what they had already decided was the better rule, not just for animals and hunting but for ideas of property generally, weirdly, it seems to us now, ignoring the antisocial consequences of the capture rule. We live knowing we are in the Anthropocene in a way that was not (or only dimly) appreciated in the last century, when animal rights were seen as more of a fringe issue and awareness of the inter-connections between the treatment of nonhuman animals and environmental degradation was less well known. To the twentieth-century legal mandarins using *Pierson* to elucidate general views of property was probably more important to them than norms (legal rules or customs) relating to actual wild animals unless they also happened to be hunters or had another interest in animals. It makes sense that the hot pursuit rule ended up making its way into works that were focused less on *the law of property* and more on *the law of animals* (e.g. John Ingham's treatise on animal law and Harry Chase's handbook for game wardens), in which one thinks less about property (and the degree of certainty desirable for clear rules) and more about the hunt or the chase (and what would be fair or plain old clear enough).

Take away the frolic, viewing it as a serious contender to the capture rule, Livingston's hot pursuit rule might be understood in the following sliding-scale way: If the hunter gives up and goes home over night, there is no legal possession (*Buster* v. *Newkirk* – absent a waif or some other custom to deal with situations of abandonment); if the situation is truly

[96] Gordon, "Holmes's *Common Law* as Legal and Social Science," 60.

one of *mere* pursuit, i.e. with a great, sizable or significant chance of escape, there is no legal possession (how Tompkins understood the facts of *Pierson*); if there is continued (i.e. hot) pursuit with an imminent taking, there is legal possession (what Livingston seemed to be assuming in his dissent relying on Barbeyrac and being "within reach"); if there is continuous/"vigorous" pursuit and escape is "highly improbable, if not impossible" and the control is such "that actual possession is practically inevitable," there is legal possession (*Liesner et al.* v. *Wanie*). Absolute capture of the wild animal is not required in order for there to be legal possession, as Kent always said (agreeing on that point with Colden and Barbeyrac). Conversely, killing is not necessarily all that would need to be done (the seal cases and custom relating to dead whales). Pothier was correct, then, to say that the key question was the *power* of the pursuer and what was sufficient power given the type of animal and what was involved in hunting it.

Lastly, there is no reason to assume that the capture rule must apply to other fugitive resources, especially where that creates environmental waste. A common-law court might well decide that a different kind of fugitive resource should not come under the capture rule. If different animals ought to be governed by different rules (whales versus seals versus fish), then why assume one rule should apply to a wide array of different resources, each of which has different properties and raises very different considerations?

Hunting itself might be a bit difficult for many people today to relate to, at least to younger urban dwellers. A modern-day example more familiar to Generation Xers and Millennials is the "kill stealing" in video game playing. This is a practice considered dishonorable by many gamers in which one player gets the points for completing a kill when the original player was the one who did most of the work weakening the health points of the enemy or who is actively engaged in taking it down.[97] "In the large crop of quasi-medieval games, with their strongly fantastic overtones, the capture of wild animals is nothing less than the principal source of wealth. The single most profitable 'industry' is hunting monsters and looting their corpses."[98] It is difficult to imagine one of these disagreements resulting in a legal dispute. However, one can see how a fight like this can easily get

[97] See https://en.wikipedia.org/wiki/Kill_stealing.

[98] James Grimmelmann, "Virtual Worlds as Comparative Law," 49 *New York Law School Law Review* (2004–2005): 147–84, 155. *Pierson* is discussed and cited on "[t]he Taking of Wild Monsters" and whether possession or labor should be rewarded. See 154 n. 24.

very heated in an online community, with taunts rising to the virtual equivalent of Melville's "Coke-upon-Littleton of the fist."[99] "Griefing," or deliberately annoying other players by engaging in kill stealing, is something for which a player can have their account suspended if enough complaints are received.[100] If one of the gamers were to sue another (or the gaming company for suspending their account or making changes to their character or other things about the game), it is not inconceivable that the judge might choose to write a solemnly foolish opinion to dismiss a situation in which there was no valid legal claim or the game company's right to do those things was governed by the contract between gamer and game company.[101] Augmented reality games for handheld electronic devices such as "Pokémon Go," where the app uses a cell phone's GPS and clock to superimpose virtual character-animals for a player to hunt in their physical environment, promises to result in a variety of real-world problems and conflicts if it continues to be popular or is replaced by a new similar fad.[102]

In this book I have applied Brian Simpson's legal archaeological method to *Pierson*, not just uncovering every possible scrap and shard of evidence relating to its original circumstances but also telling the history of how the case came to be so central to the legal profession, how it came to be a leading case, important in a wide, indeed bewildering variety of circumstances, from virtual worlds to home run baseballs to dwindling environmental resources. A case is nothing unless the members of the legal profession, primarily its elite members, decide it is important and in what sense. This is an inherently historical, variable, person-driven

99 *Moby-Dick*, 433.

100 Gimmelmann, "Virtual Worlds as Comparative Law," 155–56 (explains that Sony used to do this for their game EverQuest, at least in 2004).

101 See generally John William Nelson, "Fiber Optic Foxes: Virtual Objects and Virtual Worlds through the Lens of *Pierson* v. *Post* and the Law of Capture," 14 *Journal of Technology Law and Policy* (2009): 5–28 (arguing that the common law of property should not extend to virtual objects).

102 "Pokémon Go" is currently limited to solo hunters. That is why news stories to date have focused on players falling off cliffs, wandering into landmine areas in Bosnia, falling victim to a crime while out hunting at night, or being lured there by someone using the game to do that and so on. However, its original advertising promised multiplayer functions, which will allow people to play against each other. This would create the possibility of kill stealing conflicts in the moment, as hunters encounter each other in the real physical world. This problem arose with the first augmented reality game "Ingress." However, the number of incidents will increase if "Pokémon Go" remains as popular as its launch indicates. For an explanation of the game and some of these issues see www.vox.com/2016/7/11/12129162/pokemon-go-android-ios-game.

process, even if it is the decisions of many different people, arbitrary and contingent in just the same way anything is. These are the persons in the law John Noonan wrote about, even if he was apt to focus on the litigants and the judges, rather than the law reporters, the case book editors, and the law journal or treatise writers that I have privileged in telling the intellectual history of *Pierson.*[103] Legal rules and principles do not fall from the sky; they are made. The first context is the local messy situations that are probably never properly translated into legally found fact in an often lopsided adversarial process.[104] These situations are remade by the legal professionals: first, the lawyers and the judges and then, later, the legal academics. The making and remaking process is complicated and often difficult to decode and understand. It happens in its own time and place, with its own concerns and confusions. Given the two-sided nature of Livingston's dissent, serious and not serious, it has been especially difficult to understand *Pierson*. The methodology in this archeological process has been to dust off each level, while trying to preserve an appreciation of the decision's inherently mixed nature, serious and silly, and where, given the many different considerations, the doctrine should sit.

Once we see that the majority and the dissent in the case were actually dealing with two different situations, *Pierson* becomes a lot less appealing for the clear contrast it creates. Tompkins understood himself to be dealing with a situation of *mere pursuit*, and Kent later agreed. This is just different than the way Livingston saw things, namely, as a situation of *reasonable* or perhaps even *imminent taking*. Tompkins wrote that "[t]he case now under consideration is one of mere pursuit."[105] Livingston stated that the pursuer must be "within reach, or have a *reasonable* prospect (which certainly existed here) of taking."[106] As we have seen, Post's lawyer Colden conceded that "pursuit alone does not give a right of property."[107] That concession was important and supported Livingston's understanding that Post's catch was reasonably certain if not imminent. It was supported in the pleadings by the idea that Pierson in view of Post and his hounds took the fox. However, if it was indeed true that Post or

[103] See John T. Noonan Jr., *Persons and Masks of the Law: Cardozo, Holmes, Jefferson, and Wythe as Makers of the Masks* (New York: Farrar, Straus and Giroux, 1975). See also Fernandez, "Legal History as the History of Legal Texts."

[104] See e.g. Maute, "*Peevyhouse*"; Threedy, "A Fish Story."

[105] *Pierson*, 179. Tompkins also wrote, 177, relying on Justinian's *Institutes* that "pursuit alone, vests no property or right in the huntsman"; 178 "mere pursuit, gave Post no legal right to the fox."

[106] Ibid., 182 (emphasis in the original). [107] Ibid., 176.

one of his hunting companions was just about to take the fox when Pierson intervened, it was not made out as clearly as it could have been or should have been. And so the majority could simply ignore the point and proceed to decide the case as if it were a situation of mere pursuit. Post or his original lawyer probably did not anticipate that this question would become so significant. We should remember that at least at the outset neither Post nor his lawyer, if he had one, was thinking about property in the fox, and how one establishes possession in a wild hunted animal.

For Post the dispute was in origin a matter of honor. As we saw in Chapter 5, Post did not originally sue for property in the fox. He sued in trespass-on-the-case for the malice with which he felt Pierson had intervened in the hunt and taken the fox "well-knowing" that Post and his friends were in pursuit of the animal. In other words, Post was looking for an award for the injury done him when Pierson knowingly killed the fox in Post's sight in order to prevent Post from getting it. This was the setup for a tort case gone "defective," as McDowell put it.[108] Sanford emphasized at the start of his argument that "[i]f [...] Post had not acquired any property in the fox, when it was killed by *Pierson* [...] he had no right in it which could be the subject of injury."[109] Post needed property in the fox in order to be able to claim an injury for which he could be compensated. Post's lawyer's claim that this was not a case of mere pursuit was ignored by Tompkins. Yet, in order to answer the question whether or not Post had established a legal possession in the fox, we need an answer to a crucial question: Was Post about to take the animal, as Livingston assumed, or was there still significant opportunity for the fox to escape, as Tompkins believed? The answer to this question is lost it seems in the sands of time and of that Long Island beach.[110]

Given the basic mismatch between the way that Tompkins and Livingston saw the facts of the case, it is difficult to comprehend how *Pierson* could have become a candidate for computer coding or artificial intelligence. The two rules cannot simply be fed into a computer or robot as binary either/or code. The majority and the dissent are not contemplating the same factual scenario. Nuance regarding fact is often said to be the hardest part of legal analysis. The law, it is sometimes said, is easy; cases

[108] McDowell, "Legal Fictions in *Pierson* v. *Post*," 735. [109] *Pierson*, 175.

[110] A similar factual ambiguity led the judge in *Swift* v. *Gifford* to apply what he termed "custom" to the whaling dispute rather than the common law. See Deal, "The Judicial Invention of Property Norms," 88–89 ("[I]t would be impossible to determine whether the [first pursuer] 'though continuing the chase, had more than a possibility of success'").

are won and lost on the facts. Stating and parsing the facts of a case are the skills that the case method has always been taken to be good at inculcating in law students. Even in a future of self-driving cars, it is difficult to imagine that a computer or robot could ever really be taught to "think like a lawyer" in this way.[111] This clash and difference in factual understandings, and the way that the opinions in the case are speaking past each other, are difficult to see amidst all the Latin of Tompkins's majority decision and all the foolery of Livingston's dissent. And I daresay it has often been missed given the dominant way of teaching the case as two contrasting situations: clear rule of capture versus fuzzy hot pursuit. But we must note that the two contrasting approaches simply do not work when we accept that the two judges were actually describing two different situations.

In a forum in which Robert Deal challenged Ellickson's writing about whaling industry norms and issues relating to animals as various as whales, seals, and foxes were considered, Ellickson charged me with being anti-rule.[112] Admittedly, that is a position difficult to inhabit consistently as a law professor. However, I have spoken up pretty consistently in favor of the allegedly fuzzy standard of hot pursuit in *Pierson*, mostly in an attempt to provide some fair counterweight to the received wisdom about the case, which has heavily tipped the other way. At least among property scholars the capture rule is clearly considered better. Their problem is that there is a lot of evidence to show that this is just not true.

My intention in this book is to disrupt any previously dominant understanding of *Pierson* by changing the way that we think about it. The most common thing people say to me about my *Pierson* work is "you have completely changed the way that I think about this case; I cannot go back to thinking about it the way that I did before." *Pierson* v. *Post*, the classic property case, turns out not to really have been a property case at all. Its structure as a "defective torts case" means that the majority and dissent, so often taken to be perfectly mirroring each other or offering a clear rule for contrast with an allegedly fuzzy standard, are not in fact even

[111] The computerization of all legal knowledge promises to take up beyond rules and standards. See e.g. Anthony J. Casey and Anthony Niblett, "The Death of Rules and Standards," 92 *Indiana Law Journal* (2016–2017): 1401–47.

[112] See Ellickson, "The Entitlements of Unallied Hunters After a Sequential Capture," ("Fernandez [...] is rather consistently anti-rule and pro-standard. Perhaps she is unhappy with lawyer-economists because they don't share her across-the-board aversion to rules").

discussing the same thing. Added to that, the troubling (and confusing) mixture of serious and silly in *Pierson* makes it so unstable that it is a mistake to approach it as a straightforward legal text; it ought instead to be approached as a slippery and wily fox, a literary as much as a legal text. One relies on it, as one would on Melville's account of whaling law, at one's peril.

Does this make *Pierson* unusable? I think it opens the case up for a variety of other uses and deployments with a deeper awareness and understanding of the different levels reverberating in it. We can be more careful and more thoughtful in the way that we use it in other words. It is not to say, as Ellickson believed I was suggesting, that there is only one way to teach or think about *Pierson*.[113] I can be accused of a lot of things for presenting *Pierson* in the way I have in this book, but a failure to be sufficiently pluralist is probably not among them! My entire approach is rather one that is adamantly anti-reductionist.

Melville knew how whaling rules and customs worked. But just because he did, does not mean that he deployed his knowledge about whaling in a reliable way. He had other aims and purposes in mind; other (and probably in his mind bigger) fish to fry. So too, Livingston was using his dissent to do a number of things. These aims and objectives might have been more obvious at the time, and this would have been especially true if Livingston had intended the opinion to be just for these lawyers, who he could fairly assume would more easily penetrate his layers of solemn foolery than the world at large. His aims and objectives are more opaque to audiences across large distances of time and space for whom Livingston's solemn foolery will have become almost entirely inscrutable, impossible to encompass in some easy reduction.

If we were forced then to sum it up, what would we say Livingston was up to? First, he appears to be tutoring the lawyers (and perhaps Tompkins too) on the use of the foreign sources in which he was himself an expert, and chastising them for their misuse. You cannot simply follow the authorities slavishly and treat litigation as a one-upmanship game of who can produce the best authority without thinking through its

[113] Ellickson, "The Entitlements of Unallied Hunters After a Sequential Capture," 133 (responding to the discussion of how *Pierson* has appeared in property law casebooks over the years, Ellickson categorizes this as the work of a particularizer rather than a synthesizer like Blackstone, and writes that methodological pluralism values the work produced from both perspectives. "Fernandez's conception of how the famous fox case should be taught is intriguing. But might not it be just one of many viable pedagogical options?").

application to American conditions. Likely, it was precisely because he valued the authorities that it annoyed him to see them so cavalierly thrown around in argument by the lawyers and rather robotically adopted by Tompkins. Instead of pointing out, as he probably would have had he been toe-to-toe with Kent, that Justinian did not properly speaking apply to the facts at hand and that Barbeyrac did, he calls for the lawyers to abandon Justinian and turn to the arbitration of sportsmen. Instead of presenting Barbeyrac as a serious source, which he certainly could have done, Livingston makes it seem like his choice of Barbeyrac was a flippant decision determined by the size and breed of Post's dogs.

Why take that tone? Because, secondly, Livingston was probably expressing exasperation with the lawyers that the case had gone on for so long and received so much attention when it was obvious (at least to him) that the jury verdict should be upheld in its (admittedly) small award to Post and a reversal in the circumstances would be unfair, especially if it was a situation of hot pursuit, reasonably inferred from the original statement of facts and from Colden's insistence that it was not a case of mere pursuit. Confronted by litigation whose modern equivalent would be a lawsuit over a video game "kill stealing" incident, or the feuding neighbors in Toronto's neighborhood of Forest Hill, the judicial humor might have been thought by Livingston to be appropriate in a situation where Pierson had persisted in a dubious appeal, his lawyer having raised a bevy of unfounded procedural challenges, wasting the court's time and resources. He would, like the judges in the modern cases we examined in Chapter 2, turn to judicial humor born out of frustration with the process and with his colleagues, adding through his Rabelaisian play another (confusing and confused) burst of excess. The playfulness invited by a trivial dispute over an animal of insignificant economic value would make his own trivialization of the situation appropriate, at least in his own mind. And he might well have never intended the case to be widely read or a matter for public record, as Caines decided it would be.

The hot pursuit rule is (and always was) a serious contender to the capture rule. I have excavated many sources to support this, along with explaining why the intellectual trajectory on the capture rule took the route that it did. A historical analysis makes more sense of the case than previous interpretations of a stripped-down kind and makes it difficult if not impossible to continue to treat the case in the way property theorists have done. There has always been too much pithiness and reduction in *Pierson*, both in the way it was decided and in the way that it was received. In this sense, it was like Melville's overly-compact presentation of fast-fish, loose-fish and iron-holds-the-whale, so apt to mislead. Indeed, one might say that the literary, in both Melville's case and in Livingston's, pushed away information that it turns out was crucial in order to evaluate the competing rules on offer. Yet even though the literariness of Livingston's dissent has made it more difficult to see and understand what was happening in *Pierson*, it offered the first and best clue that there was something here worth unravelling and trying to understand. If the authors had thought less about wit and more about truth to form, a lot of misunderstanding might have been avoided, in both Livingston's and Melville's case. Yet that is to bring to bear a set of assumptions that might be entirely fair from a legal perspective but do not speak to ambitions to legal literariness that embody very different priorities.

The need to use different standards of evaluation is obvious in the case of *Moby-Dick*, widely acknowledged to be a literary masterpiece and a whale of a book. It might seem to be less so for Livingston, who was, after all, an officer of the law speaking in this capacity as a judge when he penned the dissent, whether or not he intended for it to appear in public print. After the archeological exploration, we now have a better sense of what we need to do. First, accept that text for what it clearly always was – an instance of legal solemn foolery – and exercise extreme care in handling it. And second, see in it something nevertheless meant to be taken seriously, the hot pursuit rule.

The hot pursuit rule is relevant for hunting of all kinds, not just non-human animals. It is good for video game "kill stealing" and other issues that will become important in future new property claims, such as asteroids, and for all those forms of common property that will become more and more important as natural resources become scarcer as global warming increases. This case study of *Pierson* makes an additional point, which is to show the costs of reductionism in legal thought, particularly in the case of the economical approach to and presentation of law and legal theory very popular in academic legal approaches in the last fifty years. The seriousness of later generations of legal mandarins failed to attend to the foolery in the case even though this was what attracted so many people to it, both students and other legal scholars.

Here we have engaged in a careful process of archaeological restoration, a building back, that has allowed the recovery of a story that is both a tale of a whale and a tale of a flea. The flea is the small history, the fox and the fight he or she started; the whale is the big history, the place of *Pierson* in a story of law and legal professionalization in American legal culture. They are, however, two sides of the same coin, a bright and shiny coin it turns out, encapsulated in this ill-understood yet influential fragment of communal legal thought, culture, and history. The big and the small, the whale and the flea, both animals that deserve their due, alongside Reynard – him- or herself.

The argument in this book has been that *Pierson* exhibits an important combination of the mock and the serious, a poorly understood, underdocumented, and undertheorized historical legal or lawyerly mode of solemn foolery. In it we have the solemn and serious treatment of an anciently and seriously discussed and debated point of legal and philosophical interest (how does one establish occupation of and therefore possession in a wild animal) but in a context which one of the judges saw fit to make comical. Both aspects, the solemn and the silly, continue to reverberate in lawyers' use of this text and should be part of our understanding of it, both its history and its current use. This book has aimed not to capture (or reduce) but to keep both dimensions in play, so that they may be properly appreciated by future consumers of this (bizarre) fragment of American legal history.

What people decide to do with the information is up to them. I would like to see some change, however, in both the serious and not-so-serious ways in which the case is used. Those who approach the case as a kind of joke and use it in a flippant way should think about the ideological and other kinds of implications it carries. Those who approach the case in an utterly serious economical or reductionist way should consider what it means to strip out its foolery and turn it into an object very different from what it originally was. Perennial objects of scholarly study such as *Pierson* have a lot to say about those who choose to perennially study them. What we hear the case saying changes over time and we are ourselves adding to the record as we go along, discussing and essentially recreating the text in the process. This book has delved into both sides of the solemn foolery of *Pierson* in a way that might be difficult to sum up in a law review footnote. That, however, is as it should be.

APPENDIX A

Citation History

	Animal-Related Cases	Non-Animal Cases
1810	*Gillet* v. *Mason*, 7 Johns. 16 (N.Y. Sup.Ct., 1810) (bees)	
1822	*Buster* v. *Newkirk*,20 Johns. 75 (N.Y. Sup.Ct., 1822) (hunted deer)	
1835	*Fleet* v. *Hegeman et al.*, 14 Wend. 42 (N.Y. Sup.Ct., 1835) (poached oysters)	
1861		*Eads et al.* v. *Brazelton*, 22 Ark. 499, 1861 WL 699 (Ark. Sup. Ct., 1861) (sunken steamboat and cargo of shot and lead)
1872	*Swift et al.* v. *Gifford*, 2 Low. 110 (MA: Dist. Ct., 1872) (hunted whale)	
1877	*Wright* v. *Clark*, 50 Vt. 130 (Vt. Sup. Ct., 1877) (dog shot while hunting a fox)	
1881		*Rowell* v. *Doyle*, 131 MA: 474, 1881 WL 11343 (MA: Sup. Ct.,1881) (snow-cleared ice)

(*continued*)

	Animal-Related Cases	Non-Animal Cases
1892		*Walradt* v. *Phoenix Ins. Co. of Hartford*, 64 Hun 129, 19 N.Y.S. 293 (N.Y. Sup. Ct., 1892) (dry goods destroyed in a fire)
1894	*People* v. *Doxtater*, 75 Hun 472, 27 N.Y.S. 481 (N.Y. Sup. Ct., 1894) (fishing regulation)	
32-year gap		
1926	*Dapson* v. *Daly*, 257 MA 195, 153 N.E. 454 (MA: Sup. Ct., 1926) (hunted deer)	
51-year gap		
1977	*Douglas* v. *Seacoast Products Inc. et al.*, 431 U.S. 265, 97 S.Ct. 1740 (U.S. Sup.Ct., 1977) (Virginia fishing regulations) (in dissent by Rehnquist J.)	
1978	*United States* v. *Long Cove Seafood Inc.*, 582 F.2d 159 (U.S. C.A., 2nd Cir., 1978) (stolen clams)	
1979		*United States* v. *Weintraub*, 613 F.2d 612 (U.S. C.A. 6th Cir., 1979) (stale tax prosecution) (in dissent)
1979	*State of Maine* v. *Goyette*, 407 A.2d 1104 (Maine Sup. Ct., 1979) (illegally shot moose)	
1980	*People of the State of Michigan* v. *Burtt*, 100 Mich.App. 122, 298 N.W.2d 684 (Mich. C.A., 1980) (questionable illegal fishing)	

(*continued*)

	Animal-Related Cases	Non-Animal Cases
1981		*Hener* v. *United States*, 525 F. Supp. 350 (South. N.Y. Dist. Ct., 1981) (sunken cargo of silver)
1983	*Idaho ex rel. Evans* v. *Oregon*, 462 U.S. 1017, 103 S.Ct. 2817 (U.S. Sup. Ct., 1983) (Idaho suing Oregon and Washington for equitable apportionment of fish in a shared river)	
1988		*State of New Jersey* v. *Schmidt*, 110 N.J. 258, 540 A.2d 1256 (N.J. Sup. Ct., 1988) (cocaine)
1989		*Mercury Bay Boating Club Inc.* v. *San Diego Yacht Club*, 150 A.D.2d 82, 545 N.Y.S.2d 693 (N.Y. Sup. Ct., Appel. Div., 1st Dept., 1989) (America's Cup boat race)
1990	*Dycus* v. *Sillers*,557 So.2d 486 (Miss. Sup. Ct., 1990) (fishing hole)	
1990		*Beltway Management Co.* v. *Lexington-Landmark Ins. Co.*, 746 F.Supp. 1145 (U.S. Dist. Ct., Dist. of Col., 1990) (leased premises)
1991		*Knightonet al.* v. *Texaco Producing Inc.*, 762 F. Supp. 686 (U.S. Dist. Ct., W. Dist. of Louis., Shreveport Div., 1991) (minerals)
1993	*In re Oriental Republic Uruguay*, 821 F.Supp. 950 (U.S. Dist. Ct., Delaware, 1993) (ducks killed by oil spill)	
1994	*Clajon Prod. Corp.* v. *Petera*, 854 F.Supp. 843	

(*continued*)

	Animal-Related Cases	Non-Animal Cases
	(U.S. Dist. Ct., Dist. of Wyoming, 1994) (constitutional challenges to the state regulation scheme governing the allocation and distribution of hunting licenses for elk, deer, and antelope by landowners) *State of Texas* v. *Bartee*, 894 S.W.2d 34 (C.A. Texas, San Antonio, 1994) (is theft of white tailed deer possible)	
1996	*Alliance Against IFQs et al.* v. *Brown*, 84 F.3d 343 (U.S. C.A., 9th Cir., 1996) (challenge to federal fishing regulations implementing a sablefish and halibut fishery management plan in Alaska)	
1999	*Bilida* v. *McCleod*, 41 F. Supp.2d 142 (U.S. Dist. Ct., R.I., 1999) (seizure and destruction of pet raccoon)	
2000		*Chappell* v. *United States of America*, 119 F.Supp.2d 1013 (U.S. Dist. Ct., W. Dist. of Missouri, W. Div., 2000) ($82,000 of abandoned drug money found hidden in the gas tank of a car purchased from the government)
2001	*In re Exxon Valdez*, 270 F.3d 1215 (U.S. C.A., 9th Cir., 2001) (commercial fishery damaged in massive 1989 Alaska oil spill on $5 billion punitive damages award)	

(*continued*)

	Animal-Related Cases	Non-Animal Cases
2002		*Popov* v. *Hayashi*, 2002 WL 31833731 (Cal. Sup. Ct., San Francisco County, 2002) (record-breaking home run baseball)
2004		*The City of San Marcos* v. *Texas Commission on Environmental Quality*, 128 S.W.3d 264 (Texas C.A., 3rd Dist., Austin, 2004) (groundwater)
2010	*Sheffield* v. *City of Fort Thomas, Kentucky*, 620 F.3d 596 (U.S. C.A., 6th Cir., 2010) (constitutional challenges to city deer population control ordinances)	

APPENDIX B

Judgment Roll

1. CONTEXT

The familiar text of *Pierson v. Post* is the report of the New York Supreme Court created by New York's first official law reporter George Caines.[1] What appears in law school casebooks is an edited version of Caines's report containing a brief statement of the facts, followed by the majority decision by Justice Daniel Tompkins and the witty dissent by Justice Brockholst Livingston.[2] The Judgment Roll, a transcript of which I provide here in this Appendix, is admittedly a less lively and engaging read but it is important for those interested in the history of the *Pierson* case. I include it here so that readers of the book can easily follow through on references to the Judgment Roll in the footnotes (e.g. "See Judgment Roll, p. 2, Appendix B"). I have not included the handwritten text the transcript is based on. A scan of the photocopy of each page of the handwritten text is electronically available for download at https://dataverse.scholarsportal.info/dataset.xhtml?persistentId=doi:10.5683/SP/3HJKJ7.

As the Judgment Roll is an unfamiliar presentation of information for most of us, spoiled as we are by the easy and elegant presentation in appellate reports, I provide here a brief overview of its contents. What we have is a copy (probably made by a clerk) of the documents Pierson's lawyer Nathan Sanford filed in his writ of *certiorari* to the New York Supreme Court.[3] As explained in detail in Chapter 3, this was a process in

[1] See Chapter 6 on George Caines and the reporter role.
[2] See Chapter 7 on an evolution of the casebook presentations.
[3] See Figure I.2 in the Introduction showing Sanford's name and the filing date of September 10, 1805.

which the loser before a Justice of the Peace (here Pierson) could appeal the decision made in a magistrate's court by asking the New York Supreme Court to command that the Justice of the Peace explain what had been done in the original trial (here a jury trial in which Post was awarded 75¢ and $5 in costs). It was the job of the New York Supreme Court to check, yes, all the "i"s were dotted and "t"s were crossed and if they were not, Pierson (the "now plaintiff" before the New York Supreme Court) was justified in winning a reversal of Post's $5.75 award.

Included in the papers Sanford filed were, first, the command to the Justice of the Peace in the case, John N. Fordham, to return documentation relating to the jury trial and how it was conducted, which Fordham dutifully does (see Transcript pp. 1–10). I describe the pieces of this in more detail below. Next were Sanford's six specific grounds of appeal filed in January 1803 (pp. 11–14). That is followed by repetition of the words the New York Supreme Court used in order to hold the case over from year to year (pp. 15–19).

Pierson was described in the published New York Supreme Court report as the "now plaintiff," because he was *now the plaintiff* appealing from the jury verdict given for Post in the court below.[4] This was true even though Post was *the original plaintiff* who brought the action forward before that Justice of the Peace and jury. He did that in order to obtain redress for the harm he felt had been done to him by Pierson's interference with his hunt. We learn here that Post alleged that interference was done "maliciously" (Transcript p. 5), an aspect of the case that was not included in Caines's published New York Supreme Court report.

The record begins on pp. 1–2 with the New York Supreme Court's, January 29, 1803, demand/command that all the "process[,] order[,] proceedings[s] and judgment" be produced by Justice of the Peace John N. Fordham and sent up to the New York Supreme Court by the third Tuesday in April in order to be heard in the May term of 1803 in New York City. It was witnessed by then Chief Justice of that court Morgan Lewis at the City Hall in Albany. Following this, pp. 2–10 are copies of what Fordham sent in response.

First we have Fordham's account of how he issued a summons to "any of the Constables of the County of Suffolk" in order to command Jesse Pierson to appear on December 30 at 2:00 pm in order to answer Lodowick Post in his plea of trespass-on-the-case under the 1801

[4] *Pierson*, 175.

version of the *Twenty-Five Dollar Act* (p. 3). Fordham attached his personal seal, represented in the clerk's copy by the letters "Ls" (see p. 2).

Fordham records Post's allegation that on December 10 1802 Lodowick was hunting a fox on the beach ("wild and uninhabited[,] unpossessed[,] and waste land") with his "dogs and hounds" and Jesse, knowing Post was in pursuit, did "maliciously" kill the fox (p. 5). Fordham goes on to describe how he empowered Constable Thomas Harris to summon twelve men for a jury and how a jury of six was chosen from the venire of twelve following the procedure set out in the *Twenty-Five Dollar Act* (p. 6). We learn the juror's names (p. 7). It also includes the jury's verdict for Post, 75¢ for his damages plus $5 in costs (p.8).

The first-hand account by Fordham is signed and dated April 26, 1803, so it was ready in time to make the May term in New York City, where it was presumably sent. This would explain why when I found the Judgment Roll it was at the Division of Old Records in New York City rather than Albany even though Caines included the report in the August term for 1805 and August was typically an Albany term, a fact that had confused previous researchers.

Next Fordham included the sealed document to Constable Harris to summon Pierson issued on December 22 1802, eight days before the trial was to take place (pp. 8–9), sworn by Harris who attested to having read the summons within Pierson's hearing (p. 9). Fordham also enclosed his sealed command to Harris on December 30 to summon twelve men for the jury to gather at the house of Hugh Gelston Jr. for the trial to be held on the same day (p.9). The record refers elsewhere to this location as the house of Hugh Gelston (p. 3).[5]

The papers and proceedings Fordham included consisted of three more items: (i) Harris's endorsed compliance regarding his summons of the twelve prospective jurors (p. 9); (ii) a list of the jurors summoned (p. 10); and (iii) a list of the court fees in the case, recording that amongst other things there were seven witnesses at the jury trial (p. 10). Those costs amounted to just over $5 (p. 10).

After Justice of the Peace Fordham's account and supporting documents, we have a list of the six grounds Sanford alleged were "manifest error" justifying reversal (pp. 11–14). Post's lawyer, Cadwallader D. Colden, is recorded as having denied the errors (p. 14). And then the case is carried over from term to term for well over two years (pp. 15–18), until finally the judgment reversing the lower court decision is decided and signed by Daniel

[5] See Figure 3.4 and information on the Gelstons and the house in Chapter 3.

D. Tompkins on September 10, 1805 (p. 19). It was filed by Pierson's lawyer, Nathan Sanford, the same day (see Figure I.2 in the Introduction). See Figure B.1 below for Tompkins's signature on the decision and a sample of what a page of the Judgment Roll looks like.

The hearing took place on August 7, 1805.[6] The costs recorded here as $121.37 (p. 19) actually ended up being $126.37.[7] That number would include the $5 in costs from the court below, to which Pierson as the triumphant "now plaintiff" was entitled having won through this professionalized and lawyerized legal process a reversal of the jury verdict from Fordham's lay court.

This transcript was prepared with the assistance of Joseph Van Nostrand at the Division of Old Records. Joe added to the transcript in a number of instances where what was written was not legible from the photocopy I worked with – I indicate these spots with underlining. Significant input also came from my colleague at the University of Toronto Faculty of Law Stephen Waddams, who helped with reading some of the manuscript handwriting. And Charles Donahue of the Harvard Law School caught some transcription errors. Mistakes certainly remain, and so I would encourage consultation of the electronically available handwritten text by anyone seeking to use it for research purposes, especially if in doubt of what I have transcribed.

There are portions of this text that have an odd mixed up character, some of which were probably generated by clerical copying error. I have not interfered with these passages in order to avoid inadvertent changes in meaning. I have added punctuation and other minor changes in order to make the text easier to read, as well as a system of bolding cities and dates on pp. 16–19, as it is particularly difficult to distinguish here where each term breaks and the next one begins as the case was carried over from term to term.

I have attempted to reproduce the handwritten text faithfully in what is known as a "diplomatic transcription," leaving the formatting and number of words on each line as they appear in the original document (in order to enable side-by-side comparison between transcript and handwriting) and using a cursive script somewhat similar to the one used in the clerk's copy.

[6] Supreme Court of Judicature (New York), General and Special Term Minute Books, J0130-82, New York State Archives, Albany, NY.

[7] Supreme Court of Judicature (NY), Docket of Judgments, J0131-82, vol. 4, New York State Archives, Albany, NY.

FIGURE B.1 Judgment Roll, Tompkins's signature, originally filed as Law Judgment #1805 P-33. Division of Old Records, New York County Clerk's Office, New York City, NY. Now available as a download as "Pierson-Post-19.jpg" at https://dataverse.scholarsportal.info/dataset.xhtml?persistentId=doi:10.5683/SP/3HJKJ7

Generally, I use square brackets to indicate textual emendation, including punctuation, capitalization, and added words to help make the text more readable. Where there is a word in the source text that could not be read or there is some doubt about it, either a guess is placed in square brackets ("*[?word?]*") or "*[?]*" is used. "*[?]*" is used where there is an inexplicable mark. More than one word that is illegible is represented by "*[???]*" or a longer series of "*?*" for an illegible line. Square brackets are used to complete or correct some spelling, although generally spelling and random capitals are left as is (e.g. "*Fox*"). Slips of the pen are not marked by *sic*. Proper names are as they are spelled (e.g. for juror's names). I have left "*Peirson*" as is in the Transcript despite the standard way the name is spelled, i.e. "*Pierson.*" There are two places where inserted material is marked with up and down arrows ("↓↑") and scratched out text is struck through ("~~*illegible scratch out*~~"). Flourishes and decorative marks are indicated (e.g. "*swirl*" beneath signatures).

2. TRANSCRIPT

[Transcript p. 1]

New York Supreme Court — *Pleas before the Justices of the People of the State of New York of the Supreme Court of Judicature of the same People at the City hall of the City of New York of the term of May in the year of our Lord one thousand eight hundred and three. Witness Morgan Lewis Esquire Chief Justice.*

Fairlie and Bloodgood[8]

State of New York to wit[:] The People of the State of New York sent to John N. Fordham Esquire[,] one of the Justices of the said People[,] the peace of the said People in and for the County of Suffolk to keep and also divers felonies[,] trespasses[,] and other misdemeanors committed in the said County to hear and determine assigned their writ [?close?] in these words to wit[:] The People of the State of New York by the grace of God free and independent to John N. Fordham Esquire[,] one of our Justices assigned to keep our peace

[8] Clerks of the New York Supreme Court, James Fairlie, New York Office (1797–1830) and Francis Bloodgood, Albany Office (1797–1825). See Duely and Constantly Kept, Appendix E, "Supreme Court Clerks (1797–1847)," 158.

in and for our County of Suffolk and also to hear and determine divers felonies[,] trespasses[,] and other misdemeanors done and committed in the said County of Suffolk[.] Greeting[.] We being willing for certain causes to be certified of a certain plaint lately levied or affirmed in our Court before you without our writ against Jesse Peirson at the suit of Lodowick Post in a plea of trespass on the case as it is said and also of the process[,] order[,] proceedings[,] and judgment in the same Do Command you that the plaint aforesaid and also all the process[,] order[,] proceedings[,] and judgment aforesaid with all things whatever concerning the same as fully and entirely as the same remain before you by whatever name or names the parties in the same are or may be called before our Justices of our Supreme Court of Judicature at the City hall of the City of New York on the third Tuesday of April next distinctly and openly you certify and send together with this writ that our

said

[Transcript p. 2]

said Justices of our said Supreme Court of Judicature may thereupon cause to be done what of right and according to the laws and customs of our said State ought to be done. Witness Morgan Lewis Esquire[,] Chief Justice at the City hall of the City of Albany[,] the twenty ninth day of January in the twenty seventh year of our Independence and in the year of our Lord one thousand eight hundred and three.

Fairlie and Bloodgood

Sanford Att[orne]y.

And afterwards to wit on the first Monday in May in the year of our Lord one thousand eight hundred and three before the Justices of the People of the State of New York of the Supreme Court of Judicature of the same People at the City hall of the City of New York comes the said Jesse Peirson by Nathan Sanford his Attorney and the said John N. Fordham the said Justice in the said writ named now here returns the said writ and sends the record in the said writ mentioned in these words to wit.

SUFFOLK COUNTY *Ls.*[9] *I[,] John N. Fordham Esquire[,] one of the Justices of the peace of the People of the State of New York the Peace of the said People in and for the County of Suffolk to keep and also divers felonies[,] trespasses[,] and other misdemeanors in the said County [?perpetrated?] to hear and determine assigned in the said writ of the People to me directed[,] named[.] To the People of the State of New York[,] [I] do certify that before the coming to me of the said writ to wit on the thirtieth day of December in the year of our Lord one thousand eight hundred and two[,] at the town of Southampton[,] in the County of Suffolk[,] Lodowick Post in the said writ named came into the Court of the said People before me[,] the said John N.*

Fordham

[Transcript p. 3]

Fordham then being one of the Justices of the Peace for the said County of Suffolk and then and there affirmed his plaint against Jesse Peirson in the said writ also named in a plea of trespass on the case to his damage twenty five dollars and prayed of me process against the said Jesse Peirson by summons whereupon at the prayer of the said Lodowick Post and in pursuance of an Act of the Legislature of the State of New York entitled an Act for the more speedy recovery of debts to the value of twenty five dollars passed the seventh day of April one thousand eight hundred and one. I[,] the said John N. Fordham[,] did issue a summons directed to any of the Constables of the County of Suffolk where the said Jesse Peirson then resided thereby requiring the said Constable to summon the said Jesse Peirson to appear before me at the dwelling house of Hugh Gelston found in the town of Southampton in the County of Suffolk aforesaid on Thursday the thirtieth of December in the year last aforesaid at two o[']clock in the afternoon of the same day to answer unto

[9] The letters stand for *locus sigilli*, used to designate the location of the seal in the original document. Since proceedings before a Justice of the Peace were not a court of record with its own seal and clerk, this would have been Fordham's own seal. See *Duely and Constantly Kept*, Appendix C, "Inferior Courts of Law." This also occurs on Transcript p. 8 and p. 9.

Lodowick Post in a plea of trespass on the case to his damage twenty five dollars[,] which Summons was delivered unto Thomas Harris one of the Constables of Southampton in the County aforesaid who afterwards to wit on the thirtieth day of December aforesaid returned [?thereto?] that the same was duly and personally served on the said Jesse Peirson by reading the same in his hearing on which said thirtieth day of December the said Lodowick Post and the said
Jesse

[Transcript, p. 4]

Jesse Peirson appeared in their proper person in the Court of the said People before ↑me↓ the said John N. Fordham and thereupon the said Lodowick Post complained against the said Jesse Peirson as follows for that whereas he[,] the said Lodowick Post[,] on the tenth day of December in the year of our Lord one thousand eight hundred and two at the town of Southampton in the County of Suffolk aforesaid was the possessor of certain dogs and hounds and the said dogs and hounds so being then and there in the possession and under the command of him[,] the said Lodowick[,] did then and there upon a certain wild and uninhabited[,] unpossessed[,] and waste land called the Beach find and start one of those wild and noxious beasts called a Fox and the said Fox being so found as aforesaid by the said dogs and hounds was then and there upon the said wild and unpossessed and uninhabited and waste land called the Beach pursued[,] hunted[,] and chased by the said hounds and dogs and followed and pursued by the said Lodowick then and there having the said dogs and hounds under his command and direction as aforesaid. The said Jesse while the said Fox was then and there hunted[,] chased[,] and pursued as aforesaid the said Jesse well knowing that the said Fox was so hunted[,] chase[,] and pursued as aforesaid with intention to injure him[,] the said Lodowick[,] and to prevent the said hounds and dogs from catching and

*taking the said Fox and with intention to
hinder the said Lodowick from having the
said*

[Transcript, p. 5]

said Fox did on the same day and year last aforesaid at and upon the said wild and uninhabited[,] unpossessed[,] and waste land called the beach to wit at the town and County aforesaid maliciously kill the said Fox[.] [T]he said Lodowick and the said dogs and hounds aforesaid then and there being in the view of the said Jesse and actually engaged in the chase[,] pursuit[,] and hunting of the said Fox as aforesaid[.] And the said Jesse did then and there maliciously take and carry away the said Fox whereby the said Lodowick saith that he is injured and hath sustained damage to twenty five dollars and therefore he brings suit [?] [T]o which the said Jesse Peirson then and there pleaded not guilty and issue being so thereupon joined between the said parties[.] [T]he said Lodowick Post in pursuance of said Act did demand of me[,] the said John N. Fordham[,] that the said action should be tried by a jury and upon such demand I[,] the said John N. Fordham[,] holding the said Court for the trial of said cause upon the thirtieth of December aforesaid at the town and County aforesaid did issue a Venire directed to Thomas Harris[,] Constable for the town of Southampton commanding him to summon twelve good and lawful men being freeholders of the town of Southampton in the County aforesaid who should in no wise be of kin either to the said Lodowick Post Plaintiff or to the said Jesse Peirson Defendant nor interested in the said

[Transcript, p. 6]

said cause to be and appear in the said Court of the said People before me[,] the said John N. Fordham[,] immediately at the said house of the said Hugh Gelston Junr situate in the town of Southampton in the County of Suffolk aforesaid to make a jury for the trial of the same action between the parties aforesaid which said Venire is hereunto annexed and was then and there delivered to the said Thomas Harris[,] one of the Constables of the town of Southampton to be executed according to law and the said Thomas Harris then and there being such Constable as aforesaid did then and there make due return of the said Venire and annexed a pannel thereto containing the names of twelve freeholders whom he had duly summoned by virtue of the said Venire and the names of the persons so impannelled were severally written on several and distinct pieces of paper as nearly of one size as could be and were delivered to me[,] the said John N. Fordham[,] (by the said Constable who returned the said panel) rolled up by him all as nearly as could be in one and the same manner and put together into a box and thereupon the said John N. Fordham did draw out six of the said papers one after another on which the following persons were named and who being respectively called did appear and were not challenged and being approved of by me[,] the said Justice[,] as indifferent were the jury to try the said cause and were severally sworn well and truly to try the matter in [in]difference between Lodowick Post Plaintiff and Jesse

Peirson

[Transcript, p. 7]

Peirson Defendant and a true verdict to give according to evidence viz. Charles Douglass[,] Stephen Satterly, James Sayr, Silas Havens, Zaccheus Payne, and John F. Havens[.] [A]nd after the jury had been so sworn they did sit together and hear the several proofs and allegations of the said parties which were delivered in public in their presence[.] [A]nd to each of the witnesses on the said trial I[,] the said Justice[,] did administer the oath directed and prescribed in and by the twelfth section of the act aforesaid[.] [A]nd the said jury had then and there heard in the said Court the proofs and allegations. I[,] the said Justice[,] did administer to the said Thomas Harris then and there being Constable as aforesaid the oath for that purpose directed and prescribed by the section last aforesaid of the act aforesaid viz. You do swear in the presence of Almighty God that

you will to the utmost of your ability keep every
person sworn on this inquest together in some
private and convenient place without meat
or drink except water[.] [Y]ou will not suffer any
person to speak to them nor speak to them
yourself unless by order of the Justice [or] unless it be to
ask them whether they have agreed on their
verdict ↑until they have agreed on their verdict↓[10]
[A]nd the said jurors were then and
there kept together and apart by themselves in a
private and convenient place attended by the
said Thomas Harris[,] the said Constable[,] until
they had agreed upon their Verdict[.] [A]nd when the
said jury had agreed upon their Verdict they
returned into the said Court and delivered their

said

[Transcript, p. 8]

said verdict to me[,] the said Justice[.] [W]hereby they
found for the Plaintiff seventy five cents for his
damages besides his costs and thereupon I[,] the
said John N. Fordham[,] did adjudge[,] consider[,]
and determine that the said Lodowick Post
should recover against the said Jesse Peirson
his damages aforesaid in [?form?] aforesaid found
and also five dollars for his costs and charges by
him about his suit in this behalf expended
which said damages[,] costs[,] and charges in the
whole amount to five dollars and seventy five
cents and that the said Lodowick Post thereof [shall]
have execution.

Given under my hand and
seal at Southampton in the
said County of Suffolk the
twenty sixth day of April in
the year of our Lord one
thousand eight hundred
and three.

John N. Fordham
Justice

[Swirl]

10 This addition was written in a different hand. It appears to be the same as that appearing at the end of the document in the sideways text on Transcript p. 19.

SUFFOLK *Ls*[11] *To either of the Constables of the town of Southampton[:]*
COUNTY *You are hereby required in the name of the People of the State of New York seasonably to summons Jesse Peirson to be and appear before me at the house of Hugh Gelston Junr on Thursday the 30th of December instant at two oclock in the afternoon to answer unto Lodowick Post in an action of trespass on the case for killing and taking away a Fox from his chase to the damage of him the said*
Lodowick

[Transcript, p. 9]

Lodowick Post twenty five dollars as it is said Hereof fail not[.] Given under my hand this 22nd day of December 1802.

John N. Fordham Justice
(Swirl)

(Indorsed) Legally [?served?] by reading within hearing of the [?within?] named [?Jesse?] [?Peirson?] and duely returned[.]
Fees 69 cents. Atest [?for?] me.

Thomas L. Harris
Counstable

SUFFOLK *Ls.*[12] *To Thomas Harris[,] Constable[:]*
COUNTY *You are hereby required in the name of the People of the*
L.S. *State of New York immediately to summons twelve good and lawful freeholders of the town of Southampton in the County aforesaid who shall be in no wise of kin either to Lodowick Post Plaintiff and Jesse Peirson Defendant and not interested in a certain cause to be and appear before me[,] John N. Fordham[,] at the dwelling house of Hugh Gelston Junr in the town aforesaid and return their names together with this [?precept?] without delay[.] Hereof fail not[.] [G]iven under my hand and seal in Southampton this* 30th *of December[,] 1802.*

John N. Fordham Justice
[Swirl]

11 "Ls" is standing for location of the seal that would have been on the original document that is here being copied.

12 This time the location of the seal is represented twice by "Ls," once inside a diamond in the margin beneath "Suffolk County."

(Indorsed) In compliance of the [?within precept?] I have summons the [?persons?] whose names are annexed. Fees 37 ½ Cents. Atest [?per?] me.

Thomas L. Harris
Counstable
[Swirl]

[Transcript, p. 10]

(Jurors Summoned) Stephen Satterley[,] John F. Havens[,] William R. Halsey[,] John Norris[,] Thomas Beebe[,] Silas Havens[,] Theophilus Cook[,] Charles Douglass[,] Isaac Jessup[,] James Sayre[,] Abraham Tapping[,] Zacheus Payne (Jurors ~~illegible scratch out~~) Ch[o]s[en][:] Douglass[,] Steph[en] Satterley[,] James Sayr[,] Silas Havens[,] Zacheus Pain[,] J[oh]n F. Havens.

John N. Fordham
Lodowick Post *Court*
against *Fees*
Jesse Peirson

Summons	9½
Constable serving	69
5 [?Subpoenas?] and serving	96
7 Witness attending	87½
Venire	19
Constable taking jury	37½
Swearing jury	12½
Swearing of Evidence	42
Swearing Constable	6
Jury Feas	75
Jury attending & not sworn	37½
Judgment	12½
	$5..4[13]

[? I tax?] of the above bill Five dollars which is the Plaintiff[']s Cost.

John N. Fordham Justice
[Swirl]
~~*[?Signature?] scratch out*~~

And the said Jesse Peirson having had hearing of the said return and of the process and proceedings mentioned

[13] Assuming ½ is 0.5¢, the total here would be $5.04 (or as it is represented here "$5..4), which Fordham probably rounded down to $5.

[Transcript, p. 11]

mentioned therein immediately says that in the said plaint[,] process[,] proceedings[,] and record and also in the rendering and giving of the said judgment there is manifest error in this that is to say[:]
That it appears in and by the said record here sent that the summons issued by the said John N. Fordham Esquire[,] the said Justice in the said action before him[,] was directed "to any of the Constables of the County of Suffolk where the said Jesse Peirson then resided[.]" [W]hereas by law every summons in actions before Justices of the peace ought to be directed to some Constable or other proper officer of the City or town where the Defendant dwells or can be found and therefore in that there is manifest error.

There is also manifest error in this that is to say that it appears in and by the said record here sent that the said Lodowick Post came into the Court of the People of the State of New York before the said Justice on the thirtieth day of December in the year of our Lord one thousand eight hundred and two and then and there affirmed his plaint against the said Jesse Peirson in the said action and prayed process against the said Jesse Peirson by summons and that thereupon the said Justice at the prayer of the said Lodowick Post issued a summons requiring the Constable to summon the said Jesse Peirson to appear before him[,] the said Justice[,] on Thursday the thirtieth day of December in the year last aforesaid at two o[']clock in the afternoon of the same day to answer to the said

[Transcript, p. 12]

said Lodowick Post in the said action which said thirtieth day of December last mentioned was the same day on which the said plaint was affirmed and the said summons was issued[.] [W]hereas by law every summons in actions before Justices of the peace ought to be made returnable not less than six nor more than twelve days from the time of issuing such summons and every such summons ought by law to be served at least six days before the time of appearance mentioned therein and therefore in that also there is manifest error[.]

There is also manifest error in this that is to say that the declaration[,] complaint[,] or demand of the said Lodowick Post against the said Jesse Peirson specified and set forth in the said record here sent upon which the said judgment was rendered and given and the matters contained therein are not sufficient in law for the said Lodowick Post to have[,] maintain[,] or support his said action against the said Jesse Peirson and therefore the said judgment thereupon rendered and given is vicious[,] erroneous[,] and void in law and therefore in that also there is great and manifest error.

There is also manifest error in this that is to say that it appears by the Venire annexed to the said record here sent that the said Venire issued by the said Justice in the said action [?required?] the Constable to whom it was directed to summon twelve good and lawful freeholders of the town of Southampton to be and appear before him the said justice and without specifying the purpose for which the said twelve freeholders

[Transcript, p. 13]

freeholders were to appear before him[,] the said Justice[.] [W]hereas by law the said Venire ought to have commanded the Constable to whom it was directed to summon twelve good and lawful men being *freeholders of the said town to be and appear before him[,] the said Justice[,] to make a jury for the trial of the action between the parties mentioned in the said Venire and therefore in that also there is manifest error.*

There is also manifest error in this that is to say that it appears in and by the said record here sent that the jury who tried the said cause between the said parties found a Verdict for the plaintiff with seventy five cents damages and it farther appears that the said jury did not find[,] award[,] or assess any costs whatever in the said action for or in favor of the said Lodowick Post and nevertheless it farther appears in and by the said record that the said Justice did adjudge[,] consider[,] and determine that the said Lodowick Post should recover against the said Jesse Peirson five dollars for his costs and charges by him about his suit in that behalf expended[.] [W]hereas by law no costs of increase or other costs whatever can be adjudged or awarded to the plaintiff in any such case unless the jury who try the cause find and assess costs for and in favor of the plaintiff separately and distinctly from the damages which they find and assess for and in favor of the plaintiff and therefore in that also there is manifest error.

[Transcript, p. 14]

There is also error in this that is to say that it farther appears in and by the said record here sent that the judgment rendered and given in the said action by the said Justice was rendered and given for the said Lodowick Post against the said Jesse Peirson[.] [W]hereas by the law of the land judgment ought to have been rendered and given in the said action for the said Jesse Peirson against the said Lodowick Post and therefore in that also there is great and manifest error.

And hereupon the said Jesse Peirson prays that the said judgment for the errors above specified and assigned and also for many other errors apparent in the said plaint[,] process[,] proceedings[,] record[,] and judgment may be reversed[,] annulled[,] revoked[,] set aside[,] and altogether held for nothing and that he[,] the said Jesse Peirson[,] may be restored to all the things which he has lost by reason of the said judgment [?] and that the said Lodowick Post may rejoin to the said errors [?].

And hereupon the said Lodowick by Cadwallader D. Colden[,] his attorney[,] voluntarily comes here into Court and having heard the errors aforesaid forthwith says that neither in the plaint and proceedings aforesaid nor in the giving the judgment aforesaid is there error and prays that the Court of the said People before the said Justices now here would proceed to the examination as well of the plaint and

proceedings aforesaid as of the matters above
assigned for error and that the judgment
aforesaid

[Transcript, p. 15]

aforesaid may be affirmed [?].

[14]*And because the Court of the People of*
the State of New York now here[15] *are not*
yet advised
of giving their judgment of and upon the
[???] of and upon the same premises for
that the Court of the People of the State of New
York now here is not yet advised thereof[.] On which
day before the Justices of the People of the State of
New York of the Supreme Court of Judicature of
the same People at the City hall of the City of
Albany *come the said parties by their said*
Attornies[.] [/] *And because the Court of the People*
of the State of New York now here[16] *is not yet*
advised of giving their judgment of and upon
the premises [a] day thereof is given to the said
parties until the second Monday in **November**
next before the Justices of the People of the State
of New York of the Supreme Court of Judicature of
the same People at the City hall of the City of
New York *to hear their judgment of and upon*
the same premises for that the Court of the
People of the State of New York now here is not
yet advised thereof. On which day[17] *before the Justices of*
the People of the State of New York of the Supreme Court of
Judicature of the same People at the City hall of the City of
New York *come the said parties by their said Attornies[.]* [/]
And because the Court of the People of the State of New
York now here is not yet advised of giving their
judgment of and upon the premises [a] day thereof is
given to the said parties until the first Monday in
February *next before the Justices of the People of the State of*

[14] I bold the alternating cities and dates, placing them in a different font, along with an inserted [/] section break where I take the case to be carried over from term to term, in order to help facilitate reading of this swath-like part of the document.

[15] Presumably the May Term 1803 (New York City), which the case was originally intended for.

[16] Presumably August Term 1803 (Albany).

[17] November Term 1803 (New York City).

[Transcript, p. 16]

New York of the Supreme Court of Judicature of the same People at the City hall of the City of **Albany** *to hear their judgment of and upon the same premises for that the Court of the People of the State of New York now here is not yet advised thereof. On which day*[18] *before the Justices of the People of the State of New York of the Supreme Court of Judicature of the same People at the City hall of the City of* **Albany** *come the said parties by their said Attornies[.]* [/] *And because the Court of the People of the State of New York now here is not yet advised of giving their judgment of and upon the premises [a] day thereof is given to the said parties until the first Monday in* **May** *next before the Justices of the People of the State of New York of the Supreme Court of Judicature of the same People at the City hall of the City of* **New York** *to hear their judgment of and upon the same premises for that the Court of the People of the State of New York now here is not yet advised thereof. On which day*[19] *before the Justices of the People of the State of New York of the Supreme Court of Judicature of the same People at the City hall of the City of* **New York** *come the said parties by their said Attornies[.]* [/] *[A]nd because the Court of the People of the State of New York now here is not yet advised of giving their judgment of and upon the premises [a] day therefore is given to the said parties until the first Monday in* **August** *next*
[???] at the City Hall
of the City of **New York** *come the said parties by their said Attornies[.] And because the Court of the People of the State of New York now here is not yet advised of giving their judgment of and upon the premises [a] day thereof is given to the said parties*
until

[Transcript, p. 17]

until the first Monday in **August** *next before the Justices of the People of the State of New York of the Supreme Court of Judicature of the same People at the City hall of the City of* **Albany** *to hear their*
[???]
premises [a] day is therefore given to the said parties

[18] February Term 1804 (Albany). [19] May Term 1804 (New York City).

to come before the Justices of the People of the State of New York of the Supreme Court of Judicature of the same People at the City hall of the City of Albany *on the first Monday in* August *next to hear their judgment of and upon the same premises for that the Court of the People of the State of New York now here are not yet advised thereof. On which day*[20] *before the Justices of the People of the State of New York of the Supreme Court of Judicature of the same People at the City hall of the City of* Albany *come the said parties by their said Attornies[.] [/] [A]nd because the Court of the People of the State of New York now here is not yet advised of giving their judgment of and upon the premises [a] day therefore is given to the said parties until the second Monday in* November *next before the Justices of the People of the State of New York of the Supreme Court of Judicature of the same People at the City hall of the City of* New York *to hear their judgment of and upon the same premises for that the Court of the People of [the] State of New York now here are not yet advised thereof. On which day*[21] *before the Justices of the People of the State of New York of the Supreme Court of Judicature of the same People at the City hall of the City of* New York *come the said parties by their said Attornies[.]* [/] *[A]nd because the Court of the People of*

[Transcript, p. 18]

the State of New York now here is not yet advised of giving their judgment of and upon the premises [a] day therefore is given to the said parties until the first Monday in February *next before the Justices of the People of the State of New York of the Supreme Court of Judicature of the same People at the City hall of the City of* Albany *to hear their judgment of and upon the said premises for that the Court of the People of the State of New York now here is not yet advised thereof. On which day*[22] *before the Justices of the People of the State of New York of the Supreme Court of Judicature of the same People at the City hall of the City of* Albany *come the said parties by their said Attornies[.]* [/] *[A]nd because the Court of the People of the State of New York now here*

[20] August Term 1804 (Albany). [21] November Term 1804 (New York City).
[22] February Term 1805 (Albany).

is not yet advised of giving their judgment of and upon the premises [a] day therefore is given to the said parties until the first Monday in May *next before the Justices of the People of the State of New York of the Supreme Court of Judicature of the same People at the City hall of the City of* New York *to hear their judgment of and upon the same premises for that the Court of the People of the State of New York now here is not yet advised thereof. On which day*[23] *before the Justices of the People of the State of New York of the Supreme Court [?of?] the Justices of the [?People?] of the State of New York of the Supreme Court of Judicature of the same People at the City hall of the City of* Albany *to hear their judgment of and upon the same premises for that the Court of the People of the State of New York now here is not yet advised thereof. On which day*[24] *before the*

[Transcript, p. 19]

the Justices of the People of the State of New York of the Supreme Court of Judicature of the same People at the City hall of the City of Albany *come the said parties by their said Attornies whereupon all and singular the premises being seen and [???] of the People of the State of New York now here fully understood and as well the process and proceedings in the said return mentioned and the judgment given thereupon as the said causes and matters by the said Jesse Peirson above assigned for error being diligently inspected and examined and mature deliberation being [?thereon first?] had for that it seems to the Court of the People of the State of New York now here that there is manifest error in the said record and proceedings and also in the rendering and giving of the said judgment. Therefore it is [?ordered?] [???] judgment [???] and given by the said John N. Fordham[,] the said Justice for the said errors and for other errors in the said record and proceedings be reversed[,]*

[23] May Term 1805 (New York City). Why the city that next appears is Albany rather than New York is puzzling.

[24] It is unclear whether this is the May Term in New York or the August Term in Albany. It would fit with the reported decision if the case was finally heard in August Term 1805 (Albany). However, the day referred to here would seem to still be the first Monday in May even though that term belongs to New York City, not Albany.

revoked[,] annulled[,] entirely set aside[,] and altogether held for nothing and that the said Jesse Peirson be restored to all things which he the said Jesse Peirson has lost by reason of the said judgment[.] And it is farther considered that the said Jesse Peirson do recover against the said Lodowick Post One hundred & twenty one dollars & thirty seven cents for his costs and charges by him the said Jesse Peirson about the prosecution of the writ of certiorari aforesaid in this behalf expended to the said Jesse Peirson according to the form of the statute in such case made and provided by the Court of the People of the State of New York now here at his request adjudged and that the said Jesse Peirson have execution thereof [?].

[25]*Judgment signed the 10th day of September in the year of our Lord one thousand eight hundred and five.*

Daniel D. Tompkins[26]
[Swirl]

[25] This text that accompanies Tompkins's signature appears sideways in the space above. The handwriting is different than the rest of the Judgment Roll, although it appears to be the same as the same as at least one other place of inserted text (the ↓↑ at Transcript, p. 7).

[26] Tompkins signature appears to be an original. Compare with examples of his signature available at p. 4 of https://www.earlyamerican.com/Auctions/PDFs/Special.Lot-2.ver-02-optimized.pdf which have the same distinctive Ds and sideways 8 swirl at the bottom).

APPENDIX C

Jury Tax Table[1]

[1] The six Jurors chosen from the panel of twelve are in bold and underlined. The number are taken from Tax Assessment Rolls for 1801, 1803, 1806, and 1818 provided by former Southampton Town Historian Henry Moëller, located in Southampton Town Hall, Southampton, NY.

Jurors	1801 Real; Personal; Total	1803 Real; Personal; Total	1806 Real; Personal; Total	1818 Real; Personal; Total
Beebe, Thomas	200 + 900? = 1100?[2]	400 + 2200 = 2600	400 + 2400 = 2800	4700 + 4700 = 9400
Cook, Theophilus	100 + 3600 = 3700	3000 + 1000 = 4000	3200 + 700 = 3900	6500 + 100 = 6600
Douglas, Charles	450 + 0 = 450	600 + 0 = 600	700 + 0 = 700	350 + 0 = 350
Halsey, William R.	1050 + 0 = 1050	1050 + 0 = 1050	1800 + 400 = 2200 "Halsey, William"	6000 + 100 = 6100 "Halsey, William Junr"
Havens, John F.	400 + 500 = 900	Not on list	150 + 800 = 950 $150 "stock store"	1600 + 400 = 2000
Havens, Silas	400 + 500 = 900	400 + 250 = 650	Not on list	Not on list
Jessup, Isaac	1000 + 0 = 1000	800 + 20 = 820	860 + 200 = 1060	Not on list
Norris, John	460 + 100 = 560	436 + 60 = 496	500 + 100 = 600	1200 + 350 = 1550
Payne, Zacheus	190 + 0 = 190	160 + 0 = 160	160 + 0 = 160	2400 + 0 = 2400
Satterly, Stephen	Not on list	400 + 150 = 550	Not on list	Not on list
Sayre, James	1050 + 120 = 1170	1050 + 120 = 1170	1050 + 150 = 1200	2350 + 100 = 2450 "Sayre, James & son"
Topping, Abraham	1150 + 90 = 1240	1100 + 100 = 1200	1000 + 150 = 1150	3200 + 0 = 3200 Listed as "Admistrar" because he died April 15, 1818

[2] I use "?" where the copy is faint and difficult to read.

APPENDIX D

Sharpe v. *Sabin*

"In an action of trespass whereupon the Pltf declares & says that he is at much expense to keep Hound Dogs Guns & ammunition for the purpose of Hunting foxes & that on our about the 1st day of September last past in Pomfret aforesd the Pltf with his hounds was hunting foxes in sd Pomfret & the Pltf's sd Hounds started a fox & were in close pursuit of the same upon his track in such manner that in all reasonable Probability the sd Hounds would either have caught & killed sd fox or would have drove sd fox within reach of the Pltf's Gun in such manner that the Pltf might have shot him. But the Pltf says the Deft well knowing the same but with an intent to wrong & injure the Pltf & deprive him of the game which his hound had so started contrary to the mind & will of the Pltf did while sd Hounds were in close pursuit of sd fox shoot sd Fox & contrary to the Pltfs will without his liberty & by force & arms carry away the skin of sd Fox & convert it to his own use which skin was well worth the sum of twelve shillings Lawfull Money which doings of the Deft in the premisses was & is against Law & the Customs & rules of Hunting."

Transcript created by Andrea McDowell from a manuscript called "Rueben Sharpe, defendant v. Jonathan Sabin, Plaintiff," located in the Connecticut State Library, State Archives, Record Group 3 (Judicial Records), Windham County Superior Court Files, Box 189, March 1795–September 1797, Item Number 35.

McDowell reproduced this in her "Legal Fictions in *Pierson* v. *Post*," 105 *Michigan Law Review* (2007): 735–78, 738, where she also reported that "[t]he lower court (with both parties appearing pro se) found the defendant 'guilty' and awarded the plaintiff 7 shillings damages and one pound, 5 shillings and 20 pence for costs." That makes the case similar to

Pierson v. Post, where the interloper, Pierson, also lost and was awarded a similar small sum, the equivalent of the bounty for an exterminated fox or a fox pelt, 75¢. However, on the same claim that "the matters therein contained are wholly insufficient in Law to support any action against the defendant," the Superior Court found no error on appeal. The defendant's claim for £6 indemnification was therefore also denied. £6 is a far cry from the $126.37 that Pierson spent and was awarded for pursuing his claim.

APPENDIX E

Corrections to Secondary Sources

- Nothing in the original documents surrounding the case or the published report suggest that the fox was shot, as is commonly stated in secondary sources discussing *Pierson*. I think it is more likely that the fox was bludgeoned to death, as one local source reports, with a piece of fence railing – source H.P. Hedges, "Pierson vs. Post" (Thursday October 24, 1895) *Sag-Harbor Express*, Suffolk County, NY.
- Correction to Donahue, "*Animalia Ferae Naturae*" and Tompkins J. – the jury trial took place in Suffolk County, not Queen's County – source Judgment Roll, Appendix B.
- Correction to Berger, "It's Not About the Fox" – Nathan Sanford attended Clinton Academy (not Hayground Academy) and was related to the Piersons on his father's side, not his mother's side (see Chapter 3).
- Correction to Berger, "It's Not About the Fox" and Singer et al. Casebook (6th ed. 2014) – Nathan Post was descended from original town inhabitant Richard Post, who was a proprietor, making it unlikely that the dispute was over proprietor's rights in undivided common land or "control of the village common," as the chase and capture all took place on the beach (see Chapter 5).
- Correction to Hutchinson relying primarily on Berger, *Is Eating People Wrong?* – it is difficult to state given ibid. that the case was about a "particularly heated [conflict] over the town's common lands" and its connection to "common land, which was used by the Pierson family and others to pasture their livestock" (pp. 70, 74) (see Chapter 5).

- Correction to Fernandez, "The Lost Record" – Post was ordered to pay $126.37, not $121.37 as recorded in the Judgment Roll – source Supreme Court of Judicature (New York), Docket of Judgments, J0131-82, vol. 4, New York State Archives, Albany, NY.
- Correction to Fernandez, "The Lost Record" – the hearing was probably held on August 7, 1805, and not the Riverhead Courthouse in September 1805 – source Supreme Court of Judicature (New York), General and Special Term Minute Books, J0130-82, New York State Archives, Albany, NY.
- Addition Fernandez, "A Great Debate" – Kent was present the day *Pierson* was probably argued – source ibid.
- Correction to Fernandez, "A Great Debate" – the type and size-of-dog discussion by Livingston was not random (see Chapter 1).
- Correction to Fernandez, "The Lost Record" – lawyers were not expressly banned from appearing before a Justice's Court by the 1801 version of the *Twenty Five Dollar Act* – source Dan Ernst (see Chapter 3).
- Correction to Fernandez, "The Lost Record" – Pierson was duly served – source Donahue, "Papyrology" a better reading of the handwriting in Judgment Roll, Appendix B (see Chapter 3).
- Correction to Fernandez, "A Great Debate" – the issue whether or not one could have property in vermin is more complicated than I stated there (see Chapter 5).

Index

CPSIA information can be obtained
at www.ICGtesting.com
Printed in the USA
LVHW010008210519
618494LV00008B/185/P

9 781107 039285